REPORTING
for the
MEDIA

REPORTING
for the MEDIA

Second Canadian Edition

John R. Bender | Lucinda D. Davenport | Michael W. Drager | Fred Fedler

Siobhan Moore | Charles Hays | Maxine Ruvinsky

OXFORD
UNIVERSITY PRESS

OXFORD
UNIVERSITY PRESS

Oxford University Press is a department of the University of Oxford.
It furthers the University's objective of excellence in research, scholarship,
and education by publishing worldwide. Oxford is a registered trade mark of
Oxford University Press in the UK and in certain other countries.

Published in Canada by
Oxford University Press
8 Sampson Mews, Suite 204,
Don Mills, Ontario M3C 0H5 Canada

www.oupcanada.com

Library and Archives Canada Cataloguing in Publication
Bender, John R., author
Reporting for the media / John R. Bender, Lucinda D. Davenport,
Michael W. Drager, Fred Fedler, Siobhan Moore, Charles Hays, and
Maxine Ruvinsky. — Second Canadian edition.

Includes bibliographical references and index.
Issued in print and electronic formats.
ISBN 978-0–19–903121–4 (softcover).—ISBN 978-0–19–903122–1 (PDF)

1. Reporters and reporting—Problems, exercises, etc. I. Title.

PN4781.B46 2019   070.4'3   C2018-904009-2
                                                              C2018-904010-6

Cover images (*from left on first occurrence*): © Sergey Nivens/Shutterstock; © Microgen/Shutterstock;
© wellphoto/Shutterstock; © Fred Mantel/Shutterstock; © Ion Sebastian/Shutterstock;
© 1000 Words/Shutterstock; © guteksk7/Shutterstock

Cover design: Laurie McGregor
Interior design: Sherill Chapman

Oxford University Press is committed to our environment.
This book is printed on Forest Stewardship Council® certified paper
and comes from responsible sources.

Printed and bound in the United States of America
1 2 3 4 — 22 21 20 19

Brief Contents

Contents

Preface

A young woman knew she wanted to become a reporter even though she was very shy. While she didn't want to tell her own story, she was very interested in listening and telling other people's stories.

She found her voice through others.

The woman worked summers at a newspaper while finishing university. She got a full-time newspaper job a week before her graduation.

That was about 35 years ago—when there were no cell phones and computers were just starting to replace typewriters in newsrooms. People found out about news stories hours, sometimes a day, after the stories had happened.

Today, news is available every second of every day. The avalanche of information, brought on and enhanced by digital and technical innovation, and the search for effective business models to harness the economic potential of this innovation has had a dramatic impact on how journalism works as a business and how journalists are taught, are trained, and do their jobs.

So why would a person want to be a journalist?

Some journalism students have said their reasons include their high school creative writing teachers telling them they would be excellent writers; they want to write about the music and entertainment industry; they need to become more involved in the world; or they thought writing would be a good area of study because they were not very good at math or sciences.

All of these are good and valid reasons.

However more recently, students are saying they want to become journalists because they want their voices heard. They want to have an impact; they want to be part of societal change for the better.

And this shows that while journalism has been hit with monumental change through digital innovation in the years since that young reporter started out, the commanding trait for a journalist now is still establishing a voice to be heard and understood by others.

To be heard and understood, a professional journalist needs to master the fundamental principles of journalism, which have been reinforced rather than diminished by digital advancement. The demand for quality journalism is stronger now with the increasing need to sort the fact from the fiction produced by information overload in a chaotic world.

The starting point to becoming a quality journalist is a curiosity about society and the world, a persistence in finding out factual truths, and an appreciation of and dedication to learning how to be a professional journalist who communicates clearly.

This second Canadian edition of *Reporting for the Media* has been streamlined to focus on showing journalism students how to develop the best professional practices to establish their voices as journalists to inform audiences; to gather facts and viewpoints from all sides of a story; to report responsibly; to be factual, accurate, and objective; to write in a clear and concise style; and to be ethical and emphatic.

The design and format of this second edition has been condensed from 22 chapters to 13 to focus on a complete update on content, figures, and statistics; to give a stronger Canadian focus; and to emphasize digital and mobile platforms.

The first five chapters explain and demonstrate how to develop story ideas and angles; how to gather, confirm, and verify information; how to be legally and ethically responsible in reporting; and how to write to clearly to reach and inform an audience responsibility and accurately. Chapters 5 to 11 show how to develop story ideas and sources, how to interview and interact with sources, and how connect with the audience using different story structures. Chapters 12 and 13 focus on polishing stories, with grammar, spelling, and style guidelines to perfect the editing process.

There are two appendices: the first is a comprehensive copy-editing practice, and the second is the answer key for some of the end-of-chapter exercises.

In all, the second Canadian edition of *Reporting for the Media* will guide student journalists on their path to telling other people's stories in this digital age.

A Note of Thanks

I am grateful to Oxford University Press for the opportunity to revise and update this text to help Canadian journalism students and educators address the demands on journalism by constant digital innovation. I would also like to thank the reviewers—both anonymous and named—who provided valuable feedback on this text. This list includes Gavin Adamson, John Bermingham, Richard Dunstan, Leonard Gervais, Bruce Gillespie, Danielle Harder, Lezlie Lowe, Anne McNeilly, and Eric Spalding. Finally, I would like to thank the many journalists, writers, and artists whose work has been inspirational and motivational, and is featured throughout this second Canadian edition of the text.

Siobhan Moore
March 2018

About the Authors

Siobhan Moore is a professor in the journalism degree program at Humber College in Toronto, Ontario. Moore is a former newspaper journalist who worked in newsrooms in Nova Scotia and Toronto until she decided to contribute more by helping journalism students learn how to work in an industry beset by the tumult of the internet. Siobhan has an honours in English literature from Mount Allison University and Masters of Arts in Journalism from the University of Missouri, where her thesis examined how *The Toronto Star*'s attempt to produce a PDF newspaper affected how reporters did their jobs.

Charles A. Hays is an assistant professor in the School of Journalism, Faculty of Arts, at Thompson Rivers University. During a career in U.S. broadcast journalism, Hays worked as a radio producer and reporter at Oregon Public Broadcasting, followed by a move to the Northern High Plains in South Dakota, where he worked as a commercial television and radio reporter. He has been active as a freelance magazine writer and freelance broadcast correspondent for cbs Radio News. Hays holds a bachelor's degree in technical journalism and broadcasting from Oregon State University, a master's degree in journalism from South Dakota State University, and a doctorate in mass communications from the University of Iowa, where he held the Moeller Doctoral Fellowship in Mass Communication and won an award for his classroom teaching.

Maxine Ruvinsky is a former associate professor in the School of Journalism, Faculty of Arts, at Thompson Rivers University in Kamloops, British Columbia. She also worked as a print and wire service reporter and spent two decades in the newspaper business, working for a variety of Canadian dailies and for the national wire service Canadian Press in Montreal.

Siobhan Moore
Journalism professor
Degree program
School of Media Studies and Information Technology
Humber Institute of Technology and Advanced Learning
3199 Lake Shore Blvd. West
Toronto, ON M8V 1K8
siobhan.moore@humber.ca
@moore_siobhan

Charles A. Hays
School of Journalism
Thompson Rivers University
900 McGill Road, P.O. Box 3010
Kamloops, BC V2C 5N3
chays@tru.ca

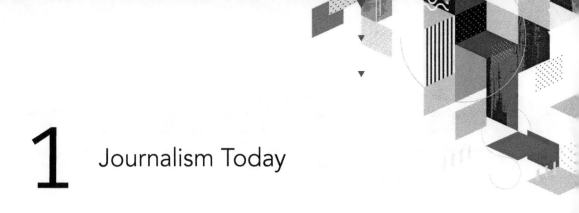

1   Journalism Today

"Good prose is like a windowpane."

—Author and journalist George Orwell in his 1946 essay *Why I Write.*

George Orwell is famous for his novels *Animal Farm* and *1984*. Orwell is also known as an accomplished journalist. His writing, or to use his term "prose," was direct, concise and clear in its exacting depictions of his view through the windowpane to the world. Digital journalists working today have the same goal—to write with honesty and clarity to help people see clearly through the journalist's window view to the world or a neighbourhood.

Digital Revolution

Throughout the 20th century, technology has changed how journalists gather facts and deliver stories to their audience. Television and radio changed how newspaper and magazine journalists did their jobs and how stories were told. But the change brought on by the internet in the 1990s has been the most revolutionary in how fast it happened and the effects that it and subsequent digital technologies had on journalism.

The business of journalism for both print and broadcast through the 1900s was very profitable—until digital technology changed everything. The World Wide Web invaded newsrooms in 1995 and changed how journalism worked as a business and how journalists worked as professionals. While the web brought great promise, it also was feared because of the threat it posed to how traditional media—newspapers, magazines, television, and radio—operated. Today, newsroom editors and producers need journalists to have both traditional newsgathering savvy and social media abilities with advanced technical skills to produce audio, text, and video pieces for multiple platforms. The web also led to the development of multimedia packages of content in which journalists produce text, audio, and visual pieces that cover the same story.

This book explains the fundamental practices and routines journalists use to gather, communicate, and deliver factual information to the mass media audience using the best professional, ethical, and legal practices in these changing digital times.

The Business

In Canada, there have been a number of federal government commissions that have examined media ownership, concentration, and business models. More recently, the report *The Shattered Mirror* by the Public Policy Forum examined how the old way of doing business for print and broadcast media has been disrupted by digital technology.

The report was released in January 2016 and detailed how traditional media (print and broadcast) has had to adapt and incorporate digital technology in order to continue. Media managers are making investments to become successful in digital journalism. At one time, owners and managers feared that online news would replace print news. They had hoped if they ignored the internet, it would just go away. This was a mistake. Digital journalism is no longer a competitor and is essential to journalism today.

> For two decades, the transformation of the news industry has largely been viewed in terms of technology—digital versus print and broadcast. But now such thinking is beside the point; everyone is digital, or had better be. Where differentiation now occurs is in the approach to the gathering and dissemination of news.
>
> The Shattered Mirror report, January 2016

The digital impact on newsrooms has been dramatic. Job titles have changed, newsroom routines and practices have altered, deadlines that generally used to be every two to three hours are now as-soon-as-something-happens-and-can-be-confirmed.

And while some reporting *by* the media *about* the media has been bleak when looking to the future, it is clear that the role journalists play in gathering, verifying, and telling the public what it needs to know is more important than ever. In the model before the digitalization of society, the media told the audience what it wanted. Now the digital world has changed that relationship, and the audience is in control.

Toronto media theorist Marshall McLuhan is known for his phrase "the medium is the message." For the practical purposes of this text, McLuhan's prophetic words can be interpreted to mean how the information is delivered takes on more importance than the message itself. To extend the interpretation further, we conclude from the two surveys presented in this chapter that Canadians say they want credible news, but *how* they get their news is their motivation.

The Audience

The Shattered Mirror's survey of 1,500 Canadians shows that people rely on journalism for news, but they want to be able to choose how and when they access it, and they do not want to pay for it. Another intriguing result is that Canadians trust news from traditional media sources more than online ones, but they also see a future where all of their news will come from online sources (Figure 1.1).

These results are given additional support by a larger survey of 38,000 Canadians from January to December 2016 by Vividata, the agency that measures cross-platform readership for the country's newspapers and magazines. The Vividata report shows readership is strong with 90 per cent of Canadians reading print every week. Fifty-nine per cent say they read on a digital device, with 70 per cent using a mobile device. The study showed "significant growth in digital platforms, with more than half of Canadians (54 per cent) now reading their daily newspaper digitally."

Media owners use results from these independent surveys along with their own research to find the best combination of traditional and online platforms to reach the biggest audience. The connections among online products are used as a lure to bring the audience deeper into all of the media product's platforms. For example, a newspaper reporter live-tweeting the NHL draft must also embed a video hit and a link back to the newspaper's website. The reporter should make Facebook, Instagram, and Snapchat postings. All of these posts tease the bigger content package of analysis of what happened, which players were traded to which teams, and what does it all mean slated for the next day's newspaper. It is a bread crumb trail of content that leads the audience to the long-form story.

As the media works on trying to get the audience's attention, other groups also work on getting the media's attention.

Cision is a marketing survey firm that gathers information for public relations and marketing professionals. It released the 2016 Canadian Social Journalism Study to detail what it called journalists' love-hate relationship with social media. The goal of the report is to show public relations and marketing professionals how to effectively get in touch with journalists to get their stories out. This relationship between public relations professionals and journalists will be discussed in Chapter 2.

The report found 78 per cent of the journalists surveyed use social media for work, and 95 per cent use it every day (Figure 1.2). Social media also rated high on the importance scale for sourcing information, verifying content, publishing and promoting content, and interacting with audiences.

People have offered many views about news that appears online compared to news that appears in non-digital media like television and newspapers. For each of the following statements, please indicate whether you strongly agree, agree, disagree, or strongly disagree.

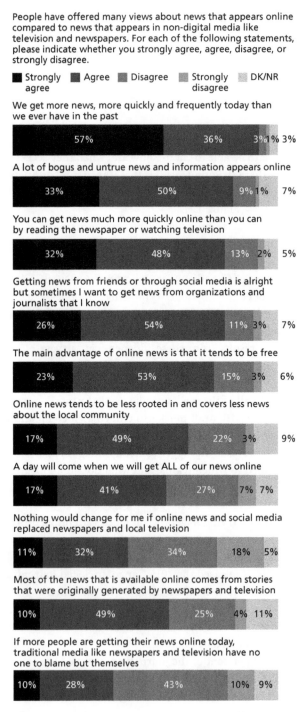

Figure 1.1 Views on news

Source: From *The Shattered Mirror: News, Democracy and Trust in the Digital Age*, Public Policy Forum (January 2017) © 2017 Public Policy Forum.

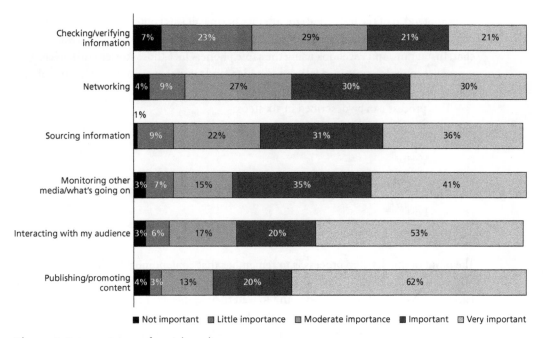

Figure 1.2 Importance of social media
Source: Copyright © 2018 Cision Canada Inc. Reproduced with permission.

The Journalism

Traditional media has expanded to include digital media platforms in order to meet the new demands of an audience that has rapidly engaged with social media. Media companies have turned to social media to keep old audiences and attract new ones.

Social media has revolutionized journalism in two ways. It helps journalists gather and deliver the news, and it helps media business managers track, evaluate, target, and tap into audience growth potential. Both outcomes mean that newsrooms have had to adapt to social media and digital innovation, retrain willing journalists, and hire new journalists whose knowledge of digital software adds essential value to newsroom practices and routines. Traditional media has had to adapt to change in order to survive.

Journalists are expected to hold traditional media values in being experts in reporting news with passion, accuracy, and authority, but now they must also have skills as photographers, videographers, editors, and formatters of content. Journalists put their stories on multiple platforms and always combine text with multimedia elements like photographs, video clips, and information graphics. They have expanded their skills to create blogs and podcasts, which the audience can download to their own phones, laptops, and whatever future digital gadgetry and software are available by the time this book sees print.

For example, a journalist covering the summer street fashion of the Osheaga music festival in Montreal must be able to use a cell phone to interview people, take pictures, and shoot video of the festival. Right after gathering all this content, the journalist writes, edits, and formats that content into stories that are posted online through Twitter, Snapchat, Instagram, and Facebook using the same phone. Once those stories are delivered, the journalist compiles more in-depth audio, video, and textual pieces for the traditional news platforms—print, radio, or broadcast.

This process can be described in six steps:

1. Gather
2. Verify
3. Write
4. Edit
5. Post
6. Compile

The point of this six-step process is to remember that content must be delivered to online platforms first, and traditional media second. All traditional media outlets use Twitter and Facebook to deliver breaking news and to lead their audiences back to their specific products. Reporters rely on Twitter and Facebook to inform their audiences, build their stories, and get news tips. Twitter has made instant access to information possible. Now, Twitter is the primary platform journalists use to get information to an audience. Facebook comes a close second as the platform used to post longer text and visual content. Reporters use content-sharing applications to post content to both platforms simultaneously. Media managers expect journalists to post stories first to social media so the audience is encouraged to go further and click on the web link, go to the website, buy the original product—the newspaper, magazine, etc.—or switch on the television or radio station. Of all the social media outlets, Twitter has so far proved to be the most valuable tool for journalists and media business managers to measure audience access.

Canadian journalists have used Twitter to cover a wide range of stories, from breaking news to political commentary. One of the most prolific and skilled journalists using Twitter has been Kady O'Malley, who works for iPolitics, an online media outlet that covers Canadian politics. O'Malley is known for her effective use of tweeting factual news items as well as her biting political commentary on what is happening on Parliament Hill. Her media experience is vast, having worked for newspapers, magazines, broadcasters, and digital media. An *Ottawa Magazine* profile of O'Malley published before her move to iPolitics wrote that O'Malley had "built the bulk of her reputation through on-the-scene reporting directly to the internet as a live blogger, with plenty of snarky commentary tossed in for good measure. . . . The *Hill Times*, the newspaper of record in the parliamentary precinct, has named her one of the 100 most influential people in government and politics for the past two years running. Put simply, O'Malley is trending."

Another Canadian journalist who made his mark for his effective use of Twitter is *Toronto Star*'s Washington, D.C., correspondent, Daniel Dale, who used Twitter for up-to-the-minute reporting from the 2016 U.S. presidential campaign trail. As Dale's tweets about Donald Trump's outlandish comments became more popular, editors decided to use the content from those tweets in another story form called "Daniel Dale's Trump Checks" on the newspaper's website. Dale's journalism was quickly noticed around the world as more people began to follow him online because of his Trump Checks. The more ridiculous things Trump said, the more people read Dale's work online. Documentary filmmaker Michael Moore tweeted about Dale's daily fact-checking, and called out the U.S. media for not being more thorough in their digging for the truth behind each of Trump's statements. Other media outlets took note of Dale's work and began adopting the idea in their online storytelling.

Daniel Dale's fact-checking is not new for the media. Two of the basic principles in journalism have always been to report the truth accurately and to hold public officials accountable. Reporters are also expected to check the information they receive to confirm that it is true. Social media gives journalists an extra tool to do this effectively. Unfortunately, social media is also a platform for gossip, innuendo, lies, sensationalism, propaganda, and fake stories. This means journalists must do an even better job of exposing untruths by continuing to push for accuracy and accountability.

Michael Moore, in his tweeted endorsement of Dale's reporting, also criticized U.S. journalists for falling into the common social media trap. The 24/7 access that the internet gives everyone to information whenever and however they want it means that competition for people's attention is the highest it has ever been. And this means journalists struggle with the need to be first over the need to be right when reporting. This book will demonstrate that the key to success in this journalistic juggling act is ***to be the first one to be right***. Many of the journalists covering the U.S. presidential campaign in 2016 were reacting instead of reporting. They were tweeting as soon as something was said when they should have been proactive—verifying what was said and checking the truth of what was said before deciding how to report the information. When reporters react instead of following press principles, they risk losing credibility. Journalism will survive and thrive in the digital age if the media follows traditional principles of solid reporting. The first two principles are accuracy and accountability.

Solid reporting is evident in the work of Pulitzer Prize–winning reporter David Fahrenthold of the *Washington Post*. Fahrenthold's diligent and persistent research into the trail of Trump's donations during his 2016 election campaign through the Trump Foundation showed the soon-to-be-president's claims of financial donations to charities were distorted and false. Twitter played an important role in Fahrenthold's journalism. Specifically, he used Twitter to ask his readers for help in his research and reporting on the discrepancies and exaggerations of Trump's charitable claims.

Fahrenthold says he decided to follow Trump's money claims when he was covering an event in January 2016 at which the presidential candidate said he had raised $6 million for veterans. Fahrenthold started a handwritten list of money donations Trump said he gave, but the list did not add up to the $6-million tally. When Trump's campaign refused to give Fahrenthold a breakdown of the details behind the donations, the reporter didn't give up—because good reporters don't.

tmyusof/Alamy Stock Photo

Figure 1.3 A journalist uses modern technology and equipment to work on her story.

Along with the principles of accuracy and accountability, a third principle of reporting is persistence. Fahrenthold used other ways to dig for the truth of the donations to veterans. Brad Scriber (see the suggested reading section at the end of this chapter) detailed Fahrenthold's process. The four key tools Fahrenthold used—a pad of paper, a phone, email, and Twitter—show the clear relationship between traditional and today's journalism. From their first assignment right through to their last one, reporters with good professional practices will always use these four key tools. They are used to talk to people and record what they say. Chapter 2 explains how to use these four tools properly as a journalist.

Journalism Training

Long before the advent of digital media, journalism schools debated the best ways to train reporters, asking whether they should emphasize critical thinking or production skills.

Journalism schools offer core courses that drill the fundamentals of news judgment and gathering, writing, and organizing information. Once students understand the basics of good reporting skills, they can adapt stories to other media platforms with added training in the different equipment and technology. In traditional curricula, students would eventually have to pick one stream of study: either print or broadcast. Now, more journalism schools are introducing their students right away to the presentation of news on a variety of platforms. Students are taught how to operate audio equipment, smartphones, video cameras, and computer software for different types of online presentations. Assignments consist of adapting the same story to print, audio, video, voice-over slide shows, stand-ups, video packages, online, pod- and webcasts, and multimedia combined.

Many journalism educators and newsroom managers maintain that the essential elements for journalists depend not only on online gadgetry but also on the traditional skills of critical thinking and storytelling along with quintessential human qualities like integrity and compassion. One researcher of digital journalism surveyed some 450 online managers and producers and found that the top requirements for story editing were news judgment and knowledge of grammar and style; requirements for content creation were the ability to report and write original stories and edit photos; and for attitudes and overall skills, the successful digital reporter needed to be detail-oriented, a good communicator, and able to multitask and learn new technologies.

This book explains the newsgathering process step by step, with review checklists and exercises at the end of most chapters. Each chapter examines a specific part of this step-by-step process that journalists use in developing news stories. The first half of the book, Chapters 2 through 5, focuses on the gather-verify-write steps. Chapter 2 examines how to find and develop news story ideas; Chapter 3 explains the importance of clear writing to inform an audience on multiple platforms; Chapter 4 details the ethical and legal considerations a journalist has to always keep in mind; Chapter 5 outlines how to interview sources, with tips and tools to help start the conversation between reporter and source. The rest of the book, Chapters 6 through 13, shows the various story structures and editing tools journalists use to present and interact with the audience. These final chapters key on the final three steps: edit-post-compile.

There are two appendices included in this second Canadian edition: Appendix A offers students copy-editing tests, and Appendix B provides the answer key to exercises at the end of some of the chapters.

The objective of this book is to act as a springboard into reporting, explaining the fundamentals of journalistic critical thinking, news judgment, and writing. This includes gathering, organizing, and presenting information across media professions and platforms. Once students are thoroughly educated and practised in the basics of journalism, they can continue to adapt and expand their knowledge and expertise to all types of reporting for the media.

Suggested Readings and Useful Websites

Cision. n.d. "2016 Canadian Social Journalism Study." Cision. Accessed June 4, 2018, http://www
.cision.ca/resources/white-papers/2016-canadian-social-journalism-study/
McCarten, James, ed. 2015. *The Canadian Press Caps and Spelling*, 21st edn. Toronto: The
Canadian Press.
———, ed. 2017. *The Canadian Press Stylebook: A Guide for Writers and Editors*, 18th edn. Toronto:
The Canadian Press.

Ottawa Magazine. 2011. "Profile: Queen of the Hill." *Ottawa Magazine*. March 8. Accessed
    June 4, 2018, https://ottawamagazine.com/people-and-places/profiles/from-the-print-
    edition-queen-of-the-hill/

Poisson, Jaime. 2017. "How Toronto Star Reporter Daniel Dale Fact-checks Trump." *Toronto Star*.
    June 16. Accessed June 4, 2018, https://www.thestar.com/news/canada/2017/06/16/how-
    toronto-star-reporter-daniel-dale-fact-checks-trump.html

Public Policy Forum. 2017. *The Shattered Mirror: News, Democracy, and Trust in the Digital Age*.
    Ottawa: Public Policy Forum. Accessed June 4, 2018, https://shatteredmirror.ca/wp-content/
    uploads/theShatteredMirror.pdf

Scriber, Brad. 2017. "The Fact-checking Tools David Fahrenthold Used on Trump's Charity
    Claims." Poynter Institute. January 4. Accessed June 4, 2018, http://www.poynter.org/2017/
    the-fact-checking-tools-david-fahrenthold-used-on-trumps-charity-claims/443233/

Taras, David. 2015. *Digital Mosaic: Media, Power, and Identity in Canada*. Toronto: University of
    Toronto Press.

Exercise 1   Chapter Review Questions

1. What are three principles of solid reporting mentioned in this chapter?
2. Find an example from recent news coverage and show how the reporter used or did not use these principles well.
3. What does the phrase "first to be right" mean? Why is this important to remember?

2 Selecting and Reporting the News

"I had an editor give me this advice when I was just starting out and it was really good advice . . . in your first years, you want to master the art of news reporting. Do different beats, be a general assignment reporter. Get a look at what is out there and meet people, develop sources . . ."

—*Globe and Mail* reporter Robyn Doolittle in a 2017 interview with Torontoist about her award-winning investigative journalism series *Unfounded**

Journalism is about learning new things every day. The best journalists know that no matter how many years they have worked in the business, they always need feedback from their editors and producers, and they will always have help from their newsroom colleagues.

A reporter's first role is covering general assignment stories. General assignment means the reporter writes about a range of topics—a press conference at city hall, a parade, or a car crash involving students leaving a house party. Editors and producers work directly with reporters on story development. They assign and guide reporters through the process of completing stories for print, broadcast, and online. Digital developments have led to the creation of another newsroom role: the multimedia editor or producer who helps reporters tell stories using all three media layers of text, audio, and visuals.

Reporters must know how to handle their first assignments by developing news judgment and learning the basics of reporting. Once rookie reporters are confident using their news sense and have grasped the basics, they can move on to mastering the art of news reporting.

The Characteristics of News

News judgment is instinct, research, and hard work. A reporter knows a forest fire forcing the evacuation of a town of 300,000 residents is a newsworthy story. Emergency officials

---

* Reprinted with permission of Newstex, LLC; permission conveyed via Copyright Clearance Center, Inc.

need reporters to get the information out so people know they have to leave the area, which routes to take to get out, and the locations of evacuation centres.

News events like a serious fire have obvious news value. In other cases, the news value may not be as evident. Journalists rely on their instincts and research skills to determine news value.

Selecting news stories to publish or broadcast is a subjective process—an art. No scientific test helps journalists measure newsworthiness. Journalists have tried to define news, but no single definition has won widespread acceptance or acknowledges all of the factors affecting the process.

Even if journalists cannot agree on a definition of news, they do agree news stories possess certain characteristics. They agree a good news story highlights the dramatic by presenting people who face challenges. Sometimes the people overcome the challenges, sometimes they are beaten by them. Either way, the structure and method of telling their stories is the fabric of journalism.

News events contain at least some of the following nine news pegs:

1. Timeliness
2. Consequence
3. Conflict
4. Human interest
5. Prominence
6. Proximity
7. Progress
8. Suspense
9. Singularity

News pegs are also called hooks. They help journalists decide if something has news value and is worth producing a story. News pegs also help determine how journalists report, write, and deliver a story. A story does not have to have all nine news pegs to be newsworthy, but it should have some of them. And if a story does not have any of these pegs, the audience is left asking "so what?" and "who cares?"

1. Timeliness: When Did It Happen?

Journalists stress current information and try to report it immediately. In the past, print followed broadcast media in reporting the basic facts of a breaking news story, but the internet has changed the nature of print and broadcast journalism. As discussed in Chapter 1, all journalists must file stories on Twitter and other digital platforms before longer stories are prepared for their traditional media outlets. Social media has increased the immediacy of journalism by allowing all journalists to get stories to the public sooner than they can with their traditional media platforms. The audience wants to know what is happening right now. This focus on reporting as quickly as possible through mobile journalism also means the rush to be first to post new information has led to many mistakes. This is why it is important to verify information before sending it out to the audience.

The timeliness peg refers to content, and to the pressure on journalists to get information out quickly—but this push must be balanced with accuracy. Some media outlets get around this hurdle by retweeting with attribution. For example, if an evacuation centre closes down because it has reached capacity, a radio reporter covering the story may tweet this information out. A newspaper reporter on the same assignment may decide to retweet the same information, crediting the radio reporter before confirming the information with officials. This can backfire, however, if the original tweet by the radio reporter is incorrect. Confirm first, tweet second is the guideline to follow.

Investigative pieces are distinctive when it comes to timeliness. Sometimes in investigative journalism, a reporter's research uncovers historical information. The *Globe and Mail* says Robyn Doolittle's investigative team

> . . . spent 20 months filing Freedom of Information requests and collected data from about 175 police forces in Canada and found that one in five people who reported sexual assault over a five-year period to police had their case dismissed as "unfounded"—a code used when an investigating officer believes an allegation is baseless and that no crime occurred. The data showed that sexual-assault complaints are nearly twice as likely to be designated unfounded as physical assault allegations.

Doolittle's investigative series shows timeliness because the findings became immediate when the reporter made the information public.

2. Consequence: What Is the Impact?

Reporters stress important information that affect, involve, or interest their audience. As reporters evaluate events, they must consider the importance of those events on the audience. A family's dispute with their neighbour over a backyard fence may not affect the audience, but if the dispute grows into an issue debated at city council because there is a proposal to change the bylaw restriction on backyard fence heights, that would affect the audience.

3. Conflict: What Are the Opposing Views?

Two people arguing about a social issue is more newsworthy than two people who agree on everything. The tension between subjects creates the conflict that often makes a story dramatic and interesting to read. Although conflict between government officials or agencies, private organizations, or private individuals can be viewed as negative news, it often provides readers and viewers with different opinions about policies and problems. Conflict can exist in any story. A single mother working her way through college faces the conflict of time to care for her child and time needed for her education. A man fighting AIDS faces the conflict of trying to live his life. An athlete fighting her competitors in a championship game faces the conflicts of the limits of her body's endurance and the talent and strength of her competition.

4. Human Interest: What Makes It Compelling?

A necessary part of reporting is talking to people who are affected by the story. In the fire story used at the beginning of this chapter, one angle for a reporter would be to talk to people about what they left behind when the fire forced them to leave their homes. Human interest is one of the most important hooks to develop in a story because of its potential to make the story more compelling to the audience. *New York Times* journalist N.R. Sonny Kleinfield wrote a feature entitled "The Lonely Death of George Bell." Kleinfield's reporting detailed a non-suspicious death of a hoarder in a New York City apartment. The death would have had no news value had Kleinfield not probed deeper to find out what happens when people die alone. Kleinfield's story was a finalist for the Pulitzer Prize, journalism's highest award in the United States.

5. Prominence: Who Was Involved?

If an insurance salesperson or a plumber catches a cold, no one cares except that person's friends and family. If the prime minister of Canada catches a cold while hosting an economic summit, the Toronto stock market may lose 600 points. Even routine events become newsworthy when they involve prominent individuals, such as politicians, business leaders, or celebrities. Almost everything the prime minister does is news because of the public title.

Reporters should not cover public figures to the exclusion of stories about ordinary people. However, the 24/7 news cycle and social media's demand for content in addition to the public's insatiable appetite for celebrity information has seen a rise in entertainment and sports coverage. Twitter, Instagram, and Snapchat, along with publications like the magazines *Hello!* and *Sports Illustrated*, are filled with information about celebrities.

Ordinary people become prominent when they are involved in a news event. When a crime is committed or an accident occurs, the news media (barring publication bans) will name the suspects or the victims, and they will be considered newsworthy as long as the event is newsworthy. Once the story runs through a news cycle and is no longer considered newsworthy, the prominence of the story's subjects diminishes, unlike the prominence of public figures who are always in the news.

Sometimes ordinary people become even more prominent in the news, with coverage of their stories lasting weeks, months, or even years. In 1974, a naked man streaked across the stage during Hollywood's Oscars ceremony just before the announcement for the best picture award. The naked man has been named every year since in lists of the top 10 odd events at the Academy Awards.

6. Proximity: Where Did It Happen?

The closer an event is to home, the more newsworthy it becomes. Murders are important news stories locally. Sometimes murder cases attract national attention. British Columbia pig farmer Robert William Pickton was convicted in 2007 for the murders of six women abducted from Vancouver's Lower Eastside (Figure 2.1). After the verdict, Crown prosecutors decided not to go ahead with a further trial on an additional 27 counts of murder despite a substantial amount of evidence. Pickton was sentenced to life in prison with no chance of parole for 25 years.

The remains or DNA of 33 women were found on Pickton's property in Port Coquitlam. Global News reported Pickton told an undercover police officer that he killed a total of 49.

The story also focused attention on issues of drug addiction, prostitution, and missing and murdered Indigenous women. Most murders are not serial cases, so they draw little

THE CANADIAN PRESS/Darryl Dyck

Figure 2.1

Jayson Fleury, brother of Mona Wilson, whom Robert Pickton was convicted of killing, holds a sign as friends and family members of Pickton's victims hold a drum circle outside the British Columbia Court of Appeal where the serial killer's appeal was taking place in Vancouver, B.C., on Monday, March 30, 2009.

national attention. Journalists say readers and viewers are most interested in and affected by stories about their own communities.

Proximity may also be more psychological than geographical. Two individuals separated by thousands of kilometres but who share a characteristic or interest may want to know more about each other. A Canadian mother may sympathize with the problems of a mother in a distant country. Canadian college students are likely to be interested in the concerns of college students elsewhere.

7. Progress: How Does the Story Move Forward?

Some events have news cycles that continue long after the first story is produced. Using the previous fire story example, many follow-up pieces could be produced in the days after the fire started. It is important for reporters to develop the progress peg by asking their sources what happens next. Questions to ask officials could include the following:

- Will more evacuation centres be needed? If so, when will they be opened?
- Where are evacuation centres located?
- Are more firefighters needed?
- When will firefighters arrive?

These questions could prompt answers about what could happen in the future, and provide other story angles. In continual coverage, it is important for reporters to keep the progress peg in mind to move their stories forward with information that keeps the audience up to date.

8. Suspense: What Could Happen?

Suspense is different from the progress peg because it leaves the question of what happens next unanswered. With this peg, the media and the audience do not know what will happen next. The media keep reporting information as soon as it becomes available and is confirmed. A suspense peg could be coverage of the police search for a serial killer, waiting for a jury in a criminal trial to return with a verdict, or waiting for election results.

9. Singularity: What Makes the Story Exceptional?

This final hook is also known as the oddity, quirky, or novelty peg. None of these terms adequately describe this story hook, which covers all emotions from amusement to devastation. Deviations from the normal—unexpected or unusual events, conflicts or controversies, drama or change—are more newsworthy than the commonplace.

The stories about the Ontario government spending $120,000 in 2017 to bring a giant rubber duck to bobble on the provincial waterways for Canada's 150 birthday celebrations is an example of a novelty story (Figure 2.2). The follow-up stories showed the $120,000

THE CANADIAN PRESS /Christopher Katsarov

Figure 2.2
A giant inflatable duck sits on Toronto's Harbourfront as part of the Redpath Waterfront Festival, on Friday,
June 30, 2017.

cost was small when compared to the boost to local economies from money spent by the
crowds who came to see the duck.

News pegs help editors, producers, and reporters evaluate information to determine
if it is worthy of coverage. As journalists progress in their careers, their news sense and instincts mature, and these guidelines are not as important. For beginners, these nine pegs
are a handy guide to find news ideas and research first assignments.

First Assignments

There are two types of stories a journalist works on as a general assignment reporter: the
assigned story and the enterprise story. Both rely on the three principles of reporting discussed in Chapter 1: accuracy, accountability, and persistence in newsgathering. A fourth
principle is curiosity. These principles are not in any particular priority. Each principle
carries equal weight and importance in how journalists conduct themselves. Curiosity
is important because it helps reporters question facts and look for the nine news pegs; it
provokes them to examine all sides of a story; it forces them to dig deeper in their research

to ensure what is presented as fact is not shaded by a source's opinion or interpretation; and it challenges them to use all of their observational skills and talents to gather enough details to produce an interesting and informative story.

The Assigned Story

Assigned stories are generally scheduled events, like press conferences, public meetings, or speeches. Newsrooms are notified in advance of these events by media releases sent through email and social media platforms, and by notices and website calendars for public organizations. For example, a city council website will have a link to media releases detailing upcoming meetings for transit, health, and budget committee meetings. A local board of trade will send notices about prominent businesspeople giving luncheon speeches, and an authors' group will promote a night where famous writers host a discussion on freedom of expression for writers in war-torn countries.

Handling Media Releases

A standard media release has details that inform reporters about an event: where it will be held; when it will be held; what time it starts; why it is being held; who will be there; and how and why the event is being held. The release includes the name and contact information for the public relations (PR) spokesperson.

It is important to remember a media release is a starting point and not the end of newsgathering. Reporters should use a media release to get the basic information needed to start researching a story. As soon as they receive a media release, they should read it through once, then read it again while taking point-form notes and writing a list of questions in their notebook. There is a checklist at the end of this chapter with tips about best practices for keeping a reporter's notebook.

First-time reporters often struggle with developing questions, particularly with an assigned story when it seems as if all the information needed is included in the media release. However, reporters must always verify information before reporting it to an audience and need to continue to ask questions about verified information in case there are new developments. There are six questions reporters always ask. These are collectively known as the 5Ws plus H: Who? What? Where? When? Why? and How?

Talking to a Media Spokesperson

Once reporters take notes from the media release and write down questions, they then get in touch with the PR spokesperson listed on the release. Reporters always **both phone and email** a spokesperson—never just do one or the other when making that all-important first connection with a spokesperson. Reporters make contact with the spokesperson to confirm the details in the media release, to see if there have been any changes or developments, and to ask if the spokesperson can connect them to sources for the story. Once the email is sent and the voice mail recorded, they continue to research the story or work on other stories while waiting for the spokesperson to get in touch with them. Patience seems like a misnomer since journalism is a deadline-driven profession, but patience is required when waiting for a spokesperson to respond. Reporters need to tell sources their deadlines and when they need a response.

Once a source returns the phone call, reporters need to be ready to take notes as well as record the conversation. Digital newsrooms rely on all three mediums of audio, visuals, and text to provide multimedia content. Reporters routinely record-on-on-one conversations with sources as Canadian law allows it. But there is a catch. Under the Canadian Radio-television and Telecommunications Commission (CRTC) rules, as long as one party (the reporter) knows the conversation is being recorded, no permission is needed in a two-person conversation. But if the recording is going to be used for broadcast in any form, including online, all parties involved in the conversation must be made aware it is being recorded and agree to parts or all of the conversation being broadcast. Reporters develop the habit of telling sources from the beginning that the conversation is recorded. Media spokespeople are trained to deal professionally with journalists and should be well aware of this practice. But is still a good idea for reporters to remind them.

After reporters identify themselves by full name and media affiliation, they start to ask their prepared questions. It is important for reporters to listen to the answers to see if there are any followup questions. It is okay to stray from prepped questions if something more interesting or another story angle comes up. They can always return to the prepared questions later in the interview. Chapter 5 explains how to prepare and interview sources.

Beginning Research

Once the details have been confirmed with the media spokesperson, reporters start researching the event, the guest speakers, any of the people involved, and previous reports on this event, the topic, or the people. The research is done using the news outlet's own archives—what it has reported on in the past—and a broader internet search. There are new apps created every week that help journalists streamline their online research. Basic keyboarding shortcuts have also been developed to help this research process.

Reporting Basics

An assigned story could be a press conference, a speech, or a community meeting. When reporters arrive at an event, whatever it is, they introduce themselves to the organizers and ensure their notebooks, digital recorder/cell phones, and press credentials are accessible and visible. Reporters take notes about the surroundings and the location of the event. Curiosity, observation, the nine news pegs, and the 5Ws plus H guide a reporter in gathering as much factual detail as possible. Traditionally, reporters would concentrate on one medium. Newspaper reporters gathered facts for written pieces, while broadcast journalists looked for visuals to work with their story scripts. With digital journalism, reporters have to gather textual, visual, and audio content. Reporters have to be prepared to file social media reports first and compile enough detail for long-form stories later. It seems like an impossible task to try to notice and gather content for all three media. But reporters do not try to do everything at once. Here are some tips:

- On arrival, find the organizer.
- Ask for any text, visual, or audio handouts.
- Take notes about the location and factual descriptions of who is there.
- Take establishing photos of the local and prominent people at the event.
- Send a tweet establishing the reporter's presence at the event. Proofread the tweet before sending it.
- If the event is a press conference or a speech, tweet as facts are spoken and prepare to interview sources after the event ends.
- Be sure to interview both scheduled sources—those directly connected to the event, such as organizers and speakers—and unscheduled sources—everyday people who are not directly involved in the event, but who have informed comments that contribute to story by presenting other viewpoints.

A reporter's notes should not be subjective or emotional responses to a source. A reporter's observations must use facts to be descriptive. Factual descriptions include details about facial characteristics—if the source has eyeglasses, a beard, moustache, different coloured eyes, or visible tattoos. Facts are used to describe clothing, height, hair, and eye colour. These are details to help find a source for an interview, and also to use later as description to enhance storytelling. For example, a reporter attends a community forum where the public gets to ask municipal politicians about road construction and one person's question prompts a lively discussion. If the reporter wants to interview this person at the end of the forum, the reporter quickly jots down some descriptive notes that will help find the person when the forum ends. Table 2.1 shows the differences between factual descriptive note-taking and subjective or emotional notes.

The Enterprise Story

Once reporters have shown they can cover assigned stories and have proven to their newsroom bosses that they are accurate, accountable, and persistent in their newsgathering, they move on to enterprise reporting. Assigned or breaking stories develop on their own and reporters cover them as they happen. With enterprise reporting, reporters develop the story. For example, a weather warning about a possible tornado would be an assigned story.

Table 2.1 Factual vs. Subjective Note-Taking

Factual Note-Taking (Do this)	Subjective Note-Taking (Do not do this)
Man in his 30s, goatee beard, wire round glasses, silver nose ring, rose tattoo on right arm, yellow Hawaiian shirt, stained cargo pants, red sandals	Scruffy guy with attitude in his 30s, beard I'd be embarrassed to have, weird glasses, bizarre nose ring, botched tattoo, garish Hawaiian shirt, awful cargo pants, hippy sandals

A tornado touching down would be a breaking story. A reporter writing a piece about the day-in-the-life of a storm chaser tracking the tornado would be an enterprise story. Enterprise stories are the result of thorough research and the reporter's curiosity to always ask why and dig deeper for more answers to more questions. A good reporter is never content with just covering the event detailed in a media release. A solid reporter investigates further to try to get a story different from the other media covering the same event.

The three articles in Box 2.1 on the same topic show the evolution from the media release to the assigned story to the enterprise report. The media release is the reporter's starting point, a source of information for a story idea. The assigned story is the result of the reporter's work researching the story angle outlined in the media release more thoroughly by finding and interviewing people connected to the angle. The enterprise story takes the story angle outlined in the media release and investigates further to see if there are other more interesting angles to the topic for the reporter to pursue.

Box 2.1   Development of an Enterprise Story

Media Release

City of Toronto staff continue to closely monitor and assess conditions on Toronto Island Park. Full efforts are underway to resume park operations as soon as conditions permit. Currently, the reopening of sections of Toronto Island Park remains on schedule for Monday, July 31. Adjustments to that date may occur and the actual reopening could be sooner or later, depending on conditions. Updates on the timing will be forthcoming.

"The high lake levels and associated flooding have had a significant impact on island residents and businesses—as well as the tens of thousands of people who would normally visit the islands every week during the warm weather," said Mayor John Tory. "This has been an unprecedented event. I thank everyone for their patience. City staff are working hard to get the islands reopened as soon as possible."

The water level in Lake Ontario is receding from this 100-year event, but more slowly than hoped. The water level is still about 30 centimetres above the pre-flood conditions of early April and it is not expected to significantly subside until well into the summer.

While staff are planning for the reopening of certain sections of Toronto Island Park targeted for July 31, some portions of the park will remain closed to the public for the entire summer. . . .

Wynna Brown
416-919-6503
wynna.brown@toronto.ca

LINK: http://wx.toronto.ca/inter/it/newsrel.nsf/7017df2f20edbe2885256619004e428e/5f3b1a902a4de6ae852581590055aff7?OpenDocument. Credit: Reprinted with permission of the City of Toronto.

continued

Assigned Story

Crews are on track to have parts of Toronto Island Park reopened to the public by July 31, though that date is far from written in stone, according to a media release from the city issued Monday.

City staff continue to monitor flood conditions on the islands, however, levels still remain 30 cm above pre-flood levels measured in early April before a days-long deluge drenched the Greater Toronto Area. Toronto Island Park has been closed and regular ferry service has been suspended since early May.

While Lake Ontario continues to recede from the "100-year event," it is happening more slowly than anticipated and is expected to remain far above seasonal averages until well into the summer.

"The high lake levels and associated flooding have had a significant impact on island residents and businesses—as well as the tens of thousands of people who would normally visit the islands every week during the warm weather," said Mayor John Tory.

According to the release, Toronto Island Park, which sees up to 1.46 million visitors annually, may open sooner or later than the projected July 31 date. Even if it does reopen on time, many areas will still be off-limits.

Further, some portions will be closed to the public for the rest of summer. These areas include:

- Olympic Island.
- Gibraltar Point.
- Hanlan's Beach.
- Sections of Centre Island, including the grandstand. . . .

LINK: http://www.cbc.ca/news/canada/toronto/toronto-island-park-flooding-reopening-ferries-1.4197788. Credit: CBC licensing.

Enterprise Story

When the waters of Lake Ontario began to rise around Toronto Islands in May, Julian Ganton wasn't worried.

"At first, I was very hopeful, because every season the water does go up and down. It's the natural cycle," he said.

"But once it started flooding almost close to the road, the hope starts to fade a little bit."

Mr. Ganton, a lifelong islander who owns a paddle-boarding business there, has never seen the water this high.

He isn't the only one who has begun to worry. When the islands were closed to visitors at the beginning of May, businesses such as Mr. Ganton's were left without the thousands of tourists who would normally begin visiting the islands (Figure 2.3). The ferries are providing

Deborah Baic/The Globe and Mail

Figure 2.3

The crowds have stayed away in droves at the amusement park on Centre Island because of the flooding. In a normal June, the park might see up to 10,000 people on a weekday.

passage to anyone who has a reservation with an island business, but not many people knew this, he said.

"When I realized that it was more serious, near the end of May, I upped my marketing like crazy because I somehow had to get the word out there that people were allowed to come over," he said. "And it worked, to an extent."

During June of any other year, Mr. Ganton said he would have up to 100 groups of people coming to his business every week, whether for a paddle-boarding tour or to rent equipment. This season, he said, that number is closer to 10.

"I've been sort of shifting my tours to talking about the flood and its natural cycles and bringing people to some of the flooded areas," Mr. Ganton said. "It's not a good thing, but it's quite a unique thing that is interesting, especially if you're not familiar with the island or the Great Lakes."

Shawnda Walker, director of marketing for Centreville Amusement Park, said the numbers aren't clear yet on how much the park has lost.

"We've definitely lost a lot of money. It's already been one third of our season, and we're only open for a very short time," Ms. Walker said. In June, the park might see up to 10,000 people on a weekday.

continued

Centreville found out about the closing of the islands three days before its opening date, which was the first Saturday in May.

While the water is nowhere near as high as it was in May, sandbags still line the roads and shores of Ward's Island, and at the amusement park, a portion of the train tracks, as well as several benches and a bridge, are still underwater.

Ms. Walker said they had hoped to be able to announce the reopening on June 20, but the water was still too high.

"We'd like to be able to announce something soon . . . but until it hits that level, we can't," she said. "Once the city says 'go,' we can open it within 48 hours."

Ralph McQuinn, the owner and operator of Toronto Harbour Water Taxi, would be ready to go even sooner than that. He has two brand-new boats sitting in the docks that have yet to see the traffic June normally brings for his business.

"I've got everything in place. I'm ready," Mr. McQuinn said. He has four people working for him now, when normally he would have 10. But the other six would come back to work at a moment's notice.

Mr. McQuinn said that, although his business has lost a lot from the islands' closing, he remains optimistic about the rest of the season. He knows his isn't the only business that is waiting for good news once the water is low enough.

"We're all gonna get together and get things going," he said. "That island will open up, then we're going to get back to work, and I still think this summer is going to be a great summer."

Luc Cote of Tiki Taxi, another water-taxi company, said he is cautiously optimistic that the islands could be open soon.

"We've noticed a lot of activity," Mr. Cote said of Centre Island, where the amusement park is. He's seen washrooms being cleaned, grass being cut, and other signs that, just like the taxi companies, the park is getting ready for business. "You don't clean a bathroom now for July 31st," he said.

Mr. Cote's business normally picks up around the May long weekend, when it got a notice from the city about the closing. "They cashed our cheque for the permits, and then told us the next day that permits were suspended," he said.

His first thought was of his staff. He told his employees he would do his best to keep them busy part-time. Mr. Cote wanted to keep as many of them on as possible so that if the islands are opened up, Tiki Taxi would be ready.

Like Mr. McQuinn, Mr. Cote has two brand-new boats for the summer. He estimates that, so far, his business has lost around $70,000. But he thinks this year's flooding may have a positive effect on islands' businesses after all the media attention the flooding has received.

"It's incredible how many people don't even know that there's an island," he said. "So now that people's curiosity is piqued . . . I think it may end up having a good effect in the long term."

Types of News

Journalists recognize two major types of news: hard and soft. "Hard news" usually refers to serious and timely stories about important topics. The stories may describe a major crime, fire, accident, speech, labour dispute, or political campaign. Journalists call hard news "spot news" or "straight news." "Breaking news," a similar label, refers to events just occurring, or "breaking" now.

"Soft news" usually refers to feature or human-interest stories. Soft news entertains as well as informs. It may make readers laugh or cry, love or hate, envy, or pity. Although still newsworthy, soft news is often less timely than breaking news. Consequently, editors can delay soft stories to make room for more timely stories. Soft stories also may use a less formal style of writing, with more anecdotes, quotations, and descriptions.

The Importance of Accuracy

A reporter's reputation depends on getting the facts right. Editors and producers work with reporters to verify that the information they gather for their stories is accurate, factual, and objective, as well as shows multiple points of view. Social media adds pressure to this gathering and verification because the volume of information available online is immense and a lot of it is not always accurate. This has potential for false news to have disrupting effects on a journalist's job. The three political journalists mentioned in Chapter 1—Kady O'Malley, Daniel Dale, and David Fahrenthold—are like all responsible reporters who use Twitter in two distinct ways: to tweet out short, concise sentences that report on the story they are covering, and to have Twitter users help them research a story. Journalists report on Twitter by tweeting out their original content, in short bursts of information and also by retweeting what others have written. Journalists also use Twitter for source development—to find out additional information about a topic they are covering or further their research efforts by asking other Twitter users who are not journalists to help them.

Fahrenthold relied on Twitter users to investigate story ideas for him. These reporting and research uses of Twitter are valuable but can also be disruptive to a reporter's process because online information is often posted and re-posted by search engines themselves, or people motivated by spreading gossip, innuendo, speculation, and propaganda. Journalists need to sift through this stream of information to sort the truth from the lies. The verification process takes time, and in the 24/7 news world the pressure to be the first to report a news story can overwhelm the journalistic need to verify first. It is essential to a reporter's work ethic to verify before posting.

The Washington, D.C.–based Newseum developed the E.S.C.A.P.E. checklist for fake news. E.S.C.A.P.E. teaches young reporters how to look for evidence that content is credible, to check the sources used, to examine how the story fits into the bigger picture, to determine the audience, and to look at how the story is presented. The Newseum poster in Figure 2.4 outlines the six ways to judge if the information is true or false. This E.S.C.A.P.E. route can be used to verify any story from any platform.

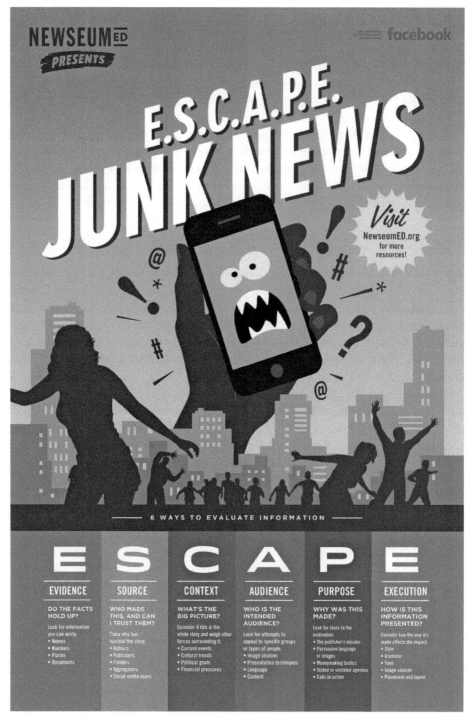

Figure 2.4 The E.S.C.A.P.E. checklist for fake news

Journalistic errors affect the public's perception of the media and ultimately the media's credibility within the public. The media's reliance on Twitter has created more errors than ever because of the urge for reporters to tweet first and confirm later. Many reporters have had to send out tweets correcting previous tweets. The motto "better to be right than first" is just as important as "correct an error as soon as it is discovered." Never hide a mistake—your journalistic integrity depends on it.

Accuracy in Facts

Professionals who manage news organizations do their best to report the news as fairly and accurately as possible. Editors require reporters to confirm every important fact with at least two sources.

Some factual errors are embarrassing. One daily newspaper was forced to publish a correction after a reporter mistakenly quoted a dead sheriff. The reporter had called the sheriff's office to obtain information about an accident and assumed the man who answered the telephone was the sheriff. He was the sheriff, but a new one; his predecessor had died a few weeks earlier. In writing a story about the accident, the reporter—who failed to ask the sheriff his name—attributed all the information to his dead predecessor. A fundamental rule is never to assume anything. Reporters should make it a routine practice to always ask sources to say and spell their full names and titles.

Carelessness and laziness cause most factual errors. Too often reporters rely on editors to catch mistakes in their copy, from misspelled names to math that doesn't add up, to figures that are out of date. With the push to post to social media first, reporters have to be their own editors on the run. This means reporters must know how to check not only the correct spelling of their sources' names and their proper titles but also the calculations in any numerical data. To self-edit, read over each sentence of a story to check the facts against reporting notes. Make sure all names are spelled correctly against the notes, and then that the spelling is consistent in the story. For basic figures, check against reporting notes, and what each source has said about the figures. If there are any discrepancies, call the sources back to clear up any discrepancies and confirm what the figures mean. It could be that each source has a different interpretation, and it is important that all interpretations are presented in the story. Reporters should do all of this work before sending their stories to editors for vetting. If the sources are unavailable or unable to provide the information, reporters should wait until sources are available, delete portions of the story, or kill the story. Reporters should never guess or make any assumptions about the facts.

Conscientious news organizations check their stories' accuracy. Reporters are expected to provide contact information for their sources for fact-checking. Copy editors double-check reporters' math by calculating percentages and statistics. Many errors occur because reporters fail to check their stories; numbers must add up. For example,

> Of the 10 men and women who were interviewed, five favoured the proposal, three opposed it, and three said they had not reached a decision.

Reporters also must understand a topic before they begin to write about it. Too often, when asked about a fuzzy sentence or paragraph, beginners respond, "I really didn't understand that myself." If reporters do not understand something they have written, neither will the audience. Reporters who do not understand a topic should go back to their source and ask for a better explanation or find a source who can explain it.

Accurate writing requires specifics instead of generalities. Getting specifics requires more effort, but in the end the story will be clearer, more accurate, and more interesting to readers and viewers. The key is to double-check—even triple-check—all the information, ask for specifics, ask for spellings, and ask whether the information is correct. Reporters whose stories contain factual errors are reprimanded. Reporters who repeatedly have errors in their work could face suspension or lose their jobs.

Sometimes inaccuracies appear in news stories because reporters have engaged in misconduct, such as fabricating quotations, sources, or facts; selectively reporting information; or committing plagiarism. News organizations fire reporters caught engaging in these behaviours. A news organization's most important asset is its credibility, and that asset must be protected.

Accuracy in Names

News organizations are particularly careful in their handling of names. Spelling errors damage a journalist's reputation, infuriate sources, and frustrate audiences.

Other errors arise because of a reporter's carelessness. A source may say his name is Shaquille, and a reporter may assume his name is spelled with one "l" instead of two. Never assume anything—always check and check again.

Absolute accuracy may be impossible. Because of the need to meet strict deadlines and social media demands, reporters work quickly and sometimes lack the time to perfect their stories. Reporters also are vulnerable to misinformation. They get much of their information from sources who may have impressive titles and may sound knowledgeable. But some sources may be ignorant of the facts, and others may lie.

Public/Civic Journalism

More than 25 years ago, a movement emerged in many newsrooms. The internet expanded the dialogue between journalists and the public, making it an open one rather than a one-way communication where the media told the audience what was news. The internet gave people the means to talk back to the media by contributing content and telling the media what they are concerned about in their communities. This movement of public/civic journalism has grown into a permanent connection that the media depends on to develop everything from the daily coverage of breaking news stories to longer work of investigative projects. The home page of most media websites has a link for members of the public to file information, photographs, or videos they have captured from a news event. Journalists routinely scan social media and use applications to gather content posted by citizens about news events and as well as interview people who witnessed them.

Public/civic journalism is also reflected in the rise of both independent media and joint investigative projects between journalism schools and news organizations. Rabble.ca is an example of independent media that is sponsored by individual donations from the public and organizations, including many labour unions. An example of collaborative investigative public interest journalism was the release in October 2017 of *The Price of Oil* series. The series is the result of the largest ever collaboration of journalists in Canada, from the *Toronto Star*, Global News, and the *National Observer* and journalism schools at Concordia, Ryerson, Regina, and UBC. It was published in the *Toronto Star* and broadcast over Global News.

David Beers, founding editor of the award-winning, Vancouver-based online publication The Tyee, is a leading Canadian advocate of public journalism. In an interview with Lauren McKeon at J Source, Beers explained the effects online media have had on the rise of public journalism:

> Unlike print, online is immediately accessible wherever you are. Its publishing schedule is minute to minute. It allows "coopetition"—the aggregating and sharing of other people's content to create media aligned with your community's interests. It's tied into the immense power of social media. And, done right, it can be productively interactive.

Supporters of public journalism link it with fundamental concepts of democracy: by participating in self-government, people preserve democracy. The role of the press in a democracy is to keep the public informed, provide a forum for public debate, and help citizens make informed choices.

Advocates of public journalism say journalists cannot live in a vacuum as neutral observers. Reporters should listen to all voices, not just the loudest, and listen particularly to people whose views on issues fall near the centre, not just those at the extremes. Supporters of public journalism suggest that the routine 5Ws plus H questions work well but should be expanded. In public journalism, reporters should ask:

- Who—cares, is affected, needs to be included, has a stake, is missing from this discussion?
- What—are the consequences, does it mean to citizens, would this accomplish, values are at work?
- When—were things different, can things be different, should talk lead to action?
- Where—are we headed, is the common ground, should debate take place, is the best entry point for citizens?
- Why—is this happening, is discussion needed, are things not happening, should people care?
- How—does it affect civic life, did the community react, does the story encourage action or help the public decide?

Civic journalism done well pays off in a more informed community and in a stronger media audience.

Checklist for a Reporter's Notebook

A reporter's notebook has a specific size and format. Here are some tips for the proper notebook.

- The notebook should be small enough to fit into a pocket.
- The spiral coil should be at the top of the notebook, not along the side. This makes the pages easier to flip in one hand while writing with the other hand.
- Practise holding the notebook, a digital recorder, and/or cell phone with the same hand.
- Put the reporter's full name and the date on the cover of the notebook.
- Some notebooks have bands to hold the pages in place. If not, use a rubber band to keep it closed and the pages together.
- Tuck reporting business cards under the band.
- Always have business cards to give sources, even the ones who are reluctant to talk. Giving a business card is a polite, professional way of ending an interview, even a difficult, unresponsive one, because sources may want to talk at another time.
- Date each notebook page and number the pages.
- Order notes by drawing a line down the middle of the page, if the line isn't already part of the page format. One side is used to write observations and questions for a source, and the other side is used to write quotations from the source.

Checklist for Email and Voice Mail

- Always put a pertinent subject line on an email.
- The salutation in the email should be the person's full name. Do not use honorifics. Be gender neutral and do not write "Hey!"
- Keep emails concise—one to two sentences—stating reporter's full name, media affiliation, interest in covering the story, and need to verify the details.
- Sign off with full name and all contact information—email, cell phone, and professional social media addresses (Twitter, Instagram, Snapchat, etc.).
- Save the email as a draft and proofread it before sending it. All names should be spelled correctly and there should be no errors in spelling, grammar, or punctuation.
- After sending the email, call the source. To leave a voice mail message, speak clearly saying your full name, media affiliation, and the purpose of the call.
- Speak clearly and slowly so the message is audible.
- Advise that an email has also been sent.
- Advise source of deadline.
- Leave a contact number.
- Always end with a thank you.

The Writing Coach

Better by the Dozen: 12 Quick Tips for Being a Smarter Reporter

Greg Hardesty is a former journalist for the *Orange County Register*. Hardesty is vice-president of Cornerstone Communications and an adjunct faculty member in journalism at Cal State Fullerton in the United States. His 12 tips for being a better reporter can be found on the Society of Professional Journalists. This is an edited and condensed version of Hardesty's list.

By Greg Hardesty

Orange County Register

Be a human being first, and a reporter second. This especially applies when covering tragedies. Show empathy. Keep your notebook and pen out of sight until after you look a person in the eye and introduce yourself, and chat briefly. Make a connection, then get to work.

Listen, listen, listen. You will get your best material by shutting up and not interjecting often when a source is talking. You can interact, of course, but keep it to a minimum.

Clearly explain the angle of your story before you interview someone, including when the story will run (if you know). People feel more comfortable when you spell things out to them however briefly.

Always get a phone number/email to confirm facts. This is crucial. Never get out of the habit of fact-checking (from a printout of your story; never from the computer screen). Also, you never know when you will need an extra quote or more information from your source. So you better know how to reach them.

Never be afraid to ask someone to repeat what they have said. Your source wants you to get things right. So get things right. Don't feel shy about re-confirming even the most basic stuff (i.e., name spelling).

Reconfirm facts via research. For example, go on the internet to confirm the full, official name of an organization to which a source belongs. People often speak in short-hand. It's your job as a journalist to confirm all factual stuff in your story. Get things right.

Urge your source to let you know what they thought of your story. Doing so makes a source feel as if he or she is part of a team (in a sense) and sometimes leads to great follow-up story ideas. Don't act like some snobbish reporter on high who is immune from criticism (and praise, too, for that matter).

Think visually when writing. Visualize a story like a movie in your head. Try to place the reader at a scene. You can still do this, to a degree, when writing straight news—even briefs. Don't get lazy just because your story may be short.

continued

When writing, pay attention to the rhythm of the words. Read your story out loud if you must, but good writing should be inviting to read—it should be effortless and pleasing, like listening to a favourite song. Good stories should have zest, bounce, and energy.

Remember: If you are bored with your story, your reader will be doubly bored. Attack each story by challenging yourself: How can I make this the most interesting story possible? How can I grab the throat of my reader?

Always cultivate story ideas. Urge sources to call you if they ever think they may have a good story for you—even if it has nothing to do with the story you are working on when you talk to them. And when going about your daily lives outside of work, do the same if the subject of what you do comes up. Use the eyes and ears of the community to your advantage.

LINK: http://www.spj.org/rrr.asp?ref=56. Credit: Reprinted with permission of Greg Hardesty.

Suggested Readings and Useful Websites

Bajak, Aleszu. 2017. "A Classroom Card Game to Teach Digital Storytelling Skills." Storybench .org. October 23. Accessed June 4, 2018, http://www.storybench.org/classroom-card-game-teach-digital-storytelling-skills/

Brumley, Nicole. 2017. "In Conversation with Robyn Doolittle: The Reporter Behind the *Globe*'s Unfounded Investigation." Toronto: The Torontoist. February 22. Accessed June 4, 2018, https://torontoist.com/2017/02/conversation-robyn-doolittle-reporter-behind-globes-unfounded-investigation/

Cameron, Stevie. 2007. *The Pickton File*. Toronto: Alfred A. Knopf Canada.

Cribb, Robert. 2017. "A Call to Arms for Public Journalism in Canada." *National Observer*. October 24. Accessed June 4, 2018, https://www.nationalobserver.com/2017/10/24/analysis/call-arms-public-interest-journalism-canada

Frechette, Casey. 2012. "How Wireframing Can Help Journalists Plan & Communicate Ideas." Poynter.org. September 24. Accessed June 4, 2018, https://www.poynter.org/news/how-wireframing-can-help-journalists-plan-communicate-ideas

Gladney, George Albert, Ivor Shapiro, and Joseph Castaldo. 2007. "Online Editors Rate Web News Quality Criteria." *Newspaper Research Journal* 28(1): 55–67.

Hackett, Robert A. 2000. *The Missing News: Filters and Blind Spots in Canada's Media*. Ottawa: Centre for Policy Alternatives.

Hardesty, Greg. n.d. "Better by the Dozen: 12 Quick Tips for Being a Smarter Reporter." Society of Professional Journalists. Accessed June 4, 2018, http://www.spj.org/rrr.asp?ref=56

Journalistic Standards and Practices. 2004. Toronto: Canadian Broadcasting Corporation.

Kleinfield, N.R. 2015. "The Lonely Death of George Bell." *The New York Times*. October 17. Accessed June 4, 2018, https://www.nytimes.com/2015/10/18/nyregion/dying-alone-in-new-york-city.html

McKeon, Lauren. 2011. "Five Questions for David Beers." Toronto: J Source. Accessed June 4, 2018, http://www.j-source.ca/article/five-questions-david-beers

Minsberg, Talya. 2015. "Snapchat: A New Mobile Challenge for Storytelling." *The New York Times*. May 18. Accessed June 4, 2018, https://www.nytimes.com/times-insider/2015/05/18/snapchat-a-new-mobile-challenge-for-storytelling/?_r=1

Policy Options. 2017. "The Future of Canadian Journalism." Policy Options. January 23.
    Accessed June 4, 2018, http://policyoptions.irpp.org/magazines/january-2017/the-
    future-of-canadian-journalism/
Silverman, Craig, ed. 2014. *Online Verification Handbook*. Maastricht, Netherlands: European
    Journalism Centre. Accessed June 4, 2018, http://verificationhandbook.com/
Wallace, Catherine. 2017. "Journalists Are Vanishing. Who Will Fill the Void?" *Toronto Star*.
    February 4. Accessed from https://www.thestar.com/news/atkinsonseries/2017/02/04/
    journalists-are-vanishing-who-will-fill-the-void.html
J Source: The Canadian Journalism Project: http://www.j-source.ca/
The Tyee: www.thetyee.ca
Rabble: http://rabble.ca

Exercise 1   News Judgment

Using the nine news pegs, discuss in class why these items are newsworthy.

1. Your province's Ministry of Education released a report today saying high school stu-
    dents in your city have reached an all-time high in scoring on their literacy exams.
2. The province approved a plan to build a six-lane bypass around your city that
    will cost $284 million and destroy thousands of acres of prime agricultural and
    developable land.
3. A city man was charged in an arson that destroyed an apartment building and
    killed eight people, including five children.
4. CSIS investigators visited the public libraries in your city to check on the reading
    records of several local residents who CSIS believes may be linked to terrorism.
5. Three Israelis and 10 Palestinians were killed in a suicide bombing at a bus stop
    in a suburb of Tel Aviv.
6. The parents of quintuplets in your city saw their five children off to school for the
    first time, as the three boys and two girls were picked up by a bus that took them
    to kindergarten.
7. More than 100 people were killed and another 800 injured when a runaway pas-
    senger train collided with a freight train in Tanzania.
8. City officials agreed at their Tuesday night council meeting to spend $128 million
    to build a new trash incinerator that would burn trash from the city as well as
    from six surrounding counties.

Exercise 2   Accuracy in Facts

Patricia Richards, a 52-year-old businesswoman in your city, today announced that she
is running for mayor. You know and can prove all the following facts but have never reported them because she was a private citizen. Mark the facts you would report today and
discuss in class.

A.   _____Richards has been divorced three times.

B.   _____At the age of 17, Richards and two friends were charged with stealing a car. The charges were dropped because the car was recovered undamaged and the car's owner, a neighbour, declined to prosecute.

C.   _____Richards has diabetes.

D.   _____Richards has had two abortions.

E.   _____Richards is a recovered alcoholic; she has not had a drink in 20 years.

F.   _____Before going into business for herself, she was fired from two other jobs because of her drinking.

G.   _____Her campaign literature says she attended McGill University, yet she never graduated.

H.   _____She established, owns, and manages the city's largest chain of furniture stores.

I.   _____Various tax and other public records reveal that her chain of furniture stores is valued at $20 million and last year earned a profit of $2.3 million.

J.   _____Each year Richards donates more than $1 million to local charities that help troubled young women but always avoids publicity, insisting that the charities never mention her donations.

Exercise 3   Accuracy in Facts

Your provincial MLA Constance Wei was involved in a traffic accident that resulted in the death of another driver and his passenger. Which of the following details would you use and which would you discard? Discuss in class.

A.   _____Wei is married and has two children.

B.   _____As an attorney, Wei successfully defended two people who had been accused of vehicular manslaughter.

C.   _____Wei was speeding and ran a red light.

D.   _____A woman, who didn't want to be identified, called your newsroom and said the minivan she and her children were riding in was almost struck at an intersection one time by a car driven by Wei.

E.   _____Friends of Wei said she often joked about having a "lead foot."

F.   _____Police said Wei refused to co-operate with them when they arrived at the scene of the accident.

G.   _____Wei has had five tickets in the past four years for speeding and reckless driving.

H.   _____Wei was first elected to office nine years ago.

I.   _____Wei was driving on an expired driver's licence.

J.   _____ Wei once sponsored a bill to eliminate the point system used to penalize drivers stopped for motor vehicle violations. Drivers would lose their licences after accumulating a certain number of points.

3 The Language of News

> *"Get to the point as directly as you can; never use a big word if a little one will do."*
>
> —Emily Carr, Canadian artist and writer*

Reporters have a challenging task. They must convey information, often complex information, to their audience. They have to tell a story by providing facts in a clear and concise manner, using simple language. Simplicity of language matters because reporters are trying to reach people whose interests vary greatly. Some may be only interested in world events, while others may be fascinated by entertainment and celebrities. To communicate effectively to a mass audience, reporters must learn to present information in a way that will allow almost everyone to read and understand it.

Basic newswriting style presents factual information succinctly, impartially, and objectively. One principle of journalism is the separation of fact and opinion when writing basic news stories, and reporters and editors work hard to avoid expressing opinions when writing. It can be a struggle for reporters to maintain a neutral stance, especially in the current environment where the news cycle never ends and the public has 24/7 access to publicize their points of view and criticisms of the news media—no matter how hateful or destructive. David Corn, the Washington, D.C., bureau chief of the online magazine *Mother Jones*, says, "It is more important not to be objective, but to be accurate." Accuracy is the reporter's best defence against accusations of slanted reporting.

The first step to any well-written and accurate story is planning and preparation. Before writers attempt to construct a news story, they need to identify the main idea they want to convey to their readers. This main idea is called the story angle.

---

* From: Carr, Emily. *Growing Pains: The Autobiography of Emily Carr*. Douglas and McIntyre, 2005. p.4. Reprinted with permission of the publisher.

Mapping Your Story

Identifying the Story Angle

Writing, whether about simple or complex topics, requires preparation and organization, also referred to as mapping your story. This preparation begins even before reporters start gathering information—when the story is just an idea in the mind of the reporter, editor, or producer—so that they know what information is needed for a balanced story. Once reporters have gathered all the necessary information, they then must organize the information into a story structure. The best way to do this—whether for long or short stories—is to decide on the story angle and write a brief outline.

The angle for a news story is a one- or two-sentence summary of what the story is about and why it is newsworthy. It is a statement of the topic—and more. Several stories may cover the same event, but the angle of each of those stories should be unique. In digital journalism, reporters also produce multimedia packages of content covering the same story. Each layer of media used—text, audio, visuals—in the packages covers another aspect of the story.

For example, if a plane crashed on landing at an airport, the multimedia package would have several stories about the crash. Each story would cover a unique angle (Figure 3.1). One story might have as its angle: "Wind and rain made airport runways

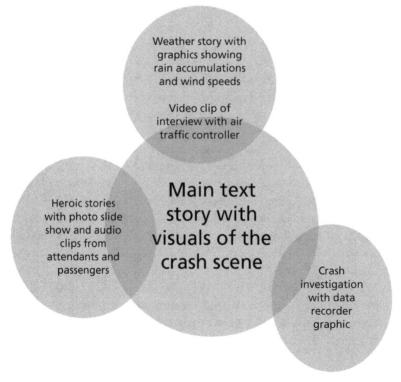

Figure 3.1 Different story angles for one event

treacherous, but other planes made successful landings." That story would report on weather conditions at the airport and whether air traffic controllers and other pilots considered them to be severe. The text piece would be accompanied by visual graphics showing wind currents and rain levels at the airport and a video clip interviewing an air traffic controller. The angle for another story might be: "The heroism of passengers and flight attendants saved the lives of dozens of people." That story would report what happened in the passenger cabin after the crash and how those who survived made it to safety. It could also include a photo slideshow of the people involved, with audio clips of their interviews. A third story's angle might be: "Federal investigators have recovered the flight data recorders but will need days or weeks to figure out what caused the crash." That story would focus on what will likely happen in the investigation of the crash and might include a graphic of how a data recorder works to record information. Although each of these stories would be about the plane crash, each would have a distinct angle, and each would have only information relevant to that angle. Collectively, all the content covers the main event: the crash.

News stories may have many possible angles. Which one reporters use depends on their news judgment, the information they gather, and their estimation of what their audiences want to and should know. If the CEO of a major corporation resigns when the business is forced to pay millions of dollars in damages after losing a lawsuit, the story for a local newspaper might focus on whether the company will have to eliminate jobs. A story on a financial news site might have as its angle the impact of the lawsuit on investors' confidence in the company. A digital newsletter that covers legal affairs might emphasize the failure of the company's courtroom strategy. Although these media and their reporters would select different angles for their stories, each choice would be appropriate for the media outlet's audience.

Story Outlines

Reporters usually have a good idea what the angle of their stories will be even as they begin gathering the information. Often, however, unexpected information emerges that forces them to rethink the story angle. Therefore, reporters always review their notes and other gathered materials before they start writing. Reviewing assures reporters they have identified the most newsworthy angle and have the information they need to develop it. It also helps them decide what the major sections of their stories will be. A reporter covering a local resident's decision to run for mayor might decide the angle is "Singh announces plans to run for mayor." The reporter then might decide that the story should have these major sections:

- Why the candidate is running
- What the candidate plans to do if elected
- Who the candidate's opponents are
- What the opponents' plans are if elected
- What the reaction is to the candidate's announcement

The angle combined with the brief outline of the sections form the skeleton of the story. Now, the reporter needs to develop each section.

Once reporters have selected an angle and written a brief outline, they can go through their notes again to decide what information belongs where. Some reporters number passages according to what section of the story they will be placed. Others use coloured pens or markers to indicate where to put particular facts, quotations, or anecdotes. They leave out information that does not fit in any of the sections.

Reporters who fail to identify a story angle or who lose sight of that angle risk writing stories that are incoherent and incomplete. No one sits down and writes great stories. Writers must plan their work. Only once they have mapped their story angle and outlined its sections, then it is time to write. A reporter's writing needs to be clear and concise so their audience can follow the flow of the story and understand it. A reporter needs to be skilled at choosing the right words and building coherent sentences and structured paragraphs, all of which work to present meaningful facts in a story that informs its audience.

The Effectiveness of Words

People expect more of journalists, who must master language. When news organizations hire a new reporter, they look for someone who understands and respects language, knows spelling and grammar, possesses an extensive vocabulary, and can write content for all the news outlet's platforms. Reporters need to have the ability to write using sentence and paragraph structures that are specific to where the stories appear (Figure 3.2). For example, a newspaper reporter covering a city council meeting where a motion to raise bus fares is passed must quickly tweet a short sentence about the fare increase. Then the reporter would write a straight news story for the newspaper, using short paragraphs that are two to three sentences long, with sentences longer than the tweet. The story would appear in the newspaper and on the paper's online site. The reporter may have a longer piece for the weekend that examines the effect the bus fare increase will have on the community. This feature would be written using longer sentences and paragraphs than the news story for the newspaper. The development of wearable devices means delivering news has to be done in even shorter sentences, almost in headline-like information bursts. Push notifications are written with brevity.

The people who devote their lives to journalism develop a respect for language. They value writing that is clear, concise, and accurate. They strive to select the exact word needed to convey an idea, use the word properly, and place it in a sentence that is grammatically correct.

When a major breaking news event occurs, such as a mass shooting in a public place, journalists rush to the scene, gather information, and then transmit it to the public. All journalists write about the same event, but some stories are much better than others. Why?

Some reporters are particularly adept at gathering the information needed to write exceptional stories. Other reporters produce exceptional stories because of their command of the English language. Their language is forceful, and their stories are written so

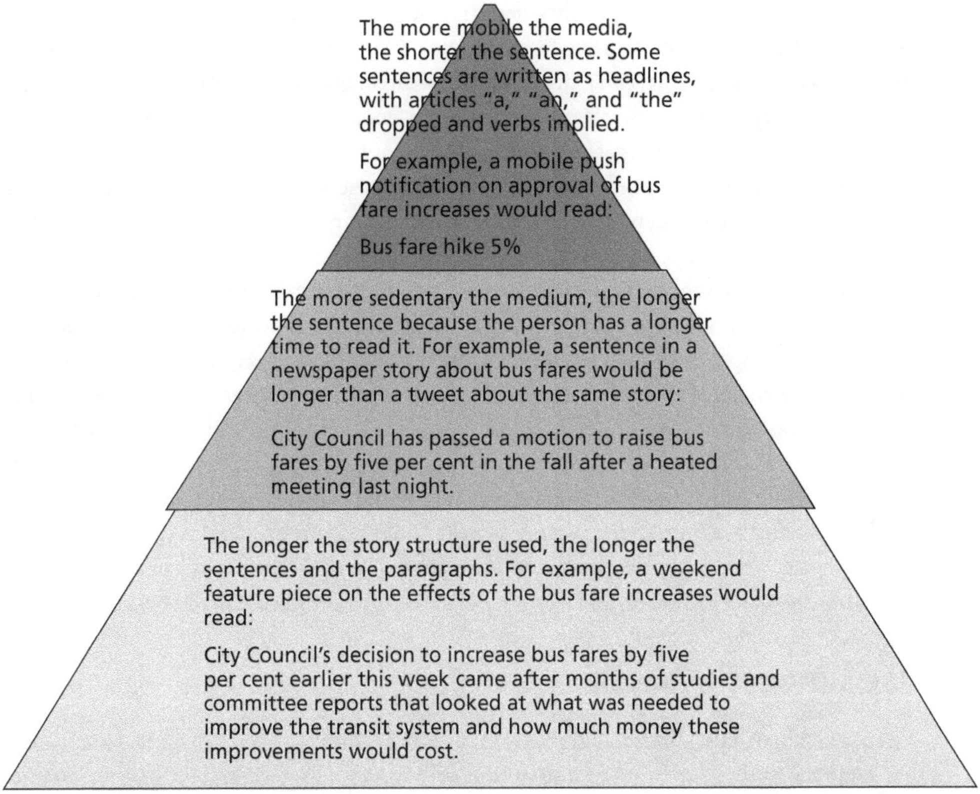

The more mobile the media, the shorter the sentence. Some sentences are written as headlines, with articles "a," "an," and "the" dropped and verbs implied.

For example, a mobile push notification on approval of bus fare increases would read:

Bus fare hike 5%

The more sedentary the medium, the longer the sentence because the person has a longer time to read it. For example, a sentence in a newspaper story about bus fares would be longer than a tweet about the same story:

City Council has passed a motion to raise bus fares by five per cent in the fall after a heated meeting last night.

The longer the story structure used, the longer the sentences and the paragraphs. For example, a weekend feature piece on the effects of the bus fare increases would read:

City Council's decision to increase bus fares by five per cent earlier this week came after months of studies and committee reports that looked at what was needed to improve the transit system and how much money these improvements would cost.

Figure 3.2 Paragraph lengths vary depending on where the story is published.

clearly and simply that everyone can understand them. These reporters describe people, places, and events involved in news stories and use quotations that enable the sources in their stories to speak directly to the public.

Skilled reporters can transform even routine events into front-page stories. A reporter who is unimaginative about or indifferent to a topic may write a three-paragraph story that because of its mediocre writing will not be used. Another reporter, excited by the same topic, may go beyond the superficial topic and write a three-paragraph story about unusual developments, injecting colour into the story.

Word Choice

To communicate effectively, reporters must be precise, particularly in their selection of words. The perfect word choice makes a sentence forceful and interesting; imprecision creates confusion and misunderstanding.

Some words are inappropriate in news stories. Few editors or news directors allow words like "cop" or "kid" (they prefer the more formal and proper "police officer" and "child").

News executives allow profanity only when it is essential to a story's meaning; even then, they refuse to publish the most offensive terms. Some editors have particular pet peeves and ban the use of contractions (isn't, can't, don't) except in direct quotations. Other editors may allow contractions. Reporters quickly learn there is an in-house style for the media outlet they are working for, and then there is the particular style of the individual editor/producer they are working with on any given day. But in spite of these idiosyncrasies, reporters need to choose words that accurately convey the factual meanings they need to properly tell their stories.

Some errors occur because the reporter is unaware of a word's exact meaning, or is trying to use more formal official language. The guidelines are to use words that are accurate and to use a shorter, more colloquial word that would be used in everyday language rather than a formal word. Journalists would write a car "hit" a tree instead of a car "collided" with a tree.

Confusion sometimes arises because words look or sound alike. Some commonly confused words are "buses" and "busses," "naval" and "navel," and "reckless" and "wreckless." The word "busses" refers to kisses, not the vehicles people ride. A "navel" is a belly button, and some motorists drive "wrecks" but are convicted of "reckless" driving. It is important to remember the spell-check function is a tool that checks only for spelling; it does not check for meaning and proper word use. Our eyes are still the best proofreader.

Use Powerful Verbs

When journalists talk about using powerful or strong verbs in their copy, they mean verbs that help the audience visualize the action of what is being described in the sentence. Verbs can transform a routine sentence into an informative one that captivates an audience. Powerful verbs paint a vivid picture to help the audience envision the events. The following sentences are colourful and interesting because the students who wrote them used descriptive verbs:

> A cargo door *popped* open, tearing a hole in the plane's side. Eleven passengers *sucked* out of the hole *plunged* 30,000 feet to their deaths.

> A gunman *jumped* behind the customer service counter of a department store Monday, *grabbed* a handful of money—then *fled* on a bicycle.

Powerful verbs describe one specific action and help to make your sentence factual. Weak verbs cover a number of different actions and are too vague. The first sentence in the following example is general and lacks detail because it uses a weak verb. The last three rewrites use specific, descriptive verbs and are more informative:

> His brother got a personal computer.
> His brother bought a personal computer.
> His brother won a personal computer.
> His brother stole a personal computer.

Other sentences that are weak and bland can be improved by powerful verbs:

ORIGINAL: A historic railroad bridge that was once the tallest and largest in the world was destroyed by strong thunderstorms that crossed the province Monday afternoon.
REVISED: Blustery thunderstorms *sweeping* across the province Monday afternoon *toppled* a historic railroad bridge that was once the tallest and largest in the world.

There are two other reasons why accurate word choice and using strong verbs are important in media writing. Accurate words and strong verbs support the proper sentence structures used in media writing where the most important information—the news—is placed at the beginning of a sentence. In the storm example above the news is what the storm did to the bridge. The interesting detail about the bridge's history is secondary information, but not the news.

Follow S-V-O Sentence Structure

A journalist's use of sentence structure can also make a sentence more dynamic and clear. The best structure for a sentence in a straight news story follows the order of subject-verb-object (S-V-O). The subject appears first, followed by an active verb, followed by an object. S-V-O sentence structure works using active verbs. An active verb means the subject of the sentence is doing the action of the verb. The object of the sentence is receiving the action of the verb. Take this sentence as an example:

The bodies were **located** by **rescue workers** shortly after 6 p.m.

Rescue workers is the subject, *located* is the verb, and *the bodies* is the object. This sentence is in the wrong order—O-V-S—which makes it awkward and too wordy. It is better to rewrite using S-V-O:

Rescue workers located the bodies after 6 p.m.

Now the sentence has impact, clarity, and brevity, using eight words instead of 11.
Avoid the repeated use of forms of the verb "to be," such as "is," "are," "was," and "were." These verbs are overused, weak, and dull—especially when a writer uses them in combination with a past participle to form a passive-voice verb, such as "were located." Sentences using passive verbs are also wordier than those with active ones:

ORIGINAL: It <u>was</u> discovered by the company lawyers that the financial records were incorrect. (13 words)
REVISED: Company lawyers discovered the financial records were incorrect. (8 words)

ORIGINAL: The program <u>was</u> created by parents and students. (8 words)
REVISED: Students and parents created the program. (6 words)

ORIGINAL: The defendant <u>was</u> sentenced by the judge to 10 years in prison. (12 words)
REVISED: The judge sentenced the defendant to 10 years in prison. (10 words)

ORIGINAL: Police officers were summoned to the scene by a neighbour. (10 words)
REVISED: A neighbour called the police. (5 words)

Simplify Words, Sentences, and Paragraphs

To simplify stories, avoid long, unfamiliar words. Whenever possible, substitute shorter and simpler words that convey the same meaning. Use the word "about" rather than "approximately," "build" rather than "construct," "call" rather than "summon," and "home" rather than "residence."

Also, use short sentences and short paragraphs. Rewrite long or awkward sentences and divide them into shorter ones that are easier to read and understand. Research has consistently found a strong correlation between readability and sentence length: the longer a sentence is, the more difficult it is to understand.

This does not mean that all stories should have nothing but short sentences. Too many short sentences strung together makes writing sound choppy. Long sentences, constructed and used with care, can be effective tools for the writer. Overuse of either long or very short sentences can make the writing awkward and difficult for the reader to understand.

Reporters should write for the ear, listening to the natural rhythm, or flow, of the words and sentences they put on paper. They should test their stories by reading them aloud to themselves or to a friend. If the sentences sound awkward or inappropriate for a conversation with friends, the writer must rewrite them and avoid complex phrases and long, awkward sentences.

Here is what the late Jimmy Breslin wrote for the *New York Herald Tribune* in November 1963 when he covered the funeral of assassinated U.S. president John F. Kennedy.

Clifton Pollard was pretty sure he was going to be working on Sunday, so when he woke up at 9 a.m., in his three-room apartment on Corcoran Street, he put on khaki overalls before going into the kitchen for breakfast. His wife, Hettie, made bacon and eggs for him. Pollard was in the middle of eating them when he received the phone call he had been expecting. It was from Mazo Kawalchik, who is the foreman of the gravediggers at Arlington National Cemetery, which is where Pollard works for a living. "Polly, could you please be here by eleven o'clock this morning?" Kawalchik asked. "I guess you know what it's for." Pollard did.

He hung up the phone, finished breakfast, and left his apartment so he could spend Sunday digging a grave for John Fitzgerald Kennedy.*

The sentences are simple and short, as are the words. There are no needless adjectives and adverbs. Breslin makes sure every word counts and adds meaning to his column. If read aloud, there is a cadence and a somber rhythm to the piece that reflects the tone of that time when the nation was in shock and in mourning. Breslin's column, which uses the human interest news peg discussed in Chapter 2, shows how clarity and simplicity in writing can have a powerful impact on the audience.

Writing coaches note that concise writing can be just as dramatic and have as much impact as long narrative passages. Many writers tend to overwrite when seeking drama or impact. Yet a few carefully selected words can better convey the story to readers.

Also, be certain the ideas in each sentence are related. If they are not, even short sentences can become confusing:

Elected president of the student senate, he went to Parkdale Elementary School.

Planning on being the first person in line for the concert, she bought her first car when she was 16.

Long introductory phrases and subordinate clauses overload sentences, making them more difficult to understand:

ORIGINAL: Fighting the wildfire from two fronts to keep the flames from engulfing the entire town, firefighters decided to let the house burn.
REVISED: Firefighters decided to let the house burn. They had been fighting the wildfire on two fronts to keep the flames from engulfing the entire town.

Sometimes beginners pack too many ideas into a single sentence:

ORIGINAL: The mayor said he was happy that the city council had passed the resolution increasing the public library tax to provide more funds to expand the library's book collection, build a website, and add a new wing to house government documents, but the amount of the increase was not enough to do everything that has to be done because repairs are needed to the roof of the public library building and facilities must be improved for accessibility.
REVISED: The mayor said he was happy that the city council had passed the resolution increasing the public library tax but added that the amount of the increase is not enough to do everything that has to be done. The tax increase will provide funds to expand the library's book collection, build a website, and add a new wing

---

* Reprinted with permission of the estate of Jimmy Breslin. All rights reserved.

to house government documents. Other work that needs to be done, the mayor said, includes repairs to the library's roof and accessibility improvements in facilities.

Paragraph length, as well as sentence length, varies from publication to publication. A paragraph should demonstrate relationships between ideas. It is a means of making complicated material clear. Like the words that form sentences, the sentences that form paragraphs should flow together, logically combining similar thoughts or ideas. Paragraphs should not combine unrelated ideas. But ideas that are related or belong together should not be artificially separated just to create shorter paragraphs. If you needlessly separate ideas, you risk producing choppy writing. Skilled writers are able to connect related ideas and material in a logical sequence that flows smoothly throughout the story.

Eliminate Unnecessary Words

Unnecessary words confuse readers and make reading difficult. Reporters must eliminate unnecessary words but retain enough detail to make their stories informative. By writing concisely, reporters present readers with as much information as possible. Brevity also helps readers grasp the main idea of each story. Writers who use two or more words when only one is necessary waste time and space. Some words are almost always unnecessary: "that," "then," "currently," "now," and "presently," for example. Because some nouns and the verb tense tell when an action occurred—in the past, present, or future—it is redundant to add a second word reiterating the time, such as "past history," "is now," and "future plans."

Notice how easily several unnecessary words can be cut from the following sentences without changing their meaning:

ORIGINAL: She was able to begin college classes her senior year in high school.
REVISED: She began college classes her senior year in high school.

ORIGINAL: At the present time he is planning to leave for Vancouver at 3 p.m. in the afternoon next Thursday.
REVISED: He plans to leave for Vancouver at 3 p.m. Thursday.

Be especially careful to avoid phrases and sentences that are redundant—that unnecessarily repeat the same idea. The following phrases contain only two or three words, yet at least one—the word in italics—is unnecessary:

dead body
exactly identical
hurry *up*
mutual cooperation
reason *why*
armed gunman

split *apart*
unexpected surprise
past experiences
free *of charge*

Improving some redundant sentences requires more thought and effort:

ORIGINAL: Deaths are extremely rare, with only one fatality occurring in every 663,000 cases.
REVISED: One death occurs in every 663,000 cases.

Redundancy often arises because writers introduce a topic and then present specific information about it. Usually, the more specific information is enough:

ORIGINAL: Trying to determine who was responsible for the burglary, police checked the door frame for fingerprints.
REVISED: Police checked the door frame for fingerprints.

Repetition is more common in longer passages involving several sentences. Sentences appearing near the end of a paragraph should not repeat facts implied or mentioned earlier:

ORIGINAL: This is not the first elected office she has held in the city. She has been a city council member, a member of the library board, and a Canada Revenue Agency accountant.
REVISED: She has been a city council member, a member of the library board, and a Canada Revenue Agency accountant.

Remain Objective

Journalists should strive to be as impartial or "objective" as possible. Reporters are neutral observers, not advocates or participants in straight news coverage. They can express their opinions and analysis through longer journalistic pieces such as features, editorials, and commentaries.

A reporter's tendency to identify with sources is natural, but good reporters strive to keep their stories free of opinion. When reporters inject their opinions into a straight news story, they risk offending readers and viewers who may not want reporters telling them how to think.

One way reporters keep their opinions out of news stories is to avoid loaded words, such as "demagogue," "extremist," "radical," "racist," "segregationist," and "zealot." Such words are often unnecessary and inaccurate. Many times, these loaded words state the obvious—that an argument was "heated," a rape "violent," or a death "unfortunate." Reporters can eliminate opinions in some sentences simply by deleting a single adjective or adverb: "alert witness," "famous author," "gala reception," "thoughtful reply." Here are two more examples:

> **ORIGINAL:** The pricey tickets are available only at the door.
> **REVISED:** The tickets are available at the door.

> **ORIGINAL:** The tragic accident killed three people.
> **REVISED:** The accident killed three people.

Writers can avoid loaded words by reporting factual details as clearly and thoroughly as possible.

Entire sentences sometimes convey opinions, unsupported by facts. Good editors will eliminate these sentences. Often, deletion is the only way to correct the problem. Here are two examples of sentences that need to be removed from copy:

> The candidate looks like a winner.
> Everyone is angry about the mayor's decision.

Reporters can report the opinions expressed by other people—the sources for their stories—but must clearly connect those opinions to the source. This connection to a source is called *attribution* and is required for proper media reporting and writing. All facts in a straight news story must connect to a source. If reporters fail to provide the proper attribution, readers may think the reporters are expressing their own opinions or agreeing with the source:

> **ORIGINAL:** The family filed a lawsuit because the doctor failed to notice the injury.
> **REVISED:** The family's lawsuit charges that the doctor failed to notice the injury.

The initial sentence does not show attribution (connection) to a source and reads as if the reporter is writing "the doctor failed" as a stated fact. The revised sentence properly attributes this detail ("the doctor failed") to a source, in this case the lawsuit.

Unacceptable Language

Offensive, condescending, or patronizing terms or phrases in defining individuals or groups by gender, race, age, religious belief, cultural practices, or mental, physical, or emotional disabilities are unacceptable. A person's race, religion, or ethnic background should only be used in copy when the fact is clearly relevant to a story. The *Canadian Press Stylebook* advises identifying a person "by race, colour, national origin, or immigration status only when it is truly pertinent" and providing a full description, "including but not limited to colour," only if "a person wanted by police is at large." Avoid occupational terms that are gender specific: "fireman," "chairwoman," for example. Use gender-neutral language—"chairperson," "spokesperson," "firefighter." As well, use the gender-neutral "they" rather than the specific "he" or "she" in your writing.

Words to Avoid

Adjectives and Adverbs

Reporters avoid adverbs and adjectives because they tend to be less forceful, specific, and objective than nouns and verbs. William Strunk, Jr., and E.B. White, authors of the influential book *The Elements of Style*, wrote, "the adjective hasn't been built that can pull a weak or inaccurate noun out of a tight place."

Adverbs and adjectives in the following sentences editorialize. Rather than simply reporting the facts, they comment on those facts:

> **ORIGINAL:** It was not until Monday that university officials finally released the report.
> **REVISED:** University officials released the report Monday.

> **ORIGINAL:** Upon hearing about the frivolous lawsuit, the mayor made it quite clear that she plans to fight the outrageous complaint.
> **REVISED:** The mayor said she plans to fight the lawsuit.

The word "finally" in the first sentence implies that university officials were negligent and should have released the report sooner. Similarly, reporting the facts in the second story clearly and concisely eliminates the need for words like "frivolous" or "outrageous." And saying the mayor made something "clear" implies she is stating a fact, not an opinion.

Clichés

Clichés are words or phrases that writers have heard and copied over and over. Many are 200 or 300 years old and are so overused they have lost their original impact and meaning. Clichés no longer startle, amuse, or interest the public. Because they eliminate the need for thought, clichés have been called the greatest labour-saving devices ever invented.

The news media can take a fresh phrase and overuse it so that it quickly becomes a cliché.

Journalists employ clichés when they lack the time to find words more specific, descriptive, or original (Box 3.1). A reporter under deadline pressure may say that a fire "swept through" a building, an explosion "rocked" a city, police officers gave a suspect a "spirited chase," or protesters were an "angry mob."

While clichés are overused, sometimes they can be twisted into a fresh expression or used in a surprising way. Here is a headline the *Toronto Star* ran in 2017 for the fourth birthday of Britain's Prince George.

> Will and Kate release fresh prints of swell heir.

The headline used the title of 1980s sitcom *Fresh Prince of Bel-Air* for its catchy play with words for the heir to the throne. This type of writing is effective in grabbing the audience's attention and elevates the story above what the competing media does.

Box 3.1   Clichés

There are thousands of clichés and slang phrases that are just too easy to use, especially when reporters are pressured by deadlines and a catchy phrase comes more quickly to mind than one that is accurate and fresh. Clichés can be replaced by writing the real meaning of the phrase. The more facts reporters gather, the more details they have to write in the story. Details help convey meaning and can eliminate clichéd writing.

Here are some examples of how information can turn clichés into clear, concise sentences packed with facts:

1. They worked **around the clock** to get the store ready for the grand opening.
    The employees worked **from 6 p.m. yesterday until 7 p.m. today** to prepare the store for the grand opening.
2. The hockey team has made it to the playoffs **at long last**.
    The hockey team has made it to the playoffs **after 35 years of struggling at the bottom of the national rankings**.
3. **It was a baptism by fire** for the rookie paramedics who pulled people from the burning truck.
    It was the first day on the job for the rookie paramedics who pulled people from the burning truck.
4. Today's weather was **the calm before the storm** of tonight's thunder showers.
    Today's **sunny skies and high temperature of 25 degrees ended** with the sudden thunderstorm that dropped the temperature down 15 degrees.
5. The councillor said the motion to increase taxes was **dead and buried**.
    The councillor said the motion to increase taxes was **voted down in a 13 to 5 vote**.
6. The cruise ship **limped into port** after its engines failed.
    Five tugboats **brought** the cruise ship **into port** after its engines failed.

Slang

Journalists avoid slang, which tends to be trendier than clichés. Some words that began as slang have won acceptance as standard English. "Blizzard" and "flabbergast" are among such terms. Most slang never makes this transition, however.

Feature stories and personality profiles sometimes employ slang effectively, but it is inappropriate in straight news stories because it is too informal and distracting.

Slang is often specific to a single generation and rapidly becomes dated so that a term used in a story may already be obsolete. During the 1970s and 1980s, young people overused such terms as "cool" and "freaked out," and over the years those terms underwent subtle changes in meaning. Other colloquial expressions have simply become outdated and fallen out of use. By the 1990s, young people found a whole new set of "slammin'" slang terms and "dissed" anyone still using the slang of the 1980s as a "Melvin." A young woman of the early 2000s might show "props" to friends who know the "off the hinges" films showing at the "grindhouse" and get "stoked" about "poppin' tags."

Slang also conveys meanings journalists may want to avoid. It often expresses a person's attitude toward something. Thus, slang terms such as "flaky," "ego trip," and "flatfoot" convey evaluations—often negative and stereotypical—of the things described. Reporters, however, should leave to editorial writers or readers and viewers the job of making evaluations.

Technical Language and Jargon

Nearly every trade and profession develops its own technical language or jargon. When professionals use jargon to impress or mislead the public, critics call it gobbledygook, bafflegab, doublespeak, or bureaucratese. Most jargon is abstract, wordy, repetitious, and confusing. For example, a government agency warned, "There exists at the intersection a traffic condition which constitutes an intolerable, dangerous hazard to the health and safety of property and persons utilizing such intersection for pedestrian and vehicular movement." That sentence contains 31 words. A good journalist could summarize it in four: "The intersection is dangerous."

> **JARGON:** Identification of the victim is being withheld pending notification of his next of kin.
>
> **REVISED:** Police are withholding the victim's name until his family has been notified.

Euphemisms

Euphemisms are vague expressions used in place of harsher, more offensive terms. Some etiquette experts say good manners require the use of euphemisms. Prudishly, some people may say a woman is "expecting" rather than pregnant. Whatever value euphemisms have for etiquette, they detract from good newswriting in which clarity and precision are the most important goals.

Because news stories are written for a general audience, words or phrases that could offend members of the audience are rarely, if ever, used. But sometimes news events force reporters to use descriptive words in place of confusing and awkward euphemisms. An example is the 1993 case of Lorena Bobbitt, the Virginia woman who used a kitchen knife to cut off her husband's penis. The word "penis" had rarely appeared in news stories, and some news organizations were squeamish about using it, especially in headlines. Euphemisms like "member," "organ," or "offending organ" appeared instead. The widespread coverage the Bobbitt case received apparently diminished journalistic sensitivity to the word. A computer search found more than 1,000 news stories that used the word "penis" in the six months after the Bobbitt story broke, compared to only 20 mentions in the previous six months.

A similar phenomenon occurred with the Monica Lewinsky scandal during former U.S. president Bill Clinton's time in office as many reporters and news anchors found themselves writing and talking about oral sex and semen stains.

As with sex, death is frequently referenced by euphemism. People may say a friend or relative "passed on" or "is no longer with us," not that they have died.

During a recession, major companies lay off thousands of employees. Few admit it, however. Instead, corporate executives say they are "restructuring," "downsizing," or "rightsizing" to get rid of "excess workers." Some executives insist such "reductions in force" offer their employees "career enhancement opportunities."

War spawns grotesque euphemisms, perhaps, as some critics say, to hide the human pain and suffering every war causes. Killing the enemy has become "servicing the target." Airplanes no longer bomb enemy soldiers; instead, they "visit a site." And if during the bombing of enemy troops, some civilians are killed, that is "collateral damage." The United States calls the largest of its land-based nuclear missiles "Peacekeepers." Finally, modern armies no longer retreat. Instead, they "move to the rear," "engage in a strategic withdrawal," or "occupy new territory in accordance with plan."

Other Problems to Avoid

Avoid Stating the Obvious: Platitudes

Dull, trite, or obvious remarks are called *platitudes*, and journalists must learn to avoid them. Platitudes that have appeared in news stories include the following:

> **ORIGINAL:** Superhighways, high-speed automobiles, and jet planes are common objects of the modern era.

The example appeared in a story about technological changes that had occurred during the life of a 100-year-old woman. The sentence would have been more interesting if it had described the changes in more detail and clearly related them to the woman's life:

> **REVISED:** Lila Hansen once spent three days on a train to visit relatives in California. Now, she flies there in three hours every Christmas.

When people stop reading a story, they rarely think about why it bored them. If they re-examine the story, they might realize it is just a series of platitudes. Platitudes say nothing that hasn't been heard before. People may stop reading the story because it is no longer interesting or newsworthy.

Avoid First-Person References

Except in extraordinary circumstances, journalists should remain neutral bystanders. They should not mention themselves in straight news stories. Reporters should use the third person perspective and not the first person in news stories.

> **ORIGINAL:** He said we must work harder to improve the city's schools.
> **REVISED:** He said parents must work harder to improve the city's schools.

ORIGINAL: The prime minister said we are being hurt by inflation.
REVISED: The prime minister said Canadians are being hurt by inflation.

Avoid the Negative

For clarity, avoid negative constructions. Sentences should be cast in positive rather than negative form, as in the following examples:

ORIGINAL: The student did not often come to class.
REVISED: The student rarely came to class.

ORIGINAL: The defence attorney tried to disprove her client's sanity.
REVISED: The defence attorney tried to prove her client was insane.

Sentences containing two or three negatives are wordy and even more difficult to understand. Aim to write your sentences to be clear, concise, and straightforward in their meaning. As you read the following examples, you may have to pause to determine their meaning:

ORIGINAL: The women said they are not against the change.
REVISED: The women said they favour the change.

ORIGINAL: The MP said she would not accept any campaign contributions from people who do not live in her riding.
REVISED: The MP said she would accept campaign contributions only from people living in her riding.

In most cases, the problem can be corrected by changing a word or two:

ORIGINAL: Most people are not careful readers.
REVISED: Few people are careful readers.

ORIGINAL: The financial planner said he could help people not go into debt.
REVISED: The financial planner said he could help people avoid debt.

Avoid Gush

Reporters also avoid "gush"—writing with exaggerated enthusiasm. They write news stories to inform members of a community, not to please their sources. News stories should report useful information. They should not praise or advocate.

Two ways to avoid gush are to always use more than one source for a story and to demand that sources provide specific details to support their generalizations. Using multiple independent sources prevents reporters from being misled or manipulated by sources seeking favourable publicity. By insisting that sources provide details and specific examples to support their claims, reporters can minimize the tendency of sources to engage in the kind of self-praise found in these examples:

> "We feel we are providing quality recreational programs for both adults and children," Mohammed Oza said.

> Police Chief Noor Sidhu said the city's mounted horse patrol, which began one year ago, has become a great success.

Each of these sentences needs to be followed with more detailed information in the stories to answer why the recreation program is a quality one and why the horse patrol is a success.

When a journalist finishes an article, it should sound like a news story, not a media release. Yet one travel story gushed that Mexico is a "land of lush valleys and marvelous people." Other examples of gush:

> The fair will offer bigger and better attractions than ever before.

> The event will provide fun and surprises for everyone who attends.

This gush cannot be rewritten, because there is nothing of substance to rewrite. It simply should be deleted.

There is a second type of gush because of an escalation in modifiers. Columnist Donna Neely explains that what used to be called "funny" is now called "hilarious" and what used to be "great" is now "fantastic" or "incredible." Exaggerations appear everywhere: in news stories, media releases, advertisements, and everyday speech. Sportswriters call athletes not just "stars" but "superstars." Advertisers call their inventories "fabulous" and their sales "gigantic." Delete all such modifiers or replace them with facts and details, and let readers and viewers decide for themselves what adjectives are appropriate.

Time References

Avoid using "yesterday" or "tomorrow" in your copy. Digital journalism has changed the traditional newspaper style of using "yesterday" and "today" to being specific about days and dates. Reporters should use the day of the week—or even the specific date further down in the copy—to explain when an event happened.

If breaking news is updated online, the dateline at the top of the web page will give the dates and exact time of publication (Figure 3.3).

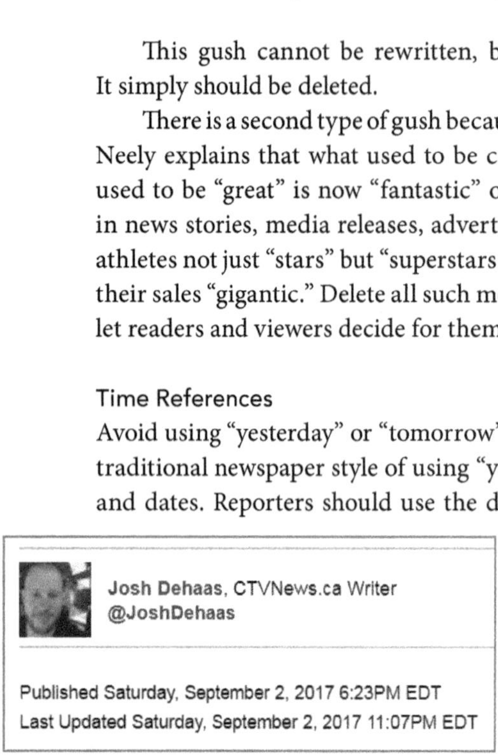

Verb Tense

Stories written for immediate publication on a website or for broadcast use the present tense. When the story is likely to reach readers or viewers as the

Josh Dehaas, CTVNews.ca Writer
@JoshDehaas

Published Saturday, September 2, 2017 6:23PM EDT
Last Updated Saturday, September 2, 2017 11:07PM EDT

Figure 3.3
This article was published at 6:23 p.m., but continued to be updated after publication.

events are unfolding, the present tense may be more accurate and more compelling than the past tense.

Print reporters avoid the present tense because many of the events they report end before readers receive the paper.

The following example shows copy that a broadcast or online reporter may publish immediately as a fire is burning. In contrast, the print copy gives more details about what happened because it will be published in the next day's paper.

> **BROADCAST/ONLINE COPY:** A fire at the Grand Hotel threatens to destroy the entire block.
> **PRINT COPY:** A fire at the Grand Hotel caused $1 million in damages when it destroyed an entire city block yesterday.

Avoid Excessive Punctuation

Journalists avoid excessive punctuation, particularly exclamation points, dashes, and parentheses. Exclamation points are rarely necessary and should never be used after every sentence in a story, regardless of that story's importance. Parentheses interrupt the flow of ideas and force people to pause and absorb additional, often jarring bits of information:

> **ORIGINAL:** He (the premier) said the elderly population (people 65 and older) had grown twice as fast as any other segment of the province's population in the last 20 years.
> **REVISED:** The premier said the percentage of people 65 and older had grown twice as fast as any other segment of the province's population in the last 20 years.

Sources use a lot of pronouns and vague references. Students often quote these sources, adding explanations within parentheses. If an explanation is necessary, then a direct quotation is not a good idea. Instead, reporters use partial quotations or paraphrase what a source has said:

> **ORIGINAL:** "I wish they (school administrators) would quit fooling around," she said. "They say they don't have enough money (to hire more teachers), but I don't believe that. I know they have it (the money); it's just a matter of priorities— of using their money more wisely."
> **REVISED:** She said the school administrators should "quit fooling around." She explained she doesn't believe that they do not have enough money to hire more teachers. "It's just a matter of priorities—of using their money more wisely," she said.

✓ Checklist for Newswriting Style

Follow these guidelines when writing a story:

1. Identify the story angle.
2. Write a brief outline of the three or four major parts of the story.

3.   Use short, familiar words.
4.   Use short sentences and short paragraphs.
5.   Eliminate unnecessary words.
6.   Avoid overloading sentences with unrelated ideas.
7.   Use relatively simple sentences that follow normal word order: subject-verb-object.
8.   Avoid statements of opinion.
9.   Avoid stereotyping people by race, gender, age, ethnic group, religion, cultural practices, or disabilities.

Checklist for the Language of News

Choose words that convey meaning as precisely as possible. Write a story with detail so it answers all the questions an audience might ask about the topic.

1.   Use active verbs and vivid nouns.
2.   Prune adjectives and adverbs from sentences.
3.   Avoid clichés, journalese, slang, and euphemisms.
4.   Avoid loaded words and opinionated or artificial labels.
5.   Avoid using the words "I," "me," "we," "us," and "our" except in direct quotations from a source.
6.   Avoid misleading statements about the time of the story. Use the specific day of the week or the date—not yesterday," "today," or "tomorrow."
7.   Avoid gush, exaggeration, contrived labels, and excessive punctuation.
8.   Avoid repetition: Do not unnecessarily repeat the same word in a sentence.
9.   Avoid platitudes: Do not state the obvious.
10. Use present tense for broadcast and online; use past tense for print media.

 The Writing Coach

The section on common writing faults in *The Canadian Press Stylebook* pays a lot of attention to the fundamentals of newswriting style. Here are some excerpts:

The most common faults in writing are lack of imagination, muted curiosity, and a deaf ear and closed eye for the reader's interests. These faults lead straight to stories that are predictable, unfocused and boring.

By turn or together, they may confuse readers with conflicting information, leave them gasping for missing facts or infuriated at what they know is misinformation.

Such stories can puzzle readers with fog and bafflegab and have them wondering what the news means to them and their everyday lives.

Bluntly put, they turn readers off.

Active vs. passive: Think of active verbs as power words—words that drive your sentences, keep the reader's attention, and move her briskly along.

Not: The economy experienced a quick revival.
But: The economy revived quickly.
Not: At first light there was no sign of the ship.
But: The ship vanished in the night.

Use the passive when a switch in emphasis is helpful, for instance, to put the news ahead of the source:

Not: A grievance board has ordered the reinstatement of a counsellor fired for kicking a patient.
But: A counsellor fired for kicking a patient has been ordered reinstated by a grievance board.

And the passive may lighten a sentence by removing secondary information that can wait: A banker wanted for questioning in the disappearance of $1 million is believed to have flown to Mexico, police said today. (But be sure a later paragraph gives reasons for the belief.)

More than words: Tell the reader what has happened, certainly. But also help the reader understand why and how it has happened in terms that strike home.

Not: The hurricane caused widespread damage to buildings, farm equipment, trees and hydro lines.
But: The hurricane's winds lifted roofs off houses and barns and flipped over cars, tractors, and even lumbering dump trucks used to carry grain. Almost every fruit and shade tree in the region was knocked over, and linemen said about 3,000 hydro poles had been snapped off.

Suggested Readings and Useful Websites

Barry, Dan. 2017. "Jimmy Breslin, Legendary New York City Newspaper Columnist, Dies at 88." *The New York Times*. March 19. Accessed June 4, 2018, https://www.nytimes.com/2017/03/19/business/media/jimmy-breslin-dead-ny-columnist-author.html?smid=fb-nytvideo&_r=0

Cumming, Carman, and Catherine McKercher. 1994. *The Canadian Reporter: News Writing and Reporting*. Toronto: Harcourt Brace Canada.

Jacobi, Peter. 1982. *Writing with Style: The News Story and the Feature*. Chicago: Lawrence Ragan Communications.

McCarten, James, ed. 2015. *The Canadian Press Caps and Spelling*, 21st edn. Toronto: The Canadian Press.

———. 2017. *The Canadian Press Stylebook: A Guide for Writers and Editors*, 18th edn. Toronto: The Canadian Press.

McFarlane, J.A., and Warren Clements, eds. 2003. *The Globe and Mail Style Book: A Guide to Language and Usage*, 9th edn. Toronto: *The Globe and Mail*.

Plotnik, Arthur. 2007. *Spunk & Bite: A Writer's Guide to Bold Contemporary Style*. New York: Random House Reference.

Stepp, Carl Sessions. 2000. *The Magic and Craft of Media Writing*. Chicago: NTC Publishing.

Strunk, William, and E.B. White. 1999. *The Elements of Style*, 4th edn. White Plains, NY: Longman.

Wells, Jackson. 2017. "Journalists Talk Societal Discontent Toward Media in Trump Era." *Brown Daily Herald*. October 23. Accessed June 4, 2018, http://www.browndailyherald.com/2017/10/23/journalists-talk-societal-discontent-toward-media-trump-e

Yagoda, Ben. 2004. *The Sound on the Page: Style and Voice in Writing*. Toronto: HarperCollins Canada.

Zinsser, William K. 2006. *On Writing Well: The Classic Guide to Writing Nonfiction*, 30th anniversary edition. New York: HarperCollins.

Canadian Association of Journalists: www.caj.ca

Canadian Journalism Foundation: www.j-source.ca (English); www.projetj.ca (French)

Comma Queen video series with Mary Norris: http://video.newyorker.com/series/comma-queen

Exercise 1   Editing

Answer Key provided: see Appendix B.

Section I: Being Concise

Eliminate the unnecessary words from the following sentences. The sentences do not have to be rewritten; simply cross out the words that are not needed.

1. The contractor did a totally complete job on the renovation.
2. The candidates for mayor will conduct a poll of the residents.
3. She said the new innovation would save the company money.
4. He said the birthday party was an unexpected surprise.
5. The police officer tried to calm down the accident victim.

Section II: Rewriting Wordy Sentences

Rewrite the following sentences, eliminating unnecessary words and correcting any other errors.

1. The mayor said everyone had to co-operate together or someone would file a lawsuit against the city.

2. It would appear that the new school mascot, which got a stamp of approval from alumni, will make an appearance at Saturday's game.

3. As a matter of fact, some of the tickets were free of charge to the contest winners while other tickets cost the sum of $50 for handling fees.

4. Police claimed the armed gunman was carrying a dangerous weapon when he entered the bank with the underlying purpose of robbing it.

5. Local residents said they planned to evacuate in the event that the floodwaters reached the banks of the river and completely destroyed the town.

Section III: Using Powerful Verbs

Rewrite the following sentences, using stronger verbs. Also use subject-verb-object (S-V-O) sentence structure.

1. The car is in need of a new paint job.
2. He was planning to open a restaurant in Moncton.
3. The professor was able to interest many students in his classes.
4. The preschool nutrition program is set up so that the cost is paid by the province.
5. A short circuit in the electrical wiring at the church was the cause of the fire.
6. The cost of a ticket for admission to the amusement park is $25.
7. A trip to the beach is what Karen and David are planning for this summer.
8. To obtain extra money to pay for university, John has picked up a second job.
9. It was suggested by the moderator that the panel participants may want to take a break.
10. The reservations she made at the hotel were for three rooms.

Exercise 2   Vocabulary

Words with different meanings often look or sound similar. As a journalist, you should be familiar with these words and use them correctly. Cross out the wrong words in the following sentences, leaving only the correct ones.

1. The mayor (accepted/excepted) the offer from the university board of directors to (aide/aid) the city in its (clean up/cleanup) efforts after the storm.

2. The professor (alluded/eluded) to the chapter in the book that mentions that people will (altar/alter) their behaviour if they are (assured/ensured/insured) their efforts will be rewarded.

3. The (cite/site/sight) of the new World War II memorial (peaked/peeked/piqued) the interest of many (people/persons) in the neighbourhood.

4. (Personal/Personnel) were asked to evaluate their (peers/piers) in regard to (their/there) job performance.

5. She was afraid the club members would (waiver/waver) in defence of their actions when it was determined the (principle/principal) planned to (censure/censor) them for demonstrating in front of the school.

6. The restaurant (complemented/complimented) the meal with a delicious (desert/dessert).

7. The team's (moral/morale) was higher (than/then) ever after (their/there/its) undefeated season became a reality.

8. Police said the car was (stationary/stationery) when the truck (collided with/struck) it, causing a quite a (cite/sight/site) for passersby.

9. The beautiful (weather/whether) was one of the reasons that thousands of Canadians turned out to demonstrate at the (Parliament Buildings/Parliament buildings/parliament buildings).

10. The snowstorm during the (assent/ascent) of the mountain peak hampered the rescue workers from reaching the climber who (received/sustained/suffered) a broken leg (due to/because of) a fall from a ledge.

4 Media Ethics and Law

"What is right? What is just? What is for the public good?"

—Joseph Howe, *Novascotian* newspaper editor, 1835

Joseph Howe was a journalist, an orator, a newspaper owner, and a politician during a time in Canadian history when newspapers generally were the mouthpieces for political parties. Howe resonates for this chapter discussion on media ethics and law because he is considered one of the first Canadian journalists to speak publicly in defence of a free and responsible press. Howe was charged with criminal libel for publishing a letter in his newspaper criticizing provincial politicians and police for misuse of public funds. Howe's speech in his own defence at his libel trial in Halifax, Nova Scotia, in 1835 was eloquent for the time and lengthy (more than six hours). He argued for the necessity of a free press that watches and checks on those who hold power over citizens. He was acquitted of the charge. The Howe case is a pivotal one for Canada's free press because it set out the goals of all journalists to find out what is right, what is just, and what is for the public good. This chapter discusses the ethics guiding journalists in these goals and the legal precautions they take to guard against being charged with libel.

Ethics

Journalists follow a code of ethics to keep their profession transparent, credible, and responsible. The Canadian Association of Journalists (CAJ) details this code at http://caj.ca/ethics-guidelines. The code's principles are updated by the CAJ board of directors annually and followed by journalists and media organizations.

Reporters use ethical guidelines and moral direction to help chase down the truth of a story—to sort through the avalanche of 24/7 information to find out what is true and what is not. In their newsgathering process, journalists have four important connections: their sources; the public; the stories; and their editors/producers. Each connection is built on a foundation of trust and responsibility, and all of these relationships must work together for a journalist to be an ethical and moral professional. A crack in one connection can weaken others and damage a journalist's reputation.

Reporters have an ethical duty to protect their sources. This is acknowledged in the *Journalistic Source Protection Act*, which became law on October 19, 2017. This act amends both the *Criminal Code* and the *Canada Evidence Act* to give more weight to a journalist's promise of confidentiality to a source. Before the act became law, if police asked to a journalist to reveal a source, it was up to the journalist to convince the court the source's identity needed to be protected. Now with the *Journalistic Source Protection Act*, the onus is on the police to convince the court the source's identity should be revealed.

The Sources

Journalists connect with and interview people who can be sources for their stories. A source can be an everyday person who is involved with the story or an official source who is an authority on a particular issue. Journalists seek sources with different opinions so all sides of an issue are presented. They should always look for a range of sources with different views.

Using Friends and Relatives

Reporters cannot use their friends and relatives as sources because it compromises their integrity and objectivity. Friends and relatives can be used as a network to gain access to other sources with whom a reporter is not connected. Journalists are expected to be transparent when they have a connection to a story, whether as a family member, friend, or acquaintance (a mechanic or landlord, for example). Reporters must disclose what their connections are and let their editors/producers know before proceeding with a story, so they can be reassigned if needed.

Where's the Line?

Journalists need to know where to draw the line between being friendly and being friends with sources. Once the line is crossed, it is harder for reporters to stay objective. Sources who become friends may expect to be treated favourably, and this puts journalists in a compromising position.

Sources give credibility to stories, offer ideas, add a different perspective, and help with leads for information. However, it also is important to keep connections professional and avoid becoming too friendly. Reporters can have coffee with sources, but should not invite them over for a family barbeque. When journalists find they are becoming too chummy with a source, they should ask their editor for a change in assignment.

Official sources know how journalism works. They know a journalist's goal is to gather information from all sides and report a balanced, objective story. But official sources can still try to manipulate the reporter–source connection. Reporters should be mindful of how official sources may try to steer them toward their way of thinking.

Non-official sources do not necessarily understand a journalist's role and can be bewildered when they see stories telling their opponent's version of events as well as their own. Rookie reporters quickly learn part of their job is to educate and remind both official and non-official sources about the profession's rules. They should never assume sources understand how journalists work, and always be clear about professional guidelines. The CAJ code of ethics is a handy resource to refer sources to so they understand how journalism works.

Source Attribution

Journalists make clear at the beginning of an interview everything is on the record and attributable. However, there are times when sources may want anonymity because they fear retribution for talking to the media or they do not want to be held accountable for what they say. In cases where a source may supply information but doesn't want to be attributed to the story, the reporter has to corroborate the story by finding other sources willing to go on the record. There are the four ways the source–reporter connection works.

1. On-the-Record
An on-the-record interview publishes a source's full name and appropriate identifying information that connects them to the story (a job title, for example). The reporter takes handwritten notes and records the interview. Both the source and reporter provide each other with necessary contact information.

2. Off-the-Record
Sources must go off the record before giving a reporter the information they want to protect. They cannot tell the reporter the information first and go off the record after the fact. Reporters working on sensitive stories need to inform their sources of this practice. Off-the-record means the information cannot be used for publication. The only way this information can be used is if the reporter gets the information independently through documentation or from another source who voluntarily gives the information without being asked for it by the reporter.

3. Not-for-Attribution
Not-for-attribution means a reporter can use a source's information but cannot identify the source by name. A source can only be identified by their general connection to the story, for example, as a government official or as a source close to the investigation.

4. Deep Background
Deep background means a source's information can be used but without attribution. The source does not want to be identified in any way, even on condition of anonymity.

Reporting about Grief

The public is especially critical of the way the media covers death and tragedy by photographing and interviewing victims and grieving relatives. Journalists need to be sensitive to victims and the public's sense of decency.

Interviewing Victims

Reporters have been criticized for their lack of compassion in their quests to interview victims of tragedy. Media competition and the desire to get the human interest news peg in a story put pressure on reporters to get these interviews. One horrible idea of old-school journalism was to get to the victims quickly while they were still in shock and the story was still breaking because there was a better chance of them wanting to talk to the media. Victims often complain later they were in shock at the time of the interview and are unable to recall even talking to a reporter. They sometimes recant their stories or accuse reporters of making up the interview. Most journalists find they get more accurate and complete stories if they wait to interview victims. Hard news stories can be written immediately after an event, with accurate, informative follow-up stories later.

Victims or their family members sometimes choose to speak to one reporter during their time of grief. Usually families select reporters who are respectful and considerate. These reporters ask to talk to the family's representative, who might be another family member or close friend. In addition, reporters give their names and telephone numbers to the victim or the victim's representative, not asking for an immediate interview but asking the victim to call if and when the victim feels ready to talk. Compassionate journalists who do not pressure victims and their families receive more in-depth information about them and the event.

Hurting Victims Again

A news story can inflict a second injury on victims and family members who have lived through a disaster and experience the trauma again when the story is produced.

Compassionate photojournalists, reporters, and editors often ask themselves how they would want the media treat them or their own family members if they were in the victim's situation. Journalists discuss the purpose of the story, what the public needs to know, and alternative ways to portray the emotion. They also weigh these crucial questions: Who will be hurt, and how many? Who will be helped, and how many?

Reporting on Victims

In their zeal for presenting facts, journalists can give the wrong impression. When reporters do not know why things happen, they sometimes speculate. Their speculations, however, often err and mislead the public. Journalists should refrain from guessing the "why" or "how" until the information is known for a follow-up story. In a case where a car had gone over the edge of a bridge, reporters investigated the bad driving record and drinking habits of the victim, leading readers to believe he might have been intoxicated. In reality, the victim had been depressed and ended his life. In another example, reporters said a victim of a shooting was a single man who kept pornography. In reality, the victim was divorced and supported two children who lived with him. This former public official, who was a victim of a gunman's shooting spree, had one 1950s *Playboy* magazine in a stack of other old magazines in his garage.

Reporters can transform heroes and victims into bad guys by presenting allusions and incomplete facts. When two teenage boys were sitting outside one of the boys' homes, they saw and tried to stop a burglar from getting into a neighbour's home. One of the boys was killed in the scuffle. One newspaper reported the victim was out at 4 a.m., smoking, had a gun, and was a high school dropout. An anonymous source said the boy "liked to party." Very little information was presented about the burglar. A different newspaper called the boy a hero and quoted the positive things his family and friends had to say. This newspaper story reported the boys were sitting on the porch because smoking was not allowed in the house. The victim was enrolled at an alternative school for dropouts because he was determined to graduate, and he had a job. The gun belonged to the other boy, whom the victim was defending when the burglar stabbed him. The burglar had been arrested several times prior for burglary and aggravated assault with a deadly weapon.

Responsible journalists avoid sensationalism, are respectful of an individual's privacy, and are mindful of the objective of the story: to report the facts and withhold reporting what you do not know.

Using Visuals: Newsworthy or Sensational?

The visual coverage of disasters has challenged many editors. They seek the proper balance between providing the public what it needs to see and presenting traumatic images. Too much repetition of the same graphic—the planes flying into the World Trade Center towers, for example—can numb viewers' reactions to the horrific events. Yet, visuals of young people and children dying show the reality of war.

Editors and producers run photographs and videos because they help tell a story. People upset by the images accuse the media of acting sensationally. Critics denounce a news organization's decision if a photo or video is used for shock. Media critics complain a numbing, saturation effect takes place as viewers become less sensitive to such acts of violence. They are concerned about a visual's effects: whether the footage is gratuitous and tasteless.

Editors and producers often feel cornered. Should they shield the public from unpleasantness or educate them? All media make ongoing decisions, sometimes on a case-by-case basis. At times, words alone do not convey the situation as well as photographs do.

Photojournalist Nilüfer Demir was working for the Dogan News Agency when she covered the drowning deaths of Syrian refugees whose bodies had washed up on the beach in Bodrum, Turkey, on Sept, 2, 2015. Demir took photos of the body of Aylan Kurdi, 3, who died along with his brother and their mother when an inflatable dinghy capsized while trying to sail to Greece. Demir's photographs were posted on social media and went viral immediately (Figure 4.1).

The images of Kurdi's body were seen around the world. Many media organizations used a warning about their graphic and disturbing nature.

Demir explains the ethical struggle a journalist experiences wrestling with the emotions that come with the duty to report tragedy responsibly. She describes in an interview in 2015 with *VICE* that while taking the photo of Aylan's body had a profound and permanent effect on her emotionally, she is also glad her photojournalism helped inform and alter the public's view of immigration and refugees.

AP Photo/Nilüfer Demir

Figure 4.1
Nilüfer Demir's photo of Aylan Kurdi's body was shared around the world.

Photo Technology

The digital revolution has caused great debate about altering photos. Photojournalists can use Adobe Photoshop or similar image-editing software to remove a distracting object in the background of a photo without changing the essence and meaning of the picture. Initially, many argued it was no different from the earlier practices of cropping photos or burning images to provide more contrast. Today, the pendulum has swung back, and photojournalists are loath to change the content of their photos. Why? Because it is dishonest and unethical. Just as writers do not lie about the content of their stories, photographers do not lie about the content of their captured images. Yet clearly, the advent of digital and online communications will continue to raise ethical questions in photojournalism.

Reporting Rumours and Speculation

Journalists are supposed to publish facts but are often tempted to publish rumours. When a gay blogger claimed U.S. Senator Larry Craig had had sex with men, the *Idaho Statesman* started to investigate. But reporters were unable to find information to confirm the rumours, which Craig had vigorously denied. Months later, Craig was arrested in a Minneapolis airport and charged with disorderly conduct for having tried to solicit sex from an undercover male police officer in an airport restroom. Craig pleaded guilty, and the *Idaho Statesman* decided it could publish its story. Although the *Statesman* might have had a more dramatic scoop if it had published the story earlier, it adhered to journalistic standards by publishing only what its reporters and editors knew to be true. Even when a rumour seems credible, journalists risk publishing false information if they have not verified it.

Sometimes, reports of unsubstantiated information can have serious impact, as in the case of reporters covering a mine disaster that trapped 12 miners. When one tired reporter pulled away to return to his motel for the night, he heard shouts of "They're alive!" People were crying with joy, and he thought he heard an official say that miracles could happen. Like most of the reporters at the scene, he immediately called his editor, and the happy news ran on the front page. Unfortunately, it was incorrect news. Only one of the miners was rescued. The reporter ran with second-hand information and did not substantiate it.

When an event occurs, some of the news elements, such as the "who," "what," "where," and "when," are readily available. It might take several days, weeks, or months to find out the "why" and the "how." Yet journalists sometimes try to provide their readers and viewers with the "why" and the "how" through speculation and interpretation. Theories and conjectures are not news and waste readers' time.

The Public and the Story

Journalists must also keep their connection with the audience in mind when pursuing a story. Will the audience understand the story? Is it clear and balanced in presenting all sides? Has the journalist been clear in identifying their role in the story? Do the text, visuals, and/or audio accurately convey the truth of a story? Reporters must take into account these considerations while compiling the information they have gathered into a story.

Conflicts and Gifts

A conflict of interest exists when journalists, their friends or relatives, or news organizations are in a position to benefit directly from a story being covered. These benefits can be financial or political, or other perks that can taint a journalist's objectivity and credibility. Most media outlets have policies against conflicts of interest and accepting gifts.

Journalists should refuse to accept money or anything else of value from the people about whom they write. Businesses usually do not give gifts without expecting something in return. Although journalists might believe their stories are not biased by gift-giving, they cannot control the public's perception of their reporting once it is known they accepted a gift. Gift-givers may assume they are influencing positive relationships, unless told their gift cannot be accepted because of policy. Some news organizations allow their journalists to accept items worth only a few dollars: a cup of coffee or a souvenir T-shirt, for example. Other newsroom guidelines require journalists to return the gift, share the gift with everyone in the newsroom, or send the gift to a charity.

Accepting Trips: "Junkets"

Free trips, called "junkets," do happen. Fashion writers are invited to New York, and television critics to Hollywood, with most if not all expenses paid. Sportswriters might accompany their local teams to games in distant cities, with the teams paying all the writers' expenses.

Many travel writers insist they could not afford to travel if hotels, airlines, or other sponsors did not pay for them. Their stories are often compromised and unrealistic, however, because people on holiday do not get complimentary trips with first-class travelling and managers' red-carpet treatment. Thus, the reporter's experience neither resembles that of most travellers nor helps them decide how to spend their vacations. Full disclosure is usually made in the copy of what was provided to the reporter.

Participating in the News

Reporters have lives outside the newsroom, and sometimes those outside activities turn reporters into newsmakers. When that happens, editors worry that their reporters' involvement in events might undermine public confidence in the news organization's objectivity. Editors insist reporters' first obligation should be to their primary employer, and they say journalists continue to represent their employers as objective news gatherers and reporters even after they leave work. Journalists should not join associations and activities that could compromise their integrity or damage their credibility.

Reporters should not hold public office, either elected or appointed, nor should they serve as party officials or help an election campaign. A lifestyle reporter running for city council might not pose a direct conflict as they may never cover the city council, but the public might suspect that other writers would slant the news in favour of their colleague's campaign. When in doubt about a possible conflict, journalists should talk with their supervisors.

Witnessing Tragedy

Reporters and photographers might witness tragedies, such as people drowning, falling to their deaths, or fleeing from fire. Journalists help other people who are in danger, particularly if they are the only ones on the scene. Journalists say they would react the same way that they would if they saw a member of their family in physical danger. But when a victim is already receiving help from rescue workers, police officers, firefighters or medical technicians, journalists will stay out of the rescuers' way and concentrate on reporting the event.

Ottawa Citizen parliamentary reporter Lee Berthiaume was one of many journalists who covered the shooting on Parliament Hill in October 2015 where Cpl. Nathan Cirillo was killed as he stood guard by the War Memorial by Michael Zehaf-Bibeau (Figure 4.2). Berthiaume was interviewed by his colleague Doug Fischer in an article that was published on the *Ottawa Citizen* website on October 22, 2015.

> I grabbed my notepad and recorder and ran out the door. As I raced down Queen Street I wasn't hearing anything so as I got close to Elgin I slowed down because I thought, well, what if the gunman, or gunmen, are still there. I didn't know what I was running into. I had a new baby and a wife, and so I kind of peeked around the corner. I could see the crowds of people and some reporters who were already there.
>
> It's strange but when I looked at Cpl. Cirillo he looked like he was sleeping. His eyes were closed. I didn't see any blood or signs of violence. Several people were trying to resuscitate him. Unaware of what was happening on Parliament Hill, I started interviewing witnesses. In the midst of one interview, I realized I should probably take a picture and so, with one hand holding my audio recorder as a witness talked, I snapped a picture with my camera practically over my shoulder. At the time I didn't think much of it. The only thing I knew was I wasn't comfortable tweeting it, even though I didn't know at the time that Cirillo had died or would die. I felt the decision whether to make it public should rest with editors. So I sent it to the *Citizen* photo desk and continued to interview witnesses before Cirillo was taken away by ambulance. It was only the next day that a colleague pointed out that my photo was on the front page of the *National Post.**

* Reprinted with the express permission of: *Ottawa Citizen*, a division of Postmedia Network Inc.

Reprinted with the express permission of: *Ottawa Citizen*, a division of Postmedia Network Inc.

Figure 4.2

Ottawa Citizen parliamentary reporter Lee Berthiaume took this picture of people trying to save Cpl. Nathan Cirillo after he was shot in October 2015.

Reporting on Terrorism

Terrorists have learned to create news that news organizations cannot ignore. The terrorists provide genuine drama: hijackings, demands, deadlines, and the threat of mass murder—such as the attacks on the World Trade Center in New York and the Pentagon in Washington on September 11, 2001.

To attract even more publicity, terrorists conduct press conferences. Some allow journalists to photograph and interview their captives. Others make videos of their captives, sometimes showing the hostages pleading for their lives, reading the terrorists' demands, and warning that they will be killed if the demands are not met.

Some critics insist media coverage encourages terrorists. They believe if the media ignored terrorists, they would become discouraged and abandon their acts of violence. Other critics note people have a right to know what is happening in the world and that a news blackout might result in rumours about the terrorists' activities that are more frightening than the truth. They also fear terrorists will escalate their violence if reporters ignore them.

Trust

Editors and producers trust their reporters to follow all ethical and legal guidelines when researching, writing, and reporting a story. The connections reporters make with their sources and the public are based on honesty and transparency. Editors and producers trust their reporters to be professional on the job. Reporters destroy that trust if they commit any of three journalistic crimes: fabrication, plagiarism, and misrepresentation.

- Fabrication is making something up—a quotation, a person, a detail, staging a video or audio clip—anything fake that pretends to be real.
- Plagiarism is taking someone else's work. It is illegal for a journalist to use another's work. It also is unethical and says something about the journalist's moral character. Journalists who plagiarize or fabricate information are fired.
- Misrepresentation is not properly identifying yourself, your media affiliation, the purpose of your reporting, twisting facts or story angles, or what sources have told you.

Unique Cases

There are unique instances where reporters are selective in how and when they identify themselves as journalists. Restaurant reviewers would be ineffective if everyone knew their identities. Restaurant owners, eager to obtain favourable publicity, would cater to the reviewers, offering them special meals and special service.

Other journalists might want to shop anonymously at a store where employees have been accused of misleading customers. Or reporters might want to attend a protest rally. If protesters realized several reporters were present, they might either act more cautiously or perform for the reporters, behaving more angrily or violently to ensure that they got into the news. Protesters might also harass or attack reporters who identified themselves.

Usually instances of passive posing present few ethical problems. The reporter is gathering information that is publicly available to any person. More serious ethical— and legal—problems arise when reporters go "undercover" and actively misrepresent themselves to gain access to places and information closed to the general public.

Typically, editors allow their reporters to pose only when a story is important and no other safe way exists to obtain it. A good example is the investigation by two *Toronto Star* reporters of fraudulent telemarketing scams in the city's downtown core, a probe that revealed Canada's dubious distinction as an international haven for the multibillion-dollar industry. The reporters went undercover for the assignment, getting jobs at one of the downtown "boiler rooms," as the establishments were called. They collected scripts and other documents and at one point even wore concealed mini-cameras; their "eyewitness" and insider status allowed them to document the fraud. Still, going undercover is difficult and risky, and the technique is used only when there is no other way to get the story.

One of the *Toronto Star* reporters described the process of deciding to go undercover on the telemarketing scam story:

> It took us a while to get to that point. It's a sort of last-ditch strategy—you always try to figure out other ways to do a story. It's complicated, it's time consuming, it's dangerous. So we had long debates about how to do the story. And at the end of the day, you have to justify this ten ways to Sunday, to editors, before you can do undercover—it's very controversial. It has to be ethically justifiable. . . . You have to sit before the senior editors and make a pretty compelling case that this is ethically defensible. Because, of course, the standard operating procedure in journalism is to present yourself as who you are and identify yourself and be up front and open and clear.
>
> So when we take this step, at least at the Star, it's not taken lightly. You have to answer two basic questions: Is there a strong enough public interest in the story? In other words, is it important? And is there any other way to get the information?

Reporters should admit their use of undercover work in the stories. When reporters go undercover, they need to explain to the audience why it was necessary to do so. They also give all the people involved in the story the opportunity to respond.

Media Law

Libel

Libel is defamation by written words or by communication in some other tangible form. Slander is defamation by spoken words or gestures. Both libel and slander are defamatory statements that are untrue and damaging to someone.

Libel is a major concern for the media. People who feel injured by a media report might be quick to sue. The costs of a lawsuit can be great. Damage awards in Canada tended to be modest until the late 1980s, when the Reichmann family brought a $102-million libel suit against *Toronto Life* magazine. More media organizations have been sued for libel since then, and the damages awarded to plaintiffs have been increasingly large.[1]

Even when media organizations win libel suits, they still might spend hundreds of thousands of dollars on court costs and attorneys' fees. And libel suits place at risk not only the news organization's pocketbook but also their reputations. Their reputation is built on fairness and accuracy. A libel judgment blemishes that reputation, sometimes irreparably. Individual reporters, producers, and editors also depend on their reputations for accuracy, thoroughness, and responsibility. If they lose a libel suit, they could lose that reputation. They might even lose their jobs.

In the case of *Munro v. Toronto Sun Publishing Co.*,[2] a cub reporter for the *Toronto Sun* wrote a story accusing the plaintiff, then a member of Parliament, of corruption and conflict of interest in the matter of a lucrative government contract for Petro-Canada service stations. The reporter, in a meeting with superiors and legal counsel shortly before the story ran on the front page, claimed to have documentary evidence of the allegations on a microfiche. Incredibly, none of the reporter's superiors at the meeting asked to view the evidence; they simply took the reporter's word for it. Further, the reporter never confronted the plaintiff with the allegations before the story ran; he never offered the right of reply to the target of his "investigation." The plaintiff won his case, and the truth emerged: the reporter had simply made up the story. The reporter was fired.[3] As the presiding judge in the case observed, the processing of this story broke the basic rules of good reporting and editing:

> [T]here must be a separation of functions between the reporter and the editor, it being the responsibility of the editor to confirm the accuracy of the contents of a story before publication. . . . [T]here must be constant supervision maintained by the editor over the reporter, with a regular reporting requirement. . . . [I]t is the editor's responsibility to know in detail before publication, the documentation to support the story and the reliability of the sources and so ensure its accuracy.[4]

The Elements of a Libel Suit

The person who sues for libel is called the plaintiff. The plaintiff's libel suit must establish a case by proving three things: (1) defamation, (2) identification or reference, and (3) publication. The person sued for libel is called the defendant.

Defamation

A defamatory statement is an untrue statement about someone that damages the person's reputation, lowering them in the estimation of the community, deterring people from associating with that person, or exposing the person to hatred, contempt, or ridicule. Some statements obviously have the power to injure reputations—for example, statements that a person has committed a crime; is incompetent in their business, trade, or profession; or has engaged in corruption, conflict of interest, or other serious misconduct. It is up to the jury (or judge sitting alone) in each case to determine whether defamation has actually occurred. Defamation is an untrue statement about someone to that person's discredit; if the statement is true, then no defamation has occurred.

In Canada, the law of libel does not require the plaintiff to prove the allegedly defamatory statements false; instead, it requires the defendant to prove the truth of what was published. Critics argue this reverses the presumption of innocent until proven guilty that is a cornerstone of the Canadian criminal justice system. In libel, the defendant is guilty until they prove their innocence. This presumption leads to "libel chill"—where journalists will shy away from hard-hitting stories for fear of attracting a libel suit.

While libel plaintiffs usually sue over statements made in the body of a news story, they may also sue over pictures, cartoons, headlines, or some combination of words and pictures that create a defamatory meaning.

In the case of *Vander Zalm v. Times Publishers*, a political cartoonist criticized a politician by depicting him tearing the wings from a fly; the court deemed the cartoon fair comment. As long as the author honestly believes what he says and isn't motivated solely by malice, the opinion does not have to be reasonable; it can "even be exaggerated or prejudiced, as long as it is an honest view that could be held by someone."[5]

Reference (Identification)

The libel plaintiff must also prove that the defamatory statements refer to them, that the audience would associate the plaintiff with the defamatory statement. This requires proving that reasonable readers, listeners, or viewers would have understood that the statement was about the plaintiff.

Usually, libel plaintiffs have no trouble establishing identification in cases involving the news media. News stories normally identify sources or subjects clearly by name. In fact, detailed identification protects reporters against libel suits. Many suits arise from situations in which similar names create confusion. If a Sam Johnson is arrested for selling cocaine, the commonness of the name creates the possibility of confusion. By identifying the person arrested as Samuel H. Johnson, Jr., 31, of Forest Street, the reporter eliminates the possibility of inadvertently defaming other Sam Johnsons in town.

Publication

Obviously, when a statement has appeared in a newspaper or been broadcast, it has been published. However, a statement does not have to be so widely disseminated for a person to sue for libel, because the legal definition of publishing is transmission to a third party. All the law requires is that the defendant made the defamatory statement to someone other than the person defamed. Thus, one person slandering another is not actionable, but if a third person overheard the insulting remarks, that would, technically, amount to publishing. The point is that the basic issue of liability doesn't depend on how many third parties were exposed to the libel; one third party is enough. Any repetition of a libellous statement is considered a new instance of publication, for which the publisher can be held liable (i.e., there's no protection in not being the first to publish libellous statements).

What about online content? The Supreme Court has ruled that hyperlinking to defamatory material on the internet does not constitute publishing the defamatory material itself. But the decision also says if someone presents content from the hyperlinked material in a way that repeats the defamatory content, they can be considered publishers and are therefore at risk of being sued for defamation.

Posting defamatory comments online carries the same legal risk as publishing them in a newspaper, magazine, or book or broadcasting them. Anonymity does not protect from liability; the owners and operators of online sites have been ordered by the courts to reveal the identities of those who post defamatory comments online. Even bloggers who provide hyperlinks to defamatory comments on other sites could be held liable.

In one recent case, the court ruled that website owners could be held liable for defamation if they intentionally provide on their sites hyperlinks to defamatory material. In *Crookes v. Newton* (2009), the B.C. Court of Appeal said that while in themselves hyperlinks are not dangerous, they could implicate the website owner if that person "endorses or adopts the defamatory content, or explicitly encourages the reader to link to the offending material."[6] Merely providing a hyperlink or website address to the libellous material or referring to it in a neutral way does not constitute publication, the court held. Refusing to remove defamatory statements from an online site once the owner or host of the site has been notified of their potentially libellous nature is another matter. A court ruling in the 2001 B.C. case of *Godfrey v. Demon Internet Ltd.* suggests that the website host could be held liable for re-publication of the offending matter.[7]

Major Defences to Libel Suits

The main defences available to media organizations against a charge of libel are these: truth, also called justification (for matters of fact); fair comment (for matters of opinion); absolute privilege (for government and judicial proceedings); qualified privilege and responsible communication (for matters of the public interest, where there is a duty to report); and consent (for cases in which the would-be plaintiff had agreed to the publication).

Truth or Justification
For a media defendant to succeed with the defence of truth, it must prove at trial the truth of the statements it published. This can be difficult. In all provinces except Quebec, truth is considered a complete defence. Because media defendants who raise the defence of truth are required to prove the alleged facts of the case, reporters should keep all their notes and any other documentary evidence (including digital recordings) used to write the story and ensure the sources are credible and trustworthy.

To prove the truth of a statement or assertion, the defendant may present only direct (not second-hand) evidence, which means journalists should corroborate information with at least two or more sources.

The defence of truth can also fail when insufficient scrutiny is applied to the motive or agenda of the source, especially if the source seeks to remain anonymous. Unless there is good reason to grant a source anonymity (for example, when the source is a bona fide whistleblower whose well-being would be threatened by identifying that person and there is other corroborating evidence to prove the truth of what the whistleblower contends), reporters should refrain from granting anonymity to sources.

Finally, the defence of truth does not protect the accurate re-publication of defamatory charges made by other people. For example, a news organization that reports a defamatory statement that a bank president makes about a competitor cannot escape liability by proving that it accurately quoted the bank president. The news organization is respon-sible for proving that the underlying statement is true, not merely that it has quoted the source accurately. There are some exceptions to this rule, the main one being the defence of absolute privilege that news organizations have to report on official government and legal proceedings.

The requirements of a successful truth defence against a libel action may seem onerous to the media defendant, but they are none other than the requirements of good journalism and truth remain the touchstone. While it may be difficult to prove the truth of a story in court, truth is also a "pre-emptive" defence, because if the story is true, the target is unlikely to sue.

Fair Comment

The law of defamation distinguishes between assertions of fact and those of opinion. Everyone has the right to an opinion. Section 2b of the Canada's *Charter of Rights and Freedoms* states:

> Everyone has the following fundamental freedoms: a) freedom of conscience and religion; b) freedom of thought, belief, opinion and expression, including freedom of the press and other media of communication; c) freedom of peaceful assembly; and d) freedom of association.

But the law distinguishes opinion based on fact and relevant to the public interest from opinion based on rumour or speculation and motivated by malice (defined in law as "intent to injure"). For the fair comment defence to succeed at trial, the comment must be on a matter of public interest, based on fact, and recognizable as comment, though the commentary must still be based on fact to be considered fair. As well, it must satisfy the "objective" test: could anyone honestly express that opinion on the proved facts? Finally, there must be no actual or express malice underlying the comment.

The defence of fair comment exists to protect the right to free expression so critical to a democratic society and to encourage the kind of full public discourse necessary to preserve free-speech rights. But the defence does not protect all editorials, columns, and reviews or even news stories that offer opinion along with reportage. Any published opinion based on or implying false facts can be the basis of a libel suit. The defence of fair comment does not exist to protect anyone's right to say anything, however harmful and ill-based, at any time; as with other constitutionally guaranteed rights, the right to express an opinion is not absolute.

The fair-comment defence is reliable when the opinion involves a matter of genuine public interest and does not amount simply to idle gossip or rumour-mongering.

The case of *Pearlman v. Canadian Broadcasting Corp.* arose after the CBC produced a hard-hitting report about a landlord in Winnipeg. In the piece, the plaintiff was called a slum landlord and a person with "no morals, principles or conscience." The plaintiff sued for libel. The CBC report was researched and reported, leaving no doubt as to the conditions the plaintiff's tenants endured. The court ruled in favour of the broadcaster, judging the opinion expressed as fair comment made without malice.[8]

In an another case, the Supreme Court of Canada bolstered the defence of fair comment with a landmark decision—the first consideration of the limits of fair comment—that overturned a court ruling against Vancouver radio broadcaster Rafe Mair. In the case of *Simpson v. Mair and WIC Radio Ltd.*,[9] the high court clarified the boundaries of free speech when it struck down a B.C. Court of Appeal ruling that found against the defendant, the controversial host of a radio talk show. In the original suit, Mair was accused of defaming Kari Simpson, a family values advocate who objected to the province's practice of allowing schools to use books that portrayed homosexual parents. In the 1999 on-air editorial that became the subject of the suit, Mair criticized Simpson's position as bigotry and compared her views to Hitler.

The Supreme Court said freedom of expression rights demand a wide berth for commentary on matters of public interest and must be balanced against the right to protect personal reputation. Supreme Court of Canada Justice Ian Binnie said:

> Public controversy can be a rough trade and the law needs to accommodate its requirements. . . . An individual's reputation is not to be treated as regrettable but unavoidable road kill on the highway of public controversy, but nor should an overly solicitous regard for personal reputation be permitted to "chill" freewheeling debate on matters of public interest.[10]

Absolute Privilege

The law recognizes certain occasions when people need absolute protection from libel suits. News organizations and their journalists are covered by absolute privilege when they report on official legislative and judicial proceedings. People called to testify in court, for example, cannot be sued for defamation because of what they say on the witness stand, even if what they say turns out to be untrue or motivated by malice. Members of legislative bodies, such as Parliament and provincial legislatures, cannot be sued over remarks they make in the course of their official duties (though the privilege ends outside those forums—for example, after the trial on the courthouse steps or outside the House of Commons in a hallway media scrum). This same privilege, in limited form, is extended to journalists so that they can cover government and open court proceedings without fear of attracting libel suits, but the following conditions generally apply: The report must be a fair and accurate account, must be published contemporaneously, must contain no comment, and must be free of seditious, blasphemous, or obscene content. This is in keeping with the overriding principle of openness that is supposed to safeguard the Canadian justice system by ensuring that such proceedings do not occur behind closed doors and that news media are able to cover them, acting as the eyes and ears of the public.

In *Geary v. Alger*, the journalist lost his case because he had added to his report the name of a person whose identity had not been revealed in open court. In *Mitchell v. Times Printing and Publishing Co.*, the court said that the defence of absolute privilege would be destroyed by any extra comment or statement imputing guilt. (The report had described the suspect, who was ultimately found not guilty, as a "long-sought killer" who had "finally been caught.") But the decision in *Wesolowski v. Armadale Publishers Ltd.* underlines the potential strength of the defence when it is used to protect a fair and accurate report. "In this case, a person was named in the indictment with the accused, but was not charged. The court said the newspaper's reference to the person as 'an unindicted co-conspirator' was fair and accurate because it adequately described that part of the judicial proceedings."[11]

Qualified Privilege

While the defence of absolute privilege allows for free speech and debate by public representatives in certain public forums, qualified privilege defends statements reported in the public interest. There has to be a moral obligation on the part of the sender to publish and on the part of the receiver, a corresponding right to know. To succeed at trial with the common-law defence of qualified privilege, the report must be a fair and accurate account, free of malice, on a compelling matter of legitimate public interest. It would seem that qualified privilege is the right defence for at least some major investigative projects, yet until recently, Canadian courts defined the intended receiver or audience narrowly (expressly excluding the public at large), and Canadian media had little success trying to use the defence in defamation cases.

But in a landmark ruling late in December of 2009, the Supreme Court of Canada affirmed a form of qualified privilege, the so-called "public interest responsible journalism" defence, which had been used in two Ontario newspaper cases.[12]

The defence was adopted by the Ontario Court of Appeal in 2007 and had earlier been accepted by leading British and American courts as necessary protection for free-expression rights. The new defence gives the media greater insulation against libel chill as long as the story was properly researched, fact-checked, written, and edited, and the matter is one in which the public has a legitimate interest. In other words, if the story meets the public-interest criteria and standards of responsible journalism, it should be protected by qualified privilege.[13]

In the groundbreaking case of *Cusson v. Quan*,[14] an Ottawa police constable with the Ontario Provincial Police decided on his own initiative to go to New York to help in the rescue operation after the September 11, 2001 attacks on the World Trade Center. He was recalled by superiors to his duties at home, but many articles portrayed him as a hero, and the stories provoked controversy. The *Ottawa Citizen* questioned the storyline of the officer as hero and suggested he might have misrepresented himself as an RCMP officer and been a hindrance rather than a help to the rescue effort. The newspaper argued at trial that because the articles in question were matters of the public interest published without malice, they should be protected by qualified privilege. The judge disagreed, finding that there was no compelling moral duty to publish the articles, and awarded the plaintiff $120,000 in damages. In 2007, however, the Ontario Court of Appeal accepted the new defence after considering the classic dilemma presented by the case and the defence of qualified privilege: how to weigh the right to protect reputation against the media's right to free expression.

Now that the Supreme Court of Canada has affirmed the new defence, courts in all provinces, not just Ontario, are required to follow the ruling, which is widely regarded as a progressive modernization of the defence of qualified privilege and an encouragement of public-interest reporting. According to one expert, it will require the courts to "shift their focus away from deciding whether there is truth or some other defence available, to whether the conduct of the media defendant met the standards for responsible journalism. In the view of Ontario's appeal court, 'this is an acceptable price to pay for free and open discussion.'"[15]

Note that the defence of qualified privilege should not be confused with the defence of fair comment. Fair comment defends not the validity of a given opinion expressed but rather the individual's right to hold an honest opinion and to express it. The essence of qualified privilege, by contrast, is the obligation to report—the idea that the person who makes the statement has an ethical duty to do so and those who receive the information, a legitimate interest in hearing it. Until recently, it was difficult for media defendants to succeed with the claim of qualified privilege against a charge of libel because the courts did not regard the defence as applicable to publishing to the general public. The advent of the responsible journalism defence at the dawn of 2010 may also encourage more journalists to produce more stories involving matters of the public interest.

Consent

This defence is rarely raised because normally, no one would consent to be defamed. This was the defence raised, however, in the 1976 case of *Syms v. Warren*. The plaintiff, chair of the Manitoba Liquor Commission, had agreed to appear on a radio call-in show to address rumours about him that were circulating in the community. During the show, a caller accused him of being an alcoholic, and the man sued the radio station. The station raised the defence of consent, arguing at trial that because the plaintiff had agreed to appear on the program, he in effect gave his consent to the broadcast comments.

> The court agreed that a defence of consent existed, but said it did not arise in this case. The mere fact that this individual consented to appear on the open-line radio show could not be taken to mean that he consented to the publication of anything that anyone might say about him. It should be added that it is foolhardy for a radio station to air an open-line show without employing a delay mechanism.[16]

Civil Libel

The remedies in a libel action are basically twofold: damages, which are awards of money meant to compensate the injured party, and injunctions, which are court orders that either compel a party to the suit to do something (called mandatory injunctions) or forbid a party to do something (called restrictive injunctions).

Damages and Special Damages

Of damages, there are two main sorts. General damages are awarded for losses that cannot be easily quantified (so-called non-monetary losses such as pain and suffering) to compensate the plaintiff for the injury to his or her reputation. Special damages are awarded for specific monetary losses. Theoretically, special damages (like general damages) have no limit, but to collect special damages, the plaintiff must provide proof that publication of the libel resulted in monetary loss (for example, lost wages if the libel caused him or her to lose a job).

In *Hill v. Church of Scientology*, a plaintiff successfully sued the church and was awarded $1.6 million in damages. During a news conference, a lawyer acting for the church defamed the plaintiff. At trial, the defendants tried to argue that the law should apply more stringently to public officials, requiring them to "prove knowledge of falsehood or a reckless disregard for the truth." The court stressed the importance of protecting the reputation of public officials and said the defendants "failed to raise enough evidence to establish a constitutional challenge of defamation law."[17] The church, in raising the issue of defamation as it applies to public figures, was referring, albeit inappropriately, to a famous ruling of the U.S. Supreme Court.

Nominal Damages

The next group, nominal damages, falls within the same compensatory category as general damages, but the amount of nominal damages is minimal. Such damages are awarded to plaintiffs who succeed but whose reputations were initially poor. A good example is the 1956 case of *Leonhard v. Sun Publishing Co.*, in which a *Vancouver Sun* article described the plaintiff as a "drug king." At trial, the newspaper brought evidence that the plaintiff was well-known in the community as a gangster with no good name to protect. The plaintiff won his case but was awarded a single dollar in damages. "The risk in this tactic is that if the defendant's evidence as to the plaintiff's generally bad reputation fails to persuade the court, the defendant, as a result, may pay even more in damages."[18]

Compensatory Damages

A final category of compensatory damages is aggravated damages, for cases in which the injury to reputation is particularly serious and the defendant has behaved particularly badly. Part of the award ($500,000) in *Hill v. Church of Scientology* was composed of aggravated damages. The courts have ruled that aggravated damages take into account "the additional harm caused to the plaintiff's feelings" by the defendant's bad conduct.[19]

Punitive Damages

The final category of damages to be considered is punitive damages. They are in a different class because unlike other kinds of damages, which seek to compensate the victim, punitive damages exist to punish the defendant for outrageously bad behaviour and to deter others from following suit. When a media defendant loses a libel case and is ordered to pay aggravated or, especially, punitive damages, something has gone badly wrong in the newsroom. Consider the *Munro v. Toronto Sun Publishing Co.*, in which punitive damages were awarded after a cub reporter fabricated a story and, by crowing around the newsroom about having "got" the target, handed the court ample evidence of malice.

Intention to Sue

A plaintiff must serve notice of his intention to sue a media defendant (within the time period set out in provincial statutes), and the defendant must then decide whether to raise one of the recognized defences or issue an apology. An early and sincere apology may serve to avoid a libel suit altogether or to lower the amount of damages awarded if the case goes forward and the media defendant loses. Notices of intention to sue, however, are more numerous than libel actions that go forward to trial.

Injunctions

One last remedy—injunctions—may occur in response to charges of defamation. Injunctions are sought by plaintiffs to prevent the publication, or re-publication, of defamatory material. But again, there are serious problems inherent in the issuing of injunctions by courts in civil cases, especially in libel actions:

> The first is that a plaintiff can apply for an interim, or temporary, injunction without having to give notice of such application to the other party. Concretely this means that an injunction could be made against a newspaper or a broadcaster without that newspaper or broadcaster having been given an opportunity to argue against it. The second problem is that an injunction issued during a libel action is as clear an example as one could ask of a prior restraint on publication—censorship in its most basic form.[20]

The Role of Malice in Civil Libel

To say that truth is a complete defence to a charge of libel means that malice is irrelevant when this defence is raised. But remember that the media organization or individual journalist who raises this defence in a lawsuit is required to prove the truth of the published allegations at trial and that if the defendant is unable to do so (i.e., loses the case), any evidence of malice will tend to increase the damages awarded. But what constitutes malice?

Actual malice can be difficult to prove; it refers to more than the commission of simple errors, even though such errors may well indicate sloppy reporting. Evidence that the journalist disliked the plaintiff is also in itself insufficient. But generally, the courts have ruled that malice can be found when the defendant:

- knew facts that would call the story into question but did not include them in the story;
- refused to examine evidence that would prove or disprove an allegation;
- relied on an inherently unbelievable source;
- relied on an anonymous source without seeking corroborating evidence;
- published a story without adequate investigation;
- exhibited reckless disregard for the truth;
- failed to give the target of an investigation a chance to respond to allegations; or
- conveyed defamatory innuendos about the plaintiff in the published article.

Box 4.1 provides tips for avoiding libel suits.

Box 4.1   Steps for Avoiding Libel Suits

No checklist or set of steps can guarantee that a news organization will never face a libel suit. The best defence against a charge of defamation is first-rate journalism: good reporting and good editing. Here are some of the things journalists can do to protect themselves and their employers:

1. Make sure everything in the story, especially any potentially defamatory statement, is newsworthy. Nothing is gained by risking a lawsuit over a statement that has no news value.
2. Identify everyone mentioned in the story as fully as possible.
3. Give people who are attacked or criticized in news stories adequate opportunity to respond, and include the response in the story, even if it is just a flat denial. If a person refuses to respond, say so in the story.
4. If a person who has been attacked or criticized presents credible evidence to support his or her denials, check out that evidence.
5. Interview every relevant source, and read every relevant document; do not ignore sources or information that might contradict the central point of a story.
6. Find out what basis a source has for making a defamatory charge and what the source's motives might be.
7. If a source for a story has credibility problems, explain in the story what those problems are.
8. Avoid confidential or anonymous sources. Reporters might be asked to reveal their sources at a libel trial. If the reporters refuse to do so, they may be charged with contempt of court, or the judges and jurors may assume the reporters made up the information.
9. Never use confidential or anonymous sources for making attacks on a subject. Use them only for factual information that can be verified by other sources or documents.
10. If a story uses documentary sources, make sure the documents are understood and quoted accurately. Double-check the information in any documents; even official records may have errors.
11. If a story is not breaking news, take additional time to make sure the investigation is thorough and the story is accurate.
12. Adhere to organizational policies regarding keeping notes, recordings, and other materials. If the policy is to keep all such materials, be sure everything is kept. If the policy is to destroy materials, make sure all are destroyed. Do not destroy some and keep others.

Privacy

Journalists need to be aware of their rights to gather and publish information, especially when these rights may conflict with the legitimate rights of others to protect their own privacy and confidential information.

In general, privacy rights are increasingly seen as relevant when a third party is required to disclose information related to health history, financial status, education, or employment status, or that indicates a person's race or ethnic origin, gender, or age.

It is legal for journalists to record telephone interviews, and they do not require the consent of the person being recorded unless the interview is to be broadcast. It is a criminal offence, however, to publish or broadcast a phone conversation that was illegally taped by a third party. For broadcast reporters, CRTC rules forbid airing interviews or conversations without the consent of the interviewees, but journalists are generally free to repeat or refer to what was said during the interview. The use of hidden microphones and cameras is generally prohibited but can be defended in the case of journalists working on investigative stories that expose matters involving the public interest.

In terms of photographs and video, standard journalistic practice requires seeking the consent of a person before publishing or broadcasting that person's image. When filming or photographing groups of people, individuals are generally not identifiable, but if a person is singled out in a crowd, journalists will seek that person's permission before publishing. On the other hand, journalists are not prohibited from covering a matter of public interest occurring in a public space (where there is generally no expectation of privacy), such as a protest march down city streets.

Newsgathering Issues

Section 2(b) of the *Charter of Rights and Freedoms* expressly protects the right to speak and to publish, but it says nothing about the right to gather information. The Supreme Court of Canada has recognized that freedom of the press means very little if there is no right to gather information, but what rights news reporters have to information are largely denied by a hodgepodge of provincial and federal statutes. This section covers three newsgathering issues: access to non-judicial events and records, access to judicial proceedings, and confidentiality for sources and information.

Reporters should always remember that the *Charter*'s free press guarantee does not protect them from prosecution if they engage in illegal conduct to gather news. Posing as a police officer, stalking the subject of an investigation, buying drugs, stealing documents, and communicating with a prostitute are all illegal activities, and reporters who are prosecuted for engaging in illegal activities will not be allowed to plead that they were doing so to gather information for a news story.

Access to Non-judicial Events and Records

When a river floods a city, a murder is discovered, or a fire destroys a building, police, rescue workers, and firefighters try to control the area to save lives and protect property. Sometimes officials also try to control what news reporters and photographers see and how they report what they see.

Reporters and photographers covering the protests accompanying meetings of the World Bank and International Monetary Fund and the Iraq War sometimes were arrested along with the demonstrators. Journalists covering protests, demonstrations, and riots face many risks, but they can do some things to minimize the chances of being harassed by police:

- Always carry press credentials.
- Don't trespass on private property or cross clearly marked police lines.
- Don't take anything from a crime scene.
- Obey all orders from police officers, even if doing so interferes with getting the story or the photo. (The alternative might be going to jail.)
- Don't argue with arresting officers.

The normal desire of the authorities to manage crisis scenes intensified after the September 11, 2001 terrorist attacks in the United States. The federal and some provincial and municipal governments have tried to use the terrorist attacks as a rationale for restricting access by reporters to government buildings and government information. Privacy concerns also have been cited as the rationale behind some decisions to curtail access to news scenes in recent years.

✓ Checklists for Libel, Privacy, and Newsgathering Issues

Elements of a Libel Suit

1. Defamation. Chances are that the story is defamatory if it contains any statements or suggestions about any of the following, whether stated expressly or only implied: criminal, immoral, or improper behaviour; information about someone's financial status or health; insults, slurs, or critical comments related to a person's business, trade, or profession; assertions that would lower the person in the eyes of ordinary people (as opposed to insiders or specialists) or deter them from associating with the person.
2. Reference (Identification). The defamatory matter refers to an individual, either directly or indirectly. The element of reference is fulfilled even if the potential plaintiff is not named—for example, if enough details are provided that the person could be identified or if the ordinary reader could assume from the details

provided that the plaintiff is that person. A member of a group may also be identified for the purposes of a libel suit if even one person might think the defamatory matter refers to a specific individual.

3. Publication. The element of publication is obviously met if the statements are published in a newspaper or magazine or broadcast. But the element is also satisfied—the comments are regarded as published—once those comments are relayed to a third party. Posting defamatory matter to the internet is considered publishing.

Libel Defences

1. Truth. To rely on the defence of truth, you need proof of the defamatory statements, such as the following: documents; credible witnesses with first-hand knowledge who are able and willing to testify in court; corroboration from at least two other sources; detailed notes and recordings from key interviews.

2. Fair comment. The defamatory matter is an expression of someone's honest opinion on a matter of public interest; it is based on provable facts and is free of malice.

3. Absolute privilege. The defence of absolute privilege applies to the occasion of a statement rather than to its content; absolute privilege applies to a fair and accurate account of the proceedings of an open court or legislature.

4. Qualified privilege. The defence of qualified privilege involves a kind of reciprocity; it applies when the sender has a social and moral duty to publish on a matter of the public interest and the intended audience has a corresponding right and responsibility to know or hear about it.

5. Responsible journalism in the public interest. A form of qualified privilege, this defence was affirmed in 2009 by the Supreme Court of Canada. It applies in matters of serious public interest in which the journalists have taken every step to ensure the accuracy and quality of the final story or series, from initial research to final editing.

Notes

Note on legal citations: After the name of a case, the year of the judgment is given in parentheses; however, some reporting series also use the year of publication in square brackets to identify the case. If the judgment year and publication year are the same, only the latter is included, in square brackets; if they are different, the judgment year is given first in parentheses, followed by the publication year.

1. Michael Crawford, *The Journalist's Legal Guide*, 5th edn, Toronto: Carswell, 2008, p. 27. The suit was settled out of court in 1991. "In the end, bloody and bowed, *Toronto Life* publicly apologized and admitted it made 'serious mistakes in the writing, editing and presentation' of an article about the family's history." See also Michael Skene and Evan Cooke, "Canadian Defamation Verdicts, October 23, 2007, to September 30, 2008," accessible on the Ad Idem website, http://www.adidem.org

2.   *Munro v. Toronto Sun Publishing Co.* (1982) 39 O.R. (2d) 100 (H.C.).

3.   "The Toronto Sun, Its Editors and Its Top Investigative . . ." United Press International. June 10, 1982. Accessed June 4, 2018, http://www.upi.com/Archives/1982/06/10/The-Toronto-Sun-its-editors-and-its-top-invest investi/8832392529600

4.   Robert Martin, *Media Law*, 2nd edn. Toronto: Irwin Law, 2003, pp. 165–6.

5.   Cited in Crawford, footnote 81, p. 62; *Vander Zalm v. Times Publishers* [1980] 4 W.W.R. 259 (B.C.C.A.).

6.   David Crerar and Michael Skene, "*Crookes v. Newton*," Ad Idem. Accessed June 4, 2018, http://adidem.org/Crookes_v._Newton. See *Crookes v. Newton*, 2009 B.C.C.A. 392.

7.   *Godfrey v. Demon Internet Ltd.* [2001] Q.B. 201; and *Carter v. B.C. Federation of Foster Parents Assn.*, 2005 B.C.C.A. 398.

8.   *Pearlman v. Canadian Broadcasting Corp.* (1981), 13 Man. R. (2d) 1 (Q.B.).

9.   *Simpson v. Mair and WIC Radio Ltd.* (2006), 55 B.C.L.R. (4th) 30 (C.A.).

10.   Quoted by Tracey Tyler, "Top Court Ditches Libel Case against B.C. 'shock jock': Decision on Boundaries of Fair Comment Will Make It Easier to Engage in Freewheeling Debate," *Toronto Star*, June 28, 2008, p. A4.

11.   Crawford, footnote 53, p. 46. See the following cases: *Geary v. Alger* [1925] 4 D.L.R. 1005 (Ont. C.A.); *Mitchell v. Times Printing and Publishing Co.* (No. 2), [1944] 1 W.W.R. 400 (B.C.S.C.); *Wesolowski v. Armadale Publishers Ltd.* (1980), 3 Sask. R. 330 (Q.B.).

12.   Ottawa: Canada News Wire (CNW), December 22, 2009: "The high court affirmed a new 'public interest responsible journalism' defence in two cases involving the Ottawa Citizen's reporting on Ontario Provincial Police officer Danno Cusson and the Toronto Star's reporting on businessman Peter Grant."

13.   Crawford, p. 3.

14.   See *Cusson v. Quan* (2007), 2007 CarswellOnt 7310, 2007 CarswellOnt 7311, 2007 ONCA 771 (C.A.), leave to appeal to the Supreme Court of Canada allowed (2008), 2008 CarswellOnt 1862 (S.C.C.), and *Douglas Quan et al. v. Danno Cusson.*

15.   Crawford, p. 56.

16.   Martin, p. 191. See *Syms v. Warren* (1976), 71 D.L.R. (3d) 413 (Sask. Q.B.).

17.   Crawford, footnote 78, p. 60. See *Hill v. Church of Scientology* [1995] 2 S.C.R. 1130, affirming (1994), 114 D.L.R. (4th) 1 (Ont. C.A.).

18.   Martin, p. 199. See *Leonhard v. Sun Publishing Co.* (1956), 4 D.L.R. (2d) 514 (B.C.S.C.).

19.   Martin, p. 201.

20.   Martin, p. 107.

Suggested Readings and Useful Websites

Crawford, Michael. 2008. *The Journalist's Legal Guide*, 5th edn. Toronto: Thomson Carswell.

Cribb, Robert, Dean Jobb, David McKie, and Fred Vallance-Jones. 2006. *Digging Deeper: A Canadian Reporter's Research Guide*. Don Mills, ON: Oxford University Press.

Fischer, Doug. 2015. "The Story behind the Story of the Oct. 22 Shooting Rampage on Parliament Hill." *Ottawa Citizen*. October 22. Accessed June 4, 2018, http://ottawacitizen.com/news/national/the-story-behind-the-story-of-the-oct-22-shooting-rampage-on-parliament-hill

Jobb, Dean. 2006. *Media Law for Canadian Journalists*. Toronto: Emond Montgomery Publications.

Kovach, Bill, and Tom Rosenstiel. 2001. *The Elements of Journalism: What Newspeople Should Know and the Public Should Expect*. New York: Three Rivers Press.

Küpeli, Ismail. 2015. "We Spoke to the Photographer Behind the Picture of the Drowned Syrian Boy." Toronto: *VICE* Canada. September 4. Accessed June 4, 2018, https://www.vice.com/en_ca/article/zngqpx/nilfer-demir-interview-876

Taylor, Lisa, Brian MacLeod Rogers, and Ryder Gilliland. 2017. "Understanding Canada's New Shield Law." J Source. October 23. Accessed June 4, 2018, http://j-source.ca/article/understanding-canadas-new-shield-law-confidential-sources/

Ward, Stephen J. 2006. *The Invention of Journalism Ethics: The Path to Objectivity and Beyond.* Montreal: McGill–Queen's University Press.
Canadian Association of Journalists: http://www.caj.ca
Canadian Committee for World Press Freedom: http://www.ccwpf-cclpm.ca/
Canadian Journalism Foundation: http://www.j-source.ca (English); http://www.ProjetJ.ca (French)
CanLII (Canadian Legal Information Institute—for rulings): http://www.canlii.org
Criminal Code of Canada: http://laws.justice.gc.ca/en/C-46/index.html
Federal statutes and regulations: http://laws.justice.gc.ca/eng/
Juristat (Statistics on crime and justice): https://www150.statcan.gc.ca/n1/pub/85-002-x/index-eng.htm
Legislation (provinces and territories): https://www.canlii.org/en/
New Media Canada: http://www.nmc-mic.ca
Reporters without Borders: http://www.rsf.org/en
Pew Center for Civic Journalism: http://www.pewcenter.org/index.php
Poynter Institute for Media Studies: http://www.poynter.org

Exercise 1   Ethics

Discussion Questions

Read the following situations, marking those actions you would take. Discuss your decisions with the class.

1. Without your knowledge, a talented young reporter on your staff breaks into the computer system at a second daily in your city, a bitter rival. The reporter gives you a list of all the stories the rival's staff is working on. Discuss in class if you would:

    A. _____ Compliment the reporter on her initiative and quickly assign your own staff to cover the stories so you won't be scooped?

    B. _____ Destroy the list and tell the reporter to never again enter the rival's computer system?

    C. _____ Reprimand the reporter, suspending her for a week?

    D. _____ Notify your rival and apologize for the reporter's actions?

    E. _____ Notify the police that the reporter may have unknowingly violated a law?

2. One of your reporters is writing about a local private club that, he learns, excludes Jews, African Canadians, and Indigenous peoples. The reporter also learns that your publisher and other influential members of your community are members of the club. Discuss in class if you would:

    A. _____ Abandon the story?

    B. _____ Inform your publisher about the story and suggest that she (the publisher) resign from the club?

     C.   _____Tell your reporter to interview the publisher and give her an opportunity to explain her membership in the club?

     D.   _____Publish the story but never identify any of the club's members?

     E.   _____Publish the story, listing your publisher and other prominent citizens who belong to the club?

     F.   _____List all 1,200 of the club's members?

3. Each year, a professional organization in your province sponsors an awards competition. Minutes ago, you learned that a reporter on your staff won second place in feature writing and that your chief photographer won third place in another category. However, another newspaper in the city—a bitter rival—won five awards, and a local television station won four. How would you handle the story? Discuss in class.

     A.   _____Ignore the story.

     B.   _____Report all the awards, beginning with the first-place awards.

     C.   _____Report only the two awards won by your staff.

     D.   _____ Start by reporting the two awards won by your staff, then briefly mention the awards won by all the other media in your city.

4. You run the evening news, and a sports reporter mistakenly credited the wrong football player with scoring two game-winning touchdowns. Would you:

     A.   _____Broadcast a correction the next evening?

     B.   _____Broadcast a correction and identify the reporter responsible for the error?

     C.   _____ Broadcast a correction and punish the reporter, placing him on probation?

     D.   _____ Broadcast a correction that identifies the reporter and reports his punishment?

     E.   _____Order the reporter to write a letter to the school, apologizing for his error?

     F.   _____Privately punish the reporter, placing him on probation, but publish nothing, treating the incident as a private personnel matter?

     G.   _____Do nothing, hoping nobody noticed?

Exercise 2   Ethics

Ethical Dilemmas

Read the following ethical dilemmas. Make a decision as to what you would do in a similar situation. Support your answer. Discuss your responses with the class.

1. There has been a shooting at a local high school. One student brought his father's gun to school and shot another student. The school security guard shot the student and killed him. In the course of an interview, the school principal says that the student with the gun was "a troubled child." Immediately after stating this,

she asks you to please not publish it, that she shouldn't have said it. Would you publish it, and why?

2. After a deadly car accident, you interview the mother of a deceased driver. She tells you that he would have lived if the hospital had not acted so slowly. In describing the hospital, she uses several expletives. For your small-town paper, would you use the expletives or not? Would you use them in a bigger paper like the *Toronto Star*?

3. While listening to a police scanner, you hear that a man has been arrested for raping a 16-year-old girl. You go to the police station, and you talk to the arresting officer. While talking about the case, the officer says that he "believes that this man should fry." Is it ethical to publish this, or is it editorializing? Is there a better way to use the quotation?

4. You are assigned to do a profile of a local African-Canadian businessman who has just donated a large amount of money to fund helping the urban black community. While discussing it, he drops a racial slur. Should you use it in your story, even though it takes away from the good deed he has done?

5. Your regular beat includes stopping by the mayor's office most days of the week, and you regularly talk with the mayor's secretary. One day the secretary says that she will treat you to lunch and the two of you can discuss what goes on "behind the scenes." Should you accept the offer of the free lunch, even though she says that it is the only way you will get the information?

6. A local woman who volunteered to serve with the armed forces was killed during a skirmish eight days ago. During the soldier's funeral in town, your videographer shoots a photo of the deceased's five-year-old son wiping away a tear and holding a stuffed bear dressed like a soldier. Should you use the video in your television story? Would it be different if it were online or print? Should you attend the funeral, or would you be invading the family's privacy?

Exercise 3   Law

Libel

Decide which of the following sentences and paragraphs are potentially libellous. Place a D in the space preceding each statement that is dangerous for the media and an S in the space preceding each statement that is safe.

1. _____The police officers said they shot and wounded Ira Andrews, a 41-year-old auto mechanic, because he was rushing toward them with a knife.

2. _____Testifying during the second day of his trial, Mrs. Andrea Cross said her husband, Lee, never intended to embezzle the $70,000, but that a secretary, Allison O'Hara, persuaded him that their actions were legal. Her husband thought they were borrowing the money, Mrs. Cross said, and that they would double it by investing in real estate.

3. _____A 72-year-old woman, Kelli Kasandra of Eastbrook Lane, has been charged with attempting to pass a counterfeit $20 bill. A convenience store clerk called the police shortly after 8 a.m. today and said that she had received "a suspicious-looking bill." The clerk added that she had written down the licence number of a car leaving the store. The police confirmed the fact that the $20 bill was counterfeit and arrested Mrs. Kasandra at her home about an hour later.

4. _____Margaret Dwyer said a thief, a boy about 14, grabbed her purse as she was walking to her car in a parking lot behind Memorial Hospital. The boy punched her in the face, apparently because she began to scream and refused to let go of her purse. She said he was blond, wore glasses, weighed about 120 pounds, and was about 5 feet 6 inches tall.

5. _____Police said the victim, Catherine White of Bell Ave., was too intoxicated to be able to describe her assailant.

6. _____"I've never lived in a city where the officials are so corrupt," Joyce Andrews, a Cleveland developer, complained. "If you don't contribute to their campaigns, they won't do anything for you or even talk to you. You have to buy their support."

7. _____The political scientist said that Americans seem unable to elect a competent president. "Look at whom they've elected," she said. "I'm convinced that Carter was incompetent, Reagan was too lazy and senile to be even a mediocre president, the first George Bush cared nothing about the people, Clinton was a scoundrel, and the second George Bush—the worst of the bunch—was a liar and a buffoon."

8. _____The newspaper's restaurant reviewer complained: "I've had poor service before, but nothing this incompetent. The service at The Heritage Inn wasn't just slow; it was awful. When she finally did get to us, the waitress didn't seem to know what was on the menu. Then she brought us the wrong drinks. When we finally got our food, it was cold and tasteless. I wouldn't even feed it to my dog. In fact, my dog wouldn't eat it. The stuff didn't even smell good."

9. _____Police Chief Claire Christopolous said: "We've been after Guiterman for years. He's the biggest drug dealer in the city, but it took months to gather the evidence and infiltrate his operations. His arrest last night was the result of good police work, and we've got the evidence to send him away for 20 or 30 years."

10. _____A police officer in your city, George Ruiz, today filed a $100,000 personal injury suit against Albert Tifton, charging that Tifton punched him in the nose last month while the police were responding to a call about a domestic dispute at Tifton's home. "It's the third time I've been hit this year," Ruiz said. "I'm tired of being used as a punching bag by these criminals, and I'm doing what I can to stop it."

11. _____There was an emergency meeting of about 100 angry parents at the Wisconsin Avenue branch of the YMCA at 8 p.m. yesterday, with its director, Rian

Singh, presiding. Singh said he called the meeting to calm the parents' fears and to respond to rumours. A parent asked whether it was true that the YMCA's janitor had been dismissed for molesting several boys. Singh responded that there had been some unfortunate incidents and the janitor had been discharged, but some of the allegations were exaggerated. When asked whether the police had been called in, Singh answered that they had and that their investigation is continuing. He assured the parents that the YMCA will see that the matter is resolved appropriately.

5 Interviews

> *"One of the axioms I use: Answers are a function of the question asked. If there are problems in the answer, it usually starts in the question."*
>
> —John Sawatsky, 2008

The interview is a basic tool of all journalists, not just investigative ones. The journalistic interview can be extremely effective when used properly. Reporters use interviews in a variety of situations. They may interview legislators about their plans to introduce a bill or police officers about a recent crime. They may gather the views of a number of citizens on a matter of public concern. Some reporters specialize in writing profiles of famous or interesting people. They usually conduct long interviews with the subjects of their stories.

No matter what kind of story a reporter writes, it usually will require one or more interviews. Successful interviews, however, do not just happen; they are the product of thought and planning by reporters.

Preparing for the Interview

Reporters planning to interview a source should ask themselves: Why am I conducting this interview? What kind of story will I write from this information? The answers will determine what kinds of questions they ask, what kinds of sources they seek, and how they conduct themselves during an interview. The reasons for interviewing are as varied as the stories themselves, but most often reporters are seeking information for one of three types of stories: the news story, the feature story, or the investigative story.

Reporters who cover a news story, such as a crime or a city council action, usually need to interview several people to gather all relevant information. From each source, reporters may want no more than a few facts, but from all of the interviews, reporters build a complete story. This means reporters must interview sources who will provide the following:

- facts and details, including dates, names, locations, and costs
- a chronology showing the unfolding of events
- relationships among the people or interests involved
- context and perspective, including the significance of events or issues and their relationships to other issues
- anecdotes that illuminate events or issues and make them more dramatic and understandable for the audience

Reporters interviewing sources to write a feature story, such as a personality profile, need everything they would need to write a news story plus descriptions of the following:

- the environment in which the subject lives or works
- how the subject appears and dresses
- the subject's mannerisms
- smells, sounds, and textures associated with the subject's home or work, using every sense to create an image of the interview subject

Interviews for personality profiles take more time. In-depth interviews conducted for investigative stories produce more tension. The purpose of the investigative story often is to expose wrongdoing, and sources may fear losing their jobs and reputations. Reporters working on the investigative story must obtain the same information as those working on more routine news or feature stories, but they also go further to seek some additional data:

- The subject's version of events, which may differ from that of other sources and records.
- Explanations of contradictions. If a subject of a story tells a version of events that differs markedly from that of other sources, reporters must ask for an explanation. A subject's explanation may be reasonable and may resolve the conflict—or it may not.
- Replies to charges and allegations. During an investigation, reporters may gather charges and allegations against a subject of a story. Those charges and allegations should be presented to the subject, who should have the opportunity to reply to them.

Many experienced interviewers think of an interview as a conversation, but it is a conversation with a specific purpose: gathering information for an unseen audience. To accomplish that purpose, interviewers must maintain control of the conversation, which they can do by properly planning for the interview. In the case of in-depth personality interviews or investigative interviews, the planning process can take longer, but even with simpler interviews, it can involve several steps.

- Define the purpose. Is this a news, feature, or investigative interview? What information is necessary for the story?
- Decide whom to interview. For some stories, the people to interview may be obvious, but for others, the reporter may have to do some research to determine the best sources.
- Assess the character of the interviewee. This may be crucial for feature and investigative interviews in which the reporter will have to shape the interview strategy to the interviewee's character. For news interviews or interviews of public officials the reporter already knows, this step is less crucial.
- Identify the areas of inquiry. What topics will the interview focus on? What questions will help the reporter gather the information necessary to write about these topics?
- Anticipate possible answers to questions. Reporters often can predict an interviewee's answers from their advance research. On the basis of these predictions, they can prepare possible follow-up questions and plan how the interview will develop.

Selecting the Sources to Interview

Once reporters know the purpose of the interviews, they must decide who to interview. If reporters are preparing a personality profile of a prominent person, the subject of that profile and their friends, enemies, and co-workers should be interviewed. But when the story is about an issue or an event, the reporters may have to figure out which people have the information they need to write the story. Reporters who don't have a deadline looming can try to interview everyone who might have relevant information. They can ask every interview subject for the names of more people who might contribute information, repeat the process until the list of sources has been exhausted, and then go back and re-interview sources to fill in gaps and clear up discrepancies in their stories.

Reporters working on deadline must be more selective. The basic principle reporters follow is to seek the best available source. Such sources possess knowledge, expertise, or insight relevant to the story. Sources also should be articulate; they should be able to make complicated matters clear and interesting.

Reporters should remember that sometimes the best available source is a document or record rather than a person. They can save themselves and the people they interview time and trouble if they begin by searching for documents or public records that provide the factual background for a story.

Finding sources who can provide insights and information can challenge a reporter's skill. A number of resources can help reporters locate the people they need. Many of the most frequently used sources work in local governments: cities, municipalities, and school districts. All of these official sources should have their contact information listed on the organizations' websites, and in online government directories and databases. In some communities, directories of local officials are published by civic groups. Local, provincial, and federal governments operate websites and online directories that can lead reporters to sources.

The federal government maintains the Government of Canada website (http://canada.gc.ca) that contains links to federal ministries and agencies, with contact information and names of employees.

Reporters can find helpful sources at local colleges and universities. Faculty members often provide background, explain complex issues, and offer insights. College and university public relations offices usually help reporters identify and contact the faculty members who can provide the most useful information.

Finding sources in private businesses may be more challenging than finding government sources. One resource is the directories of members published by local service clubs like Rotary and Kiwanis. Many club members are local business leaders who will be identified by company and title. Most businesses have to file documents and reports with local, provincial, and federal governments. Financial statements for all companies incorporated under the *Canadian Business Corporations Act* (CBCA) must be filed with Industry Canada's Corporations Directorate. Provincial agencies may have the names of principal officers of companies incorporated or doing business in that province. Local governments often issue business licences, which might name key executives.

Reporters should never let any organization, governmental or private, allow its public relations person to take the fall. The job of the reporter is to hold the real decision-maker accountable. The PR person usually is not the best source.

How Many Sources Are Enough?

Rookie reporters sometimes wonder how many sources they need for a story. The answer depends on at least four factors:

1. deadline pressure
2. the expertise of the sources
3. the degree of controversy raised by a topic
4. the complexity of a topic

When stories involve breaking news, which must be published or broadcast as soon as possible, reporters lack the luxury of searching widely for sources and information. They must construct a story from the materials readily available. Still, reporters should get as complete an account of the event and include as many points of view as possible. If they cannot interview a key source before the deadline, the story should say so clearly.

If sources possess broad expertise in a topic, three or four might be enough. If they have more limited experience, reporters may need to speak to many people. A reporter writing a story about the economic health of a city, for instance, may be able to produce a complete and accurate picture after talking to just a few people with broad expertise, such as academic and government economists, chamber of commerce officials, bank executives, and union leaders. The reporter would have to interview many individual business owners for the same story. Individual business owners may know the conditions for their own businesses, but they probably don't know the economic health of the community as a whole.

The degree of controversy also affects the number of sources reporters should interview. If a topic is not controversial—the route for a weekend parade, for example—then one source may be sufficient. However, if the topic is the likelihood of developing cures for diabetes or Alzheimer's disease from fetal stem cells—about which experts disagree vigorously—then reporters must include all reasonable points of view in the story.

As a story becomes more complex, the number of sources needed will grow. A story about a particular crime committed by a particular teenager would be fairly straightforward. Reporters could get a complete picture from only a few sources. A story about the causes of teenage crime in general is much more complicated and would require talking to dozens of sources from such fields as law enforcement, criminology, psychology, and social work.

No matter how many sources reporters talk to, they must evaluate those sources. Journalists should do more than simply pass along quotations from other people, even those considered experts. The obligation to evaluate information increases as the complexity of the story increases. Evaluating sources requires reporters to ask how the source knows what he or she purports to know: What is the basis of the source's knowledge? How credible or reliable is the source? The first question calls on reporters to find out and weigh the manner in which the source obtained the information. Water-cooler gossip is not as valuable as information from an eyewitness. When a source makes an assertion, ask, "How do you know that?" The credibility and reliability of the source require asking about the source's credentials and cross-checking information from one source with that from others. The process is not simple or easy, but it is essential if reporters are going to produce sound, accurate news stories.

Researching Sources and Topics

Veteran journalists agree the successful interviewer must be well informed. That means spending time reading books and articles by or about the person the reporter will interview, researching a company's annual reports, reviewing public documents, and learning the jargon of an industry or the organization of a company. For example, preparing to interview a well-known writer would entail reading at least a representative sample or portion of that writer's work.

Investigative journalist John Sawatsky typically went after stories that mainstream media either were oblivious to or ignored. In newspaper articles and later in his books, Sawatsky tore the veil of secrecy from important organizations, including Canada's RCMP, to reveal their inner workings. Another great Canadian journalist, Cecil Rosner, in his much-praised book on the history of investigative reporting in Canada, *Behind the Headlines*, noted the significance of Sawatsky's pioneering efforts to bolster the impact of investigative reporting with journalistic technique:

> Sawatsky developed a methodology of investigative work that tried to put research on a more scientific footing. His ideas about organization and classification of material, along with the mindset he brought to approaching sources, were important factors in his success at ferreting out information. Most importantly, he became a student of the mechanics and linguistics of the interview. He demonstrated, in both theory and practice, that the specific sequencing and wording of questions was crucial in providing the highest quality of journalistic information.

Why do reporters attach so much importance to conducting research before they interview people? Reporters who have conducted thorough research have the following advantages:

- They will not waste time by asking about issues that have already been widely publicized.
- They will have more interesting questions. People who are interviewed frequently get bored answering the same questions over and over. Interviewers who have researched their subject will have fresh questions that will elicit fresh answers from their source.
- They are more likely to have documented all relevant facts. Once the reporter and the source agree on what the facts are, they can move on to discussing the meaning of those facts.
- They will not embarrass themselves by appearing ignorant. On the other hand, reporters sometimes want to feign ignorance about a topic to elicit more in-depth, revealing explanations.
- They are more likely to recognize newsworthy statements and ask intelligent follow-up questions about them.
- They are more likely to spot inconsistencies and evasions in a source's responses.
- They learn about secondary sources, people who are familiar with the main source and who might have insights and information that will help reporters interview the main source.
- They are less likely to have to re-interview the main source. If they interview the main source before doing their research and interviews with secondary sources, their subsequent research may uncover important topics they failed to cover in the initial interview.
- They encourage their sources to speak more freely because sources are more likely to trust reporters who seem knowledgeable.

Reporters who fail to prepare for an interview will not know what to ask or how to report the information they get. Some sources will try to manipulate ignorant reporters or avoid difficult topics. Sometimes, sources will immediately end an interview—and scold unprepared reporters.

Preparing Questions for the Interview

Good questions elicit interesting quotations and details. Reporters begin the process of constructing good questions when they select a unifying angle for their story. With a story angle in mind, interviewers can decide whom they should interview and what questions they should ask. Say a reporter is planning a profile of a local bank executive who has won several marathon races. The angle for the story may be that long-distance running enhances the bank executive's personal and professional life. That angle suggests certain questions the reporter may ask the bank executive and his friends and family. If the reporter is investigating the bank's treatment of minorities, however, the reporter may want to interview the same bank executive, but the angle will be different. It may be the way the bank's lending practices affect minorities who want to buy homes or start businesses. The questions reporters would ask to develop a story about treatment of minorities would be much different from the questions they would ask for a feature about running in marathons.

Once reporters have selected an angle and have researched the topic, they write their questions in advance. They need not write out full questions. Often it is enough to jot down a word or phrase to remind themselves what to ask.

Reporters craft their questions to get as much information as possible. This means asking open-ended rather than closed-ended questions. A closed-ended question is one that sources can answer with a yes or no: "Will the province's new tax limitation hurt schools?" If reporters want more information, they have to ask follow-up questions. An open-ended question would be, "What will be the effect of the province's new tax limitation on schools?" The question requires the source to provide an analysis of the problem with some supporting facts.

Sawatsky advises journalists to ask short, neutral questions that begin with "what," "how," and "why" and to a lesser extent "who," "when," and "where." Questions structured as Sawatsky suggests encourage interviewees to tell their stories and reveal their feelings. Questions like "Are you angry?" or "Were you scared?"—besides inviting only yes or no answers—suggest that the interviewer has a preconceived notion about how the subject should have acted or felt. The subject might not want to tell their story to a reporter who appears to have already decided what happened.

When sources have a story to tell, such as how they survived a plane crash or what happened during a bank robbery, reporters should simply let that person tell the story. Something like "Tell me what happened to you" might be enough to encourage people to talk. This gives them a chance to tell their story as they remember it. Often the most useful information emerges during this phase of an interview. As interviewees talk, reporters should listen carefully. Reporters might think of more questions as the subject tells the story, but they should not interrupt the interviewee. Rather, they should wait until the source has finished and then ask follow-up questions.

Reporters ask for clarification when they do not understand things sources say. Sometimes that means asking a question that might appear naive or silly. Reporters should not fear asking those questions, however. Reporters who assume they understand what a source said or who fail to ask a critical question out of fear of appearing ignorant could make serious and embarrassing mistakes when they write their stories.

When reporters seek more specific details, they choose questions that will elicit anecdotes, examples, and quotations. Here are examples of such questions:

- What crime was the most difficult for you to solve in your career as a detective?
- What television shows do you consider most harmful for children?
- What do you fear the most when you perform before a live audience?

When news sources generalize or give vague answers, reporters ask for anecdotes and examples that support the generalizations or make the vague responses clearer and more specific. Reporters can use the anecdotes, examples, and quotations to make their stories more colourful, interesting, and understandable.

For feature interviews or personality profiles, some reporters have questions they often use to try to gain insight into the subject. Here are some examples:

- What do you read?
- Who are your heroes?
- What goals do you have?
- What is a typical day like for you?
- What are your weaknesses or drawbacks?
- How do you compensate for those weaknesses?
- What caused the most significant change in your life?
- How did you cope with that change?

Reporters have an infinite number of approaches they can take to conducting an interview, but they should avoid some traps:

- Ask questions rather than make statements: Questions will elicit the subject's opinions and ideas, but statements might make the subject fearful of expressing ideas that conflict with the reporter's. The interviewee may conclude that the reporter is biased and will not fairly report the interview.
- Don't ask double-barrelled questions, which might have more than one correct answer. For example, one interviewer asked former U.S. president Bill Clinton, when he first ran for president, "Was Gennifer Flowers your lover for 12 years?" Clinton answered, "That allegation is false." But which part was false? The part

about Flowers being his lover or the part about the 12 years? By splitting the question into two parts, the reporter might have received better answers.

- Don't use loaded words in questions: "Mayor Datolli, will your budget scheme save the city from bankruptcy?" The word "scheme" seems to judge the mayor's proposal. A more neutral term would be "plan."

- Don't ask leading questions that suggest what the reporter thinks the answer should be: A question like "Was the robber carrying a shotgun?" implies the questioner thinks the robber was. If the source is uncertain, they might be tempted to confirm that suspicion, even if it is incorrect.

Conducting the Interview

Selecting a Location for the Interview

Some sources are anxious about being interviewed. This can prevent them from answering any questions in a natural manner. Reporters reassure their sources by conducting interviews in places where sources feel comfortable. Reporters can learn more about sources by seeing them in their home or office. Take the time to look around for clues and details. The photos sources display on their desks and walls, the lapel pins they wear, or the items they have clipped from newspapers and taped to their refrigerators could give reporters insights about sources or suggest questions to ask them.

Here is an excerpt from the beginning of a feature profile by Chris Koentges about noted Canadian chef Michael Noble. The profile, published in *The Walrus* magazine, is entitled "The Noble Effect: Can a $15-a-plate restaurant chain apportion the genius of one of Canada's greatest chefs?" The piece begins in a test kitchen, and Koentges starts with a lengthy opening that details the environment of the test kitchen before he first quotes his source. Notice how he uses details he observed to give readers a sense of Noble and his working environment as well as to prefigure the profile's main theme: Haute cuisine is haute cuisine because of the mystique of its chef.

There is nothing remarkable about the Earls Test Kitchen, which is known to insiders as TK1. It is stainless steel and tile, six burners, two long counters, a double fridge, some gadgets. With the door closed it feels like a subway car, its windows revealing the hallway of a much larger kitchen. This larger kitchen opens out to a shiny, boisterous room called Earls Tin Palace, which in turn gives way to the world outside, where fifty-one other Earls are strewn from Fort McMurray almost to the Mexican border. Fifty-three, fifty-four and fifty-five are on the way.

I have spent my life avoiding Earls. Then Michael Noble started working there.

If you live in the east, you may not know Earls, which surfaced in the west, with oversized papier-mâché parrots dangling from its rafters, about the same time as U2 and Tom Cruise. Earls is known for inventing and reinventing much of our casual-dining canon, most notably the dry rib and the hot chicken Caesar salad. It is known for servers who are not exactly hard on the eyes. It is arguably the safest bet for a first date in the history of dining out.

Until recently, a typical Earls was 7,000 square feet and averaged $3 million in annual sales. However, the newest generation of stores have flashier décor and tonier locations like Polo Park in Winnipeg, with sales averaging $5.5 million. One competitor I spoke with equated the Fuller family, which runs Earls and several other high-end chains, to NASA scientists, so systematically have they stayed a teaspoon ahead of the public's tastes. What they've shown in their latest incarnation is that the essential qualities of elite cuisine can be reproduced, packaged, and delivered—without the elitism.

In the autumn of 2004, Michael Noble left Catch, a $5-million fine-dining experiment in downtown Calgary that critics had christened "Canada's best new restaurant," to become Earls' Director of Culinary & Product Development. In the weeks leading up to Christmas, he travelled five times from Calgary to TK1, summoned each time by Earls' Executive Tasting Panel. On this, his sixth trip, things would get interesting. In a span of thirty hours, he would attempt to crank out ten dishes, representing the final crack at his first full-fledged Earls menu. And then, because this is how the stars sometimes align, he would prepare a single course for La Confrérie de la Chaîne de Rôtisseurs, an international gastronomic society dating back to Louis IX's Royal Guild of Goose Roasters that is dedicated to safeguarding fine dining as we know it.*

Newsrooms are poor places for interviews. They are noisy and chaotic. Sources unfamiliar with newsrooms might find them intimidating.

Restaurants have several drawbacks as interview locations, too. Crowd noise and interruptions from servers can interfere with the conversation. Reporters who record interviews might find that the background noise muffles the interview.

No matter where reporters conduct interviews, they should always arrive early and keep the interview within the agreed-on time. They also should dress appropriately for the interview setting, usually in business clothes.

Organizing the Questions

Reporters should start an interview with a clear statement of its purpose, if that's not already understood. For brief interviews, reporters try to get right to the main questions. For longer interviews, reporters often begin with a few minutes of small talk to put a source at ease.

Once the serious questioning begins, reporters should take charge of the conversation, decide what questions to ask, keep the interview on track, and make sure the source fully answers each question. If a source wanders or tries to evade questions, reporters bring the conversation back to the story angle and politely but firmly ask the source to respond to the questions.

* Reprinted with permission of Chris Koentges.

Questions should be grouped by topic. A reporter who is planning to profile a candidate for mayor, for example, may want to cover the person's education, work history, family life, community service, political experience, and plans for running the city. Reporters try to organize the topics, making it easy for the source to move from one to the next. Chronological organization is one way of organizing the topics. For a reporter interviewing a scientist about the effects of global warming, chronology is meaningless, so a different organization makes more sense, such as moving from effects on oceans and ocean life to effects on land animals and finally to effects on humans. In still other situations, the reporter might let the conversation follow its own course and let topics arise naturally, simply making sure that the source covers all essential points.

Reporters organize the questions they ask as well as the topics they want to cover. One approach—sometimes called the funnel—starts with a general question and moves to progressively more specific ones. For example, a reporter interviewing a police chief about how an influx of immigrants is affecting law enforcement might ask the questions in this order:

- Has the presence of large numbers of immigrants changed the way the police force operates?
- What kinds of changes has the department made?
- Has the department changed any of its policies to deal with immigrants?
- Is the department requiring or encouraging officers to learn additional languages?

Sometimes reporters might organize their questions in a reverse funnel, starting with specifics and moving to more general matters. The same interview with the police chief using a reverse funnel might go like this:

- How many officers does the department have who can speak a second language?
- Is the department considering encouraging officers to learn a second language?
- What changes might the department make to deal with growing numbers of immigrants?
- How has the presence of large numbers of immigrants affected law enforcement generally?

Many experienced reporters recommend starting an interview with some comments or soft questions that will break the ice and get the conversation going. Once the source becomes comfortable talking, the reporter can ask more difficult questions. As banal as it might seem, even a polite question about the weather can start the conversation. Another way of breaking the ice is to ask the interviewee about some personal effect—a photograph or an award—on display in the person's office or home. Talking about a mutual interest or people both the reporter and the interviewee know is another way to start the conversation.

Reporters save their most embarrassing or difficult questions for the end of interviews. By then, their sources should be more comfortable answering questions. Moreover, if a source refuses to answer embarrassing questions and abruptly ends an interview, the reporter will have already obtained most of the information needed for the story.

Experienced interviewers will have prepared well enough before an interview that they will encounter few surprises, but occasionally an interview yields unexpected information. If the new information is newsworthy, reporters must abandon their original plans and pursue the new angles.

At the end of an interview, reporters should always ask sources if they have anything to add. Sometimes the most surprising and newsworthy information emerges in response to that question. Reporters should also ask sources for the names of other people to interview or for documents that might provide additional information or verification. They also should ask the best time to call sources back if they have follow-up questions. Finally, reporters should thank sources for granting the interview.

Dealing with Reluctant Sources and Asking Tough Questions

Most sources co-operate with reporters because they welcome the opportunity to tell their side of a story; however, a few dislike talking to reporters or are hostile. They may fear a topic is too difficult for reporters to understand; they may have been embarrassed by reporters in earlier interviews; or they may suspect the resulting story will portray them in a bad light.

Reporters first try to learn why the source is hesitant to speak to them. After learning the reason, they may be able to overcome that specific objection. In some cases, sources fear the interview will turn into an interrogation. Reporters might be able to lessen the interviewee's anxiety by showing empathy and adjusting their personal style to fit the mood of the person being interviewed. Good interviewers convey the feeling they are more interested in sources than in themselves.

When sources fear reporters will distort or misunderstand what is said, reporters can demonstrate their knowledge of the topic and background by asking intelligent questions or pointing to other stories they have written on the topic. The interviewees may then be willing to fill in the gaps in the reporters' knowledge. Explaining the purpose of the interview and the story also can help convince sources that reporters are knowledgeable and trustworthy.

Interviewers have a variety of tactics for getting reluctant sources to talk. If interviewees are unresponsive, reporters may try switching topics, trying to find something that will get the source to talk more. In some instances, reporters can build rapport with sources by expressing admiration (if it is genuine) for something a source did or said. Or reporters might draw on their background to establish a connection with a reluctant source. If the interviewee is a college president, the reporter might mention that her father was a college professor (if that is true).

Some sources fear the story will put them in a bad light and cause them to lose their jobs or money or even to face criminal prosecution. Reporters can soothe these fears by explaining that the interview is an opportunity for sources to put their side of a story before the public and that failure to do so will make them look worse.

Many interviews—whether done for feature stories or investigative stories—require reporters to ask tough questions that the source might find embarrassing or potentially harmful. Failure to ask the questions, however, means an interview will be incomplete and lack news value. Asking tough questions is easier if reporters maintain their neutrality. If interviewees believe reporters are simply asking questions and not expressing opinions, they are more likely to submit to tough questions without ending the interview or criticizing the reporter. Sometimes reporters can enhance this sense of neutrality by asking questions in ways that distance themselves from the opinions the questions may imply. They can, for example:

- Attribute the question or point of view implied in the question to a third party or to public opinion generally. For example: "Chancellor Smith, some faculty members have said you attach more importance to intercollegiate athletics than to academics. What is your response?"
- Sugar-coat questions. Asking a person, "Is there anything about your marriage that you now regret?" is easier than asking, "Did you attack your partner?"
- Ask interviewees to explain their previous statements or actions or give their versions of controversial events.
- Ask interviewees to talk about others. Once they start talking about what other people have said or done, it might be easier to shift the interview to their own conduct.
- Ask interviewees for the names of people who support or criticize them. Then ask the interviewees to guess what their critics are most likely to say about them. This tactic often elicits information as well as tips for additional interviews.
- Be persistent. If sources refuse to talk, hang up the phone, or slam the door in reporters' faces, reporters should go back the next day or the next week and try again.

Sources pressed to talk about sensitive topics may sometimes try to evade the question or may even lie. When sources avoid an issue or give fuzzy answers, reporters can restate the question, forcing sources to be more forthcoming. Reporters can also simply remain silent if answers seem incomplete or evasive. The silence tells sources their answers are insufficient and pushes them to elaborate. In some cases, reporters might want to confront sources directly about evasive answers, saying they will note evasions in the story.

Reporters who have done their homework often will know when a source is lying. American reporter Eric Nalder lets sources he suspects of lying spin out their tales. He interrupts them only to ask for elaboration or more detail. Once he has the source's entire story, he can begin to use the facts he has already gathered to pick the source's story apart and get that person to tell the truth.

Reporters should never try to bully or intimidate hostile sources or try to deceive them about the purpose of an interview. Information obtained from a source who has been intimidated may be unreliable. Sources who have been led to believe an interview will be about one topic when the reporters want information about something else will feel unprepared to respond fully and accurately.

Special Situations

Phone Interviews

Reporters conduct many interviews by phone. When they do, they always identify themselves and their news organizations clearly at the start of the conversation. They never pose as someone other than a reporter. As discussed in Chapter 2, reporters should always ask permission to record the interview.

Experienced reporters wear headsets, keeping their hands free to type notes as they interview their sources. Some sources become upset when they hear the clicking of the keyboard and realize that reporters are typing everything they say; they begin to speak more cautiously or try to end the interview. If a source cannot be soothed, reporters can take notes more quietly in longhand. Sources used to dealing with reporters become accustomed to the noise.

Phone calls save enormous amounts of time, since reporters do not have to drive to a source's home or office, wait until a source is free, conduct the interview, and then drive back to their offices. Another advantage is that some sources are more comfortable talking without someone watching them.

Phone interviews have disadvantages too. Some sources might be hesitant to talk. Even if reporters have identified themselves, sources may want to call reporters back to make sure they are who they say they are. More important, phone interviews need to be brief. Sources usually have other work, and long phone conversations may annoy them. Particularly frustrating for reporters is playing phone tag or not being able to reach a source while on deadline. Reporters simply have to be persistent and keep calling. They should not wait for sources to return phone calls.

Reporters also have to be alert to the possibility that they may be calling at an inconvenient time for the source. If reporters are calling sources in different time zones, they need to be aware of what the time is where the source lives. A reporter working in Vancouver at 8 p.m. should realize that it is 11 p.m. for a source in Toronto, a time when many people are asleep.

Phone calls are an unsatisfactory means of conducting in-depth interviews about controversial or complex issues and personalities. It is difficult to cultivate sources known only by phone and never seen face-to-face. Sources might be reluctant to answer over-the-phone questions about embarrassing or personal matters; thus, phone interviews tend to be brief and superficial. If reporters want to conduct longer, in-depth interviews, they must visit the source in person.

Email Interviews

Email has opened up another way of interviewing sources. Reporters use email to contact hard-to-reach or reluctant sources. Even people who travel a lot make time to check their email. Sources who dodge phone calls or hesitate to return phone messages may answer a reporter's email. A reporter who is trying to contact several sources for similar information can use email to send the same message to each of them. Email is also a way of keeping in contact with sources, exchanging ideas with colleagues, or communicating with the audience.

Reporters are as polite in their emails as they are in person or on the phone. They use a salutation (such as "Dear Isabel Ramirez,") and identify themselves and the news organization they represent. They usually review the background of an event or issue before they ask their questions. Reporters also tell sources their deadline, and they thank the sources for their time and expertise. (After all, the sources are not getting paid to answer the reporter's questions but are donating their time.) Reporters do not write in all capital letters because many email users regard it as shouting. Journalists also avoid using acronyms and initialisms, such as "btw" ("by the way"), because not everyone knows what they represent.

Email interviews have some advantages over phone interviews. Besides being more convenient for some sources, email also affords them an opportunity to develop their thoughts more carefully and in more detail. That means reporters get more thorough answers to their questions. The email also provides a written record of the interviews, lessening the likelihood of misunderstanding or misquotation.

However, interviews by email also have drawbacks. Reporters are deprived of their sources' facial expressions, vocal inflections, and body language, all of which can help reporters understand their sources better. Also, although the email response might be more thorough and thoughtful, it also might be less spontaneous. The offhand responses sources make in personal or phone interviews give reporters additional information and insights on which they can follow up quickly.

Another drawback to the email interview is the possibility the respondent is not the correct person. For example, a business executive might have a public relations person draft an answer to an email from a reporter. In still other cases, email sources might simply be pretending to have credentials or experiences they do not really have. The possibility of such fraud exists even for face-to-face interviews, but posing seems to be easier over the internet or through email. Journalists always try to conduct interviews in person or on the phone and will use email only if the first two options are not available.

Interviewing for Broadcast

Reporters interviewing sources for radio or television have problems print reporters don't face. In an interview with *American Journalism Review*, Terry Gross, host of the National Public Radio program *Fresh Air* and one of the best interviewers in the business, explains the difference this way: "For most print journalists the interview is the raw material for the piece, along with everything else the reporter has seen and heard in researching the story. For me the interview is the piece." Gross tries to arrange her questions so that the answers produce a pleasing narrative, rather than something that sounds like answers to a random questionnaire. Although Gross's program is not broadcast live, giving the program staff time to check and edit responses, the production deadlines are tight enough that extensive editing is impractical (Figure 5.1).

CBC Licensing

Figure 5.1

Broadcast journalists do a lot of advance planning for interviews to make sure there is a good flow to the story. In his first television interview since his release from an Egyptian prison, Canadian journalist Mohamed Fahmy spoke with broadcast journalist Gillian Findlay of CBC's *The Fifth Estate* in Cairo, February 2015.

Television reporters need to plan their interviews in advance with the technicians who will operate the cameras and sound equipment, especially if the interview needs to be shot quickly for broadcast that day or if the source does not want to appear on camera. They also might want to show the interview subject doing more than talking. Where possible, television reporters might want the subject to demonstrate an activity or respond to a video or another source.

In digital journalism, both print and broadcast reporters have to keep in mind the content they can use for their story online. Text on social media is always more appealing to the audience with a visual or audio component, which is why in-person or phone interviews work best as these scenarios give the reporter the chance to gather audio or visual content.

Taking Notes

Reporters conducting interviews balance the tasks of note-taking and questioning. Unless reporters take detailed notes, they probably will forget much of what is said. Many interviewers take copious notes, writing down much more information than they can possibly use. During an interview, reporters may not know which facts they will need or want to emphasize in their stories. If they record as much as possible, they are less likely to forget an important point or make a factual error. They can easily ignore notes that later prove to be unimportant or irrelevant.

Few reporters know shorthand, but most develop their own shortcuts for taking notes. They leave out some words, abbreviate others, and jot down names, numbers, good quotations, and key ideas. When sources speak too rapidly, reporters can ask them to slow down or repeat important statements. Note-taking makes some sources nervous. Reporters should explain that the notes will help them write more accurate and thorough stories.

After completing interviews, reporters review their notes immediately while everything is fresh in their minds. They may want to fill in some gaps or be certain that they understand everything a source said. Reporters often write their stories as soon as possible after their interviews. The longer they wait, the more likely they are to forget some facts or distort others.

Recording Interviews

Recording interviews frees reporters to concentrate on the questions they want to ask and sources' responses to those questions. Recordings also provide verbatim and permanent records, so reporters make fewer factual errors, and sources are less likely to claim that they were misquoted. When reporters replay the recordings, they often find important statements they failed to notice during the interviews.

Recording has drawbacks too. After recording a one-hour interview, reporters may have to replay the entire recording at least once, and perhaps two or three times, before writing the story. They also may have difficulty locating important facts or quotations on the recording. By comparison, reporters may need a minute or less to find a fact or a quotation in their handwritten notes from a one-hour interview.

Fortunately, there is a third possibility: reporters may both record their interviews and take written notes. The reporters can consult their notes to write the stories, then use the recordings to verify the accuracy of important facts and quotations. Most digital recorders have a counter reporters can use to note the location of important or interesting quotations. Reporters can also use their cell phones as recorders.

Although recorders are commonplace, some sources still refuse to be recorded. Reporters should patiently explain to their sources how recording interviews ensures the sources are accurately quoted and their words are reported with the right context. Recording a conversation without the other party's consent is unethical and sometimes illegal. While it is legal for journalists to record phone interviews without the consent of the person being interviewed, consent is required if the interview is to be broadcast. Reporters may also listen in on or record private conversations if they have the consent of one of the parties (the originator or intended receiver of the communication), but it is a *Criminal Code* offence to reveal the content of the communication without the consent of one of the parties. It is also a criminal offence to publish or broadcast a phone conversation that was illegally recorded by a third party. In broadcast journalism, under Canadian

Radio-television and Telecommunications Commission (CRTC) rules, reporters are pro-hibited from airing interviews or conversations without the consent of the interviewees. Recording in secret may also present legal problems under various other provisions of the *Criminal Code*. Finally, while the use of hidden microphones and cameras is generally prohibited, the procedure may be defended in cases where it is necessary to expose the truth on a matter of legitimate public interest.

In the usual case of a reporter recording a phone or face-to-face interview, the consent-ing party would be the reporter doing the recording. Even where it is legal, though, record-ing a conversation without the other party's consent raises ethical questions. Undisclosed recording seems manipulative and invasive. The audience and jurors (if a story results in a lawsuit) may consider any information reporters obtain through secret recording tainted.

Final Thoughts

Interviewing is an art form that requires practice. Journalists who are most successful at interviewing have done it for years and have developed insights into the sources they in-terview and into their own strengths and weaknesses in relating to other people. Student journalists may find their initial attempts at interviewing difficult but they should not become discouraged. With time and persistence, they can become excellent interviewers.

Writing the Interview Story

Writing a story based on an in-depth interview, such as a personality profile, is similar to writing any other news story. An interview story does raise a couple of unusual problems, however.

One option reporters have when writing an interview story is to use a question-and-answer format. Few do so, however, because it requires too much space and makes it dif-ficult for the audience to grasp a story's highlights quickly. The Q-and-A format works best with celebrity interviews, self-help stories, and sidebars for main stories. Q-and-A stories are never verbatim transcripts of interviews, even though the format may create that impression. The interviews are usually heavily edited to eliminate boring and irrele-vant passages.

Most reporters begin interview stories with a summary lead that presents the story's angle. Reporters then present the highlights in the following paragraphs. Reporters also may use an alternative lead, such as an anecdote or description that introduces a nut paragraph containing the angle. Information in the body of the story usually is organized by topic, and facts and quotations are presented in the order of their importance, not the order in which the source provided them. Reporters must be sure, however, that in rearranging information they keep every direct and indirect quotation in its proper context. Reporters usually keep background information to a minimum and incorporate it in the story where it is most necessary and helpful for explaining a source's remarks.

Making sure an interview story adheres to its angle can be difficult. A student interested in Canada's participation in the U.S. space shuttle program interviewed a representative of the National Aeronautics and Space Administration (NASA). The NASA source overwhelmed the student with facts about the technological benefits of the Apollo and Skylab projects. Those were the facts that filled the reporter's story. They were accurate but irrelevant to the student's purpose of writing about the space shuttle program. Had the student kept the interview focused on the shuttle program, the story would have kept its focus too.

Another problem is the overuse of quotations. Some writers think they have done their job simply by stringing together quotations from their sources. Quotations should be used only for emphasis and impact. Reporters should tell most of the story in their own words and use only those quotations that show strong emotion or support a point in a particularly effective way.

Checklist for Interviewing

1. Determine whether the story will be a news story, a feature, or an investigative story.
2. For all types of stories, interview to get facts, details, chronologies, context, and anecdotes.
3. For feature stories, capture the source's environment, appearance, and mannerisms.
4. For investigative stories, get the source's version of events, explanations of contradictions, and replies to charges.
5. Identify the best available sources who can provide the necessary information for the story.
6. In deciding how many sources to interview, keep in mind deadlines, the expertise of the sources, the degree of controversy regarding the issue, and the complexity of the issue.
7. Research people and issues as thoroughly as possible before conducting any interviews.
8. Select questions that will address the angle of the planned story.
9. Use questions that will encourage interviewees to talk—and then let them talk with as few interruptions as possible.
10. Interview sources in places where they will be comfortable, not newsrooms or restaurants.
11. Organize questions by topic, and raise topics in an order that will make it easy for sources to move from one to the next.
12. If a source is reluctant to talk or hostile, find out why and try to address the concern.
13. Maintain neutrality when asking tough questions. Sources are more likely to answer tough questions from neutral interviewers than from those who seem to be advocates for a point of view.
14. Phone interviews save time, but they are unsatisfactory for long, in-depth interviews, which are better if done in person.

15. Email can be an effective way of interviewing some sources, but the interviewer is deprived of information about the source's demeanour and personality. Email should be used only when interviews in person or on the phone are not possible.

16. Reporters interviewing for broadcast need to remember that the interview is the story and not just raw material for a story.

17. Take thorough notes during the interview, making sure to write down names, dates, numbers, and good quotations.

18. Recorders provide a verbatim permanent record. It is a good professional practice to both record and take notes during interviews.

 The Writing Coach

Interviewing for Story

By Don Gibb

"What's the weather like?"

Such a simple, conversational question, and yet it led *Globe and Mail* columnist Murray Campbell to a detail that provided a lead for his story on Julia Butterfly Hill, the woman who lived for two years in a 1,000-year-old giant redwood tree in California to prevent it from becoming lumber.

His simple question—along with follow-up questions—produced rich visual detail for readers. It was a cold, cold rainy day. The protective tarp was flapping in the wind. Butterfly Hill was shivering under layers of clothing. Seven, to be exact. And all of this happening on a platform the size of a double bed—yet another detail to let readers "see" the image in their minds.

He opened the story with this:

It is beginning to hail, and Julia Butterfly Hill is shivering even though she is wearing seven layers of clothing. "It's extremely windy and it's extremely cold," she said, drawing out the syllables of "extremely" to underline the point that she has seen better days.

Ms. Hill was speaking on a cellular phone about halfway up a 60-metre redwood tree in northern California. She was huddled beneath rustling tarps and a platform about the size of a double bed.

Around her were her very few possessions: A single-burner propane stove and a bucket she uses as a toilet, some books and the cardboard on which she writes letters and poems.

What's the weather like? What does your living space look like? What are you doing now? Such simple questions produce the details, anecdotes, quotes, dialogue, and scenes

continued

writers need to create the images readers need to "see" and to be part of a story. Good writers develop a built-in alarm that goes off every time one of their senses (see, hear, smell, touch, or taste) detects a moment worth capturing in more detail:

"Like the father, his daughter abducted and murdered a year earlier, who cannot stand to hear the doorbell ring."

Why?

"It was a year ago, as he made a pot of tea in the kitchen, that the doorbell rang. He walked past his daughter's high school graduation picture on the piano in the living room, opened the front door, and faced a police constable."

What did the officer say?

"I looked straight into his eyes. He didn't have to say anything. I knew my daughter was dead. Every time I hear the doorbell, the image of the police officer—his eyes—flash back to remind me of my daughter's death." A single, simple detail of the doorbell allows the writer to capture a key moment—a telling anecdote—in the story of a father still grieving as police continue to search for his daughter's killer.

But keep going. *What did the father see in his eyes that told him she was dead? What were the first words the police officer said? Did he come in? Did he have tea with the father? Where was the mother of the girl when the officer arrived?* And then . . . keep going.

The interview is the key that opens the door to great storytelling. Every interview should be an exploration for interesting, factual, informative, and visual detail. It is not simply a question-and-answer exchange or transcribing verbatim what someone says. When done well, it involves getting to the heart of an issue and to the very soul of a person.

Feature writing often offers writers a chance to do more research and more interviews. It gives writers more of an opportunity to see their interview subjects at work, at play, and at home—in other words, to go to the scene or several scenes. And that means the chance to gather more detail. It also offers the luxury of conducting follow-up interviews with key characters in the middle or at the end of the process or after having talked to others.

To be an effective interviewer, writers need to know simple rules that form the building blocks of creating memorable features. Here are some of them:

- Listen. Perhaps this is the most crucial interviewing skill. If you're too busy thinking of your next question or checking your digital recorder, you're not paying enough attention to the words coming from your interviewee.
- Stay in charge. Listen to your sources and listen to their agendas, but don't let them take control of the interview.
- Understand the sequence of events. For the audience, nothing adds confusion to a story faster than not knowing where we are in time or place.
- Ask open-ended questions. Asking questions that cannot be answered with a simple yes or no opens the door to essential details.
- Probe for graphic details. Always ask follow-up questions, and you will quickly discover that the answers generate better and more complete responses as well as added detail to bring more colour to your stories.

- Take one thing at a time. It's a good idea not to leave a topic until you believe you have explored it fully.
- Ask for clarification. Follow this simple rule: do not move into a new line of questioning until you understand what has already been discussed.
- Ask tough questions. First, go in prepared. If you're listening carefully, you're likely to find the right spot to segue to your tough questions.
- Ask simple questions. Reporters who fail to ask simple questions risk failing to properly understand their story or explain it to readers. Too often, they allow a person's quote to substitute for a proper explanation.
- Don't accept "no" too readily. Before accepting "no" as the final answer to your request for an interview, try to determine and then address what lies behind the potential source's refusal.
- Take careful notes. Use a recorder to supplement rather than to replace note-taking. Over-reliance on recorders dulls a reporter's listening skills.
- Go somewhere. Getting out of the newsroom and to the scene of an interview allows you to experience the setting where an interview subject works, plays, or lives and, based on that experience, to build scenes into your stories.
- Trust your senses. Writers need to record what people say, but they also need to move quickly into observation mode when necessary. Seek the telling detail, and don't be afraid to look for personal objects in an interview setting and ask about them.
- Phone with your eyes open. A phone interview is second-best to a face-to-face interview, so when doing phone interviews, be sure to ask the kinds of questions that will allow you to paint pictures for your readers.
- Watch out for hazards. Reporters encounter a variety of hazards in an interview; mostly, these hazards are designed to intimidate the reporter and to wrest control of the interview. (The source who waits till the end of an interview to announce that all the preceding was of course "off the record" is a good example.)
- Snap . . . Snap . . . Snap. The best writers collect images detail by detail through questions designed to capture a story piece by piece.

Suggested Readings and Useful Websites

Cribb, Robert, Dean Jobb, David McKie, and Fred Vallance-Jones. 2014. "Getting People to Talk: The Art of the Interview." In *Digging Deeper: A Canadian Reporter's Research Guide*, pp. 118–34. Don Mills, ON: Oxford University Press.

Factor, Amanda. 2004. "Dumb and Dumber." *Ryerson Review of Journalism*. June 1. Accessed June 4, 2018, http://rrj.ca/dumb-and-dumber/

Gibb, Don. 2009. "Interviewing to Tell a Story." In Ivor Shapiro, ed., *The Bigger Picture: Elements of Feature Writing*, pp. 35–54. Toronto: Emond Montgomery Publications.

McCarten, James, ed. 2017. *The Canadian Press Stylebook: A Guide for Writers and Editors*, 18th edn. Toronto: The Canadian Press.

Sawatsky, John. 1989. *Insiders: Power, Money and Secrets*. Toronto: McClelland and Stewart.

Scanlon, Chip. 2013. "How Journalists Can Become Better Interviewers." Poynter. March 13. Accessed June 4, 2018, https://www.poynter.org/news/how-journalists-can-become-better-interviewers

Stein, M.L., and Susan F. Paterno. 2001. *Talk Straight, Listen Carefully: The Art of Interviewing*. Hoboken, NJ: Wiley-Blackwell.

Vernon, Pete. 2017. "Behind the Success of the *LA Times* Hit True-Crime Thriller." *Columbia Journalism Review*. October 30. Accessed June 4, 2018, https://www.cjr.org/local_news/dirty-john-la-times.php

BBC Academy – Journalism – Interviewing: http://www.bbc.co.uk/academy/journalism/skills/interviewing

Exercise 1   Interviews

Section I: Discussion Questions

1. How would you respond to a source who, several days before a scheduled interview, asked for a list of the questions you intended to ask?
2. Do you agree that reporters have an obligation to inform their sources when they plan to record an interview even when it's legal to do so? Why or why not?
3. If a story's publication is likely to embarrass a source, do reporters have a responsibility to warn the source of that possibility? Does it matter whether the source is used to dealing with reporters?
4. Would you be willing to interview a mother whose son just died? Would it matter whether her son drowned in a swimming pool, was murdered, or was a convicted killer executed in a state prison?
5. Imagine that you wrote a front-page story about students' use of marijuana on your campus. To obtain the story, you promised several sources that you would never reveal their identities. If, during a subsequent legal proceeding, a judge ordered you to identify your sources, would you do so? Or would you be willing to go to jail to protect your sources?

Section II: Class Projects

1. List 10 interviewing tips provided by other sources.
2. Interview an expert on body language or nonverbal communication, perhaps someone in your school's psychology or speech department, and report on the information's usefulness to journalists. You might also invite the expert to speak to your class.

3. Interview an expert on interviewing, perhaps a faculty member in your school's psychology department. You might also invite the expert to speak to your class.

4. Interview government officials who frequently deal with reporters. Ask those officials what they like and dislike about the interviews and how they try to handle the interviews and the reporters conducting the interviews.

5. Ask several government officials which local reporters are the best interviewers, then interview those reporters about their interviewing techniques. You might invite one of those reporters to speak to your class.

6. Ask every student in your class to write one paragraph about each of the three most newsworthy experiences in his or her life. Then select the students with the most interesting experiences and have each student in your class interview them, one by one, and write news stories about their experiences.

Exercise 2   Interview with an Injured Bicyclist

Write a news story based on the following interview with Marsha L. Taylor, conducted this morning, two days after she was released from a hospital after being injured in a bicycling accident. "Q" stands for the questions that Taylor was asked during the interview at her home, and "A" stands for her answers, which can be quoted directly. Taylor manages a McDonald's restaurant and lives on McKay Boulevard in your city.

Q: How long have you been bicycling?

A: I started when I was in college, but I didn't do any serious cycling until after I had graduated. I spent that first summer looking for work, and cycling was a way of filling in time and keeping fit while I waited for interviews. Eventually I got involved with some groups of cyclists and participating in weekend rides and even some races. Since then it's been a major part of my life. I can't imagine what my life would be like without bicycling.

Q: How active have you been in bicycling recently?

A: I rode a lot this year. Um, I guess I must have ridden at least maybe 5,000 kilometres, because in the spring I rode in the annual Lieutenant-Governor's Bicycle Tour, which goes across the province. And in the fall, I rode in a tour across Canada.

Q: How did your accident happen?

A: Well, a lot of it is hazy to me, but it happened shortly after I finished the tour. I had been back in town about two weeks, and I was just out for a short ride of an hour or so. I was riding down 72nd Street almost to Southland Boulevard when a car hit me from behind and sent me flying off my bike. That's all I remember until I was in the hospital.

Q: What were your injuries?

A: Gee, you might as well ask what wasn't injured. I had a mild concussion, a broken neck, six broken ribs, a broken arm, and a broken pelvis.

Q: Were the doctors worried about your condition?

A: Yeah, somewhat. They didn't think there was anything they couldn't control, but there was a lot of stuff broken. They were especially concerned about the broken neck. One doctor said I had what they call a hangman's fracture. She said it was a miracle that I wasn't paralyzed.

Q: Was your recovery pretty smooth?

A: No. In fact I got worse at first. After a couple of weeks, they sent me to a rehabilitation facility, but then I developed complications. The doctors discovered I had some internal injuries. My intestine was perforated, and my liver and gall bladder were injured. All that caused my skin to change colour, start turning bright orange. When my mother saw me she said I looked like a Halloween pumpkin. I had to go back to the hospital because of those complications. But for that, I probably would have been out in two months instead of four. I still have to go back for rehabilitation three times a week.

Q: Have you changed your attitude about cycling since your accident?

A: No. I still want to ride. If I could, I'd be out there right now, but it's hard to ride a bike when you have to use crutches. If you, you know, take precautions and are careful, bicycling's pretty safe.

Q: What kind of precautions?

A: Well, the main thing, you know, is protective clothing, especially the helmet. I never ride unless I have my helmet. It probably saved my life this time.

Q: How long have you lived here?

A: Let's see, ah, 15 years now, ever since I started work for McDonald's.

Q: How long have you been manager there?

A: Four years.

Q: How old are you?

A: Ah, 37. Old enough, yeah.

Exercise 3   Interview with a Robbery Victim

Write a news story based on the following interview with Michele Schipper, a second-year student majoring in journalism at your school. The interview provides a verbatim account of a robbery that occurred yesterday. "Q" stands for the questions Schipper was asked during an interview this morning, and "A" stands for her answers, which can be quoted directly. (This is a true story, told by a student.)

Q: Could you describe the robbery?

A: I pulled up into the parking lot of a convenience store on Bonneville Drive, but I pulled up on the side and not in front where I should have, and I was getting out of my car, and I was reaching into my car to pull out my purse when this guy, 6-foot-tall or whatever, approached me and said, "Give me your purse." I said,

"OK." I barely saw him out of the corner of my eye. And then, I, um, so I reached in to get my purse. And I could see him approaching a little closer. Before then, he was four or five feet away. So I turned around and kicked him in the groin area, and he started going down, but I was afraid he wouldn't stay down, that he would seek some kind of retribution. So when he was down, I gave him a round-house to the nose. I just hit him as hard as I could, an undercut as hard as I could. And I could hear some crunching, and some blood spurted, and he went on the ground, and I got in my car, and I went away. I called the cops from a motel down the street. They asked where he was last I seen him, and I said, "On the ground."

Q: Did the police find him?

A: No, he was gone.

Q: Had you taken judo or some type of self-defence course?

A: No, but I used to be a tomboy, and I used to wrestle with the guys, my good friends, when I was young. It was a good punch. I don't know, I was just very mad. My dad, he works out with boxing and weightlifting and everything, and I've played with that, so I've got the power.

Q: Could you describe the man?

A: I didn't see him well enough to identify him, really, but I hope he thinks twice next time.

Q: What time did the robbery occur?

A: This was about 4 in the afternoon, broad daylight, but there were no other cars parked around, though.

Q: Did you see the man when you drove up, or was he hiding?

A: There was a dumpster, and I guess he came from behind the dumpster, like he was waiting there, just like he was waiting there. And I guess he was waiting around the dumpster, because no one was standing around when I pulled up, I remember that.

Q: Were there any witnesses who could describe the man?

A: There was no one around, there were no cars parked. The clerks were inside the store. I didn't see any pedestrians around, and after I did it, I didn't wait to find if there were any witnesses because I wanted to leave right away.

Q: Was the man armed?

A: Out of the corner of my eye I realized I didn't see any weapon. And I guess I thought he was alone. You register some things; you just don't consciously realize it.

Q: What was your first reaction, what did you think when he first approached and demanded your purse?

A: I didn't think of anything, really, you know. I just reacted. I was very, really indignant. Why, you know, just because he wanted my purse, why should he have it? There was really only $10 in there, and I probably wouldn't really do it again in the same situation. And my parents don't know about it because they would be very angry that I fought back.

Q: Had you ever thought about being robbed and about what you would do, about how you would respond?

A: It just came instinctively, and after the incident, you know, I was shaking for about an hour afterwards.

Q: About how long did the robbery last?

A: It really only lasted a second, just as long as it would take for you to kick someone and then to hit them and then drive away in the car. It really only lasted a second.

6   Basic News Leads

"If you have anything to tell me of importance, for God's sake begin at the end."

—Sara Jeannette Duncan, Canadian journalist and author, 1904

The first paragraph or two in a news story is called the "lead." The lead (some journalists spell it "lede") is the most important part of a story—and the most difficult part to write. Like the opening paragraphs of a short story or novel, the lead of a news story is the part that attracts readers and, if it is well written, arouses their interest. It should tell readers the angle of the story, not hide the subject with unnecessary or misleading words and phrases.

The Summary News Lead

A basic news story answers the 5Ws plus H questions: Who? Where? Why? When? What? and How? But do not be misled by the term "summary" lead. This does not mean you need to summarize all of the answers to the 5Ws plus H questions in your lead. The summary lead means you sum up in your opening paragraph the most important part of the story. The summary lead is not the place to answer all of the 5Ws plus H questions. The summary lead should answer only the one or two questions that are most interesting, newsworthy, and unusual.

To determine which questions are most important for a story, you can use the nine news pegs we discussed in Chapter 2 to measure the news value of your story. You should also consider the following points:

1. What is the most important information? What is the story's angle? Many summary leads are written to show the story's angle.
2. What was said or done about the topic? What happened or what action was taken?
3. What are the most recent developments? This is particularly important in reporting breaking news online.

4.   Which facts are most likely to affect or interest your readers?
5.   Which facts are most unusual?

Each of the following summary leads emphasizes the answer to only one of the 5Ws plus H questions—the question that seems most important for that particular story:

WHAT: Gunfire has killed a candidate in Venezuela's controversial election for a new assembly tasked with rewriting the country's constitution, as well as an opposition activist, officials said Sunday. (CBC News)

WHO: Prime Minister Justin Trudeau says he plans to visit British Columbia's wild-fire zones in the coming days as the situation continues to shift. (*Globe and Mail*)

WHERE: The United States flew two supersonic bombers over the Korean Peninsula on Sunday in a show of force against North Korea following the country's latest intercontinental ballistic missile test. The U.S. also said it conducted a successful test of a missile defence system located in Alaska. (CTV News)

WHEN: The long-awaited weekend is here. The tall ships are finally coming to town. The Rendez-Vous 2017 Tall Ships Regatta hits Halifax with a kick-off event at the Seaport Market on Friday morning. (*Halifax Chronicle Herald*)

WHY: A Canadian Tire employee seen getting physical with an Indigenous customer refusing to leave a store in Regina is no longer with the company, a spokesperson says. (CBC News)

HOW: The two massive mechanical creatures that have been wandering through the streets of Ottawa have become so popular that organizers of the event had to hire more security guards and volunteers to manage the crowds. (CBC News)

When writers try to answer all of the 5Ws plus H questions in one paragraph, they create complicated and confusing leads. Here's an example of an overloaded lead that needs revision.

ORIGINAL: Jamal Patel Vickers, 47, of Yarmouth Drive, died, and John Aston Walters, 39, of Colonial Avenue, was severely injured Sunday afternoon when the bicycles they were riding were struck near the intersection of Weston and Falmouth Roads by a car driven by a man police said had a blood alcohol count of nearly .23 per cent and was driving without a licence because it had been revoked last year after his fourth conviction for driving under the influence of alcohol.
REVISED: One man is dead and another severely injured after the bicycles they were riding were struck by a drunken driver Sunday afternoon near the intersection of Weston and Falmouth Roads.

Because people and what they do are central to many news stories, some journalists recognize two variations on the summary news lead: the immediate-identification lead and the delayed-identification lead. Reporters use the immediate-identification lead when the identities of the major subjects in the story are important or are well known:

> U.S. President Donald Trump's chief of staff Reince Priebus has been elbowed out in a White House civil war, capping a chaotic week even by the standards of Mr. Trump's Washington. (*Globe and Mail*)

In many stories, the names of the main subjects are not as important as what those people did or what happened to them. For those stories, reporters use leads that withhold complete identification of the people involved until the second or third paragraph. The following is a delayed-identification lead:

> An Ottawa man held his girlfriend's baby at knife point for more than two hours Saturday night before police officers captured him after shooting him with a stun gun.

Leads that hold back details so the reporter can get to the angle of the story more quickly are called blind leads. Again, do not misinterpret the term. A blind lead does not hide the angle of the story, only information that the reader does not need immediately. Blind leads let the reporter tell readers what the story is about to pique their interest and get them into the story.

A catchall paragraph usually follows the blind lead to identify sources and answer questions created by the blind lead. Missing details can be placed in subsequent paragraphs. Here's an example of a blind lead:

> It was a local company that lost its appeal in court, but it's the provincial ministry charged with overseeing construction matters that's feeling the pain.

In its second paragraph, the article identified the company and what the case involved. In the third paragraph, the article identified the ministry involved and what it had done wrong.

Before reporters can write effective leads, however, they must learn to recognize what is news. After deciding which facts are most newsworthy, they must summarize those facts in sharp, clear sentences, giving a simple, straightforward account of what happened. Examine these leads, which provide clear, concise summaries of important moments in the nation's history:

> MONTREAL/CALGARY (Reuters)—Canada's Liberal leader Justin Trudeau rode a late surge to a stunning majority election victory on Monday, toppling Prime Minister Stephen Harper's Conservatives with a promise of change and returning a touch of glamour, youth and charisma to Ottawa. (Randall Palmer and Rod Nickel, Reuters, Oct. 19, 2015)

> OTTAWA—Transgender Canadians will soon have the same human rights protections as everyone else, after the government's attempt to add gender identity

to the Canadian Human Rights Act passed in the Senate Thursday afternoon. (Laura Payton, CTV Ottawa News Bureau, June 15, 2017)

Leads that fail to emphasize the news—the most interesting and important details—are sometimes described as burying the lead. Here's an example of a lead that fails to give readers the news:

Wentworth is required to give inmates the same level of medical treatment the general public receives, Corrections Director Maria Sanchez said.

The news in the story, however, was not the level of medical care provided to jail inmates. The news was the financial problems the municipality was facing because of the requirement that it provide medical care to inmates. Here's a rewritten lead that makes the significance of the story clearer:

Wentworth's costs for medical care for jail inmates doubled—from $50,000 to $100,000—last year because of a new provincial regulation.
Friday morning, municipal and provincial officials gathered to find a way to pay the bill.

Sentence Structure in Leads

Most summary leads are a single sentence, and that sentence must follow all the normal rules for punctuation, grammar, word usage, and verb tense. If an event occurred in the past, the lead must use the past tense, not the present. Leads must be complete sentences and should include all the necessary articles—the words "a," "an," and "the."

Some problems with sentence structure arise because beginners confuse a story's lead with its headline. The lead is the first paragraph of a news story. The headline is a brief summary that appears in larger type above the story. To save space, editors use only a few key words in each headline. However, that style of writing is not appropriate for leads:

HEADLINE: Heather Heyer's Mom Doesn't Want to Talk to Donald Trump After Charlottesville

LEAD: The mother of Heather Heyer, the woman killed while protesting Saturday's white-supremacist rally in Charlottesville, Virginia, said she won't talk to President Donald Trump "after what he said about my child."
(Elizabeth Wasserman/Bloomberg http://time.com/4906331/
heather-heyer-mother-susan-bro-donald-trump/)

Reporters usually write leads that use normal word order of subject-verb-object (S-V-O) discussed in Chapter 3. Most leads begin with the subject, which is closely followed by an active verb and then by the object of the verb. Reporters deviate from that style only in the rare case that a different sentence structure better tells the news. Leads that begin with long qualifying clauses and phrases lack the clarity of simpler, more direct sentences. Long introductory clauses also clutter leads, burying the news amid a jumble of less significant details. Writing coaches call this "backing in" to the lead.

> **ORIGINAL:** A new pill, approved by Health Canada after 10 years of testing and costing about $100 per pill, could relieve the pain of migraine headaches, medical researchers said today.
>
> **REVISED:** A new $100 pill could relieve the pain of migraine headaches, medical researchers said today. The pill has been approved by Health Canada after a decade of testing.

Guidelines for Writing Effective Leads

Be Concise

Summary leads on straight news stories need to be concise and straightforward. In the following example the first lead attempt is wordy, repetitious, and choppy, particularly when all the sentences are very short.

> **ORIGINAL:** Two women robbed a shopper in a local supermarket Tuesday. One woman distracted the shopper, and the second woman grabbed her purse, which contained about $50.
>
> **REVISED:** Two women stole a purse containing $50 from a shopper in a local supermarket Tuesday.

The original lead was redundant. It reported two women robbed a shopper, and then it described the robbery.

Reporters need to be mindful of the length of their summary leads, as well as the information they contain. Readability surveys show many readers find a 25-word summary lead "difficult" to read and a 29-word lead "very difficult." A better average would be 18 to 20 words. Reporters should examine their leads critically to determine whether they are wordy or repetitious or contain facts that could be shifted to later paragraphs.

Reporters shorten leads by eliminating unnecessary background information—dates, names, locations—or the description of routine procedures. A lead should report a story's highlights, not its minor details, as concisely as possible:

> **ORIGINAL:** A former Saskatoon woman, who has eluded RCMP since she allegedly hijacked a flight from Canada to Cuba using a plastic flare gun in 1983, was arrested Wednesday as she stood alone on a street corner in Montreal, according to the RCMP.

REVISED: The RCMP on Wednesday arrested a former Saskatoon woman who has eluded authorities since 1983, when she was accused of hijacking an airplane.

Although leads can be too long, they cannot be too short. An effective lead may contain only four, five or six words: "The King is dead" or "Americans landed on the moon" or "There's new hope for couch potatoes."

Be Specific

Good leads contain interesting details and are so specific that readers can visualize the events they describe. As you read the following lead, you should be able to imagine the dramatic scene it describes:

At 59, she'd never touched a gun—until someone held one to her head.

The following lead is less interesting because it is abstract and contains vague generalities. Reporters can easily transform such leads into more interesting ones by adding more specific details:

ORIGINAL: The city council passed an ordinance that will affect all parents and teenagers living within city limits.
REVISED: The city council ignored the objections of the mayor and numerous parents and voted 6–1 Monday to enact a dusk-to-dawn curfew to keep teenagers off city streets.

Some leads use worn-out clichés—a lazy way of summarizing a story. Avoid saying that "a step has been taken" or that someone has moved "one step closer" to a goal. Present specific details:

ORIGINAL: University officials moved one step closer to increasing tuition and fees for the upcoming school year, leaving students up in the air.
REVISED: University officials voted Tuesday to increase tuition and fees 10 per cent next year to offset cuts in government funding.

Use Powerful, Active Verbs

A single word—a descriptive verb—can transform a routine lead into a dramatic one. As you read the following lead, for example, you may be able to picture what happened:

VICTORIA—After rushing her seven-year-old daughter to safety, Ann Murray raced back to the docks and pounded on her friends' boats while flames and explosions tore through a marina early Friday morning.

Powerful, active verbs such as "rushing," "raced," "pounded," and "tore" paint a vivid picture of the scene in readers' minds. Strong verbs capture the drama and emotion of a news event and help readers understand the impact of the story.

The following lead uses several colourful verbs to describe the capture of a wayward Angus steer that escaped his handlers:

> The suspect tore through a homeowner's fence, ripped the wires from a satellite dish with his teeth, slammed head-on into a travel trailer, then bolted down the street on his way to a weird encounter with a canoe. (*Orlando [Fla.] Sentinel*)

Avoid passive-voice constructions, which combine the past participle of a verb with some form of the verb "to be"—such as "is," "are," "was," and "were." Strong, active-voice verbs are more colourful, interesting, and dramatic:

> **ORIGINAL:** One person *was killed* and four others *were injured* Sunday morning when their car, which *was travelling* west on the Trans-Canada Highway, *hit* a concrete bridge pillar and *was engulfed* in flames.
> **REVISED:** A car *travelling* west on the Trans-Canada Highway *swerved* across two eastbound lanes, *slammed* into a concrete bridge pillar and *burst* into flames, *killing* one person and *injuring* four others Sunday morning.

Writers can easily convert passive voice to the active voice. Simply rearrange the words, so the sentence begins by reporting (1) who . . . (2) did what . . . (3) to whom. Instead of reporting: "Rocks and bottles were thrown at firefighters," report: "Rioters threw rocks and bottles at firefighters."

Emphasize the Magnitude of the Story

If a story is important, reporters emphasize its magnitude in the lead. Most good leads emphasize the impact stories have on people. When describing natural disasters or human-made catastrophes, such as airplane crashes, earthquakes, or major fires, reporters emphasize the number of people killed, injured, and left homeless. They also emphasize the dollar cost of the damage to buildings or other objects. When describing a storm, reporters may emphasize the amount of rain or snow that fell. The following lead does not deal with a disaster or catastrophe, but it shows how magnitude can be emphasized in a story:

> Second-hand cigarette smoke will cause an estimated 4,700 deaths and about 15,000 nonfatal heart attacks in Canadian non-smokers this year, a study says. That's as much as 50 per cent higher than previous estimates.

Stress the Unusual

Leads also emphasize the unusual. By definition, news involves deviations from the norm. Consider this lead from a story about two men who were arrested for stealing a man's clothes:

> OELWEIN, Iowa—Two men have been arrested for stealing a man's clothes and leaving him to wander around naked, officials said. (Associated Press)

A lead about a board of education meeting or other governmental agency should not report "the board met at 8 p.m. at a local school and began the meeting by approving the agenda." Those facts are routine and not newsworthy. Most school boards meet every couple of weeks, usually at the same time and place, and begin by approving the agenda. Leads should emphasize the unique—the action that follows those routine formalities.

Bank robberies are so common in big cities that newspapers normally devote only a few paragraphs to them. Yet a robbery at the Burlington National Bank in Columbus, Ohio, became a front-page story, published by newspapers throughout the United States. A story transmitted by the Associated Press explained:

> A 61-year-old man says he robbed a bank with a toy gun—he even told the FBI ahead of time when and where—because he wants to spend his golden years in federal prison.

After his arrest, the bank robber insisted he did not want a lawyer. Instead, he wanted to immediately "plead guilty to anything." The man explained he recently was divorced, had no family ties, and was disabled with arthritis. He had spent time in at least three federal prisons and wanted to return to one of them. "I knew what I was doing," he insisted. "I wanted to get arrested, and I proceeded about it the best way I knew how."

Reporters must learn to recognize and emphasize a story's unusual details.

> LONDON—A Dutch driver who watched movies and ate dinner while 58 Chinese immigrants slowly suffocated in the back of his sweltering tomato truck was convicted Thursday of manslaughter and sentenced to 14 years in prison. (Associated Press)

Localize and Update

Reporters localize and update their leads whenever possible by emphasizing their communities' involvement in stories. Readers are most interested in stories affecting them and the people they know.

Reporters also try to localize stories from other parts of the world. When a bomb exploded in an Air India plane in 1985, newspapers across Canada not only ran the story of the bombing but localized the story on the basis of where the passengers had lived. Similarly, when Statistics Canada reports on the number of violent crimes committed in Canada, reporters stress the statistics for their communities:

> **BROAD:** Statistics Canada reported Tuesday that the number of violent crimes in Canada rose 8.3 per cent during the last year.
>
> **LOCALIZED:** The number of violent crimes committed in the city last year rose 5.4 per cent, compared to a national average of 8.3 per cent, Statistics Canada reported Tuesday.

Reporters update a lead by stressing the latest developments in the story. If a breaking story appears in an early edition of a newspaper, they will gather new information and rewrite the story for the newspaper's social media platforms and website.

Be Objective and Attribute Opinions

The lead of a news story, like the rest of the story, must be objective (as opposed to subjective). Reporters are expected to gather facts and convey them to their readers—not to comment, interpret, or advocate.

Although reporters cannot express their own opinions in stories, they often include the opinions of people involved in the news. A lead containing a statement of opinion must be attributed so readers clearly understand the opinion is not the reporter's.

A lead containing an obvious fact or a fact the reporter has witnessed or verified by other means generally does not require attribution. One editor, instructing reporters to "make the lead of a story as brief and clear as possible," noted: "One thing that obstructs that aim is the inclusion of an unnecessary source of attribution. . . . If the lead is controversial, an attribution is imperative. But if the lead is innocuous, forget it." So, if a lead states undisputed facts, the attribution can be placed in a later paragraph:

> Cars and motorcycles crash into deer more than 4,000 times a day, and it's taking an increasingly deadly toll—on people.

Strive for Simplicity

Every lead should be clear, simple, and to the point. Here is an example:

> Like hundreds of mobile homes throughout the province, the home where Linda McDonald and her family died Monday was built before provincial regulators required fire-retardant walls, accessible windows, and smoke detectors.

Here is an example of a lead that suffers from far too much detail:

ORIGINAL: Officials of the city and the school district are breathing sighs of relief following a Housing Authority decision to pull out of a plan to build an apartment complex for moderate-income people on 11 acres of land between Southeast Oatfield and Webster Roads.

The lead could be rewritten any number of ways. The reporter must decide what the important point is. Here are two versions of a simple blind lead for the same story:

REVISED: Several city and school district officials applauded the county's decision to scrap plans for a subsidized housing complex.
REVISED: A new subsidized housing complex will not be built, and city and school district officials are relieved.

Avoiding Some Common Errors

Begin with the News

Avoid beginning a lead with the attribution. Names and titles are dull and seldom important. Attribution should come at the end of the lead. Put attribution at the beginning of a lead only when it is unusual or significant or deserves that emphasis:

ORIGINAL: At a press conference in Ottawa today, Ontario Minister of Labour Peter Fonseca announced that last month the cost of living rose 2.83 per cent, a record high.
REVISED: The cost of living rose 2.83 per cent last month, a record high, the Ontario labour minister said today.

Originally, the lead devoted more space to the attribution than to the news. As revised, it emphasizes the news—the information the Ontario Ministry of Labour released.

Emphasize the News

Chronological order rarely works in a news story. By definition, news is what just happened. The first events in a sequence rarely are the most newsworthy. Decide which facts are most interesting and important, and then write a lead that emphasizes these facts regardless of whether they occurred first, last, or in the middle of a sequence of events:

ORIGINAL: City council began its meeting by approving the minutes from its last meeting and then approved paying omnibus budget bills and examined a list of proposed ordinances.

REVISED: City council voted 6–1 Monday night to increase the Parks Department budget by 15 per cent to hire more groundskeepers and buy new equipment.

Look for a story's action or consequences. That's what should be emphasized in a lead. The following lead, as revised, stresses the consequences of the accident:

ORIGINAL: A 15-year-old boy learning to drive his family's new car struck a gasoline pump in a service station on Hall Road late Tuesday afternoon.
REVISED: A 15-year-old boy learning to drive created a fireball Tuesday. The family car he was driving struck a gasoline pump at a Hall Road service station, blocking traffic for three hours while firefighters extinguished the blaze.

Avoid Agenda Leads

An opening paragraph that places too much emphasis on the time and place at which a story occurred is called an agenda lead. Although agenda leads are used to announce an upcoming event—public relations media releases use them to promote an organization's product or event—they should never be used in a news story. A lead should focus on the news.

ORIGINAL: James Matthews, president of International Biotech Inc., a company that manufactures recycling and composting machinery, was the keynote speaker at Monday night's opening ceremony of the Earth Preservation Society's annual conference.
REVISED: There's gold in the garbage society discards, the president of a company that manufactures recycling and composting machinery said, staking his claim on the future of recycling.

The revised lead focuses on what the speaker said, which the original lead failed to do.

Avoid Label Leads

Label leads mention a topic but fail to reveal what was said or done about that topic. Leads should report the substance of a story, not just its topic. A good lead does more than report that a group met, held a press conference, or issued a report. The lead reveals what the group did at its meeting, what was said at the press conference, or what was written in the report.

Label leads are easy to recognize and avoid because they use similar words and phrases, such as "was the subject of," "the main topic of discussion," "spoke about," "delivered a speech about," or "interviewed about." Here are two examples:

The city council Tuesday night discussed ways of regulating a new exotic dance club in the city.

Faculty and staff members and other experts Thursday proposed strategies to recruit more minority students.

The first lead should summarize the city council's discussion, clearly explaining how the council plans to regulate the club. The second lead should summarize the experts' strategies for recruiting more minority students.

Avoid Lists

Most lists, like names, are dull. If a list must be used in a lead, place an explanation before it, never after it. Readers can more quickly grasp a list's meaning if an explanation precedes it, as the following lead and its revision illustrate:

ORIGINAL: The company that made it, the store that sold it, and the friend who lent it to him are being sued by a 24-year-old man whose spine was severed when a motorcycle overturned.
REVISED: A 24-year-old man whose spine was severed when a motorcycle overturned is suing the company that made the motorcycle, the store that sold it, and the friend who lent it to him.

Avoid Stating the Obvious

Avoid stating the obvious or emphasizing routine procedures in leads. For a story about a crime, do not begin by reporting that police "were called to the scene" or ambulances "rushed" the victims to a hospital "for treatment of their injuries." This problem is particularly common on sports pages, where many leads have become clichés. For example, news stories that say most coaches and players express optimism at the beginning of a season report the obvious: The coaches and players want to win most of their games.
The following lead, before its revision, is ineffective for the same reason:

ORIGINAL: The Pearson Park school board has decided to spend the additional funds it will receive from the province.
REVISED: The Pearson Park school board voted Monday night to rescind the five per cent spending cut it approved last month after learning the district will receive more money from the province.

Avoid the Negative

When writing a lead, report what happened—not what failed to happen or what does not exist:

ORIGINAL: Canadians over the age of 65 say that crime is not their greatest fear, two sociologists reported Friday.

REVISED: Canadians over the age of 65 say their greatest fears are poor health and poverty, two sociologists reported Friday.

Remember the Readers

While writing every lead, remember the people who will read it. Leads must be factual, clear, and interesting to attract and keep readers. The following lead, until revised, fails:

ORIGINAL: Two policy resolutions will come before the Student Committee this week.
REVISED: Two proposals before the Student Committee this week would raise student parking and athletic fees by more than $100 a year.

Is the first lead interesting? Why not? It emphasizes the number of resolutions the student senate has scheduled to consider. Yet almost no one would care about the number of resolutions or, from the lead, would understand their significance: the fact that they would affect every student at the school.

Rewrite Leads

Critically examine all leads and rewrite them as often as necessary. First drafts are rarely so well written that they cannot be improved. Even experienced professionals often rewrite their leads three or more times.

Checklist for Writing Leads

1. Be specific rather than vague and abstract.
2. Avoid stating the obvious or the negative.
3. Emphasize the story's most unusual or unexpected developments.
4. Emphasize the story's most interesting and important developments.
5. Emphasize the story's magnitude and its impact on its participants and readers.
6. Use complete sentences, the proper tense, and all the necessary articles—"a," "an," and "the."
7. Be concise. If a lead exceeds three typed lines, examine it for wordiness, repetition, or unnecessary details, and rewrite it to eliminate the problems.
8. Avoid writing a label lead that reports the story's topic but not what was said or done about it.
9. Begin leads with the news—the main point of the story—not the attribution or the time and place the events occurred.
10. Use relatively simple sentences, and avoid beginning leads with a long phrase or clause.
11. Use strong, active, and descriptive verbs rather than passive ones.
12. Avoid using unfamiliar names. Any names that require lengthy identification should be reported in a later paragraph.

13. Attribute any quotation or statement of opinion appearing in the lead.
14. Localize the lead, and emphasize the latest developments, preferably what happened today or yesterday.
15. Eliminate statements of opinion, including one-word labels such as "interesting" and "alert."
16. Remember the readers. Write a lead that is clear, concise, and interesting and that emphasizes the details most likely to affect and interest readers.
17. Read the lead aloud to be certain that it is clear, concise, and easy to understand.

 ## The Writing Coach

Oh Where, Oh Where Does the Time Element Go?

If you have problems—and most of us do—deciding where the time element should go, here are some tips from the *Canadian Press Stylebook*:

Put the time element where it falls naturally in speech, usually right after the verb or at the end of the sentence.

Not: Veterans Affairs Minister Jean-Pierre Blackburn Thursday said the new policy . . .
But: Veterans Affairs Minister Jean-Pierre Blackburn said Thursday the new policy . . .

Try to put the time element at the end if putting it directly between the verb and its object is awkward:

Not: Finance Minister Jim Flaherty announced Wednesday a $2-billion job program.
But: Finance Minister Jim Flaherty announced a $2-billion job program Wednesday.

There are situations where the time element is at home either in the middle or at the end of the sentence:

Dawn Coe-Jones came out of the pack Saturday to score a five-shot victory in the Canadian women's golf championship (Saturday).

Suggested Readings and Useful Websites

Bloch, Hannah. 2016. "Leads Are Hard—Here's How to Write One." NPR Training. October 12.
    Accessed June 4, 2018, http://training.npr.org/digital/leads-are-hard-heres-how-to-write-a-good-one/
Eskenazi, Gerald. 2016. "A Look at Some of Sports Journalism Best Leads." *Columbia Journalism Review.* January 5. Accessed June 4, 2018, https://www.cjr.org/first_person/lead_or_lede_idk.php
Hart, Jack. 2006. *A Writer's Coach: An Editor's Guide to Words That Work.* New York: Pantheon.

McCarten, James, ed. 2015. *The Canadian Press Caps and Spelling*, 21st edn. Toronto: The Canadian Press.

———. 2017. *The Canadian Press Stylebook: A Guide for Writers and Editors*, 18th edn. Toronto: The Canadian Press.

Stepp, Carl Sessions. 2000. *The Magic and Craft of Media Writing*. Chicago: NTC Publishing.

Sweet, Lois, and Klaus Pohle. 2003. *Writing with Spirit: A Journalistic Guide to Effective Writing*. Kitchener, ON: Castle Quay Books Canada.

Zinsser, William. 2006. *On Writing Well*, 6th edn. New York: HarperCollins.

Purdue Online Writing Lab: https://owl.english.purdue.edu/owl/resource/735/05/

Reuters, Handbook of Journalism: http://handbook.reuters.com/?title=Reporting_and_Writing_Basics

Exercise 1   Evaluating Good and Bad Leads

In-Class Exercises

Critically evaluate the following leads. Select the best leads, and explain why they are effective. In addition, point out the flaws in the remaining leads. As you evaluate the leads, look for lessons—dos and don'ts—that you can apply to your own work.

1. A 24-year-old Toronto man was charged with multiple counts of first-degree murder and arson in the deaths of his wife and three children who died in an early morning fire in their home.
2. City Council has to return a grant it received last year to fix deteriorating road conditions on Main Street.
3. People are jumping into swimming pools and switching buttons to high on air conditioners as temperatures in the province soared to record numbers over the past three days.
4. University administrators say they are considering imposing the largest tuition and fee increases in a decade because of provincial budget cuts.
5. A petition filed by City Council member William Bellmonte to force the council into a special session to reduce local property taxes was thrown out in court Monday after it was discovered that half the names listed on the petition were dead people.
6. An 85-year-old woman stepped off the curb and into the path of a moving car. She was struck by the car and tossed 16 metres into the air. She died instantly.
7. Ray's Mini-Mart at S. Alderman St. was the location of a burglary sometime Friday night.
8. RCMP Constable Jeer Singh is concerned that crime is rising in the city.
9. This weekend will offer the best chance yet to see a brilliant performance of *My Fair Lady* at the Fairwood Community Theatre, so reserve your tickets now.
10. Loans become a popular way to cut university costs.
11. The right of students to freely express themselves may soon be cast aside if the board of governors votes to restrict access to campus public areas.

12. The tree-lined campus is home to many wild and stray animals.

13. Two men suspected of burglarizing five churches, two homes, and a pet store all in one night were captured Wednesday during another burglary attempt.

14. The union representing university secretaries and maintenance workers reached a tentative agreement Friday that will give members a 6.5 per cent raise over three years.

15. Distance education classes offer alternative to classroom.

16. Fingerprints on a candle led the RCMP to a man accused of blowing up the building he worked in to hide the shooting deaths of the man's boss and three co-workers.

17. Around 10 a.m. Wednesday a bank at the intersection of McGill and Hillside Streets was the scene of a daring daylight robbery by three armed gunmen.

18. A teenage driver lost control of his car Wednesday night killing himself and a female passenger, while a 14-year-old friend who was riding in the back seat walked away with only scratches and bruises.

Exercise 2   Writing Leads

In-Class Exercises

Section I: Condensing Lengthy Leads

Condense each of these leads to no more than two typed lines, or about 20 words.

1. Christina Shattuck, 43, and Dennis Shattuck, 45, and their three children, ages 7, 3, and 9 months, all of Third St., returned home from a shopping trip Saturday night and found their two-storey frame house on fire and called firefighters, who responded to the scene within five minutes, but were unable to save the house and its contents, which were totally destroyed.

2. The local school board held a special meeting Tuesday night so Schools Superintendent Greg Hubbard could address a group of angry parents who were demanding to know why they were never informed that a student had brought a gun to school and may have been targeting their children during an incident on school grounds last Friday.

Section II: Using Proper Sentence Structure

Rewrite the following leads, using the normal word order: subject-verb-object. Avoid starting the leads with a long clause or phrase. You may want to divide some of the leads into several sentences or paragraphs. Correct all errors.

1. In an effort to curb what city officials are calling an epidemic of obesity among young people in the city, which mirrors national data on overall obesity of the population, your local city council voted 7–0 to offer free memberships at its meeting Monday night to local youth centres and health clubs in the city for children ages 8 to 15 whose parents do not have the financial wherewithal to purchase the memberships.

2.   Despite the efforts of Karen Dees, 19, a student at your university who lives on University Avenue, and performed cardiopulmonary resuscitation for more than 20 minutes, she was not able to help Constable William McGowen, 47, of Queen St, who died while directing traffic after being struck by lightning during an electrical storm.

Section III: Emphasizing the News

Rewrite the following leads, emphasizing the news, not the attribution. Limit the attributions to a few words, and place them at the end, not the beginning, of the leads.

1.   Health Canada released a report today indicating that more than 90 per cent of all heart attack victims have one or more classic risk factors: smoking, diabetes, high cholesterol, and high blood pressure.
2.   Police reported Monday that Stephanie Sessions, 16, daughter of Jeffrey D. and Michelle A. Sessions, of Vale Drive, had just gotten her driver's licence two days before she was involved in an accident in which she rolled the Jeep Wrangler she was driving, injuring herself and two other passengers.

Section IV: Combining Multi-sentence Leads

Rewrite each of the following leads in a single sentence, correcting all errors.

1.   Gary Hubard, superintendent of schools, announced a new program for your local school district. It is called the "Tattle-Tale Program." The program involves paying students to tell on classmates who bring guns or drugs to school or violate other school rules. The program is in response to an incident last month in which a high school student was caught carrying a loaded handgun on school property.
2.   Statistics Canada released a report Monday on the number of people in Canada who have spent time in prison. Last year, about one in every 120 adult Canadians was imprisoned or had been in prison at one time. The 861,000 people who were either serving or had served time in prison represented 0.82 per cent of the adult population of 32 million people, according to the report. The figures represent people who served time in federal and provincial prisons after being sentenced for a crime, not those temporarily held in jail.

Section V: Stressing the Unusual

Write only the lead for each of the following stories, correcting errors if necessary.

1.   The city is sweltering under a heat wave. Temperatures have hit 40-plus degrees for the past week and humidity levels have hovered between 75 and 90 per cent each day. Authorities have been cautioning people, especially the very young and the elderly to stay inside in air conditioning and avoid exerting themselves outside in the sun. Interior Health Authority officials held a press conference

this morning to announce that three people had died over the past two days because of the heat. All three were elderly people who lived in the downtown area. Two of the three were a married couple. The one victim was identified as Betsy Aaron, 86, of Hillcrest St, Apartment 302. Aaron was a retired teacher who had taught elementary school for more than 30 years. The other two victims were Jeffrey Ahsonn, 84, and his wife, Teresa Ahson, 79, both of Groveland Ave. Ahsonn was a retired mechanical engineer who had worked for the city for many years. Police and health department officials were alerted to the deaths in each case by relatives who discovered the bodies. When they entered the dwellings, police told officials that they found a pair of fans and an air conditioner in each dwelling. The fans and air conditioners had been delivered by city workers to disabled elderly people to help them cope with the heat wave. But authorities found the fans and air conditioners still in their boxes. They had never been installed.

2.   Destiny Schfini is a vice president with SunBank. Schifini is divorced and the mother of two children—a 10-year-old girl and an eight-year-old boy. The children visit her once a month. Schifinis son, Ronald, was visiting this weekend. Schfini is 36 years old and lives at Timber Terrace. Ronald was injured in an accident Saturday afternoon around 2 p.m. The boy was struck by a train. Police said Schifini and her son were riding bikes along Fremont Avenue when the mother decided to take a shortcut across the railroad tracks that run along Fremont Avenue. The boy is on life support in Mercy Hospital and listed in critical condition. He was struck by a train. Witnesses said the mother saw the train coming and crossed anyway and encouraged her son to cross. The boy's bike got caught on the tracks and as he tried to free it, the train struck him. Ronald was thrown through the air and sustained broken ribs, a broken pelvis, and a bruised heart. Police charged Destiny Schifini with aggravated assault, reckless endangerment, endangering the welfare of a child, and failure to obey a train signal. Police said they charged Schfini after they learned from witnesses that Schifini did not help the boy, but taunted him as the train approached.

3.   Julius Povacz is a paramedic in your community who serves with the rescue squad in the fire department. The 34-year-old Povaz lives at East King Avenue, Apartment 4. Eight years ago he was tested for human immunodeficiency virus, or HIV, the virus that causes AIDS, and told that the test was positive. Povacz never told his superiors that he had tested positive. A routine check of his medical records last month by fire department officials found the notation that the test was positive. Povacz was relieved of his duties. Povacz said at the time he may have been infected with the virus accidentally by coming in contact with an infected patient at the scene of an emergency. When he learned that he lost his job, Povaz said it was worse than learning that he had tested positive for HIV. Being a paramedic was all he ever wanted to do. He said for eight years he has feared that

his medical condition would be discovered or that he would develop AIDS and die. The regional Health Authority computer system tracks HIV patients and periodically reviews cases. An official at the Health Authority informed Povacz and his superiors yesterday that Povacz is not and never was HIV positive. A second test that was performed eight years ago to confirm the first test indicated no presence of HIV, but the information was never placed in Povaczs medical records by his physician, Dr Nadine Caspinwall, and Caspinwall never informed Povacz. Povacz is now fighting to get his job back.

4. The RCMP in your community are investigating a two-vehicle accident. The accident occurred at 5:38 p.m. Thursday during rush hour. The accident occurred at the busy intersection of Huron Avenue and Timber Trail Road. An RCMP spokesperson said a blue Toyota Camry driven by Cheryl Nicholls, 25, of Belgard Avenue, ran into the rear of a pickup truck driven by Ronald Dawkins, 44, of Stratmore Drive. Dawkins is a bricklayer. Nichols Toyota suffered severe damage, but she sustained only bruises and a laceration on her leg. RCMP said the car was a total loss. RCMP charged Nicholls with inattentive driving and operating a cell phone while driving. The cell phone law was passed last year by the provincial legislature and banned the operation of a cell phone while driving. Nicholls was talking to her car insurance company about an error on a car insurance bill when she struck the rear of Dawkins pickup truck.

Exercise 3   Writing Basic News Leads

Pro Challenge

Write only a lead for each of the following stories. As you write your leads, consult the checklist on page 129. As you write the leads, correct any errors of spelling, diction, possessives, and style.

1. Researchers from Statistics Canada conducted a major study of Canadian marriages and announced their results at a press conference today. Of couples that marry, the researchers found that 43% break up within fifteen years, according to their study of 50,000 women. It helps if women are wealthy, religious, college-educated, and at least 20 years old when they marry. They are less likely to divorce. StatsCan found that half of Canadian women had lived with a partner by age 30. And 70% of those couples that lived together for at least five years eventually walked down the aisle. But their marriages were most likely to break up. After 10 years 40% of the couples that had lived together before marriage had broken up, compared with 31% of those couples that did not live together. That's because people who choose to live together tend to be younger and less religious and have other traits that put them at a greater risk for divorce, the researchers concluded.

2. Your citys downtown businessmen want something done immediately about the problem of panhandling and vagrants, especially on downtown city streets. Some vagrants sleep at night in parking lots or on doorsteps. Passersby they approach for money find them scary, and business leaders don't like them in front of their stores, saying they scare away good customers and give the downtown a seedy image. Businessmen say vagrants also eat, urinate, and sleep in parks, in unlocked vehicles, and elsewhere. So mayor Datolli said today she will introduce a new panhandling ordinance to the city council at its regular meeting at 8:00 pm next Tuesday night. The ordinance calls for the establishment of a program to offer homeless people one-way bus tickets to a town where they have family. A critic, Sandra Gandolf, says it is heartless, since many of the homeless have long-lasting problems including mental illness and/or drug or alcohol addiction and need real help. She favours providing programs to feed and house the homeless and to guide them toward mental health treatment, substance abuse counseling, and job assistance. However, the mayor said today the RCMP now charge vagrants with minor crimes such as indecent exposure and shoplifting, that vagrants clog the jails and the court system, and that they end up right back on the streets. Downtown businessmen have promised to raise all the money needed for bus tickets.

3. Erik Barsh is the son of Margaret and Michael Barsh of Hazel Lane. He was hit by lightning at a municipal swimming pool last summer. A friend was killed and Erik was injured. Now, Erik is suing the city for his injuries: for the cost of his mounting medical bills that total thousands of dollars each and every month. He says the citys lifeguards knew a storm was coming and were gathering their own equipment but failed to warn swimmers of the danger. He is 17 yrs old, has dropped out of high school where he was to be a senior this school year, and now takes pain medication daily and says he cannot work or even muster the strength to go to church or to a mall or to a movie theater with friends. He says he can't stand for more than ten minutes at a time. He says his body was set in a slow, painful decline of lightning-induced brain and nerve injuries that he and his lawyers contend may eventually leave him in a wheelchair and destroy his sight and memory. He adds that before the unfortunate incident he was his high schools top male tennis player, earned As in all his classes, and planned to begin playing tennis and studying engineering next year at Carleton University. Alan Farci, your City Attorney, said, "Our position on this is that we didn't have any greater knowledge than he did. The problem was obvious. It had started raining, and we've got a dozen witnesses who heard the thunder approaching and said the lifeguards had, in fact, ordered everyone to immediately get out of the pool, but this kid was horse playing with his friend. Its tragic, but they just didn't listen, and lightning hit before the lifeguards could do anything else."

4. Cynthia Lowrie of Hillside Drive, was arrested today by RCMP. She was charged by them with theft and with defrauding an adoption agency. She had said she

was pregnant. She received $12,000 from the Hope Agency to pay all her medical and other expenses while pregnant and had signed a contract to give her unborn child up for adoption. Medical tests given her today showed she isn't pregnant and never has been. She admits submitting at one point to the adoption agency test results from a friend who was pregnant. After all the money, the entire amount, was spent, she cut off contact with the agency and the prospective adoptive parents. A private detective hired by the couple tracked her down. She then said at first that her baby was born dead. Based on the results of todays tests, medical doctors concluded she was not recently pregnant, and she was arrested.

5. Construction workers for a new apartment complex were digging a trench for some underground utilities today. They hit by accident a major water main, shattering it, leaving major parts of the city with low or no water pressure. It may not be fully restored for 24 hours, authorities say. Now, water officials warn everyone living North of Hanson Avenue to boil their cooking and drinking water for the next three days. All water used for drinking and food preparation should be boiled vigorously for at least 3 minutes. The boil-water notice affects about 25,000 customers. The break occurred in a 65-centimetre pipe, a major line running from the citys main water plant. The area was flooded as a fountain of water gushed an estimated sixteen metres upward, flooding the entire construction site near the intersection of Colonial Ave. and Chapman Rd., and the intersection also had to be closed due to being under a metre or more of water. During the repair process dirt is likely to get into the lines and will have to be flushed out.

6. An RCMP constable yesterday arrested an 8 yr old boy. Today RCMP are conducting an internal investigation. The charges have been dropped but the boys mother is upset, saying const. Roger Temple who arrested her son should have simply separated the 2 children who were squabbling on a playground. The boys mother, Audrey W. VanPelt, said the girls mother was out of control and hysterical, insisting that she wanted to press charges. The boys mother said, "That dumb cop that gave my son a ticket reacted to the womans feelings instead of acting as an officer of the law and trying to calm her down." The incident happened at about 4 p.m. at Riverview Park. The boys mother had taken him there to play with several friends. A girl was trying to use a swing when the children began squabbling, and the boy slapped her on the face leaving a red mark. The girls mom immediately called police and insisted that charges be filed, so officer Tempel took the boy to a juvenile detention facility on an assault charge. An internal investigation will be done to examine the decision to take the boy to the juvenile lockup says the RCMP. The name of the boy was not released because he is a juvenile.

7. Elizabeth Anne Daigel was 102 years old and apparently in perfect health. She never used her health benefits. Investigators called at her home yesterday to find out her secret for good health and longevity. They found she had been

dead twenty years. She apparently died of natural causes and her body had been wrapped in blankets and hidden in a trunk in a locked room in the basement of her home on Central Boulevard. Her granddaughter, Annette, told police her grandmother died in her sleep and she hid the body in order to keep collecting her monthly social insurance cheque which Annette said she desperately needs as a divorced mother with four children to support. The government routinely compares the names of those receiving social insurance cheques to the rolls of eligible persons. Today police charged Annette with theft. She could not be charged with improper burial or failure to report a death because the crimes are beyond the statute of limitations. If convicted she could be sentenced to five years in prison and ordered to make full restitution for all the money she collected after her grandmothers death, a total well in excess of 200,000.00, plus interest.

8. Your city needs more money to eliminate a 6 million dollar deficit. So mayor Datolli at a press conference today proposed a fire tax. The tax would put the financial bite on all property owners, without exception, including churches, schools, and non-profits as well as residences and businesses. Under the proposal by mayor Datoli, the city would charge homeowners a $134.00 fee each year regardless of a propertys value. Apartment owners would pay $89.00 per unit. Churches, businesses, and schools would have various rates based on square footage. Datolli noted that for the past seven years there has been no tax rate increase in the city. Council member Nyad called the idea "bizarre." Nyad said, "We already pay for fire protection through our property taxes. This would tax citizens twice for the same thing. It's the dumbest thing I've ever heard of. You don't tax schools. Where would they get the money from?" But the mayor on the other hand stated, "Its painful but ultimately a good thing. We have to be fiscally responsible. We have to solve our financial problems and provide essential services. I don't want to cut back on them."

9. There's a new program to help your citys teachers. They aren't paid much. Many can't afford a down payment for a house. So local school officials today unveiled a new program that will offer mortgages with below-market interest rates to teachers and administrators in public schools. Its designed for first-time buyers and would offer eligible educators up to 10,000 dollars to help cover down payments and closing costs. They will not have to repay any of that amount provided they both continue to teach and remain in the home for a minimum of the next five consecutive years. Helping teachers buy or rent is becoming a popular incentive across the nation as teacher shortages and attrition continue to plague schools. Cash for the down payments will come from funds already used to help low to moderate income residents buy homes. Program rules have been tweaked so teachers qualify, said school supt. Gary Hubard. There are limits on applicants income and on a homes purchase price, mostly depending on exactly where a home is located.

10. Your city's Fire Chief announced today that the fire department is ending a tradition at least a hundred years old. It's the tradition of sliding down a pole to get to a fire engine. The city, he explained, is phasing poles out as it builds new one-story stations to replace older multistory firehouses. Going down the pole too fast and hitting a concrete floor can cause injuries and was therefore never a good tradition, he said. He explained that fire department records show over the past 20 years at least 12 firemen suffered injuries, especially sprained or broken ankles or legs. Still, crews improved their response time to fires by bypassing staircases from their upstairs living quarters, by cutting holes in the floors of fire-houses, and by installing and using the brass or steel poles. The last multi-storey firehouse with a pole is slated for demolition sometime early next year.

7   Alternative Leads

"And I say to you that if you bring curiosity to your work it will cease
to be merely a job and become a door through which you enter
the best that life has to give you."

—Robertson Davies, Canadian novelist, playwright,
journalist and professor, 1974

When the *Toronto Star's* Peter Gorrie set out to cover a conference of Ban Asbestos International, he didn't expect the resulting story to win a National Newspaper Award. He wasn't even sure there was a story.

"Asbestos had been around for a long time," he said, "and I thought it was pretty much a dead issue. So, I went just with that level of curiosity . . . I wanted to see what was up." He discovered a campaign by the federal and Quebec governments to "rehabilitate" the public image of asbestos (from decidedly toxic to perfectly safe). He knew he'd need to figure out how to frame the piece for readability and how to convey the complex and controversial history of asbestos without drowning readers in information overload. Because of the sheer mass of information and the wealth of technical data to explain, he "wanted to make it simple and dramatic without losing accuracy or perspective."

Gorrie is a consummate craftsman, but he says the asbestos story gave him trouble. "This one drove me nuts. . . . I started it several different ways and I wasn't happy with any of them. It was either obvious or dull or it got convoluted."

He knew the lead would be key and struggled with variations on a theme. Then came "the heaven-sent arrival of the press release written on asbestos paper. As soon as I saw it, the lead was in my head and the structure of the article finally started to emerge." He wrote:

The jolt of fright came at the bottom of an information sheet sent to reporters.
"This press release is printed on chrysotile paper."

Why should that simple statement lead to nervous tremors?

Because chrysotile is not just any old ingredient in paper. It's a form of asbestos. And asbestos is a convicted mass-killer, one of the most feared substances on Earth. (*Toronto Star*)

The lead that Gorrie wrote is an example of an alternative or soft lead. Journalists employ at least a dozen variations of soft leads, but most begin with a story's most interesting details—often an anecdote, description, quotation, or question. Stories with soft leads, which may run four or five paragraphs, usually have a nut paragraph (called the nut graph) after the lead. The nut graph states the story angle and gives the story context, serving some of the same functions as the summary news lead.

Chapter 6 describes basic summary news leads. Summary leads are more common than alternative leads—and generally easier to write. Writing an alternative lead requires thought and imagination: the ability to recognize and convey an interesting idea uniquely. It does not require an unusual story. In the following example, the lead first appears as a routine report about the first day of a smoking ban. The alternative lead captures the news better:

TYPICAL SUMMARY: A new smoking ban that ends the use of parking lots and outdoor shelters by smokers took effect Monday.

ALTERNATIVE LEAD: Terre King's Monday morning might have been rougher than just about anyone else's. Not only was it the first day in her 16 years at work that she couldn't light up, but as well her job required her to remind people at the entrance about the brand new no-smoking policy. (*Maryland Gazette*)

Good reporters can write many kinds of leads, choosing the appropriate one for each story. This versatility allows reporters to avoid the trap of following a particular formula in newswriting. Although summary leads are effective for many stories, alternative leads allow reporters to expand their writing techniques.

Even stories that at first appear minor can provide the impetus and opportunity for alternative leads. Gorrie said he "reworked and reworked" the first section of his asbestos story. "I took stuff out and put stuff in and moved it around. Unless I'm on a tight deadline, I spend a lot of time writing and rewriting. That's actually one of my favourite parts of the job."

As the former editor for the *Toronto Star's* Insight section, Gorrie worked closely with reporters on their feature stories. "One thing I tried to instill was that it's actually fun to do it: if it's not right the first time, it's not a big deal. In fact, the reshaping and working at it can be as much fun as doing the research."

Appropriateness is important when considering the use of alternative leads, whose range depends on both the nature of the publication and the stylistic restraints of the writer. When reporters finish a story, their editors expect it to be well-written: clear, concise, accurate, and interesting. If a story meets these criteria, editors are unlikely to object if its lead uses an alternative form. Nor are they likely to object to a summary lead that creatively and freshly captures the essence of a story. When Sears Canada announced it was closing in the fall of 2017, some stories used a hard news summary lead, while others used alternative leads that personalized the impact of the closure.

> **SUMMARY LEAD:** Sears Canada workers are feeling confused and angry after learning on Tuesday that the retailer plans to close its remaining 130 stores.
>
> If Sears gets court approval, it would start liquidating the stores as early as Oct. 19, putting the retailer out of business and about 12,000 employees out of work.

> **ALTERNATIVE LEAD:** Employees from Sears Canada are concerned about job losses and their pensions after the company announced plans to close its remaining 130 stores. One of those employees is Trevor Gibbons. His first day at Sears was in 1976. "(That's) 41 years, and there are people who have been there longer than me," he said. Gibbons expects to be laid off any day.
>
> "We're told we'll be receiving letters with our own personal information and also our last day of work here. So, you know they won't even come to you face to face and let you go," he said.

Criticisms

During the 1960s, large Canadian daily newspapers like the *Globe and Mail* and the *Toronto Star* began to experiment with new and emerging forms such as the soft lead. The *Globe and Mail* led the way, earning itself a reputation as a "writer's newspaper." Since then, other Canadian dailies have given their reporters more freedom to experiment with their writing. Proponents of soft leads say what matters is whether the lead works, not whether it is hard or soft. They criticize traditional summary leads as "suitcase leads"—too easy to use when packaging content. They say summary leads remove the possibility of surprise and make all stories sound alike. With digital journalism, reporters find they are using summary leads for their online content and alternative leads for traditional print and broadcast media, where space and time accommodate more in-depth narratives.

Critics call alternative leads "Jell-O Journalism." They complain soft leads are inappropriate for most news stories: too arty, literary, dangerous, and unprofessional. Critics add soft leads are too long and fail to emphasize the news. If a story begins with several paragraphs of description or quotations, for example, its most important details may be buried in the story.

The following example shows how a poorly constructed alternative lead can confuse readers who have to read more than 145 words before getting to the news—the main point—of the story:

> Eleanor Lago considers herself an intelligent, educated woman.
>
> She's read the information provided her by the Grand Rapids Township Board. She's talked to friends and neighbours. And she intends to vote Tuesday in a special election that could determine the township's future.
>
> "I just want to do what's best," says Lago.
>
> Like many residents, though, she's not sure what that is.
>
> An unusual battle is being fought in this smallest of Kent County townships, a raggedy-shaped 16 square miles set cheek to jowl against the cities of Grand Rapids, East Grand Rapids, and Kentwood.
>
> The battle is not about zoning, the more typical flash point of local politics. Nor is it about leaf burning ordinances or other grassroots laws in this suburb of nearly 11,000 people.
>
> This battle is about what the community can do to keep from being nibbled to pieces by annexation.

While the writer's intention was good, the introduction would have been more effective if it had been cut in half. The writer could have cut some description, removed the clichés, and avoided writing what the election was *not* about.

The following sections describe different types of alternative leads and offer examples of each.

Delayed Leads

A delayed lead is the most common type of alternative lead. Typically, a delayed lead begins with an interesting example or anecdote that sets a story's theme. Then a nut graph—perhaps the third or fourth paragraph—summarizes the story and provides a transition to the body. The nut graph states the angle of the story and moves it from a single example or anecdote to the general issue or problem. Like a traditional lead, it summarizes the topic. In addition, it may explain why the topic is important.

The following story by Lindsay Kines is an example of a delayed lead. Kines' story is one of the earliest stories in the case of women going missing from Vancouver's notorious Downtown Eastside, a case that ended with a conviction in what is now known as the worst case of serial killing in Canadian history.

> VANCOUVER—Every night, women stop at the WISH drop-in centre on East Hastings before going out to work the streets.
>
> And most nights, Joanna Russell gives them each a hug and, like a police staff sergeant to departing troops, urges them to be careful out there.

"And every night when they leave the centre, we're at a point, or at least I am," Russell says, ". . . where we wonder who we're not going to see tomorrow."

With each passing month, the list of the disappeared continues to grow. Vancouver city police have 20 outstanding files on missing "street-involved" women since 1995—11 from last year alone.

The delayed lead can introduce a complex or abstract problem by showing how the problem affects a single individual—someone readers may know or identify with. Or an anecdote can illustrate a problem and arouse readers' interest in the topic.

Some delayed leads surprise their readers with an unusual twist. If a story is only three or four paragraphs long, journalists may save the twist for the last line. If a story is longer, they use the twist to lure readers to the nut graph, which then provides a transition to the following paragraphs.

Multi-paragraph Leads

Other reporters think of a lead as a unit of thought. Their summary leads consist of two or three paragraphs that flow into each other as if they were one:

> CARLISLE—It didn't take Mark Toigo and Jay Shettel long to realize they had bought an aerodynamic pile of junk.
>
> They had paid $75,000 to a West Coast aircraft broker who'd advertised the early 1950s Grumman Albatross amphibious plane on the internet auction site eBay.
>
> It was a sight-unseen deal.
>
> Toigo, of Shippensburg, and Shettel, of Carlisle, didn't get a good look at the Albatross until they ventured to a Brazilian air force base outside Sao Paolo, where the venerable old bird was roosting.
>
> The Albatross was grimy, beaten-up, partially scavenged and anything but airworthy.
>
> "Right away, we named her 'Dirty Girl,'" Toigo said.
>
> Four years and about $500,000 worth of work later, Dirty Girl still needs a final face-lift, but she flies. (*Patriot-News* [Harrisburg, Pa.])

> No one would begrudge Rite Fletcher a comfy retirement.
>
> Though only 52, she has taught chemistry for 31 years in Salisbury, Md. She could have retired without regret last year after 30 years in the classroom.
>
> But when Fletcher saw what it would cost her and her self-employed husband for health insurance—nearly half of her $1,780 monthly pension—she signed on for another year. "People say, 'Oh, you could retire,' and I say, 'Only if I didn't need food, shelter or health care.'"
>
> As more teachers look ahead to retirement, many are finding themselves in Fletcher's shoes. Benefits they took for granted, such as health care, are

becoming prohibitively expensive, both for them and their school districts. (*USA Today*)

Using Quotations

Reporters usually avoid using quotations in leads. Sources generally do not provide quotations that meet three criteria for leads:

1. They summarize the entire story (not just part of it).
2. They are brief.
3. They are self-explanatory.

Some editors prohibit the use of quotation leads because they lack clarity and are often too long and complicated. As with the use of any quotation in a story, the source's statement should be so effective that the reporter cannot improve it. When used in the first line of a story, a quotation also must tell the reader the point of the story:

> "I wanted to slam the plane into a mountain so I could die with my husband," said Betty Smith, whose husband died at its controls. But then she thought of her children on the ground.

> "Our children can't read, add or find countries on a map," the award-winning teacher said Wednesday.

If a quotation is only sensational, then it fails to satisfy the criteria for a lead. It may be suitable to use elsewhere in the story, however. Reporters have other ways of writing leads that will startle readers or grab their attention. Remember that the lead provides the organization for the rest of the story. If the quotation does not lead readers into and set the stage for the rest of the story, then it will only confuse and discourage them. Even within the body of a story, a quotation should be brief. In the lead, brevity is a virtue because a complicated, long quotation will raise unnecessary questions.

Avoid quotations that begin with words needing identification or explanation, words like "he," "she," "we," "they," "it," "that," and "this." If such words open a story, readers have no way of knowing to whom or what the words refer. When the subject's identity is revealed later in a story, readers may have to reread the quotation to understand its meaning.

Leads using a quotation often can be rewritten with a brief introduction to enhance clarity:

> **ORIGINAL:** "The water was rising so fast and the bank was so muddy and slippery I just didn't think I could get away from that torrent of water." That's how a Winnipeg man described his ordeal just before rescue workers used a utility truck to pluck him out of a tree he had climbed to escape a flash flood during Monday night's thunderstorms.

REVISED: A Winnipeg man who was rescued from a tree he had climbed to escape a flash flood Monday night said, "The water was so fast and the bank was so muddy and slippery I just didn't think I could get away from that torrent of water."

Using Questions

Questions can make effective leads. Some editors, though, prohibit question leads because they believe news stories should answer questions, not ask them. Question leads often run the risk of being clichés.

To be effective, question leads must be brief, simple, specific, and provocative. The question should contain no more than a dozen words. Moreover, readers should feel absolutely compelled to answer it. Avoid questions if the readers' responses may discourage them from continuing with the story:

Are you interested in nuclear physics?

A few readers might be interested in nuclear physics, but many would think the story too complicated. This question lead also fails because readers can answer "yes" or "no," possibly ending the reader's interest in the story.

A question should concern a controversial issue that readers are familiar with and that interests and affects them. Avoid abstract or complicated questions requiring a great deal of explanation.

The following question is ineffective because it is too abstract, long, and complicated. Moreover, it fails to ask about issues that everyone is certain to care about:

If you were on vacation miles from your house and you thought the mechanics at a service station deliberately damaged your car, then demanded an exorbitant fee to repair it, would you be willing to file criminal charges against the mechanics and return to the area to testify at their trial?

The following questions also fail, but for different reasons. The first question asks about an issue unlikely to concern most readers. The second question is unanswerable and flippant, treating a serious topic as a trivial one:

Have you thought lately about going to prison?

Someone was swindled today. Who'll be swindled tomorrow?

The following questions make more effective leads. Notice that immediately after asking a question, the reporter answers it:

GAINSVILLE—How much is an inch of height worth? Nearly $900 a year in salary, a new study finds. (Associated Press)

Could this be the end of cereal aisle showdowns between parents and sweet-toothed tots? Reduced-sugar versions of popular children's breakfast cereals—everything from Fruit Loops to Frosted Flakes—certainly sound promising, but consumers might want to hold off chiming in when Tony the Tiger says, "They're Gr-r-reat!" (Associated Press)

Suspenseful Leads

Some reporters write leads to create suspense, arouse readers' curiosity, or raise a question in their minds. By hinting at some mysterious development explained in a later paragraph, this type of lead compels readers to finish a story:

It is the fire bell that signals the beginning of each firefighter's day.
  It is the same bell that summons firefighters to action.
  And it is the same bell that marks their last alarm. (*Desert Sun* [Palm Springs, Calif.])

It is difficult to run a successful business when you keep losing half of your work force year after year.
  Just ask James Griffe—or any other beekeeper. (*Patriot News* [Harrisburg, Pa.])

The first story focused on the deaths of several firefighters. The second story reported on the economic devastation an insect parasite was causing for beekeepers.

Descriptive Leads

Other leads begin with descriptive details that paint a picture for the reader before moving gradually into the action. The description should be colourful and interesting so that it arouses readers' interest. The description should also help to summarize the story.

The following examples show the effectiveness of descriptive leads. Notice the use of concrete images and active verbs in the first lead: "sirens wail," "lights strobe," and "vehicles speed."

Sirens wail in the night. Emergency lights strobe red and blue through the windows as a Lincoln Navigator and Ford Crown Victoria rush through a red light in the city's northwest, the cars ahead of them slowing, pulling to the curb. The big black vehicles speed past, straddling the solid yellow center lines. (*Washington Post*)

Parkinson's disease worked on Goldie Maurer like a slow-moving robber, taking away things one at a time.
  Baling hay. Birthing calves. Working the controls of a John Deere tractor.

Each lost activity seemed to pull Maurer further from what she was—a Midwestern-born farm girl, raised in the 1920s on a farm near tiny Lena, Ill.

The tremors and faulty sense of balance started 25 years ago, long after Maurer moved from Illinois to a farm in northern Dauphin County.

First, she surrendered garden chores, such as tending strawberry and potato plants. Then, she had to give up handling equipment, such as riding a snowmobile to far-flung parts of her farm.

It was the tremors, she said. (*Patriot News* [Harrisburg, Pa.])

The second lead sets the scene and provides background details for a feature story about a woman and her husband who suffer from Parkinson's disease. The focus of the story is the doctor who treats them and the relationship his father, who was also a physician, had with Maurer's family as their doctor many years before.

Shockers: Leads with a Twist

Reporters like shockers—startling leads that immediately capture the attention of readers. The following examples have an unusual twist that adds to their effectiveness:

APOKA—Every night, when Twanyetta Jones puts her 1-year-old son, Terry Jr., to bed, she has to stuff cotton balls in his ears.

It keeps the cockroaches from crawling in them. (*Orlando Sentinel*)

MANAGUA, Nicaragua—She had been raped. She was pregnant. And she was poor. And Rosa was 9. That gave her one more reason to want an abortion. (*Los Angeles Times*)

Ironic Leads

Closely related to shockers are leads that present a startling or ironic contrast. The use of striking details is likely to arouse readers' curiosity:

For months, second-year high school student Sara Corbett had begged her mother for permission to get her tongue pierced. On Aug. 7, 2004, Sara's mother, Robin DeBaise, relented and the two went to a nearby mall.

The next day, Sara, 16, was in severe pain. At her aunt's house, she found a couple of methadone pills—amounting to twice the recommended dosage—and took them. She passed out and was rushed to a hospital, where she died. (*USA Today*)

When union activist Oliver French goes on trial today on charges of killing two auto plant colleagues and wounding two others, he likely will be portrayed as the victim. (*Detroit News*)

Direct-Address Leads

Reporters occasionally use a form of direct address, speaking directly to their readers:

> You can now take skating to new heights—literally.
>
> Blue Mountain, the popular destination located a couple hours north of Toronto, has just announced it is opening an amazing new skating trail on top of the mountain.
>
> The trail, which debuts in January 2018, will be 1.1 km long and offer some stunning scenery viewed from way up high. It'll weave through a wooded area before opening up to offer sweeping vistas of Georgian Bay and the Niagara Escarpment. (*blogTO*)

Words Used in Unusual Ways

If you are clever and have a good imagination (or a good grasp of literature), you can use a common word or phrase in an uncommon way:

> Sufferin' succotash—Sylvester had better stay home. An impending vote could pave the way for legally shooting stray cats. (*USA Today*)

> Perhaps it was God's joke on a newly ordained priest when the Rev. Jim Farnan, former class clown and no stranger to the detention room, was asked to speak with the occasional clone of his former self at Our Lady of Fatima School. (*Pittsburgh Post-Gazette*)

This style is difficult, because what seems funny or clever to one person may seem corny or silly to another. Also, the subjects may be too serious for such a light touch:

> Oakland County Prosecutor Richard Thompson wants to be known by the criminals he keeps. (*Detroit Free Press*)

The story was about the high costs a prosecutor was creating by refusing to plea bargain with criminals.

Other Unusual Leads

The following leads are difficult to categorize. All the leads are unusual yet effective. Notice their simplicity, brevity, and clarity. Also, notice the leads' emphasis on the interesting and unusual. The first lead introduces a story describing the effects of unusually cold weather on the economy. The second lead reports the death of actor Audrey Hepburn, who played Eliza Doolittle in the movie *My Fair Lady*. The third lead introduces the man in charge of demolishing Three Rivers Stadium in Pittsburgh, Pa.

WASHINGTON—Jack Frost is nipping at our growth. (*Wall Street Journal*)

Audrey Hepburn was the fairest lady of them all. (*Detroit News*)

Circuses have ringmasters. Military boot camps have drill sergeants. The Three Rivers Stadium implosion has Greg Yesko, who's a bit of both. (*Pittsburgh Post-Gazette*)

 The Writing Coach

Some Tips for Tighter Sentences
By Don Gibb, Ryerson University

1. Re-read your story, focusing on making sentences shorter.
2. Look for clutter. Remove redundant or unnecessary words that add nothing to understanding the sentence or the story. (Examples: end result; completely destroyed; total number; serious threat.)
3. Read your story aloud to see if you stumble over words or phrases. If so, rephrase.
4. On deadline, keep those periods handy as a quick-fix for long sentences.
5. Remember: If you give readers a long sentence, treat them to a short one.
6. Reduce attribution. If you know something to be true or it's clear to readers whom you are quoting (because of an earlier reference), there is no need for attribution.
7. Use active verbs.
8. Choose short, simple words instead of long, difficult words.
9. Avoid little qualifiers (very, extremely, quite, rather). From Strunk and White: "These are the leeches that infest the pond of prose, sucking the blood of words."
10. Rewrite, rewrite, rewrite is to a journalist what location, location, location is to a real estate agent.
11. Beware of dashes and brackets. If they make sentences too long, consider a separate sentence.
12. Read *The Elements of Style* (Strunk and White), *On Writing Well* (Zinsser), or any other favourite book on writing just to remind you of the pitfalls and to encourage you to strive for better writing.

"Keep those periods handy. Give your readers a fighting chance. Keep sentences short, and limit them to one idea," by Don Gibb, Ryerson University.

Don Gibb is Professor Emeritus of the Ryerson University School of Journalism. Retired since 2009, he continues to conduct seminars and one-on-one coaching at newspapers across Canada. He is a visiting writing coach at the *Globe and Mail*. He can be reached at dgibb@ryerson.ca

Suggested Readings and Useful Websites

Benedetti, Paul. 2009. "Kick Start." In Ivor Shapiro, ed., *The Bigger Picture: Elements of Feature Writing*, pp. 206–7. Toronto: Emond Montgomery Publications.

Berton, Pierre. 2003. *The Joy of Writing: A Guide for Writers Disguised as a Literary Memoir*. Toronto: Doubleday Canada.

Bloom, Stephen G. 2002. *Inside the Writer's Mind: Writing Narrative Journalism*. Hoboken, N.J.: Wiley-Blackwell.

Cumming, Carman, and Catherine McKercher. 2010. *The Canadian Reporter: News Writing and Reporting*. Toronto: Harcourt Brace Canada.

Farr, Moira, and Ian Pearson. 2009. *Cabin Fever: The Best New Canadian Non-Fiction*. Banff Centre Literary Journalism Program. Markham, ON: Thomas Allen Publishers.

Newton, Eric. 2013. *Searchlight and Sunglasses: Field Notes from the Digital Age of Journalism*. Accessed June 4, 2018, http://www.searchlightsandsunglasses.org/

Zinsser, William. 2006. *On Writing Well: The Classic Guide to Writing Nonfiction*, 6th edn. New York: HarperCollins.

Purdue Online Writing Lab: http://owl.english.purdue.edu

Exercise 1   Alternative Leads

Evaluating Alternative Leads

Critically evaluate the following leads, each of which uses one of the alternative forms discussed in this chapter. Select the best leads and explain why they succeed. Point out the flaws in the remaining leads. As you evaluate the leads, look for lessons—dos and don'ts—that you can apply to your own work.

1. Are you ready for a big change?
2. "I saw the train coming at us, and I knew it would never get stopped."
3. No shirt! No shoes! No service!

   Unfortunately, the 350-pound black bear that wandered into the city limits and pried open a window to break into the Oakhill Restaurant couldn't read. The bear was captured by wildlife officers after it had ransacked the restaurant's kitchen and helped itself to a variety of treats.
4. Amy Clauch sat beside the rough-hewn pine fence, her fingers rubbing the worn knuckles of the knots in the rope she held in her hand.

   The sweet scent of clover hay wafted on the light breeze that blew through the barn. She sucked in a deep breath and held it. The scent lingered. She wished it always would.

   The sun hung in the early morning cobalt blue sky like a spotlight in a theatre, illuminating her, the actor on this stage. This is where she wanted to be—free from the confines of the four pale beige walls that surrounded her in clinical sterility for months.

She tugged at her jeans. Her lips pursed. "You can do this," she whispered in prayer to herself.

Clauch rocked the wheelchair to the left and reached for the stirrup hanging limply from the saddle. Pulling herself upright, she grimaced as she felt the braces tighten on her legs. The muscles in her arms clenched as she pulled herself into the saddle. The chestnut mare flinched at the load, and Clauch grabbed the worn leather saddle horn to steady herself. Her smile stretched her cheeks to their limit. She was back where she belonged.

It had been eight months since a riding accident left Clauch temporarily paralyzed from the waist down.

5. Too much work. Too many demands. Too many responsibilities. Not enough time.

Stress is killing Canadians, the Canadian Medical Association said in a report released Monday.

6. Should high school students have to take a competency test before receiving their diplomas?

7. The province's motorcycle riders won the right today to have the wind in their hair and bugs in their teeth. The provincial legislature passed a bill eliminating the province's helmet requirements for riders 18 and older.

8. How much would you pay for, say, a triple heart bypass? Or gall bladder surgery? As government officials struggle to rein in health care costs without sacrificing the quality of care, they find themselves confronted with the question of who should pay how much.

9. "If we can't solve the budget crisis today, the students of tomorrow will suffer the consequences," school superintendent Gary Hubbard said about the government's failure to pass a budget before the start of the school year.

10. Sajeel Goh pushes the blond hair away from his blue eyes, exposing the dusting of freckles on his forehead.

The 12-year-old sits in a chair that is a bit too adult for his small frame, his feet, clad in gleaming white athletic shoes, dangling several inches above the floor.

There is an air of innocence surrounding the boy that will make it hard for any jury to believe that he could have set the fire that killed his parents and baby sister. But that is what prosecutors will attempt to do as Goh's murder trial gets underway today.

Exercise 2   Alternative Leads

Writing Alternative Leads

Using techniques you studied in this chapter, write an alternative lead for each of the following stories. You may want to use complete or partial quotations, questions, descriptions, delayed leads, multi-paragraph leads, suspense, or chronological order. Or you may want to try a shocking lead, ironic lead, direct-address lead, or a word used in an unusual way. Correct any errors you find.

1. A group of ecologists and biologists at your university and other schools have come up with a unique idea. They want to transplant African wildlife to the Great Plains of North America. Julie Allen, of Lincoln Drive, is an associate professor of biology at your university. She had this to say about the idea, "I think it would be wonderful to drive across the Great Plains and see lions and elephants and giraffes roaming the prairie." The idea was developed by more than 30 scientists as a way to perpetuate species that are slowly facing extinction because of declining habitat in Africa. The scientists say there is plenty of room left in the American West for these types of animals. Relocating the animals could help them increase their numbers. The plan is being criticized by ranchers, developers, and other scientists, who say that it would be difficult to introduce animals to a place they had never lived. Ranchers, such as Jim Smithson, who lives in North Dakota and is vice-president of the Western Stockman's Association, claims such a move would devastate the regions cattle industry. "How many steers or dairy cows can a pride of lions eat in a week?" Smithson said. Supporters of the idea say the animals they want to relocate would be held in large game parks or private reserves. They would not be allowed to roam free. Other critics say the transplanting of alien creatures could have devastating effects on native creatures. The animals being brought to places they have never lived could introduce new diseases or could destroy native wildlife. In addition, taking wildlife from Africa could hurt the tourist trade on that continent.

2. It was an intense situation for police Wednesday afternoon. It was an adventure for the six-month-old daughter of Michael and Ethel Perakiss of Collins Street. Everything ended OK, police said. Megan Perakiss, the daughter of Michael and Ethel, was in the back seat of a 2006 Ford Explorer sport utility vehicle when it was carjacked by a man who had just held up the convenience store where Ethel had stopped to get gas. The robbery of the Quik Shoppe convenience store on Michigan Avenue occurred shortly after 2 p.m., according to Police Chief Shelagh Zhan. Zhan said the suspect walked into the store and waved a handgun in the face of Edwin C. Jimenez, manager of the store. He ordered Jimenez to empty the cash register into a cloth bag he threw on the counter and threatened to shoot him if he did not. The thief made off with an undetermined amount of money. Megan was unaware of what was going on. Police said Ethel pulled into the convenience store to get fuel and had just finished pumping the gas when the robber ran from the store and pushed her away from the vehicle. Reports of the carjacking sparked a massive, multi-agency search for Megan that at one point included nearly two dozen units from the city's police force. Ethel Perakiss left her keys in the ignition while she was filling the fuel tank. Police described the armed robbery and carjacking suspect as a 6 foot 1 inch tall white male in his early to mid-20s wearing a white T-shirt and long black pants. He had short, neatly cropped hair. "My baby's in the back seat," Perakiss shouted as the carjacker drove away. About 40 minutes after the ordeal began, Zhan said, police officers spotted the

missing vehicle abandoned in the parking lot of a Chinese restaurant with Megan inside. The carjacker apparently had fled, leaving the vehicle unlocked and running with the air conditioner on. Police said they were shocked but pleased that the incident ended so quickly and without harm to the child.

Exercise 3   Writing Alternative Leads

Pro Challenge

Write an alternative lead for each of the following stories, correcting any errors.

1. Patricia Richards, 23, of Tusca Trail, got married Saturday. It was a lovely ceremony. Her new husband is Grady Smith, 22, of Peach Street. Richards was arrested Saturday night and charged with disturbing the peace, criminal mischief, simple assault, and resisting arrest. Police handcuffed Richards and put her in jail. She was released Sunday and left for her honeymoon on Monday after posting a $25,000 bond. Richards said it was all a misunderstanding. The reception was held at the Downtown Club at the intersection of Washington and Virginia avenues. More than 200 guests had been invited to the reception. When the reception dinner was served, it was discovered that the wrong meal had been prepared. Instead of having prime rib au jus and salmon almondine as entries, the reception party was served baked ham and stuffed chicken breasts. Richards said she had already paid the bill and wanted a refund. She got into an argument with Walter Morton, the manager of food service at the Downtown Club. Richards picked up a stuffed chicken breast and threw it at Morton, striking him in the face. She then grabbed a serving plate of ham and threw it at a waiter. The waiter picked up some of the ham and threw it back at Richards. The ham struck Richards in the chest. Grady Smith tried to stop Richards, to calm her down, and Richards struck him on the head with a serving platter. Richards began throwing food and wine glasses at other waiters and waitresses. By the time police arrived, Richards was throwing hunks of her wedding cake at Morton and staff members of the Downtown Club. Several officers were struck by cake when they tried to take Richards into custody. Richards kicked one of the officers during the struggle. Police said alcohol was a factor in the incident.

2. There was an attempted burglary at the Wendy's Old Fashion Hamburgers restaurant, on Huron Ave. The attempted burglary occurred between 2 a.m. and 8 a.m. Tuesday. Police said the burglary was discovered by the store manager, Jenna Adams, 31, of S. Highland Ave. Police said the burglar attempted to enter the fast-food restaurant through the drive-thru window on the north side of the building. Adams is the day manager. She usually arrives at work around 8 a.m. to begin preparations for the restaurants opening at 11 a.m. Police said her normal

routine is to go directly to her office located behind the cooking and serving area of the restaurant. Adams told police she did not notice anything unusual when she first entered the restaurant. Nothing seemed to be missing. About 30 minutes after arriving at the restaurant, Adams heard a noise. She said it sounded like a whimpering animal. She began to look around the restaurant to locate the noise. What she found shocked her. A man was stuck in the drive-thru window of the restaurant. His belt and a belt loop of his pants were hooked on a metal peg used to open and close the window. The upper half of his body was inside the restaurant and the lower half was outside the restaurant, his feet dangling a foot off the ground. Adams said the man apparently had been hanging there for hours. Adams called police and officers managed to free the burglar. Police charged the suspect, Thomas C. Ahl, 19, of 6th Street, with burglary and indecent exposure. Ahl had torn the seat of his trousers while trying to free himself from his predicament. "I surrender. Now please get me out of here," Ahl said when police arrived at the restaurant.

8 The Body of a News Story

"Once we figure out how the dice are made, we may be able to figure out who is throwing them."

—Graeme Ross, correspondent in Fredericton, N.B., 1990

The portion of a news story that follows the lead is called the "body." It contains the information a reporter believes readers need to know. The information can be presented in several styles: inverted pyramid, hourglass, focus, or narrative. No technique works best with all readers, all stories, or all reporters. All require thorough reporting, and all require reporters to organize the facts and present them effectively. Whatever story style a writer chooses, the important thing for the writer is to determine how to best get the information across to the reader.

Think of writing a news story as driving a train along a track. The rails are the story's angle and give the story direction. The railroad ties—who, what, when, where, why, and how—provide a foundation. The train's engine is the lead; it must be powerful enough to pull the rest of the story. Like the whistle of the engine, a story's lead must capture the reader's attention. Each car that follows the lead represents a paragraph containing information and providing structure. The cars (paragraphs) can be arranged in whatever sequence—for example, from most important to least important—seems most effective. The train is strengthened when research, verification, multiple sources, quotations, anecdotes, and descriptions fill the cars. The amount of information needed to complete the story determines the number of cars in the train. Holding the train cars together are couplings, which represent the transitions between paragraphs. Without strong transitions, the paragraphs disconnect from one another.

This chapter discusses the writing styles and the techniques reporters often use to write effective bodies for their news stories.

The Inverted-Pyramid Style

Inverted-pyramid stories arrange the information in descending order of importance or newsworthiness. The lead states the most newsworthy, important, or striking information and establishes the story's angle. The second paragraph—and sometimes the third and fourth paragraphs—provides details that amplify the lead. Subsequent paragraphs add less important details or introduce subordinate topics. Each paragraph presents additional information: names, descriptions, quotations, conflicting viewpoints, explanations, and background data. Beginning reporters must learn this style because it helps them decide what is most important and what is least important. It also helps reporters discover "holes" in their information—details that have not been collected and need to be found.

The advantage of the inverted pyramid is it allows someone to stop reading a story after only one or two paragraphs yet still learn the newest, most newsworthy, and most important facts. The inverted pyramid also ensures that all the facts are immediately understandable. It also helps rookie reporters learn to prioritize information quickly and develop leads that can be sent out as tweets. Digital journalism relies heavily on the inverted pyramid style structure for content that is concise and gets to the point quickly.

Organizing the Information

If two cars collide and several people are injured, an inverted-pyramid story about the accident might contain the sequence of paragraphs in Figure 8.1.

Normally, reporters emphasize people: what they do and what happens to them. Consequently, in the preceding example the injuries to the people are described early in the story. Damage to the vehicles is less important and reported later. Paragraph three describes the accident itself—the recent action and main point of the story. Quotations, such as those used in paragraphs five, six, and seven, add detail and colour as well as a change of pace. Paragraphs eight, nine, and 10 add less essential information and might be deleted if space is limited.

The exact organization of a story will vary depending on the story's unique facts and most newsworthy points. The second, third and, perhaps, fourth paragraphs should provide details that develop and support the lead.

Lead	Summarizes the story
Paragraph Two	Identifies the injured
Paragraph Three	Explains how the accident occurred
Paragraph Four	Reports charges filed against driver(s)
Paragraphs Five, Six, Seven	Quotes driver(s), police officer(s), and witness(es)
Paragraph Eight	Describes unusual damage to the cars
Paragraph Nine	Describes traffic problems caused by the accident
Paragraph Ten	Presents minor details

Figure 8.1

Notice how the lead in the following story summarizes its topics and how the second and third paragraphs present the most important details. The story does not end with a summary or conclusion; instead, the final paragraphs present the least important details. The story is cohesive because the lead summarizes the main topics and because each of the subsequent paragraphs presents additional information about those topics.

> LOTHIAN, Maryland—A Glen Burnie man was in serious but stable condition yesterday, a day after he fell asleep at the wheel and collided with a box truck in South County.
>
> David A. Calligan Jr., 19, was driving a 1998 Ford Explorer east on Route 258 near Brookswood Road just before 3 p.m. when he fell asleep and crossed the center line, county police said.
>
> The Ford collided with a westbound GMC box truck, which overturned, trapping Calligan.
>
> A county fire department spokesperson said it took 15 to 20 minutes for firefighters to free Calligan, who was flown by helicopter to the Maryland's Shock Trauma Center in Baltimore.
>
> The box truck driver, 29-year-old Ulise Trujillo-Hetteta of Waldorf, and passenger Raphael Ignot, 26, of Fort Washington, were not seriously hurt. (*Maryland Gazette*)

Notice in this inverted-pyramid story example, an editor could easily remove the last couple of paragraphs if necessary (for space) and still keep the important information of the story.

Many of the facts reported in longer news stories are of approximately equal importance. These stories are more likely to resemble the diagram shown in Figure 8.2 rather than the perfect triangle shown in Figure 8.1.

Immediately after the diagram's summary lead, Section 1 presents several paragraphs that contain information of roughly equal importance. These paragraphs may present some

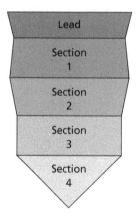

Figure 8.2

additional information about a single topic or information about several different but related subtopics. Section 2 may describe a somewhat less important aspect of the story. Section 3 presents more facts of about equal importance to one another but of less importance than the facts in Section 2. Section 4 contains the least important details, perhaps routine procedures, background information, or a reminder of related or similar incidents that occurred in the past.

Writing the Second Paragraph

The second paragraph in a news story is almost as important as the lead—and almost as difficult to write. Like the lead, the second paragraph should emphasize the news. In addition, the second paragraph should provide a smooth, logical transition from the lead to the following paragraphs.

Sometimes reporters fail to emphasize the news in a story's second paragraph. Other times they fail to provide smooth transitions. As a result, their stories seem dull or disorganized. The following sections discuss both of these problems and present some solutions.

Avoid Leapfrogging

Reporters often refer to an individual in their lead and begin their second paragraph with a name. However, many reporters fail to say clearly that the individual referred to in their lead is the person named in their second paragraph.

This problem is so common that it has a name: "leapfrogging." To avoid it, provide a one- or two-word transition from the lead to the name in the second paragraph:

> **ORIGINAL:** A man rammed his car into his wife's car, then shot her in the arm and leg before bystanders tackled him, police said.
>   Police thanked the bystanders who helped bring John McDonald, 53, of Allentown into custody Monday.
> **REVISED:** A man rammed his car into his wife's car, then shot her in the arm and leg before bystanders tackled him, police said.
>   Police thanked the bystanders who helped bring the suspect in the attack, John McDonald, 53, of Allentown, into custody Monday.

Continue with the News

After providing a smooth transition between the lead and the second paragraph, continue with information about the topic summarized in the lead. Mistakenly, some reporters shift to a different topic, a decision certain to confuse their readers:

> **ORIGINAL:** The mayor and City Council agreed Monday night to freeze wages and make city workers pay more for benefits in an effort to close a budget deficit that is now larger than officials expected.

Mayor Sabrina Datolli, who has been a lifelong resident of the city, is in her fourth term as mayor. She has seen many ups and downs over her years as mayor but hopes the city can overcome its problems.

REVISED: The mayor and City Council agreed Monday night to freeze wages and make city workers pay more for benefits in an effort to close a budget deficit that is now larger than officials expected.

Mayor Sabrina Datolli said the wage freeze and other measures are needed to prevent layoffs of city employees, cuts in programs, and more drastic fiscal surgery to balance the city's budget.

Before revision, the story seems to discuss two different topics. The lead summarizes a problem that confronts city officials everywhere: balancing budgets. The second paragraph shifts to the mayor's career and hopes. It fails even to mention the problem of balancing the budget.

Names, Names—Dull, Dull

Reporters sometimes place too much emphasis on their sources' identities. As a result, their second paragraphs fail to convey any information of interest to readers. Note how the following example can be revised to emphasize the news—what the source said, saw or did, not who he is:

ORIGINAL: A highway engineer was killed Wednesday at a TransCanada Highway construction site when a tractor-trailer owned by Shearson Trucking Inc. plowed through a concrete barrier and struck him.

A materials engineer, Riley Patterson of Independent Testing Laboratory Inc., was killed in the mishap.

Jonathan Martin, a site manager for Baldini Construction Co., saw the accident happen.

REVISED: A tractor-trailer plowed through a concrete barrier at a TransCanada Highway construction site Monday, killing a highway engineer.

The force of the crash pushed the concrete barrier into a piece of road equipment, crushing the engineer, Riley Patterson. Patterson had been using a core-drilling machine to bore a sample hole in the concrete roadbed when the accident occurred. He was pronounced dead at the scene.

Jonathan Martin, a worker at the site, said he saw the truck crash through the barrier but could not warn Patterson because of the noise of the drilling machine.

Background: Too Much, Too Soon

Avoid devoting the entire second paragraph to background information. The second paragraph in the following story is dull because it emphasizes routine, insignificant details:

ORIGINAL: Local Red Cross officials expressed alarm Wednesday that blood supplies are dangerously low prior to the beginning of the long holiday weekend.

Nancy Cross, executive director of the Broward County Chapter of the Red Cross, said the Red Cross strives to maintain an adequate blood supply for emergency situations.

"The role of the Red Cross since it was founded is to help people during times of need," she said.

The story shifts from the news—the lack of adequate blood supplies—to the organization's purpose. Yet that purpose has not changed since the Red Cross was established. Thus, the second paragraph says nothing new. Fortunately, the problem is easy to correct:

REVISED: Local Red Cross officials expressed alarm Wednesday that blood supplies are dangerously low heading into the long holiday weekend.

Restocking those supplies will require a 50 per cent increase in blood donations over the next three days, said Nancy Cross, executive director of the Broward County Chapter of the Red Cross.

"Holiday periods are often a problem because people are travelling or have other plans and don't think about the need for blood," Cross said. "But the holiday period is also a busy time for emergency rooms and trauma centres, which increases the demand for blood."

The revised second and third paragraphs describe the solution to the blood supply problem and explain the reasons for the problem—details central to the story, not minor or unnecessary ones.

Complex Stories

Some stories that contain several major subthemes may be too complex to summarize in a brief lead.

Reporters often use lists in news stories that involve several ideas, subtopics, or examples. If all the ideas or examples are important, reporters may begin a news story by summarizing one or two main points, adding a brief transition, and presenting the other ideas or examples in a simple, orderly list:

Assailants attacked three women in the college's parking lots, and Police Chief Alvin Schwab today warned other students that the attacks may continue. To protect themselves, Schwab recommended that women:

- avoid dark areas;
- park in areas that will be lighted when they return;

- tell friends where they are going and when they will return;
- keep their car doors locked and windows rolled up when driving alone;
- check their car's floor and back seat for intruders before getting into the vehicle;
- report any suspicious activities to the campus police.

Later in a story, reporters can discuss each point in greater detail. The initial summary may contain all the essential information about a topic; if so, it need not be mentioned again.

Each item in a list must be in parallel form. If one item is an incomplete sentence that begins with a verb, then the rest must have the same structure. For example, each item in the following story is an incomplete sentence that begins with a verb:

The premier said he wants to raise the province's sales tax and increase spending on education. He told reporters he would use the money to:

- raise teachers' salaries;
- test new teachers to assess their competence;
- place more emphasis on English, science, and math;
- reduce the number of students in each class;
- give schools more money to educate gifted students.

Reporters also use lists to summarize less important details placed at the end of news stories. Lists are particularly useful when dealing with chronologies, with minor details that concern several topics, or with material that would be difficult to organize.

The Hourglass Style

Roy Peter Clark, vice-president and senior scholar at the Poynter Institute, says the inverted pyramid often forced writers to tell their stories in unnatural ways. It also homogenized the news so stories about bank robberies and parliamentary debates sound the same. At the same time, writers who experimented with narrative structures for their stories often lost sight of the news. The most important and newsworthy information might be buried so far down that frustrated readers never saw it. Clark offered the hourglass style as one that combines the strengths of the inverted pyramid and the narrative format (Figure 8.3).

The hourglass story has three parts: an inverted pyramid top that summarizes the most newsworthy information, a turn or pivot paragraph, and a narrative. The inverted pyramid top, which may be only three to five paragraphs, gives readers the most newsworthy information quickly. The narrative allows the writer to develop the story in depth and detail, using the power of chronology. Clark says the key is the turn or pivot, which

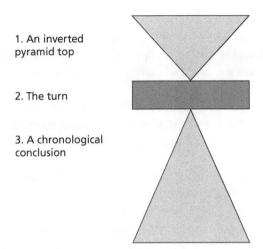

1. An inverted pyramid top

2. The turn

3. A chronological conclusion

Figure 8.3 Organization of the hourglass story

makes the transition between the two formats. Here's an excerpt from a story illustrating the hourglass style*:

By John Rieti. CBC News. Posted Aug. 8, 2018

1   Klever Freire says he and a colleague prayed and panicked as storm water started gushing into the elevator they were stranded in at their office building in north Toronto.

2   As the lift quickly filled with water, the two men found themselves in chin-deep water, despite standing on the elevator's handrails. When they only had about 30 centimetres of space between the water and the roof of the elevator, they frantically started punching a ceiling panel in an attempt to escape.

3   The effort left Freire, a 34-year-old aerospace engineer who heads the drone company DreamQii Inc., with bruised knuckles, while his coworker, Gabriel Otrin, 27, suffered cuts. But they did manage to open a crack just big enough to squeeze a cellphone out to call 911. Minutes later, two police officers arrived and set out to rescue the trapped men.

4   Const. Ryan Barnett said he could hear the men screaming for help when they arrived. His partner, Const. Josh McSweeney, estimated the men "might have had about five or 10 more minutes" before the entire elevator would have filled with water.

5   The officers said the cold, murky water was high enough that neither of them could touch the ground during the rescue's final moments.

6   Freire said when the doors opened it was a moment of tremendous relief.

---

* Source: CBC Licensing.

7   "I'm not sure how much time we had left in there," he told reporters on Wednesday at the Alliance Avenue building where his office is based.

8   Otrin credited his faith with helping him through the ordeal.

9   "I prayed about it ... and I was able to remain calm as a result because I knew God would save us."

10   The dramatic rescue happened in Toronto's northwest end around 11 p.m. on Tuesday, shortly after the city was slammed by what meteorologists are calling a "tropical downpour" that dropped upwards of 50 millimetres of rain on some areas in just one hour.

11   The two men were trying to get to the basement when the water started coming in, leaving the elevator stuck.

12   "It started gushing right away," Freire said.

13   Otrin tried to use the elevator's emergency system, but by the time they heard a response, the water was covering the speaker. Moments later, the electronics were fried.

14   The water quickly reached their waists while in the elevator, but then started slowing down. Freire said he watched the water cover different floor buttons. None of those buttons worked, nor did their cellphones.

15   "There was a period of time where, I mean, Gabriel was praying," said Freire.

16   "But I don't know, at some point, I decided that wasn't going to be the moment," he said.

17   That's when they started punching the ceiling, an effort, Freire said, that was hampered by the stinky, freezing water sloshing around inside the elevator.

18   "We were just full of adrenalin," he said.

19   Otrin told reporters he resorted to using his head to pry open the panel, as they both struggled to maintain a signal to keep a 911 operator on the line.

20   Officers Barnett and McSweeney were almost finished what had been a crazy day—police were swamped with calls for assistance due to the heavy rain—when they heard a radio call about two men trapped in an elevator with water coming in.

21   At a news conference today, Barnett said he knew they were just minutes from the building, so they crossed into the neighbouring police division to help out. As they drove, they were getting updates that the water level was climbing in the elevator.

22   When they arrrived, they realized the top hatch could only be opened about 10 centimetres, so they decided to try pry open the doors.

23   The whole time, they kept talking to the trapped men.

24   "They obviously didn't want to be in there anymore," Barnett said.

25   McSweeney tried a long crowbar first, but that wasn't working, so he swam back to get a shorter one. He said at that point, he couldn't touch the floor, but there was a railing to stand on to get the leverage required to crack open the elevator doors.

26   "There was no panic," McSweeney said.

27   Once all four men made it to safety, however, the seriousness of the situation started to sink in. Barnett said one of the men gave him a big hug. McSweeney had another realization: "we needed a shower."

28   Barnett said he found it nearly impossible to sleep last night, but said it feels great to have saved a life. "That's what we're here for," he said.

29   Freire said once he and Otrin were dry, those around them were shocked to hear what had happened as they waited for their families to pick them up (Freire's car was badly damaged in a flooded parking garage.)

30   Freire said one woman offered them a shot of vodka. They took it.

The first nine paragraphs tell this story in modified inverted pyramid fashion, reporting the newsworthy facts about the men trapped in the elevator during the sudden storm and the officers who rescued them. The tenth paragraph is the turn, and gives background information on how the men became trapped and their dramatic rescue. The eleventh paragraph picks up the rest of the story.

The hourglass style will not work for all stories. For stories that have no meaningful chronology, such as an account of a city council meeting in which topics are discussed in no particular order, the hourglass style is useless. But for stories about many newsworthy events—sports contests, criminal investigations, natural disasters, and political campaigns—the hourglass can be an effective way of organizing information.

The Focus Style

The focus style has been used for years by the *Globe and Mail*. Its news feature stories often employ this format (Figure 8.4). The focus style, like the hourglass style, tries to incorporate storytelling techniques in newswriting. But unlike the hourglass, the focus story begins with a lead that focuses on a specific individual, situation, or anecdote and uses that to illustrate a larger problem.

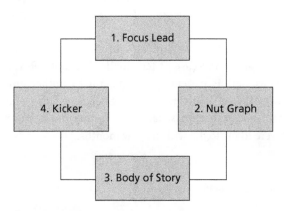

Figure 8.4 Organization of a focus story

The focus story has four parts. The first is the lead, which, unlike the lead for an inverted pyramid story, may run three, four, five paragraphs or more. Also, unlike the hard-news lead, the focus lead describes a person, place, situation, or event that may not be newsworthy by itself but exemplifies a larger problem that is newsworthy.

The second part of the focus story is a nut graph—which can actually be two or three paragraphs—stating the story angle and how the lead illustrates that point. The third part of the story is the body, which develops the angle in detail. The final part is a one-, two-, or three-paragraph close, or kicker, that brings the story to a conclusion. The kicker usually relates to the person, place or situation described in the focus lead. Here's an example of a focus story from the *Globe and Mail**:

TORONTO—The last thing Benjamin ever thought he'd have to do is help his father die.

But after a cancer diagnosis in the prime of life, his father gathered his wife, 20-year-old Benjamin and his older brother around the kitchen table in their Toronto home to discuss exactly that.

"We faced his death together, as a challenge," recalls Benjamin, who asked that his surname not be used to protect the privacy of his grieving mother. "When he knew the end was near, he asked that something good come out of it and that his body be used to help others."

Benjamin struggled to accept the fact that his father, a successful business-man and enthusiastic skier, golfer and runner in his late 50s, had only months to live. Just over a year, as it turned out, from diagnosis to his death last January. When aggressive treatment failed to stop the spread of pancreatic cancer to his internal organs, his father opted for palliative care.

"There was no sugarcoating. We knew he was going to die," says Benjamin, a poised and thoughtful business student. "We were involved in every decision. We normalized it by talking about everything, including all the therapies and procedures my father went through."

With every passing year, as life expectancies increase, there is an illusion we will all last forever. Medical stories often focus on the sexier aspect of medicine— the cure.

But palliative-care experts say the bulk of medicine is about something less cheery: how to manage the care of terminally ill people. Research shows that many doctors, as well as patients, are reluctant to initiate this conversation. A recent study by Queen's University in Kingston found that only 18 per cent of 440 patients with end-stage disease talked to doctors about their prognosis, even though most were likely to die within a few months.

---

* Reprinted with permission of Globe and Mail, Inc.

The time has come to put death back on the table for discussion, says Gary Rodin, the head of psychosocial oncology and palliative care at Princess Margaret Hospital in Toronto.

"For years there was a feeling in the medical community that you shouldn't talk about death. This created a conspiracy of silence," says Dr. Rodin, who is also a University of Toronto professor. "But someone who is seriously ill knows it, so if you don't talk about it they feel very alone."

Today, medical students are being taught empathy and communication along with anatomy and physiology.

Doctors understand that terminally ill patients don't want sympathy, or to be deprived of hope. "But hope isn't just about how long you live," says Dr. Rodin, "but about knowing you are loved, and that your life is meaningful."

Researchers have found that the final days of a person's life are often the most expensive, and medically complicated. In many cases, active treatment is maintained, or another round of chemotherapy administered, even if there is no chance it will improve the patient's quality of life.

"There are cases where futile treatment, such as chemotherapy, is given because people are reluctant to have these conversations," Dr. Rodin says, "and patients fear they will be abandoned. Far too often, people are referred to palliative care too late."

If patients plan ahead, there is a greater likelihood that their passing will be more peaceful, and that their death won't in any way diminish the life they have lived. Planning includes a discussion about how and where to die and the writing of a living will and a do-not-resuscitate order (DNR).

Though Dr. Rodin helped Benjamin and his family cope, a recent U.S. study found that 40 per cent of people with family members in hospice care were provided no information about the loved one's life expectancy, and 20 per cent were never told the illness could not be cured. The study, published last year in the *Journal of Palliative Medicine*, concluded that the most common question was: "How long does my loved one have?" and "What is happening with my loved one?" Many were afraid to ask doctors for a physical description of a dying person's last moments, which can be quite frightening.

In his recent book *The Welcome Visitor*, legendary BBC broadcaster John Humphrys writes about people who are afraid of living too long and having no control over how their lives end.

"Society's approach to death must change as we all live longer," Mr. Humphrys says. He was inspired to write the book by his father's "final sad, lingering and undignified" years. "My father's last years cast a shadow over what had been a good life," he says.

Benjamin knows he is blessed to have well-adjusted parents who helped him face death: "We saw it as our family responsibility."

Dr. Rodin also helped the family decide how to manage their father's care, including whether he should participate in a clinical trial and when to stop aggressive cancer therapies in favour of enjoying the few months he had left. Ultimately, his father decided to work a half-day at the office, and ski and travel as long as he could. The summer after his diagnosis, he even completed a two-day, 200-kilometre bike race to raise money for cancer research.

By the fall of 2008, when his illness became debilitating, he chose to be cared for at home. A palliative-care team installed a hospital bed in his bedroom, and a physician was on call 24 hours a day. His sons and wife helped him with his medication and going to the bathroom.

Two days before he died, his father checked into Princess Margaret's palliative-care unit. A colourful mural decorated the wall of his room, and soothing music from a CD player on his bedside table filled the room. A physician told the family what to expect when his time came, and explained that he wouldn't be in pain.

"He told us it could be a few days or hours. We held my father's hand and told him we loved him, because he could still feel our presence, even though he wasn't responding," Benjamin says. His breathing became laboured toward the end, which was a little scary, but the palliative-care team ensured he had the right balance of drugs.

In his grief, Benjamin felt supported by his close-knit peer group, but also found he had no script for his journey. "I didn't want my friends to pity me or for them to feel hurt. I wanted them to know that I was still the same person," he recalls.

In this, too, his father and Dr. Rodin helped him, advising him how to share news of the illness with friends.

Dr. Rodin notes that things rarely go as smoothly as they did for Benjamin's family. Sometimes, the dying person changes his wishes as he becomes sicker. There is no prescription for a "good death," as it is strongly influenced by a person's religion, culture, age, background and psychology.

But every family can benefit from open communication, early planning and attention to pain relief, Dr. Rodin says. "Birth and death are two major life events. We go to prenatal classes to prepare for birth, and we also need to prepare for death."

The first five paragraphs of the story describe the focus: a single aging father facing a diagnosis of cancer in an era of increased life expectancies. The writer introduces us to Benjamin, the 20-year-old son of the dying man, and it is through Benjamin's eyes that we come to understand how the family dealt with its loss. Those facts are interesting, but paragraphs six and seven—the nut paragraphs—explain in detail the central point of the story: research shows that despite an aging population, palliative care is a subject neglected by most patients with end-stage disease. The last four paragraphs of the story provide the kicker—tying the end of the story back to the beginning and providing a sense of conclusion to the story.

The success of the focus story depends on the selection of the lead. Some beginners start their stories with interesting anecdotes or descriptions that have little or no connection to the central point of the story. If the focus has no connection to the central point, it is likely only to confuse and frustrate readers.

The focus style also has flexibility. The body of the story can be developed in any number of ways. If the story has several subtopics, they can be arranged in descending order of importance. Or if the material lends itself to a narrative structure, the information can be arranged chronologically.

The Narrative Style

A narrative has two components: a story and a storyteller. A storyteller writes as a playwright or novelist would, depicting people interacting with other people and within their surroundings. To write in the narrative style, a reporter must find people who are crucial to the story and record their actions. This technique requires more than just interviewing sources, recording quotations, and reporting numbers. It requires keen observation.

Observation does not mean reporters are free to interject their opinions into a story. It means that reporters observe people, places, and events important to a story and describe them in vivid, factual detail. Through those details, readers get a better sense of what is occurring. But to paint a picture with words, reporters must be specific. Notice the difference between the following sentences:

Students are angry about the board of governors' decision.

Students gathered in the administration building lobby waving signs protesting the board of governors' decision.

The first sentence presents an opinion. Without using attribution, it says the students are angry at the board's decision. The reader does not know whether the writer is reporting a fact or an opinion. The second sentence, however, shows the students' negative behaviour in response to the board's decision.

The narrative approach allows reporters to be more creative. Reporters can describe the drama—even if it is not high drama—at a school board meeting, for example. What happened? What did they see? Were people shouting? Were people laughing? Did the participants exchange views? Reporters cannot answer these questions and others unless they take extensive notes.

A story written in narrative style can still lead with the news—the most important part of the story—but then quickly switch to using chronology, flashbacks, dialogue, and other storytelling techniques. Or the stories can employ a strictly chronological organization, ending with the most recent and perhaps most newsworthy information. Generally, such stories have a beginning, a middle, and an end, each of relatively equal importance. It is more difficult to cut the final paragraphs of narrative stories than of stories written in the inverted-pyramid style.

The following story about the St. Lawrence Seaway by *Globe and Mail* writer Erin Anderssen illustrates the narrative style*:

TORONTO—The official opening of the St. Lawrence Seaway was orchestrated to be a breathless moment in history—a "flossy, glossy" ceremony, to quote this newspaper. On the muggy afternoon 50 years ago yesterday, balloons soared, guns saluted, an American president stopped by and a rosy-cheeked Queen, just turned 33, leaned over the railing of her yacht and waved at the cheering crowds.

Cargo freighters had, in fact, been lumbering through the new locks to Toronto and major ports on the Great Lakes for more than a month, smoothing out kinks in advance of the *Royal Yacht Britannia*'s sleek arrival.

As it was, fog interrupted the voyage from Montreal, and the Queen turned up too late to enjoy the dinner carefully prepared for her at the hotel in Long Sault, a town created to house the many families who had lost their homes to the rising waters of the seaway and Ontario Hydro's massive new power dam.

But for most observers that day, a few lost villages was well worth giving ocean vessels access to the Great Lakes; to them, the seaway was an economic bonanza for Canada after decades of bickering with the United States. An engineering marvel finished on time and under budget, it had cost nearly $470 million (US) and taken 22,000 workers four years and nine months to build the vital 306-kilometre stretch from Montreal to Lake Ontario.

The hydroelectric dams—built at the same time and worth an additional $530 million—would fire up the bustling cities and manufacturing plants along both sides of the seaway. And this was the time of the Cold War, when the route promised secure berths for military ships and submarines, with quick passage to the ocean. The canals and locks that had widened and deepened the river path—silencing the famous Long Sault Rapids, which had 400 years earlier frustrated Jacques Cartier's travel plans—now made it possible for a transoceanic freighter the size of two football fields to deliver French perfume and Italian marble (as the first arrivals did) to inland ports such as Toronto before heading to Lake Superior to take home grain from Thunder Bay.

"It has moved the ocean a thousand miles inland," the *Globe and Mail* declared that day in 1959. "The effects of this cannot as yet be estimated, but we can be certain that they will be very great." Or, as the Queen put it: "We can say in truth that this occasion deserves a place in history."

The prediction proved to be true: The seaway, arguably the world's most impressive inland waterway, built at a cost that today would top $7 billion (US), transformed cities along its shores, opening new markets and churning out a reliable stream of electricity. But over time, the story has become less rosy, the seaway's place in history less celebrated, its future uncertain.

* Reprinted with permission of Globe and Mail, Inc.

Canada paid roughly 70 per cent of the bill, and has divided revenue with the U.S. accordingly. But that revenue has yet to cover the cost of construction, and often has barely covered operating costs.

Even worse, the seaway has wreaked so much havoc on the world's greatest supply of fresh water that some critics now propose that it be abandoned as a route for saltwater ships—the very notion that stirred its creators' imagination.

"It's pretty clear that the seaway has been an economic disappointment and an environmental disaster for the Great Lakes," says environmental writer Jeff Alexander, whose new book, *Pandora's Locks*, chronicles the project's fallout. "I think it would be disingenuous to hold a celebration without recognizing some of the unintended side effects."

Mussel Power

The seaway has always been the tale of two waters—salt and fresh, divided by nature but united by humanity. Even before construction began on the Montreal section, however, it was clear that mixing the ocean with the lakes came with risks. The building of the Welland Canal years ago allowed ships to circumvent Niagara Falls, but it also provided passage to the sea lamprey, a vicious "aquatic assassin," as Mr. Alexander describes it, that broke into the world's largest fresh-water fish market with no natural predator to stand against it.

So perhaps it shouldn't have come as such a surprise when, in 1988, two biology students found an unusual shellfish on the bottom of Lake St. Clair, which lies between Lake Erie and Lake Huron. It turned out to be a foreign intruder that had hitched a ride on an ocean freighter and, of course, in the two decades since then, the zebra mussel has become legendary for the many millions of dollars in damage it has caused to its new habitat.

But it didn't come alone: Since the seaway opened, scientists estimate that as many as 57 foreign species (about one-third of the 185 now on record and almost all of those that have been found in the past 50 years) have arrived in the ballast water shed by saltwater ships. They have displaced native plants and animals, decimated fish stocks, even disrupted power plants.

The seaway is hardly the only cause of the Great Lakes' decline—aquaculture and recreational boating have done much damage, along with pollution from industry and agriculture—but many scientists believe that it is responsible for the most harm, and certainly let in the most destructive intruders.

Even worse, environmentalists point out, government agencies that regulate the seaway and shipping have been painfully slow to react. Only in the past two years have seaway authorities on both sides of the border made it mandatory that all ships—including those with just small amounts of ballast from ports overseas—flush their tanks in the ocean before entering the seaway. Even that isn't necessarily foolproof. Flushing may kill 95 per cent of what is in the tanks, but a troublemaker could survive.

So, 20 years after the zebra mussel arrived, "the threat still remains," says Jennifer Nalbone, an analyst with Great Lakes United, a cross-border environmental coalition. "It's a very sober anniversary."

Assessing the economic value of the seaway—and whether the environmental toll and human costs have been justified—is complicated. There is no doubt that having lots of cheap hydro as well as a watery highway has been important to manufacturing cities on the Great Lakes.

Statistics released this week show that more than 2.5 billion tonnes of cargo worth more than $375 billion have passed through the seaway, most of it between Canadian and U.S. ports.

Even so, annual tallies for "salties" have never reached the predictions made on opening day, and the early glow of having ready access to European markets—the romantic focus of those "glossy, flossy" celebrations—soon faded. Demand for grain moved to the west, other markets shifted as well, and long-distance container vessels grew too big to fit in the seaway's locks.

"It was a noble idea—it's been very valuable for domestic bulk cargo," says John Taylor, a transport specialist at Grand Valley State University in Grand Rapids, Mich. "But the seaway has been 'locked' in time. The world has evolved and the seaway has not been able to evolve with it."

Today, as Mr. Alexander points out in *Pandora's Locks*, only about 5 per cent of the world's container fleet can even squeeze into the Great Lakes. By 2007, the volume of cargo carried by ocean-going vessels had dropped to nine million tonnes from a high of 23 million in 1978, and even that figure was well off early expectations.

Prof. Taylor says the salties could be replaced by as few as two 100-car freight trains running each day of the year. A study he co-wrote in 2005 calculated that the cost of closing the locks to transoceanic ships at roughly $55 million, a figure that is widely criticized by the shipping industry but is just a fraction of the $200-million environmental toll he estimates the seaway has taken on the Great Lakes.

But the seaway also has ardent defenders, who make a convincing case that it will play an increasingly important role as transportation costs rise and, ironically, the environment becomes an even greater concern. Because the loads can be so huge, transporting goods by ship uses, on average, far less fuel and doesn't clog up already congested highways.

"One ship can take 800 trucks off the road," says Bruce Bowie, president of the Canadian Shipowners Association.

In addition, the shipping industry is lobbying to have removed the 25-percent duty the government charges on vessels built outside Canada, which, he says, has prevented companies from making their fleets even more environmentally efficient. Steps have been taken to modernize the locks, and an incentive program lured nearly two billion tonnes of new cargo to the route last year, according to the seaway corporation. But drawing even more business by staying open through the winter would be costly, and major renovations required down the road will cost more than the seaway currently earns.

As for banishing the salties, Mr. Bowie calls it a "sledgehammer solution" that would only limit future economic growth. The seaway needs to be ready to capture some emerging market abroad, he says, just as lakers have suddenly picked up solid business in the past few years by carrying low-sulphur coal to power plants on the East Coast.

But future prospects aside, it has been a rocky 50 years for Highway H-2O, as the seaway has been branded by the development corporation that now oversees it, and this anniversary is not the exuberant celebration of that June day half a century past. To a large extent, the seaway's prospects depend on the global path of supply and demand. But the next half-century will decide whether it can sell itself as a clean, energy-efficient water route and earn the place in history that the Queen once said it deserved.

Notice how the writer used quotations, dialogue, and description to give the reader a sense of working on the seaway and of each source's distinctive personality. The details are ones that easily bring images to the reader's mind. Notice the length of the story. Stories using the narrative style tend to be longer, and yet the rich detail and concrete imagery make the stories easier to read than many shorter straight news stories.

Narrative style can be a refreshing change from the inverted pyramid, but it is not appropriate for all stories. Stories about breaking news events, speeches, or most government meetings, for instance, often make more sense to readers when told in traditional inverted-pyramid fashion. Narrative touches, such as dialogue and colourful descriptions, can make any story more readable, however. Regardless of the occasion, the success of a narrative story depends on the depth of the reporting. A writer who has not attentively gathered details and quotations will have difficulty constructing a narrative story.

Using Transitions

Transitions help stories move from one fact to the next in a smooth, logical order. Again, think of the story as a train. The engine is the lead, and each car that follows is a paragraph. The couplings that hold the cars together are transitions. Reporters introduce ideas by relating them to ideas reported earlier in a story. Often, the natural progression of thought, or sequence of facts and action, is adequate. Or reporters may repeat a key name or pronoun:

School board member Diana Maceda voted against the proposed cuts in the school lunch program. Maceda said cuts would hurt low-income families that rely on the program.

Police Capt. Virginia Detwieler said the accident occurred when a car cut in front of the tractor-trailer, causing the rig to jackknife when the driver slammed on his brakes.

She added that police investigators have a description of the car and a partial licence number and were searching for the vehicle to question the driver.

The first example repeats the name of the school board member. In the second example, the pronoun "she" refers to the captain mentioned in the preceding paragraph. Reporters can also repeat other key words, ideas, or phrases:

Richard Nolles, editor of the *Weekly Outlook*, said the newspaper tries to report the truth even when its readers do not want to hear it.

"A newspaper that reports only what its readers want to hear is dodging its moral obligations," Nolles said.

In a speech Wednesday, Nolles added that many readers want to avoid unpleasant news and threaten to cancel their subscriptions when he reports it.

"But if a problem exists, they need to know about it so they can correct it," he said. "Ignorant citizens can't make wise decisions."

Transitional Words

Sometimes a single word can lead readers from one idea to the next. Many transitional words refer to time: words such as "earlier" and "later," "before" and "after," "prompt" and "tardy." Below are other common transitional words that refer to time:

delayed	occasionally
eventually	often
finally	once
formerly	seldom
frequently	sometimes
meanwhile	soon
next	then
now	

Using the hour, day of the week, month, season, year, decade, or century ("an hour later," "the previous Saturday," and so on) can also provide a transition.

Other types and examples of linkage words include the following:

Addition	**Causation**
again	accordingly
also	because
another	consequently
besides	hence
beyond	since
extra	so

furthermore	then
moreover	therefore
new	thus
other	
together	
too	

Comparison	**Contrast**
agreeing	although
conflicting	but
contrary	conversely
different	despite
identical	exactly
inconsistent	however
like	if
objecting	nevertheless
opposite	simply
related	solely
separately	still
similarly	until
while	
without	
yet	

Phrases can also move a story from one idea to another:

along with	in an earlier
as a result of	in another
aside from	in contrast
at last	in other action
at the same time	in other business
due to	on the contrary
for example	on the other hand
for instance	until then
for that reason	years earlier
in addition	with the exception of

Transitional Sentences

Transitional sentences link paragraphs that contain diverse ideas, but they should do more than report that another idea was "introduced" or "discussed." They should present some interesting details about the new topic so that readers want to finish the story. Mistakenly, beginners often use vague generalities. A good transitional sentence often serves the same purposes as a lead, summarizing the topic it introduces and revealing what was said or done about it. The following paragraphs then discuss the topic in more detail:

> **ORIGINAL:** She also commented on the legislators' overriding of the premier's veto.
> **REVISED:** She said the legislators' overriding of the premier's veto would anger supporters of the death penalty.

> **ORIGINAL:** He also discussed the budget proposal.
> **REVISED:** He said the budget had been cut as much as possible.

Questions as Transitions

Transitional sentences occasionally take the form of questions. The questions should be short and, as in the following examples, should be immediately followed by their answers—the new details or topics that reporters want to introduce:

> How does he manage to play the piano so well at such a young age?
> "Practice," he said, the freckles blossoming with the smile that spread across his seven-year-old face. "I practise four hours a day—every day. I practise even when I don't feel like it."

Explain the Unfamiliar

Reporters should avoid words that are not used in everyday conversation. When an unfamiliar word is necessary, journalists must immediately define it. Stories that fail to define unfamiliar terms may annoy as well as puzzle readers and listeners. A story about a 19-year-old Olympic skater who collapsed and died before a practice session reported she died of clinical terminal cardiac arrhythmia. The journalist placed the term in quotation marks but failed to define it. Yet many people would be interested in the death of an Olympic skater and would wonder why an apparently healthy young athlete had died of what should have been explained in layman's terms as a condition when the heart muscle fails to contract and stops blood flow to other organs in the body. Because the story failed to define the term, it failed to satisfy their curiosity about the cause of the young woman's death.

Here are three techniques journalists can use to define or explain unfamiliar terms:

1. Place a brief explanation in parentheses:

    The law would ban accessory structures (sheds, pool houses, and unattached garages) in new subdivisions.

2. Place the explanation immediately after the unfamiliar name or term, setting it off with a colon, comma, or dash:

Amy and Ralph Hargis of Carlton Drive filed for bankruptcy under Chapter 13, which allows them to repay their creditors in monthly installments over a three-year period.

About 800 foreign students at the university are on F-1 student visas—which means that they are allowed to stay in the United States only until they complete their degrees.

3. Place the explanation in the next sentence:

The major banks raised their prime rate to 12.5 per cent. The prime rate is the interest rate banks charge their best customers.

Instead of using an unfamiliar term and then defining it, journalists may eliminate the term and use the definition or explanation instead:

ORIGINAL: She said the school will have K-6 facilities.
REVISED: She said the school will accept children from kindergarten through the sixth grade.

Journalists using these techniques can make even the most complicated stories understandable. For example, large numbers—millions, billions, and trillions—also need explaining. For example, few readers who saw a story reporting that failing savings and loan companies cost the US $500 billion or that the accounting frauds at Enron or WorldCom cost stockholders and employees tens of billions of dollars would really comprehend these numbers. Reporters can help audiences understand large numbers by converting them into something related to everyday life.

The *Washington Post* reported that an investment bank offered to pay US $20.6 billion to take over RJR Nabisco Inc. (The company has split since then into R.J. Reynolds Tobacco Co. and Nabisco.) At the time, the conglomerate made Oreos, LifeSavers, and Camel cigarettes. RJR Nabisco rejected the offer, saying it wasn't big enough. If $20.6 billion (US) cannot buy a cookie company, what is it good for? A writer at the *Post* calculated it could:

- provide shoes for every American for a year;
- house two million criminals in prisons for a year;
- sponsor 80 million destitute children around the world for one year;
- match the combined fortunes of the six richest people in the United States;
- cover the cost of every movie ticket bought in the United States in the past four years; or
- buy every advertisement in every magazine published in the United States for the past four years or every radio ad for the past three years.

When a sentence must explain several items in a list, the explanation should precede the list, not follow it. If the explanation follows the list, people might not immediately understand the relationship between the items or the significance of the list:

ORIGINAL: To provide children with better nutrition, better health care, and better educational opportunities were the reasons the politician voted for the bill.
REVISED: The politician said he voted for the bill to provide children with better nutrition, better health care, and better educational opportunities.

The Importance of Examples

Examples make stories more interesting, personal, and understandable. A story about a teenager who became an alcoholic and flunked out of school might include examples of the problems she experienced:

She said school became unimportant, adding: "I can remember staying up all night before my public health final. When I took the test I was smashed. And if that wasn't bad enough, then I ran the entire 10 blocks back to my apartment so I could drink some more. Of course, I flunked public health."

Examples are especially important in stories about abstract issues. Sometimes numbers help put those issues into perspective. A story about the lives of people who drop out of school might include the percentage of students who drop out of school nationally, their reasons for dropping out, and what they do afterward. In addition to reporting the general trends, a good writer would illustrate the story by describing the lives of two or three dropouts—specific examples of the trend.

Reporters can clarify unfamiliar concepts by comparing them to things that are familiar. Many readers struggle to understand business and finance, and stories of financial fraud can be extraordinarily complex. Paul Krugman, a columnist for the *New York Times*, used the following analogy to help readers understand how mutual fund managers and major investors were cheating ordinary investors:

You're selling your house, and your real estate agent claims that he's representing your interests. But he sells the property at less than fair value to a friend, who resells it at a substantial profit, on which the agent receives a kickback. You complain to the county attorney. But he gets big campaign contributions from the agent, so he pays no attention.

That, in essence, is the story of the growing mutual fund scandal.

The Use of Description

Descriptions, like quotations, make stories more interesting and help people visualize scenes. But many journalists are reluctant to use descriptive phrases; they summarize whatever they hear but are less likely to describe what they see, feel, taste, and smell. For example, a student who attended a gallery exhibit of editorial cartoons handed her instructor a story that said:

> The city's top cartoonists for the two main daily newspapers showed their work and talked about how political commentary can be just as important with illustrations as it can be with words.

The student failed to describe the work shown at the gallery or relate those works to what the cartoonists said during the opening of the exhibit.

When asked to write descriptions, most students rely too heavily on adverbs and adjectives. Nouns and verbs are more effective. Nouns and verbs are less redundant and less opinionated than adverbs and adjectives.

Reporters who want to describe an object must learn to use concrete, factual details as opposed to trite phrases and generalities. Readers should be able to visualize the scene in their minds:

> **VAGUE:** There were about 50 men and women working in the area.
> **BETTER:** About 50 men and women worked in the area, and most wore hard hats, some yellow, some white, and others red. Four of the workers had tied nail pouches around their waists. Others smoked cigarettes and looked weary in their dirty white T-shirts, jeans, and sunglasses.

Vagueness also becomes a problem when reporters attempt to describe other people. Some reporters mistake generalities or their personal impressions for factual detail:

> She spoke with authority.
> She seemed to enjoy talking about her work.

Neither of those sentences is an actual description. The first sentence concludes the woman spoke "with authority" but fails to explain why the writer reached that conclusion. The second sentence reports she "seemed to enjoy" talking about her work but does not specifically describe either the speaker or what she said.

Generalities are often inconsistent among observers. One student reported a woman "seemed relaxed and very sure of herself." Everything about her "conveyed calmness." Yet another student concluded, "She seemed nervous." The students could have avoided the problem by reporting specific details as opposed to their impressions and opinions.

Reporters train themselves to observe and describe details. If they are important to the story, include descriptions of people's voices, mannerisms, facial expressions, posture, gestures, and surroundings. Include details about or descriptions of their height, weight, age, clothing, hair, glasses, jewellery, and family if they help to bring an image alive. Each factor can be described in detail. For example, a journalist might describe a man's hands by mentioning their size, calluses, nails, smoothness or wrinkles or veins, and jewellery. Avoid generalities and conclusions:

VAGUE: He is a large man.
BETTER: He is 6 feet tall and weighs 210 pounds.

VAGUE: Butler looked as though he had dressed in a hurry.
BETTER: Butler's shirt was buttoned halfway, his socks were mismatched, his shoelaces were untied, and his hair was not brushed.

Factual descriptions help the audience see the situation or person through the eyes of the reporter.

The Use of Humour

Editors constantly look for humorous stories. But humorous stories are particularly difficult to write. Journalists should not try to inject humour into stories that are not obviously humorous. If a story is funny, the humour should be apparent from the facts. Journalists should not have to point out the humour by labelling it "funny" or "comical." Author and economist John Kenneth Galbraith once explained: "Humour is an intensely personal, largely internal thing. What pleases some, including the source, does not please others."

A story about the peculiar laws in some cities never called the laws "peculiar" or "funny." Instead, it simply listed them so people could judge the humour of the laws for themselves. The laws made it illegal to do the following:

- take a cow on a school bus
- take a bath without a bathing suit
- break more than three dishes in a single day
- ride a horse not equipped with a horn and tail light

Humour, when it is appropriate, makes news stories more interesting, but remember that understatement is more effective than exaggeration. Simply report the facts that seem humorous, and hope others will laugh.

The Need to Be Fair

Regardless of how a story is organized, it must be balanced, fair, and accurate. Reporters who write about a controversy should present every significant viewpoint fully and fairly. They must exercise particular care when their stories might harm another person's reputation. A reckless or irresponsible charge may destroy an innocent person's reputation, marriage, or career.

If a story contains information critical of an individual, that person must have an opportunity to respond—the right of reply. It is not enough to get the person's response after a story has been published and report it in a later story, because not everyone who read the original criticism will see the second story. If the person cannot be reached, editors and reporters should consider holding the story. If the story cannot be held, it must describe the efforts made to reach the person and explain that those efforts will be renewed the next day.

When the subject of a negative story is unavailable or refuses to respond, that fact should be mentioned. A brief sentence might explain:

Repeated attempts to reach a company employee were unsuccessful.
OR: A vice-president at the company declined to comment about the charges.
OR: Company officials did not return phone calls made by reporters.

The Final Step: Edit Your Story

After finishing a story, edit it ruthlessly. Novelist Kurt Vonnegut said, "If a sentence, no matter how excellent, does not illuminate your subject in some new and useful way, scratch it out." Vonnegut also urged writers to have mercy on their readers, explaining: "Our audience requires us to be sympathetic and patient teachers, ever willing to simplify and clarify—whereas we would rather soar high above the crowd singing like nightingales."

Good reporters will reread and edit their stories. Lazy reporters immediately submit their stories to an editor, thinking their stories need no editing or expecting the editor to correct any mistakes. That attitude involves some risks. If an editor misses the errors, the reporter will be the one who suffers the embarrassment and bears the responsibility. Or an editor may decide the stories require extensive changes, perhaps even total rewriting. When that happens, reporters often complain about the changes. Reporters who correct their own errors will develop reputations as good writers and earn better assignments, raises, and promotions.

✓ Checklist for Writing News Stories

Use the following checklist to evaluate all your stories:

1. Place the most important details in your lead.
2. Throughout the story, emphasize the details most likely to interest and affect your readers.

3. Include details from your observations to create a picture your readers can visualize.

4. In the story's second paragraph, continue to discuss the topic initiated in your lead.

5. Do not leapfrog. If your lead mentions an individual and your second paragraph begins with a name, provide a transition that makes it clear you mean the same person.

6. Make your sentences clear, concise, and to the point. (Avoid passive verbs. Also, use the normal word order of subject-verb-object.)

7. Vary your sentence structure.

8. Avoid overloading your sentences.

9. If your story discusses several major subtopics, mention all the major subtopics in your story's opening paragraphs so your readers know what to expect.

10. If you use a list, make sure each item is in parallel form.

11. Provide transitions to lead your readers from one sentence or paragraph to another smoothly and logically.

12. Make your transitional sentences specific; say something intriguing to sustain readers' interest in the topic.

13. If you use a question as a transition, make it clear, short, and simple.

14. Avoid generalities that have to be explained in a later sentence or paragraph. Be specific.

15. Resist the temptation to end your story with a summary, conclusion, or opinion.

16. After finishing your story, critically edit and rewrite it.

 ## The Writing Coach

Lose 10 Bad Habits in One Week

By Gregg McLachlan, associate managing editor, *Simcoe Reformer*

It's totally free and the results are guaranteed. No gimmicks, no monthly fees.

One of the greatest aids to improving your copy is to print out your work and read it as if you were a reader. Reading your work aloud is another routine step that helps produce better copy. So, how often do you include these steps in your daily routine? Sometimes not enough. Make it a habit today.

Breaking habits requires an investment in examining your copy to make the necessary changes.

We can't break habits unless we know our habits. Here's a sampling of steps that can help you improve your work. How many habits can you eliminate in one week—and sustain for the long run?

Give it a shot this week:

1. Avoid patterns
   Reread your work from the past week. Look for habits. Maybe it's that you started multiple leads all in the same way (i.e., with the name of someone) or that you filed multiple run-on sentences. Or that you started multiple paragraphs with a surname. Or that you overused certain words such as "the," "that," "and," etc. It's easy to fall into habits. Don't roboticize your work. Evolve it.
2. Eliminate awkward words
   Nobody's asking reporters to dumb down their writing. It's simply a case of being reader-friendly. Write for your readers, not above them. Look for words with fewer syllables to replace long-winded words. Look for places where one word will take the place of two words. Condense. Cut. Tighten.
3. Improve your quotes
   Evaluate your quotes. Are they quotes that add colour to your story, or are you just quoting information that can be paraphrased? Filing quotes such as "If people want more information, they'll have to contact Bob Smith in accounting next week" are a disservice to quote marks. Or, if you repeatedly file quotes that consist of three words (i.e., bit quotes) that are not colourful and add nothing to your story, it's time to work on gathering full quotes that say something worthwhile.
4. The "background" paragraph
   If you constantly forget to write a background paragraph, you need to make a note to yourself whenever you write. When you start to write your story, type BACKGROUND PARAGRAPH HERE in bold and fill in the space before you file your copy. Don't leave it to editors to fill your holes. It's your byline. It's your work.
5. The basic stuff
   Have you identified people in your story? Get the basics: who they are, title, age, occupation, home town, etc.
6. Don't fake it
   Read other papers to get up-to-date on current events. If you're localizing a national story, get the background and understand it so you're reporting accurately and with proper knowledge of connected events so you'll properly inform your readers.
7. Their/there, to/too, it's/its
   The BIG three in many reporters' copy requires special attention. Whenever you use one of these words, develop the habit of checking and rechecking. Have you got the correct word? Readers love catching these silly errors . . . and they let us know about them.
8. Don't rely just on officials
   It's easy to get into a routine of talking just to officials. Don't forget about John Public. That's who's affected. People-cize your stories.

continued

9. Junk the jargon

Beware jargon. Is there really a rule of thumb? Does fur really fly? Does a puck really bulge the twine? Jargon is like writing in code to readers. Just tell them in plain English what you mean.

10. The "what does this mean" paragraph

Add perspective to your work. It's a simple explanation of the significance of a story. It can be based on past events, opinions, or it can bring readers up to speed so they understand new developments or where a story is headed. Type WHAT DOES THIS MEAN as a reminder in your copy . . . and then fill it. Your readers will be thankful. Report what it means early in your copy.

Source: Reprinted with permission of Gregg McLachlan

Suggested Readings and Useful Websites

Hayes, David. 2009. "Telling Pictures: Reporting and Reconstructing Scenes." In Ivor Shapiro, ed., *The Bigger Picture: Elements of Feature Writing*, pp. 91–114. Toronto: Emond Montgomery Publications.

Lloyd, Robert, and Glenn Guzzo. 2008. *Writing and Reporting the News as a Story*. Boston: Allyn and Bacon.

McCarten, James, ed. 2017. *The Canadian Press Stylebook: A Guide for Writers and Editors*, 18th edn. Toronto: The Canadian Press.

Reuters. 2008. "Reporting and Writing Basics." Handbook of Journalism. Accessed June 4, 2018, http://handbook.reuters.com/?title=Reporting_and_Writing_Basics

Rowe, Dan. 2016. *Feature Writing for Journalism and Media Students*. Don Mills, ON: Oxford University Press.

Scalon, Chris. 2003. "The Hourglass: Serving the News, Serving the Reader." Poynter. June 18. Accessed June 4, 2018, https://www.poynter.org/news/hourglass-serving-news-serving-reader

Stepp, Carl Sessions. 2000. *The Magic and Craft of Media Writing*. Chicago: NTC Publishing.

Exercise 1   The Body of a News Story

Section I: Second Paragraphs

Second paragraphs are almost as important as leads. Like leads, second paragraphs must help arouse readers' interest in a topic. Critically evaluate the second paragraphs in the following stories. Judge which of the second paragraphs are most successful in (1) providing a smooth transition from the lead; (2) continuing to discuss the topic summarized in the lead; and (3) emphasizing the news—details that are new, important, and interesting. Give each second paragraph a grade from A to F.

1. A Pinkerton courier was robbed at gunpoint and fatally wounded on Tuesday while leaving Merchants Bank with the day's daily transaction records.

    Edwin James, 59, of Bell Drive, was following standard bank procedures and carrying no money. (Grade:_____)

2. A 41-year-old teacher who fell and broke an ankle while stopping for a cup of coffee on her way to work sued a convenience store Monday.

    The teacher, Tina Alvarez, has worked at Macdonald Elementary School for 21 years. (Grade: _____)

3. Two young men are presumed dead after falling off a 9-metre rock formation into the Pacific Ocean at a California park Saturday.

    The men remain unidentified, and their bodies have not been recovered. (Grade: _____)

4. Police responding to a 911 call about a shooting at 10 p.m. Sunday discovered Ralph Beasley on Bennett Road with a gunshot wound to his head.

    County sheriff's deputies arrived at about the same time in response to a radio request for assistance. An ambulance was already at the scene, as were Fire Department paramedics. (Grade: _____)

5. A 32-year-old woman who said she smoked marijuana to ease the pain of a rare intestinal disease was charged Tuesday morning with possessing illegal drugs.

    Ruth Howland was stopped at the Toronto Pearson International Airport after a K-9 dog singled out her suitcase. She and her husband, Terry, were returning from Mexico. (Grade: _____)

6. Three gunmen who entered a restaurant on Wilson Avenue at 10:30 p.m. Tuesday held four employees and 12 customers at gunpoint while taking more than $3,000 from several cash registers.

    Peggy Deacosti, the restaurant's hostess, was on duty when the robbery occurred. (Grade: _____)

7. Eileen Guion, 38, a food and beverage co-ordinator at Walt Disney World for 18 years, died at her home Tuesday of unknown causes.

    Although she was offered many other jobs at restaurants, she never accepted them. She once said, "I've loved working at Disney because I get to work with people from all over the world, and I think that is very neat." (Grade: _____)

8. Police are searching for a man who attacked a woman outside the Bayside Bar & Grill Thursday night.

    Terry Smythe, a bartender at the restaurant, said he heard a woman screaming outside the entrance at 9 p.m. Smythe darted to the foyer, where he saw the woman trapped in the entryway. Smythe said it was "kind of like a tug of war," with the assailant trying to pull the woman outside while waitresses tried to pull her inside. (Grade: _____)

Section II: Transitions

Critically evaluate the following transitions. Which would be most likely to entice you to continue reading the stories? Which provide a smooth, specific, informative, and interesting introduction to the next idea? Give each transition a grade from A to F.

1. _____ Other students said they would tell their teachers about cheaters because cheating is not fair to those who take the time to study.
2. _____ But what should happen when a husband and wife disagree about having a baby?
3. _____ A concerned citizen then addressed the commission about the fence.
4. _____ Next, the task force presented its plan for preservation and renovation of the downtown.
5. _____ In a flat, emotionless voice, Howard responded that he and Jackson stole a red Mustang convertible on the night of June 3, picked up the two 14-year-old girls, and took them to the motel.
6. _____ Gary Hubbard, superintendent of schools, then addressed his concerns about security in the city's schools.
7. _____ Police Chief Barry Kopperud said his department is trying to combat juvenile crime by changing the way officers interact with children.
8. _____ He then discussed prejudice as a problem that plagues society.
9. _____ She also spoke about the different religious celebrations and rituals.
10. _____ Parents who love, care for, and respect their children don't raise delinquents, she said.

Exercise 2   Writing Complete News Stories

Write complete news stories based on the following information. Be thorough; use most of the information provided. Because much of the material is wordy, awkward, and poorly organized, you will have to rewrite it extensively. Correct all errors in your rewrite.

1. A family that owns a farm about 2 kilometres outside your town has decided to sell it. It has been in they're family for four generations. They often bring fresh eggs, produce, and other items to the farmers market in town to sell, which is held once a month on the first Saturday. The father of the family told you they are selling because their children are nearly grown and don't want to farm, and that they will be moving to another province to be closer to other family members, but he declined to say any more than that. A real estate developer is buying the property, and he wants to subdivide it for single-family homes and town houses. There would be a total of five hundred new homes as the developer, Eugene McIntry, President of McIntry Realty, has planned it. McIntery has submitted his subdivision plan to the county commissioners. The commissioners and the County Planning Commission are extremely worried about this giant new development.

They don't believe their roads and their water and sewer systems can handle all those people. In fact, right now the water system and sewer system don't even run to the farm. The family that lives on the farm have a well and a septic tank for their house and another well for their barn. But, the county doesn't have any zoning, so the supervisors don't think they can keep McIntry from buying the farm and building all those homes. Plus, McIntry has threatened to file a lawsuit if the township tries anything to keep his plans from going through. He said he has a lot of money invested and doesn't want to lose it. Some nearby residents, however, are going to file a lawsuit of their own to keep him from building the houses. They are angry that they're peaceful, quiet stretch of road just outside the city will soon be filled with cars and their view will be ruined by hundred's of new houses. The residents attorney, Hector Salvatore, says he is finishing up the suit and will file it in County Court next week. He said the residents also are afraid they will be forced to hook up to the water and sewer systems if they are expanded out to the farm, which means several hundred dollars out of each of their pockets, which he said is unfair and possibly illegal.

2. A bad accident happened this morning on the interprovincial highway that runs right along the western edge of your city. It is Highway 790. Apparently two tractor trailers collided and started a chain reaction crash. The citys Police Department is not done investigating the accident, which happened at 6:45 a.m. in the morning, but that is what they believe preliminarily. A total of 4 tractor-trailers and fourteen cars were involved, according to Sgt. Albert Wei of the police department. One of the tractor-trailers was a tanker hauling diesel fuel; it was very lucky, Wei said, that it didn't roll over or dump any fuel or catch fire. The truck part of the tanker was damaged when a car hit it, but the truck driver managed to get it stopped along the side of the road. He wasn't hurt, Wei said, but 2 people driving cars were killed and twenty other people were injured and taken to the hospital, four of them seriously hurt. The fire chief, Tony Sullivan, said those seriously hurt people had injuries that were life-threatening. One of the ambulance drivers told him that. Sulluvan said his firefighters had to cut the roofs off three of the cars to free the drivers and passengers that were trapped inside. All five of the fire department's ambulances were on the seen, along with ambulances from four nearby citys' fire departments. Also, the "Life Flight" helicopter from Memorial Hospital in you're city was called to the scene and flew two of the worst injuries to the trauma center in Statesville, 50 miles away. Sullivan said the crash scene looked like something from a war zone when he arrived, with bodies laying along the road, people covered with blood sitting next to their cars, emergency workers running from place to place trying to help the injured, and sirens wailing in the distance as more fire trucks and ambulances were called. He had never seen anything that bad in the 18 and a half years he's been with the fire department. Wie said the police officers on the scene were having trouble figuring out which people were from which vehicles, and who were the drivers and who were the

passengers. According to Wei, the accident, which happened in the northbound lanes, closed the entire highway, north and south. The highway was still closed at 10 a.m., the deadline for your story, and Wei had no idea when it would be open again. It created quite a mess for the rush hour traffic today, since people who normally would have used Highway 790 had to go on Highway 690, on the eastern side of the city, and that backed up traffic on 690 for three hours.

Exercise 3   Writing Complete News Stories

Write complete news stories based on the following information. Critically examine the information's language and organization, improving it whenever possible. To provide a pleasing change of pace, use quotations in your stories. Go beyond the superficial; unless your instructor tells you otherwise, assume that you have enough space to report every important and interesting detail.

1.   The president of your local school board is in trouble. David DeBecker has been a member of the school board for more than 20 years and president for nearly six years. He told school officials and local authorities that he has done nothing wrong. Police have charged DeBecker with theft, fraud, extortion, and obstruction of justice. DeBecker, 57, lives on a 15-acre estate on Meadowdale Road. The property includes an 18-room white brick mansion, a barn and stable, several work sheds, and a large pond stocked with fish. Police said this is what happened. DeBecker is part owner of a janitorial service incorporated as Best Bet Cleaning Services. DeBecker did not disclose the fact that he was part owner of the business when the company bid on the cleaning contract at your local high school. His partner, James V. Stimson, 43, of Jamestown Drive, is listed as owner and operator of the company. DeBecker runs his own accounting firm, DeBecker Accounting Services Inc. DeBecker became acquainted with Stimson seven years ago when Stimson came to DeBecker seeking financial advice. Stimson was in trouble with the federal government for owing back taxes and DeBecker was able to fix the problem but demanded to be made a silent partner in the lucrative cleaning business. DeBecker helped Stimson bid on the school cleaning contract and Stimson was awarded the contract as low bidder. DeBecker recruited students from the local vocational school to work with Stimson, but often did not pay the students. DeBecker would pocket the money instead. DeBecker also had the students work on his property to clean and do construction work on various projects. The students were not paid for the work. More than 35 vocational students were involved at one time or another in the scam. Best Bet Cleaning Services was being paid hundreds of thousands of dollars to do the cleaning work at the high school with the stipulation that vocational students be among the workers. The students were never told they were to be paid. They were told by Stimson that they were getting "business experience" as their compensation. Also charged

with obstruction of justice is Ruth Gunderson who is accused of destroying email and other records in regard to the work done at the high school. Gunderson is the office secretary for Best Bet Cleaning Services. She is 45 years old and lives on Hillcrest Street with her husband, William Gunderson. Charges are pending against Stimson. A provincial court handed down the indictments after a 14-month investigation. Authorities believe that DeBecker defrauded the school district of more than $850,000 over the six-year term of the cleaning contract. DeBecker is free on $250,000 bond. He faces up to 25 years in prison if convicted of the charges.

2. It was a potential tragedy that your city's police, rescue, and fire officials say was just barely averted. James Shanahan, his two daughters, Alyssa and Adrienne, and his wife, Mary, were travelling from Kenora, Ont. They were flying near your city when the plane they were in had to make an emergency landing. James Shanahan is a licensed pilot. He has been flying for 30 years. He has never had a problem in all that time. No one was seriously injured, but James Shanahan was admitted to Mercy Hospital for observation. Mrs. Shanahan was treated for a broken wrist and a laceration on her forehead and released. Adrienne suffered minor cuts and bruises. Alyssa was not injured. The plane was a four-passenger Mooney Executive 21 propeller-driven, fixed-wing aircraft. The undercarriage of the plane sustained minor damage. There was a small fuel spill, according to the fire department. "They were very fortunate. It could have been much worse than it was. There were a lot of startled people when that plane came at them," said Fire Chief Tony Sullivan. Police Chief Barry Kopperud said the Shanahans left Kenora early in the morning. The flight was proceeding normally until the plane was 100 kilometres east of the city. The plane began to wander off course and was contacted by the control tower at City Regional Airport. A girl's voice responded to the control tower. "The girl I talked to on the radio told me the pilot was having problems. She told me he had slumped in his seat and was unconscious. I could hear the passengers screaming in the background. It was really confusing. I think they were getting a bit panicky up there," said control tower flight manager Peter Jacobs. Police said James Shanahan lost consciousness as he was about to contact the tower to request an emergency landing. His wife, Mary, told police her husband began complaining about not feeling well. He told her that he felt dizzy and couldn't get his breath. She said he suddenly slumped over in his seat and the plane went into a shallow dive. "There was nothing I could do. I was in the back passenger seat with my daughter Adrienne. I couldn't reach the controls. And even if I could have, I don't think I could have helped because I never learned how to fly. I hate flying," Mrs. Shanahan said. Kopperud said Alyssa Shanahan was seated beside her father. It was she who responded to the tower's call about the plane wandering off course. Alyssa pulled her father's arms away from the controls and his legs off the rudder pedals. She then took over the controls of the aircraft and called the tower for help to land the plane. Jacobs stayed in contact

with Alyssa and gave her instructions on what to do. He talked to her the entire time and directed other aircraft away from the airport until the emergency was over. Alyssa was able to locate the airport and brought the plane down. When the plane landed, it overshot the runway and skidded across an open field. The landing gear of the plane collapsed and the plane plowed through a chain-link fence and came to a stop just three metres from the northbound lane of Trans-Canada Highway. The highway was crowded with traffic at the time of the accident. The accident occurred at 4:05 p.m., police said. No one on the ground was injured. Alyssa is 12 years old, 4 feet 3 inches tall and weighs 88 pounds. "I've been flying with my Daddy since I was a little girl. He taught me all about flying and even let me handle the controls sometimes. I was a little scared because I couldn't reach the rudder pedals very well. But I couldn't be too scared because I want to be a pilot like my Daddy someday. I was more worried about my Daddy because I didn't know what happened to him. I just wanted to get on the ground and get help for him," Alyssa said. Doctors at Mercy Hospital said Mr. Shanahan was in satisfactory condition after suffering an allergic reaction to a prescription medicine he had begun taking that morning.

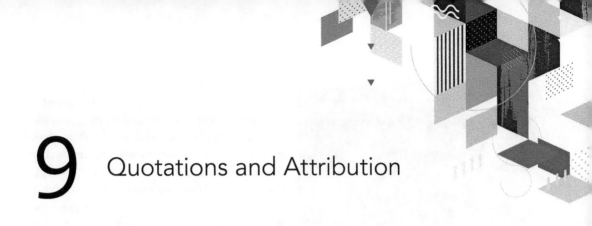

9 Quotations and Attribution

"Just watch me."

—Prime Minister Pierre Elliott Trudeau in an interview with CBC journalist
Tim Ralfe during the October Crisis in 1970. Reprinted with permission.

This quotation has become legendary in Canadian history because of how aptly it describes Trudeau's leadership style and how it foretells his declaration of the *War Measures Act* three days after this interview in response to kidnappings of British Trade commissioner James Cross and Quebec labour minister Pierre Laporte by the Quebec separatist group the FLQ (Figure 9.1).

Such a bold and blunt challenge from a leader was exceptional in 1970, and would still be considered so today. Trudeau said it during a unique discussion with the CBC's Ralfe that broke the mould on how to interview a source, let alone the leader of a country.

At that time, reporters talked to sources in person or on a rotary phone. Trudeau had just gotten out of his car at the Parliamentary buildings when Ralfe and other reporters scrummed him. Ralfe asked, "Sir, what is it with all these men and guns around here?" Trudeau's response began a seven-and-a-half-minute discussion with Ralfe about the meaning of the law and the protection of civilized, democratic society. The video of their conversation—for this was far more than an interview between reporter and source—is in the CBC Archives and is often shown in journalism classes to demonstrate, among other things, when rules of interviews can and should be broken, and the value of a good quotation.

There were no 24/7 news feeds in the 1970s, so the interview with Trudeau was not immediately delivered to the audience. Today, social media and cell phone technology means the same conversation would be immediately posted on many platforms, trend on Twitter, and become the breaking news ticker on several news websites.

Good quotations help build and support solid stories. They can be a unique way to present a strong and firm stance in times of crisis, as in the Trudeau instance. They also add depth to news stories by allowing the audience to hear many voices rather than just the voice of the writer. Quotations add credibility to a story by verifying and supporting the facts the reporter presents. Weaving many voices into one coherent news story, however, can be difficult. Experienced writers use certain techniques to help them handle these difficulties.

Figure 9.1

Reporters Tim Ralfe, right, and Peter Reilly, centre, ask Prime Minister Pierre Trudeau about the FLQ crisis.

Quotations

Reporters put quotations they get from sources in one of three forms: (1) direct, (2) indirect, and (3) partial quotations.

Direct quotations present a source's exact words and are placed entirely in quotation marks.

Indirect quotations lack quotation marks because reporters use their own words to summarize or paraphrase a source's remarks.

Partial quotations directly quote key phrases from what a source says and the reporter summarizes the rest.

DIRECT QUOTATION: "I'm a true believer in the strength of teamwork, in the power of dreams and in the absolute necessity of a support structure," Canada's new Governor General Julie Payette said.

INDIRECT QUOTATION: Canada's new Governor General Julie Payette says she believes in teamwork, dreams, and having support.

PARTIAL QUOTATION: Canada's new Governor General Julie Payette says she believes in teamwork, dreams, and "the absolute necessity of a support structure."

When to Use Direct Quotations

Reporters use direct quotations when their sources say something important or controversial or just state their ideas in an interesting, unusual, or colourful manner. *Toronto Star* reporter Linda Diebel in a 2014 feature wrote about an acerbic interview with novelist Margaret Atwood, who had this response to a question about the volume of her work:

> "That's just because I'm old. Like fluff under the bed, it's accumulative. If I'd had a list like that when I was 25 . . . It stretches out, a novel every three or four years is not that prolific," Atwood said.

It is important to use direct quotations because they add value to a story—not just to meet a quotation quota.

Here are some guidelines on when to use direct quotations:

- Use quotations to let your sources talk directly to the reader.
- Use quotations when you cannot improve on the speaker's exact words or cannot match the speaker's wit, rhythm, colour, or emotion.
- Use quotations to tie a controversial opinion to the source.
- Use quotations as evidence for a statement.
- Use quotations to reveal the speaker's character.
- Use quotations to verify information that you have gathered.
- Use quotations to confirm intangibles (emotions, feelings).
- Use quotations to show the other side(s) of a story.

In the summer of 2016, the Montreal Canadiens hockey organization announced it was trading its all-star defenceman P.K. Subban to the Nashville Predators for Shea Webber. General Manager Marc Bergevin's deal stunned Canadiens' fans. Everyone wanted to know if there was division in the team's head office. A few days after the deal was announced, team owner Geoff Molson gave a press conference to show his support for Bergevin. It was the other side of a hot media story and it was the media's responsibility to report it.

> "I'm not surprised how the fans have reacted," Molson said. "P.K. is a bigger-than-life person on and off the ice and our fans love him and still will love him.
>
> "I appreciate that, but I also appreciate what I've hired (general manager) Marc Bergevin to do and that is to make our team better. I'm confident he's done that."

Using Direct Quotations Effectively

Direct quotations should illustrate a point, not tell an entire story. Stories are structured with paragraphs that weave together quotations from sources. These transitional paragraphs help build the narrative thread. The following story contains a combination of quotations, paraphrases, and transitional paragraphs that help lead readers through the details of the story.

The most important thing women's basketball coach Vance Coleman carries in his briefcase is not a sketch of a new defensive scheme, a game plan for the up-coming opponent, or even the phone number of a basketball colleague.

It's a crumpled, yellowed piece of paper with a list full of scratches and re-dos. It's his list of five life goals. Coleman lists living a long and healthy life, playing the role of a good father and husband, and earning a million dollars as his top three goals. The other two, he said, constantly change as he ages.

But the point, Coleman said, is to always have them.

"There is an equation I use that works on the basketball court, on the playing field, in business, and in life," Coleman said, "and that is performance equals ability times motivation. You may have all the ability in the world, but with no motivation, you won't accomplish anything. Zero times anything is nothing.

"No matter what you do in life, you have to have goals. And you have to stick to those goals."

Coleman, now in his second year at the university and his seventeenth year of coaching, spoke about goals and motivation to nearly 300 students at the Student Alumni Association Conference Friday.

"The first thing you need is a good attitude," Coleman said. "When you get up at 7 a.m., do you say, 'Good morning, God,' or 'Good God, morning'? Same words, big difference in attitude."

Next, the coach shifted gears to the importance of beliefs.

"When someone asks you what you believe in, tell them with conviction," Coleman said. "Say, 'I believe in myself and what I think with my whole heart and nothing less.'"

Reporters often summarize a major point and then use a direct quotation to explain the point or provide more details about it. But the quotation should provide new informa-tion. Here's an example of how a quotation can effectively support a point. Toronto City Council voted in favour of a pilot project to let residents keep up to four hens in their back-yards. The story, in which the reporter spoke with councillors who voted for and against the plan, included this quotation that enhanced the point about the favourable vote:

But the two councillors who hatched the plan, Joe Mihevc and Justin Di Ciano, were delighted with the 23–14 vote in their favour. Both say they'll be getting chickens as soon as the pilot starts.

"To have a few pets in your backyard that also have the benefit of producing eggs, there's nothing wrong with it from a public health perspective, from a nui-sance perspective," Mihevc told reporters. "They are as clean as cats and dogs."

A quotation should not repeat, or echo, facts reported earlier in a story:

ORIGINAL: Company officials said they are not worried about the upcoming audit.

"We're not expecting anything to worry about," treasurer Peter VanNeffe said.

REVISED: Company officials said they welcome the upcoming audit.

"We're not expecting anything to worry about," treasurer Peter VanNeffe said.

When to Use Indirect Quotations

Some sources are more quotable than others, but sometimes even preferred sources say things that are not quotable. Reporters may be tempted to use whatever quotations are available. Yet a weak quotation is worse than none. If a quotation bores or confuses people, most will stop reading a story.

"It's something that's pretty unique here," she said.

"We're here for many reasons," he said.

"The positive response was tremendous," he said.

None of these speakers is saying anything interesting. Each sentence would be better paraphrased or omitted entirely.

Reporters use indirect quotations when their sources fail to say their ideas effectively. Indirect quotations allow reporters to rephrase a source's remarks and show them more clearly and concisely. Reporters also can emphasize the source's most significant remarks and revise or eliminate remarks that are unclear, irrelevant, libellous, pretentious, or otherwise unprintable:

ORIGINAL QUOTATION: Edna Czarski said, "Women do not get the same tax and insurance benefits that men receive, and they do not receive maternity benefits that even start to cover what they should."

PARAPHRASED: Edna Czarski said women receive neither the same tax and insurance benefits as men nor adequate maternity benefits.

Reporters can never justify a weak quotation by responding, "But that's what my source said." They should use their interviewing skills and judgment to elicit and report quotations that are clear, concise, dramatic, and interesting.

Sometimes sources give reporters only routine, boring quotations such as, "I really love to play football." By continuing the interview and asking better questions, reporters can get better responses. Here's the type of quotation reporters want:

"I really love football," Joe Lozado said. "I've been playing since I was seven years old, and I would feel worthless if I couldn't play. There's no better feeling than just before a game when you run out on the field with all your buddies and see the crowd. You can feel the excitement."

Asking questions that encourage the source to elaborate on their ideas or reactions often will produce good quotations.

Avoid quotations—direct or indirect—that say the obvious. The following quotations are likely to sound familiar because they appear dozens of times every year.

"We really want to win this game," Coach Riley said. (Readers already know this. Does any coach want to lose?)

"If we can score some points, we can win this game," Tran Ogbondah said. (A team that does not score points obviously cannot win.)

When to Use Partial Quotations

Reporters can get around the problem of weak or confusing quotations by directly quoting only a few words from a sentence. However, some partial quotations are awkward or unnecessary. Sentences that contain several partial quotations can be distracting. Usually, the quoted phrases can be turned into part of the sentence by taking out the quotation marks:

PARTIAL QUOTATION: He said the press barons "such as William Randolph Hearst" created "an amazingly rich variety" of newspapers.
REVISED: He said the press barons such as William Randolph Hearst created a rich variety of newspapers.

Reporters also should avoid using "orphan" quotations; that is, they should not place quotation marks around an isolated word or two used in an ordinary way.

INCORRECT: He complained that no one "understands" his problem.
REVISED: He complained that no one understands his problem.

Reporters may use partial quotations to more clearly attribute controversial, important, or interesting phrases to a specific source:

Oakland Raiders coach Jack Del Rio said "nothing really surprises you after 32 years, but that was unusual," after an NFL referee used a folded piece of paper to measure a first down in a game with the Dallas Cowboys in 2017.

Blending Quotations and Narrative

Every news story must have an angle, and everything in the story must connect to that angle. The sources whom the reporter interviewed, however, may have spoken about a number of topics, some of which may touch only slightly on the story's angle. Reporters must blend the quotations and the narrative they write to create a coherent, well-focused news story. This blending of narrative and quotations can present several problems for reporters.

Explaining Quotations

Sometimes reporters use a quotation and then realize readers need background information to understand it. They might try inserting explanatory material in parentheses. Or they might tack on the explanation after the attribution. Still others might put a large block of background information high in the story, hoping it will give readers the information they need to understand the quotations and new facts reported elsewhere in the story. None of these approaches works well.

Lazy writers solve the problems of providing explanatory material by inserting it in parentheses in the quotation. When reporters pepper their stories with parenthetical explanations, the stories become difficult to read. The occasional use of parentheses to insert brief explanations may be acceptable, but reporters should paraphrase quotations that need several parenthetical explanations. If reporters use parentheses repeatedly, they should reorganize their stories.

> **ORIGINAL:** "When (head coach Tom) Whitman decides on his starter (at quarterback), the rest of them (the players) will quit squabbling," the athletic director said.
> **REVISED:** The football players will quit squabbling when head coach Tom Whitman selects a starting quarterback, the athletic director said.

Adding the explanatory information after the quotation or attribution is little better than using parentheses. Such backward constructions force readers to complete the sentence before they can figure out what the topic is. Here's an example:

> **ORIGINAL:** "We're mobilizing for an economic war with other cities and states," the mayor said of his plan for attracting new businesses to the city.

Instead of using this "said-of" construction, flip the sentence and use an indirect quotation:

> **REVISED:** The mayor said his plan for attracting new business amounted to mobilization for an economic war with other cities and states.

Beginning reporters sometimes think they must report their questions so that readers can understand the source's answers. The news is in the answers, however, not in the questions. The use of both questions and answers is repetitive and dull. Reporters usually omit the question. If the question provides important context, reporters incorporate it in the answer:

> **ORIGINAL:** The president was asked whether he plans to seek a second term, and he responded that he would not announce his decision until next winter.
> **REVISED:** The president said he would not announce his decision regarding a second term until next winter.
> **REVISED:** During a question-and-answer session after his speech, the president said he would not announce his decision regarding a second term until next winter.

To Change or Not to Change Quotations

Sometimes the exact words a source uses may be inappropriate to use in a news story. To make a quotation usable, reporters may be tempted to alter the speaker's words. Whether writers should ever change a quotation is a matter of debate among journalists. Some journalists accept making minor changes in quotations to correct grammatical errors or delete profanity. Other journalists say reporters should never change quotations. Extensive changes in quotations are rarely acceptable (if the quotation needs that much altering, paraphrase instead of quoting, and be sure to remain faithful to the speaker's meaning). However, even those who oppose altering quotations recognize a few instances where changes are necessary. They usually involve the deletion of unnecessary words, grammatical errors, and profanities.

Deleting Unnecessary Words

Using the source's exact words eliminates questions about accuracy. Reporters who are uncertain about the source's exact words (or think a statement needs rewriting) should use indirect rather than direct quotations. Doctoring a quotation could lead to a mistake that may injure the reputation of the source and the career of the reporter. Sometimes, however, unnecessary words can be omitted when the meaning is clearly not changed.

> **ORIGINAL:** He said, "Look, you know I think nuclear power is safe, absolutely safe."
> **REVISION:** He said, "Nuclear power is safe, absolutely safe."

Reporters may use an ellipsis (three evenly spaced periods) to show where they deleted a word, phrase, or sentence. An ellipsis that appears at the end rather than in the middle of a complete sentence should have four periods. Policies vary from news organization to news organization, and some journalists do not use ellipses in reporting ordinary interviews. Reporters are more likely to use them when quoting formal statements or documents.

Reporters have an obligation to present a source's views as faithfully as possible, so they must be certain that they are not removing important context when they delete words or phrases from a quotation.

Correcting Grammatical Errors

If a quotation is so ungrammatical that it becomes difficult to understand, the reporter should paraphrase the source.

> **ORIGINAL:** "The council and the mayor is giving them corporations too much tax breaks so the load's not fair no more," Andrews said.
> **REVISED:** The council and the mayor have given so many tax breaks to corporations that the tax burden is no longer fairly shared, Andrews said.

Some public figures are well known for misusing words and creating confusing sentences. A reporter cleaning up their quotations could rob the story of its colour or charm, or more importantly its accuracy. The late Yogi Berra, a famous baseball player, manager, and coach, was famous for his jumbled sayings such as "when you come to a fork in the road, take it" and "if you don't know where you are going, you'll end up someplace else."

The following flubs by former U.S. president George W. Bush's linguistic flubs were widely reported:

"I am a person who recognizes the fallacy of human beings."
"I know how hard it is to put food on your family."
"I think that the vice-president is a person reflecting a half-glass-full mentality."

Deleting Profanities

Reporters usually omit profanities from quotations. Editors and news directors say children as well as adults read their stories and view their programs. Not only may profanities be inappropriate for children, but some adults also may find certain words offensive. News organizations are becoming more candid, however, and some publish mild profanities that are essential to a story. Casual profanities—those used habitually and unnecessarily by many people—remain forbidden in most newsrooms:

UNNECESSARY PROFANITY: "Shit, I wasn't going to try to stop that damned idiot," the witness testified. "He had a knife."
REVISED AS A PARAPHRASE: The witness testified he did not try to stop the accused because he had a knife.

For broadcast journalists, deletion of profanities may be required by federal law.

The Canadian Radio-television and Telecommunications Commission (CRTC) regulates broadcast media, forbidding obscene, profane, or indecent language. The CRTC is authorized to levy fines for transgressions, but such matters are normally left to self-regulation by the industry's Canadian Broadcast Standards Council (CBSC). But for online casts—audio and video—there are no rules governing profanity.

According to CBSC, self-regulation within the context of prevailing community standards has functioned well; television and radio stations are familiar with the requirements for content warnings and program ratings; obscene language is permitted only after 9 p.m.

Generally, broadcast journalists, like print and online journalists, should avoid profanities. The laws are still developing, and the price of guessing wrong can be steep.

Editorialization

Avoid unintentional editorials. If worded carelessly, partial quotations, and even the form of attribution used, can express an opinion:

> **EDITORIALIZATION:** The mayor made it clear that the city cannot afford to give its employees a raise.
> **REVISED:** The mayor said the city cannot afford to give its employees a raise.

> **EDITORIALIZATION:** Each month, Sen. William Proxmire presented the Golden Fleece Award "for the biggest, most ironic, or most ridiculous example of wasteful government spending."
> **REVISED:** Each month, Sen. William Proxmire presented the Golden Fleece Award for what he considered "the biggest, most ironic, or most ridiculous example of wasteful government spending."

Before revision, the first sentence editorializes by saying the mayor "made it clear," which implies that she stated a fact in a convincing manner. Others might regard the statement that the city cannot afford pay raises for employees as an opinion or political posturing. The second sentence reports as fact the claim by Proxmire that all the recipients of his "award" wasted the government's money. Many of the recipients disagreed, and some provided convincing evidence that Proxmire was wrong.

Attribution

The Purpose of Attribution

Reporters are experts in finding things out. They rarely possess expertise in the topics they write about, such as city planning, health care, finance, or international relations. Instead, reporters must rely on the expertise of their sources. Attribution lets the readers know who the reporter's sources are. Chapter 4 explains the different levels of attribution (on-the-record, off-the-record, not-for-attribution, and deep background). Ideally, the purpose of on-the-record attribution is to make sure all direct quotations, opinions, evaluations, and second-hand statements of fact are attributed to specific individuals. This information lets readers draw their own conclusions about the credibility of the story.

Reporters can attribute information to people, documents, or publications but not to places or institutions. For example, reporters can quote a hospital official but not a hospital:

> **INCORRECT:** The hospital said the epidemic had ended.
> **REVISED:** A hospital spokesperson said the epidemic had ended.

INCORRECT: Toronto announced that all city offices would be closed Monday.
REVISED: The mayor of Toronto announced that all city offices would be closed Monday.

Statements That Require Attribution

Reporters do not have to attribute statements that report undisputed facts, such as the fact that the Second World War ended in 1945 or that Montreal is in Quebec. Nor must reporters attribute things they witness. However, reporters must attribute the information they get from other people, especially the following:

1. statements about controversial issues;
2. statements of opinion; and
3. all direct and indirect quotations.

News stories that fail to attribute such statements appear to present the reporter's personal opinions rather than the opinions of the sources. Two or three words of attribution are usually adequate:

UNATTRIBUTED: The Birthing Centre is an alternative for pregnant women who prefer more personalized care.
ATTRIBUTED: Director Sally Malone said the Birthing Centre is an alternative for pregnant women who prefer more personalized care.

Reporters must attribute statements that praise or condemn, or assign credit or blame to any person or organization. Readers should immediately recognize that a story reports what someone else said, not the reporter's opinions or those of the news organization:

UNATTRIBUTED: Parliament has wasted time while the problem of unemployment has worsened.
ATTRIBUTED: The Speaker said that Parliament has wasted time while the problem of unemployment has worsened.

UNATTRIBUTED: Acting in self-defence, the officer shot the man three times in the chest.
ATTRIBUTED: The officer said she was acting in self-defence when she shot the man three times in the chest.

Statements that imply carelessness or recklessness or culpable conduct can provoke lawsuits. Careful attribution, particularly if the statements can be attributed to official sources, will reduce the risk of being sued.

Guidelines for the Placement and Frequency of Attribution

Attribution may be placed at the beginning or end of a sentence or at a natural break within it. However, it should never interrupt a thought:

> **INCORRECT:** "I shall," the general said, "return."
> **REVISED:** The general said, "I shall return."

Readers and listeners should be told who is speaking as soon as conveniently possible; they should never have to guess. If a quotation is long, the writer should place the attribution at the beginning or end of the first sentence or after the first meaningful clause in that sentence. The attribution should not be delayed until the end of the second or third sentence. Similarly, if a quotation contains only one sentence but that sentence is long, the attribution should come at or near the beginning of that sentence, not at the end:

> **INCORRECT:** "However close we sometimes seem to that dark and final abyss, let no man of peace and freedom despair. For he does not stand alone. If we all can persevere, if we can in every land and office look beyond our shores and ambitions, then surely the age will dawn in which the strong are just and the weak secure and the peace preserved," the president said.
> **REVISED:** "However close we sometimes seem to that dark and final abyss," the president said, "let no man of peace and freedom despair. For he does not stand alone. If we all can persevere, if we can in every land and office look beyond our shores and ambitions, then surely the age will dawn in which the strong are just and the weak secure and the peace preserved."

Attribution should come at the beginning of any quotation in which there is a change of speakers. If reporters fail to provide transitions from one speaker to another, particularly when the quotations are contradictory, readers may not understand who is speaking:

> The newspaper's editor said he no longer will accept advertisements for X-rated movies. He explained: "These movies are worthless. They contribute nothing to society and offend our readers. They're depressing and pornographic."
> "Newspapers have no right to pass judgment on matters of taste. If they do, they should also ban the advertisements for other products considered harmful: cigarettes, liquor, and pollutants like automobiles," a theatre owner responded.

These two paragraphs are confusing. Readers beginning the second paragraph might mistakenly assume the editor is contradicting himself. The writer can avoid the confusion by placing a brief transition at the beginning of the second paragraph, such as the following:

> However, a local theatre owner responded, "Newspapers have no right . . ."

Direct Quotations

A direct quotation should be attributed only once, regardless of the number of sentences it contains:

> **INCORRECT:** "I'm opposed to any laws that prohibit the sale of pornography," the attorney said. "The restriction of pornography infringes on civil rights," he said. "I like to picture myself as a good guy defending a sleazy thing," he concluded.
> **REVISED:** "I'm opposed to any laws that prohibit the sale of pornography," the attorney said. "The restriction of pornography infringes on civil rights. I like to picture myself as a good guy defending a sleazy thing."

Even when a direct quotation continues for several paragraphs, it needs attribution only once:

> Capt. Bonventre eliminated the police department's motorcycle squad.
> "The main reason is that there are more injuries to motorcycle officers," he said. "I want to protect my officers. They think there's no danger on a cycle. Well, that's just optimistic thinking; there's a real danger.
> "Officers have much more protection in a car. I think that's pretty obvious. If an officer gets in a hot pursuit and crashes, he stands a better chance of escaping injury when he's in a car.
> "Also, almost any situation, even traffic, can be handled better in a patrol car than on a motorcycle. There are some places a motorcycle can go more easily, but a car certainly commands more respect."

Reporters also must avoid "floating" quotations: direct quotations that lack clear attribution to a speaker. Direct quotations need attribution only once, but that attribution must be clearly attached to the quotation. Careless writers sometimes name a source in one sentence and then deliver an unattributed quotation in the following sentence or paragraph. The reader must guess whether the quotation comes from the person just named or someone who will be identified later. The uncertainty halts the reader. Several such delays can cause the reader to put down the newspaper. Clear attribution makes the reader's work easier:

> **INCORRECT:** Wendy Mitchell, a sociologist, said there is a trend toward vocationalism on college campuses.
> "Many students now demand from college not a chance to think but a chance to become qualified for some job."
> **REVISED:** Wendy Mitchell, a sociologist, said there is a trend toward vocationalism on college campuses.
> "Many students now demand from college not a chance to think," she said, "but a chance to become qualified for some job."

Partial Quotations

On the rare occasions when writers quote part of a sentence, they take care to separate it from complete sentences that are also being quoted. Combining partial and complete quotations sometimes causes confusing pronoun shifts, which can be avoided by (1) placing attribution between the partial quotation and the full-sentence quotation, or (2) paraphrasing the partial quotation:

> **INCORRECT:** Ross said he expects to find a job "within a few weeks. And when I do get a job, the first thing I'm going to buy is a new car."
> **ACCEPTABLE:** Ross said he expects to find a job "within a few weeks." He added, "And when I do get a job, the first thing I'm going to buy is a new car."
> **BETTER:** Ross said he expects to find a job within a few weeks. "And when I do get a job, the first thing I'm going to buy is a new car," he added.

The original passage is confusing because of a shift in pronouns. The first sentence uses the third person, referring to Ross as "he." But in the second sentence, which is the full quotation, Ross refers to himself in the first person. The second sentence is correct but it is awkward. Rewriting the partial quotation eliminates the confusion.

Indirect Quotations

Indirect quotations (or paraphrases) need more frequent attribution than direct quotations. Every opinion or unverified fact in an indirect quotation—sometimes every sentence— must be attributed:

> **INCORRECT:** The police chief insisted that the solitary confinement must be retained. Solitary confinement, harsh as it may seem, is designed to protect correctional guards and other inmates.
> **REVISED:** The police chief insisted that the solitary confinement must be retained. Solitary confinement might seem harsh, he said, but it is designed to protect the correctional guards and other inmates.

If the police chief's remarks have been paraphrased, the reporter may not attribute them by placing the paragraph within quotation marks because it does not contain the police chief's own words. Similarly, editors should not convert an indirect quotation written by a reporter into a direct quotation. However, reporters and editors may take a quotation out of quotation marks and reword it, provided they do not change its meaning.

Every sentence of indirect quotation should have attribution, but writers should avoid inserting phrases that may attribute a quotation twice. For example, the following sentence reports that a fire chief made an announcement, then adds that he "said":

INCORRECT: In making the announcement, the fire chief said arsonists caused 20 per cent of the blazes reported in the city last year.
REVISED: The fire chief said arsonists caused 20 per cent of the blazes reported in the city last year.

Whether reporting direct or indirect quotations, the writer should strive to vary the location of the attribution. Writing becomes dull if every sentence begins with "she said" or some variation. Moving the attribution to the end or middle of the sentence keeps writing interesting. Often the most effective location for attribution is after the first natural pause in the sentence. This is another good reason to read stories aloud to find the natural breaks.

Word Choice in Attributing Statements

The verbs used to attribute statements must be accurate and impartial. For straight news stories, they also should be in the past tense. For feature stories, present tense attribution may be acceptable. For online content, present tense is used.

Some form of the verb "to say" best describes how sources communicate information. For variety, reporters sometimes use the following verbs:

- comment
- reply
- declare
- add
- explain
- continue
- point out
- note
- urge
- suggest
- warn

Each has a more specific meaning than "say" and can be used only when that meaning accurately reflects how the source spoke. "Explain," for instance, means to make something comprehensible or less obscure. Unless the source was discussing a complicated or unclear topic, "explain" would not be an appropriate verb for attribution:

UNACCEPTABLE: The city council meeting will begin at 8 p.m., he explained.
ACCEPTABLE: He said the city council meeting will begin at 8 p.m.

The statement is obvious and needs no explanation; the most appropriate verb of attribution is "said."

Many editors prohibit the use of verbs such as "hope," "feel," "believe," "want," and "think" to attribute statements. Editors say reporters know only what their sources tell them, not what sources hope, feel, believe, want, or think.

Other words are even more inappropriate. People speak words; they do not "grin," "smile," "chuckle," "laugh," "sigh" or "cough" them. Reporters should rephrase such sentences as this:

ORIGINAL: "It's a wonderful movie," she smiled.
REVISED: "It's a wonderful movie," she said.
OR THIS: "It's a wonderful movie," she said with a smile.

The words "claimed" and "admitted" and "stated" are troublesome. "Claimed" casts doubt on a source's remarks, suggesting the remarks are controversial and possibly wrong. "Admitted" implies a source conceded some point or confessed to an error, charge, or crime. "Stated" can be too emphatic, and imply there is no other side to the story. By comparison, the word "said" is almost always appropriate. Frequent use of "said" may sound awkward at first, but it is a neutral term and can be used any number of times in a story. For online and broadcast content, "says" is used.

Attribution should also be concise. Each of the following phrases (which have appeared in news stories) can be replaced by either "said" or "added":

- made it clear that
- further stated that
- went on to say that
- let it be known that
- also pointed out that
- emphasized the fact that
- stated in the report that
- said that he feels that
- brought out the idea that
- went on to say that in his opinion
- in making the announcement said that
- continued the speech by urging that
- responded to the question by saying that
- concluded the speech with the comment that

Anonymous Sources

Why do so many stories use anonymous sources? Sometimes sources want to remain anonymous for legitimate reasons. (See Box 9.1 for guidelines on when to use anonymous sources.) Corporate or government officials who want to blow the whistle on waste, fraud, or other illegal or unethical conduct at their workplace may fear retaliation. Many have lost jobs or been demoted because they disclosed truths that made their supervisors uncomfortable. Canadian Press policy dictates that all anonymous sources be double-sourced (corroborated by two other sources) and cleared for publication by a senior editor.

Some journalists have deplored the use of anonymous sources as a threat to the independence, accuracy, and credibility of the news. In the United States, Benjamin Bradlee, famed former executive editor of the *Washington Post*, said: "Why, then, do we go along so complacently with withholding the identity of public officials? I'm damned if I know. I do know that by doing so, we shamelessly do other people's bidding: We knowingly let ourselves be used. . . . In short, we demean our profession."

In Canada, the Maher Arar affair sparked a wide and passionate debate about the use of anonymous sources. An in-depth feature written by Andrew Mitrovica and published in *The Walrus* magazine detailed how some journalists were irresponsible in their use of political sources. Mitrovica reported that Justice Dennis O'Connor ruled in 2006 that "Arar was an innocent victim of incompetent RCMP officers who produced worthless intelligence. O'Connor also concluded that a smear campaign had been orchestrated against Arar by Canadian officials, aided by members of the media."

Mitrovica also reported that O'Connor's ruling found:

> A careful review of more than 2,500 stories, editorials, opinion pieces, letters to the editor, and transcripts of newscasts between the time word broke in mid-October 2002 that Arar had been secretly shipped to Syria and early October 2006 reveals much about the sometimes incestuous relationship between anonymous government sources and parliamentary reporters. These documents also speak to the hypocrisy of news organizations and writers who demand transparency and accountability from others but fail to provide it themselves, and to a great divide between the coverage of the Arar story published by Canada's two national newspapers. (*The Walrus*, 2006)

Anonymity allows sources to try to influence the way journalists cover the news. In Ottawa, high-level government sources often demand that their briefings be on background or on deep background. The officials use these briefings to place administration policy in the best possible light. They think they can do that most effectively when their identities and their political motives are hidden from the general public. Reporters abide by the background rules officials set because of the competitive pressures they face to get the story.

The accuracy of information from anonymous sources is always a concern. Even if sources are not intentionally misleading reporters, anonymity protects them from the consequences of their mistakes. The same is not true of the news organizations that publish the information. If several newspapers cover the same prison riot and receive inaccurate information from anonymous sources, the public's right to know is not served.

A final problem with anonymous sources is that under some circumstances a promise to keep a source's identity secret can be enforced in court. Courts have ruled that a source whose identity is revealed after confidentiality was promised may sue for damages.

| Box 9.1 | Guidelines for Using Anonymous Sources |

Editors are becoming more reluctant to use anonymous sources. Journalism critics say reporters can get more information on the record by threatening to ignore all information from sources who demand anonymity. If some sources insist on remaining anonymous, reporters might seek the same information from other sources who are willing to be identified. On the rare occasions when justification exists for using anonymous sources, news directors and editors tell their reporters to follow guidelines like these:

1. Do not use anonymous sources without the approval of your supervising editor or news director.
2. Be prepared to disclose the identities of anonymous sources to your editors or news directors and, possibly, to your news organization's lawyer.
3. Use anonymous sources only if they provide facts that are essential to the story, not just interesting quotations or opinions. Be sure the sources are appropriate for the story and that they are in a position to give authoritative information. Even then, information from anonymous sources should be verified.
4. Be sure you understand the motives of the anonymous source, such as whether the source is carrying a grudge or trying to puff a program or an agency. The motives help you evaluate the reliability of the information.
5. Identify sources as specifically as possible without revealing their identities so that readers can judge their importance and reliability. For example, instead of attributing information to "an informed source" or "a key official," you might attribute it to "an elected city official." This tells the reader the level of government in which the official works and alerts the reader to the fact that the official may have political interests. Never include any misleading information about the identity of a source, even if your motive is to protect the source.
6. Explain in the story why the source does not want to be identified.
7. Never allow a source to engage in anonymous attacks on other individuals or groups. Anonymous attacks risk involving you and your employer in a libel suit and are inherently unfair to the person attacked.

Guidelines for Capitalizing and Punctuating Quotations

The Use of Quotation Marks

Use double quotation marks to set off quotations. Only the quotation, never the attribution, should appear within the quotation marks:

> **INCORRECT:** "The motorcycle slid sideways and skidded about 100 feet, she said. The driver was killed."
> **REVISED:** "The motorcycle slid sideways and skidded about 100 feet," she said. "The driver was killed."

If a quotation continues for several sentences, all the sentences should be enclosed within a single set of quotation marks; quotation marks do not have to be placed at the beginning and end of each sentence in the quotation:

> **INCORRECT:** She said: "I did not see the car when I stepped out onto the street." "But when I saw the headlights coming at me, I knew it was going to hit me."
> **REVISED:** She said: "I did not see the car when I stepped out onto the street. But when I saw the headlights coming at me, I knew it was going to hit me."

Like any other part of a news story, a long quotation should be divided into short paragraphs to make it easier to read. New paragraphs should begin at natural breaks in the quotation, usually at changes in topic, however slight. Place quotation marks at the beginning of a long quotation and at the start of each new paragraph. Place closing quotation marks only at the end of the entire quotation, not at the end of every paragraph. Here is an example from a *New York Times* feature on Carla Bruni-Sarkozy, fashion model, singer, and wife of former French president Nicolas Sarkozy:

> "With my music, I could cope," she said, running a hand through her hair, "because it was so far from the role of public life. And who was going to stop me from playing my guitar? No one. I could play at night, on the plane. I'm a poor guitar player but I write my songs on a guitar. So I would bring a small guitar, a Taylor—it's child's size but a real guitar, with very good sound—and I would play all the time.
> "The one who had the weight on his shoulders was my man. He was elected. He was the president. I was there to be with him and help when people asked me for help. It was really easy for me."

When a quotation includes another quotation, use double quotation marks to identify the overall quotation and single quotation marks (or an apostrophe on the keyboard) to indicate the quotation within the quotation:

> During the U.S. 1960 presidential campaign, Republicans were accusing John F. Kennedy of using his family's wealth to buy the election. Kennedy joked, "I got a wire from my father that said: 'Dear Jack, Don't buy one vote more than necessary. I'll be damned if I'll pay for a landslide.'"

If the passage has a quotation within a quotation within a quotation, use double quotation marks to indicate the third level of quotation, as in this example:

> The member of Parliament said: "I had a voter tell me, 'I'm fed up with tax cheats. They get away with "murder."' And I had to agree with her."

Other Punctuation

If the attribution comes before a quotation that contains just one full sentence, a comma should follow the attribution. If the attribution precedes a quotation that contains two or more sentences, it should be followed by a colon. Do not use a period after attribution that comes before the quotation:

> **CORRECT:** James Thurber said, "It is better to know some of the questions than all of the answers."
> **CORRECT:** Mark Twain said: "I apologize for writing a long letter. If I'd had more time, I'd have written a shorter one."
> **INCORRECT:** The council member said. "We need to raise the speed limit."
> **REVISED:** The council member said, "We need to raise the speed limit."

When reporters place the attribution after a quotation, they use a comma, not a period, at the end of the quotation and place a period after the attribution to punctuate the entire sentence:

> **INCORRECT:** "I'm feeling better." she said.
> **REVISED:** "I'm feeling better," she said.

The comma or period at the end of the quotation should always be placed inside the quotation marks. This rule has no exceptions. Colons and semicolons should be outside the quotation marks. Whether a question mark or an exclamation point should appear inside or outside the quotation marks depends on the meaning. If the quotation is a question or exclamation, put the question mark or exclamation point inside the quotation marks. Otherwise, leave it outside the quotation marks:

> **CORRECT:** The politician asked, "How much will the program cost?"
> **INCORRECT:** Why did you say, "It's time to leave?"
> **REVISED:** Why did you say, "It's time to leave"?

Capitalization

The first word in a quotation that is a complete sentence is capitalized, but the first word in a partial quotation is not:

> **INCORRECT:** He said, "life is just one damned thing after another."
> **REVISED:** He said, "Life is just one damned thing after another."

> **INCORRECT:** He called journalism "Literature in a hurry."
> **REVISED:** He called journalism "literature in a hurry."

Word Order for Attribution

Journalists put the name of or pronoun for the speaker and the verb of attribution in their normal order, with the subject appearing before the verb. That is the way people talk, and it is usually the most graceful way to write:

> **INCORRECT:** "Hard work is good for you," insisted the executive. "Nobody ever drowned in sweat."
> **REVISED:** "Hard work is good for you," the executive insisted. "Nobody ever drowned in sweat."

However, if you place a long identifying or descriptive phrase after the name of the speaker, the normal word order may be awkward. In that case, place the verb first and the subject second:

> **AWKWARD:** "This project will save you many times the $2 million it will cost," Smith, a 29-year-old architect employed by the Manitoba firm, said.
> **REVISED:** "This project will save you many times the $2 million it will cost," said Smith, a 29-year-old architect employed by the Manitoba firm.

✓ Checklists for Quotations and Attribution

Quotations

1. Use quotations sparingly to emphasize a point or change pace, not to tell the story or state facts.
2. Place only the exact words of the source within quotation marks.
3. Each quotation should serve a purpose, such as reveal the source's character, describe or emphasize a point, or present an opinion.
4. All direct quotations should be clear, concise, relevant, and effective.
5. Avoid awkward combinations of partial and complete quotations.
6. Report only the source's answers, not the questions you asked.
7. Eliminate orphan quotations and floating quotations.
8. Make sure the quotations do not repeat facts reported elsewhere in the story.
9. For a one-paragraph quotation that includes two or more sentences, place the quotation marks only at the beginning and end of the entire quotation, not at the beginning and end of each sentence.
10. Capitalize the first letter of all quotations that are full sentences but not of partial quotations.
11. Divide long quotations into shorter paragraphs; place open quotation marks at the beginning of each paragraph, but place close quotation marks at the end of only the final paragraph.
12. Use single quotation marks for quotations that appear within other quotations.

Attribution

1. Attribute all second-hand information, criticisms, statements about controversial issues, opinions, and all direct and indirect quotations. (Do not attribute undisputed facts.)
2. Punctuate the attribution properly. Put a comma after an attribution introducing a one-sentence quotation and a colon after an attribution introducing two or more sentences of quotation.
3. Put the attribution at or near the beginning of a long quotation.
4. Attribution that appears in the middle of a sentence should come at a natural break rather than interrupt a thought.
5. Vary sentences and paragraphs so that all do not begin with attribution.
6. Place the attribution outside the quotation marks.
7. Attribute each direct quotation only once.
8. Attribute each separate statement of opinion in indirect quotations.
9. Attribute statements only to people, documents, or publications, never to places or institutions.

10. Provide transitions between statements from different sources, particularly when a quotation from one source immediately follows a quotation from a different source.
11. Select the verb of attribution that most accurately describes the source's actual meaning and behaviour.
12. Do not use such verbs as "hope," "feel," "believe," "think," "laugh," "cough," and "cry" for attribution.
13. Make the attribution as concise as possible.

 ## The Writing Coach

Tips on Quotations from *The Globe and Mail Style Book*
By J.A. (Sandy) McFarlane and Warren Clements

Direct quotations add authority to a report, and are our first choice when the speaker is clear and concise, particularly if he or she is also forceful or colourful. But if the speaker is long-winded and confusing, a paraphrase does a better job of conveying information; we can always use partial quotations for important or colourful passages. Here are some points to watch in both direct and indirect quotes:

- If something is enclosed in quotation marks, it should be the speaker's exact words, with the exception of corrected mispronunciations and minor grammatical departures that are common in everyday speech. The spoken "gonna" and "o'" should be changed to "going to" and "of," for example, unless a particular flavour is sought for a feature. However, taking this too far can affect a newspaper's credibility, particularly since the reader may have already heard the statement on TV or radio. An "um" or "ah" may be left out, but we cannot omit such recognizable words as "like" and "you know" and pass off the quote as exact.
- We usually retreat into paraphrase if grammatical and other spoken lapses make a quote rambling or confusing. In particular, do not include such lapses if it will appear that the intention is to hold the speaker up as an uneducated person or user of quaint dialect, except in those very rare stories in which this is the point. Slang may be retained, especially when it is obviously being used for effect, as may regional words and such practices as referring to inanimate things as he or she, but regional pronunciation generally should not be reflected in spelling (pardnuh, de b'y dat builds de boat). This rule applies as well to quotations from people whose first language is not English. Do not retain profanity and vulgarity, even with letters removed, unless there are exceptional circumstances and approval is obtained from the editor-in-chief, deputy editor, Report on Business editor, associate editor, or their deputies.

continued

- There is no way of inserting "[sic]"into a quote without implying that the speaker is misinformed or uneducated, and without bringing readers to an abrupt halt while they figure out the error. If a spoken slip is likely to mislead the reader (as when a person gives a wrong date, or says Second World War instead of First World War), our first choice is to use an indirect quote to report this part of the sentence. If it is vital that the direct quote be used in full regardless of the error (rare indeed is the situation that justifies misleading or confusing the reader even for a moment), we would have to follow the quote immediately with an explanation. We should never call attention to grammatical errors in giving attribution, as in "Mr. Smith said, oblivious to the double negative."

- One common and unacceptable form of straying from the speaker's exact words involves changing tenses and personal pronouns, in effect recasting the quotation into indirect but retaining the quotation marks. For example, if someone says "I will have your jobs," we cannot use quotation marks if we report him saying he would "have their jobs."

- Can a person be misquoted even if we use the exact words? Yes, if we leave out nearby sentences that explain, modify, or qualify the remark, or do not report facial expressions and gestures that might be important parts of the context. An ironic smile or a rolling of the eyes speaks volumes to the reporter, and these must be conveyed to the reader whenever they affect interpretation.

- Do not place quotation marks around statements people "might" have made—a rhetorical device that puts words in their mouths for satirical or argumentative purposes. You may have seen such "hypothetical quotes" elsewhere (in some popular biographies or histories, for example, and even in these their use is controversial). But they are extremely rare in newspapers, whose readers are typically rushed, reading primarily for information and not expecting this sort of nuance.

- In the spirit of "never say never," there may arise some instance in which it is journalistically justifiable to use the device of hypothetical quotes, but we should take care to eliminate all confusion by tipping off the reader beforehand, not afterward, that the quote is not real, and we should set it off typographically (introduced by a colon, perhaps, or in italics if necessary), but not with quotation marks.

- Translations of direct quotes from other languages pose a special problem for our foreign correspondents and for our reporters in Quebec and Ottawa. TV and radio reports can carry the original language at reduced volume as an undertone to the voice of the reporter or translator, a technique that clearly informs the listener that the words are not exactly those of the subject. In print journalism, the lack of a comparable handy device does not reduce our obligation to the reader and the person being quoted. It has become a convention that we may use quotation marks, presenting translations as if they were direct quotes rendered in English, but we should be clear that we have done this.

- If a statement is made on Bulgarian TV, for example, our readers certainly know it was not in English. However, in reporting on interviews, etc. when this is not obvious, *Globe* writers should indicate that the interview was conducted in Spanish, that the news conference was conducted partly or mostly in French, etc. It is then unnecessary to specify the language of each quote, unless this is significant, as when a politician gives conflicting messages to different audiences. (The requirement for indicating that the direct quotes we report are actually translations is relaxed for stories from other sources if it is impossible to determine the original language of the interview or statement.)
- If a colloquial expression makes literal translation of a significant quote difficult, we should inform the reader of the problem and offer the conflicting interpretations. If we have any reason to doubt the accuracy of a translation done by others, we should tell the reader the source (said through an interpreter, etc.).

Source: Excerpted from *The Globe and Mail Style Book*, 9/e by J.A. (Sandy) McFarlane & Warren Clements. Copyright © 2003 The Globe and Mail. Reprinted by permission of McClelland & Stewart, a division of Penguin Random House Canada Limited.

Suggested Readings and Useful Websites

Canadian Association of Journalists. 2011. "Ethics Guidelines." June. Accessed June 15, 2018, http://caj.ca/ethics-guidelines

Cribb, Robert, Dean Jobb, David McKie, and Fred Vallance-Jones. 2014. *Digging Deeper: A Canadian Reporter's Research Guide*, 3rd edn. Don Mills, ON: Oxford University Press.

Jackson, Gordon. 2006. *Watchdogs, Blogs, and Wild Hogs: A Collection of Quotations on the Media*. Spokane, WA: New Media Adventures.

McCarten. James, ed. 2017. *The Canadian Press Stylebook*, 18th edn. Toronto: Canadian Press.

McClelland, Susan. 2009. "Required Elements: Details of Structure." In Ivor Shapiro, ed., *The Bigger Picture: Elements of Feature Writing*, pp. 227–250. Toronto: Emond Montgomery Publications.

McFarlane, J.A., and Warren Clements. 2003. *The Globe and Mail Style Book: A Guide to Language and Usage,* pp. 337–40, 364–70, 382. Toronto: McClelland and Stewart.

Manning, Paul. 2001. *News and News Sources: A Critical Introduction*. Thousand Oaks, CA: Sage Publications.

Mitrovica, Andrew. 2006. "Hear No Evil, Writes No Lies." *The Walrus* magazine. December 12. Updated July 5, 2017. Accessed June 15, 2018, https://thewalrus.ca/hear-no-evil-write-no-lies/

Rosner, Cecil. 2008. "Under Cover, Hidden-Camera, and Gotcha Journalism." In *Behind the Headlines: A History of Investigative Journalism in Canada*, pp. 153–64. Don Mills, ON: Oxford University Press.

Soley, Lawrence. 1992. *The News Shapers: The Sources Who Explain the News*. New York: Praeger.

Exercise 1   Improving Quotations and Attribution

Section I: Avoiding Double Attribution
Rewrite the following sentences, attributing them only once. Correct any other errors.

1. A report issued Tuesday by the Criminal Justice Branch of the B.C. Attorney General's Ministry said the number of serious crimes committed in British Columbia increased slightly last year.
2. Speaking to more than 3,000 people in the Municipal Auditorium, she continued by stating that only the New Democratic Party favours universal health care.
3. Statistics Canada issued a report today stating that, according to data it gathered in 2001, one in every 10 Canadian households is facing housing affordability issues.

Section II: Correcting Placement Errors
Correct the placement of the attribution in the following sentences. Correct any other errors.

1. People under 18, she said, should not be allowed to drive.
2. Another important step is to, she said, lower the books prices.
3. "The average shoplifters are teenage girls who steal for the thrill of it, and housewives who steal items they can use. They don't have to steal; most have plenty of money, but they don't think its a crime. They also think they'll get away with it forever," Valderrama said.

Section III: Condensing Wordy Attribution
The attributions in the following sentences are too wordy. How many of the words can you eliminate? Rewrite the attribution, if necessary. Correct any other errors.

1. She concluded her speech by telling the scouts that the jamboree will be held August 7–13.
2. He was quick to point out the fact that, in his opinion, the finance minister has "failed to act effectively to reduce the federal deficit."
3. She expressed her feelings by explaining that she believes that all those convicted of drunk driving should lose their licences for life.
4. She also went on to point out the fact that the results of federal studies show that, by recycling 1 ton of paper, you can save 17 trees.
5. In a speech to the students Tuesday, he first began by offering them his opinion that their professors should emphasize teaching, not research.
6. He continued by urging his listeners to remember the critical point that the countrys energy policy has failed: that Canada. is not developing alternative fuels, nor conserving existing fuels.

Section IV: Improving Attribution

Correct all the problems in the following attributions and quotations and any other errors.

1. He said: "after a certain number of years, our faces become our biographies".
2. Andy Rooney declared "if dogs could talk, it would take a lot of fun out of owning one".
3. "Because that's where the money is" Willie Sutton answered when asked why he robbed banks.
4. He continued by claiming that there are "two" types of people who complain about their taxes: "men" and "women."
5. "Blessed is he" said W.C. Bennett "who expects no gratitude, for he shall not be disappointed." explained Bennett.
6. Mother Teresa then spoke to the youths, telling them that. "The most terrible poverty is loneliness and the feeling of being unwanted."
7. "My views on birth control" said Robert F. Kennedy "Are somewhat distorted by the fact that I was the seventh of nine children".
8. Being a police officer is not always fun and exciting, says Griffith. "Some things you'd just as soon forget." "Some things you do forget."
9. "The art of taxation." claimed a French statesman long ago "Consists in so plucking the goose as to obtain the most feathers with the least hissing".
10. Dr. Hector Rivera said they test for aids at the clinic "but do not treat the disease." "People come in to be tested scared to death." "Some leave the clinic relieved, and some don't." he said.

Exercise 2   Quotations and Attribution

Wording, Placement, and Punctuation

Answer key provided: see Appendix B.

Make any changes necessary to improve the attribution in the following sentences and paragraphs. Also correct style, spelling, and punctuation errors.

1. "Our goal is peace". claimed the prime minister.
2. Benjamin Franklin said: "death takes no bribes".
3. She said her son refers to her literary endeavours as, "moms writing thing".
4. He is a scuba diver and pilot. He also enjoys skydiving. "I like challenge, something exciting."
5. "The dangers promise to be of indefinite duration." the prime minister said referring to the Mideast crisis.
6. "A free press can of course be good or bad, but, most certainly, without freedom it will never be anything but bad. . . ." "Freedom is nothing else but a chance to

be better, whereas enslavement is a certainty of the worse." said the writer Albert Camus in one of his books.

7. Jesse Owens expressed the opinion that "I think that America has become too athletic." "From Little League to the pro leagues, sports are no longer recreation." "They are big business, and they're drudgery." he continued.

8. The man smiled, "It's a great deal for me." "I expect to double my money," he explained.

9. When asked what she likes most about her job as a newspaper reporter, the woman responded by saying—"I'm not paid much, but the work is important. And it's varied and exciting." She grinned: "Also, I like seeing my byline in the paper."

10. The librarian announced to reporters that the new building "will cost somewhere in the neighbourhood of about $4.6 million."

10 Feature Stories

"A writer has the duty to be good, not lousy; true, not false; lively, not dull; accurate, not full of error. He should tend to lift people up, not lower them down. Writers do not merely reflect and interpret life, they inform and shape life."

—Writer and editor E.B. White in a 1969 interview with *Paris Review**

Most people remember E.B. White as the author of children's books, *Charlotte's Web* and *Stuart Little* to name just two. But beyond this popularity, White is more importantly known as an iconic editor for *The New Yorker* magazine who shaped modern writing. White also co-wrote—with his former university professor William Strunk—*The Elements of Style*, the definitive text on the fundamental principles of writing. Although it was published in 1918, it has been revised many times because it is considered invaluable to writers today for its emphasis on straightforward sentence structure, clarity of style, and depth of storytelling.

Good journalists use all of the elements of style to show the essential human interest of storytelling by taking the audience beyond the nuts and bolts of news—meetings, crimes, fires, or accidents, for example. In order to recognize and use the human element in developing a story's narrative, journalists need to have the abilities to perform the duties White described in the *Paris Review* interview. By having these abilities, journalists can use their craft to write feature stories which have an emotional centre that "inform and shape life" and move beyond the 5Ws plus H of instantaneous reporting on social media. Feature stories inform readers and viewers, but they also amuse, entertain, inspire, and stimulate. Because of these attributes, they are also called human-interest stories.

Features can describe a person, place, process, or idea rather than an event. Their topics might be less timely and less local than those of news stories, but producers and editors find time and space to run them because they are newsworthy and appeal to audiences.

* Source: E.B. White, "The Art of the Essay No. 1." *The Paris Review.* Copyright © *The Paris Review*, 1969, used by permission of The Wylie Agency (UK) Limited.

Reporters who write features use no single story structure, such as the inverted pyramid. In general, features explore topics in greater depth than news stories.

When writing a feature story, journalists can borrow techniques from short stories, often using description, sensory details, quotations, and anecdotes. They might use characterization, scene setting, plot structure, and other novelistic elements to dramatize a story's angle and to add more details.

Feature stories, however, are still a form of journalism; they are not fiction or creative writing. Nothing is made up. Like news stories, features must be factual and original. They must be fair and balanced, based on verified information. They also must be objective.

Selecting a Topic and Gathering Information

The most crucial step in writing a good feature story is making the topic fresh by discovering details and facts that are dramatic, colourful, and exciting. Journalists go to the places they write about and interview people in their customary surroundings. They also do background research to give context to the story. Reporters use all their senses—seeing, hearing, touching, tasting, and smelling. They record how people move, speak, and dress. They use descriptive verbs instead of adjectives and adverbs. They give audience members a reason to care about the subject.

Feature writers find story ideas by being curious and observant. News stories may provide spin-off topics for features. Events such as war, school shootings, and natural disasters can spark human-interest stories about the reactions of victims, heroism in crises, and other human-interest angles that bring the event into sharper focus.

After selecting a topic likely to interest a large audience, reporters must narrow the subject and find a story angle that emphasizes, perhaps, a single person, situation, or episode. For example, a profile cannot summarize a person's entire life, so a reporter will focus on just one aspect with an emotional edge: a single experience, trait, or achievement that sums up the person's character. If reporters fail to identify a story angle, their stories become long, disorganized, and superficial. This can leave readers and viewers confused, and they will quit the story because the point is lost.

While gathering the information for feature stories, reporters normally consult several sources, perhaps four or more, to obtain a well-rounded account. Good reporters gather two or three times as much information as they can need and use the most telling details.

Types of Feature Stories

Feature stories come in a wide variety. The following are a few of the most common types.

Profiles or Personality Features

Profiles describe interesting people. These people may have overcome a disability, had an interesting hobby, pursued an unusual career, or become newsworthy because of what happened to them. To be effective, profiles must do more than list an individual's achievements or important dates in the individual's life. They must reveal the person's character. To gather the necessary information, feature writers often watch their subjects at work, visit them at home, and interview their friends, relatives, and business associates. Completed profiles quote and describe their subjects. The best profiles are so revealing that readers and viewers feel as though they have actually talked to the people.

Here's a shortened version of a profile about Fred Sasakamoose, the first Indigenous NHL player (Figure 10.1). *Globe and Mail* sports reporter Marty Klinkenberg won a National Newspaper Award (NNA) for this piece published December 24, 2016.[1] The NNAs are prestigious annual awards given to Canadian newspaper journalists for their print and online work. In his piece, Klinkenberg shows his audience how Sasakamoose's life was affected when the Canadian government forcibly removed him at the age of six from his family to put him in the residential school system. Klinkenberg sets the scene in his opening paragraphs to show Sasakamoose telling his story. Klinkenberg is the unseen narrator, the observer who uses words to show his readers where they are and the story they are being told. Klinkenberg details the news angles to the story, the context, later in the structure of his article.

Reprinted here with permission of Jason Franson.

Figure 10.1
Fred Sasakamoose was photographed by Jason Franson for the *Globe and Mail* feature story. Sasakamoose stands in front of the house where he was born in 1933 on the Ahtahkakoop Cree Nation in Saskatchewan.

AHTAHKAKOOP CREE NATION, SASK.—A bitter gale whips snow across canola fields that turn gold each summer. It is a cold impossible to brace against, nearly–40 C. Fred Sasakamoose drives slowly along a road on the Ahtahkakoop Cree Nation in central Saskatchewan. He pulls into a driveway, passing a bungalow where relatives live, and stops beside the ruins of the 24-by-24-foot log home where he was born in 1933 on Christmas Day. A pile of tired boards, pitched haphazardly, is all that remains. He was one of 11 kids, only five of whom survived childhood. Four of his siblings—two sets of twins—died of smallpox. There was no electricity when he grew up, only blankets made from rabbit skins to warm him, and a lamp fashioned from rags braided together and soaked in moose fat for light.

"The beginning of my life was here," he says, and tears stream down his cheeks. "My mom and dad lived in that house. Oh gosh, I can't believe it. I can still see them." He presses on, inching his pickup truck down an embankment to the edge of the slough where his grandfather, Alexander, a deaf mute, taught him to skate. He parks, and walks out onto the ice. Wind whistles through spruce trees planted by his parents nearly a century ago.

"My grandpa used to haul me down that trail in a toboggan over there," he says, pointing. "He was the greatest teacher I ever had. He couldn't talk or hear but I understood him very well." When Fred was a toddler, his grandfather slipped five pairs of socks onto his feet, then moccasins. Then he attached tiny bob skates, and set the little boy down gently onto the ice. They spent hours together here, Freddie skating and the old man sitting on top of a pail smiling and watching and lifting his grandson up each time he fell.

"There are a lot of memories," Sasakamoose says, choking back sobs.

If it wasn't for his grandfather, Fred likely would have never become the first aboriginal person to play in the NHL. Called up from the Moose Jaw Canucks near the end of the 1954 season, he played 11 games for the Chicago Blackhawks. He was barely out of his teens when he took faceoffs against Maurice Richard and played against Gordie Howe, Jean Béliveau and Tim Horton.

"At the time, there were 125 players on six teams, and I was one of them," Sasakamoose says. "I succeeded to the highest level you could achieve. I played against the best in the game, perhaps the best that ever played.

"It is unbelievable when you face off against Rocket Richard. His eyes looked at you like a tiger."

It was Fred's grandfather who got him started, carving hockey sticks out of red willow branches that the youngster employed to whack pucks fashioned out of frozen horse droppings. It was the beginning of a journey that has always ended with him longing to return to the reserve an hour north of Prince Albert.

"I think people will understand my story and where I am coming from," Sasakamoose says. "I was striving for success in an outside world that was not meant for me. For me to be in the public life, to be in white society, was very difficult.

"It was hard to continue because my life was always away from my parents. I never received a hug or a kiss for 10 years."

Fred Sasakamoose was six when a priest and an agent from the Department of Indian Affairs took him and his eight-year-old brother from his parents.

Roderick and Sugil Sasakamoose were poor but loving people, and were threatened with jail if they refused to turn their boys over.

"A big truck pulled up out front," Sasakamoose says, sitting beside a fireplace in his living room. "I could hear kids crying. They took us and loaded us into the back. There were about 30 kids.

"There was nothing my parents could do. My grandfather, the one who couldn't talk, was yelling and grabbing for me, but he got pushed aside. He was not a big man."

After a five-hour drive, they arrived at the St. Michael's Indian Residential School at Duck Lake. It is where Fred spent most of the next 10 years.

"We got to a building that was four or five storeys high," he says. "It was so strange and huge. I couldn't believe what I saw. There was a fence surrounding it about eight feet high, with wire at the top.

"The 30 of us got off. I had beautiful braids and so did my brother. My mom was always so delicate, fixing our hair every morning. A priest cut them off. The abuse we received in that school was not human."

Canada's residential school system was established in the 1880s and in existence for more than 100 years.

Over that period, more than 150,000 children were removed from their families and placed in more than 130 schools.

The acts committed led to the largest class-action lawsuit in Canadian history and the formation in 2008 of the Truth and Reconciliation Commission (TRC).

Hearings were conducted across Canada over five years, during which thousands of victims detailed horrendous abuse. In a final report released on Dec. 15, the commission said the residential school system had resulted in a form of cultural genocide. It weakened family ties and led to the loss of pride and respect for aboriginal people.

In 2008, the federal government apologized for its actions, and since then more than $2-billion in reparations have been paid. But no amount of money can undo the damage done. Lives were stolen and families were torn apart.

Historical Features

Historical features commemorate the dates of important events; news organizations also publicize the anniversaries of the births and deaths of famous people. The profile piece of Fred Sasakamoose can also be considered a historical feature because of the story it tells about Canada's residential school system.

Other historical features are tied to current events that generate interest in their topics. If a tornado, flood, or earthquake strikes a city, news organizations are likely to present stories about earlier tornadoes, floods, or earthquakes.

Historical features might also describe landmarks, pioneers, and philosophies; changes in educational, entertainment, medical, and transportation facilities; and trends in an area's housing patterns, food, industries, growth, religions, and wealth.

A historical feature can also have a unique, novelty human-interest angle, such as the shortened version of this CBC story that trended on social media over the holidays in 2017.[2] In this example, sometimes the details of the story are unique enough for only one source to be interviewed to tell the tale.

As Canadians tear open their presents this Christmas morning, there's one dog-eared gift that an Edmonton man won't be opening that came from an old girlfriend who dumped him 47 years ago.

Back in 1970, Adrian Pearce was a 17-year-old Grade 12 student at George S. Henry Secondary School in Don Mills in suburban Toronto, and looking forward to Christmas vacation.

Then his girlfriend—his first serious girlfriend—broke up with him.

"She gave me a present at the same time and I took the present home. I had a long walk home and I was all upset and angry, and all the things you feel when somebody breaks up with you," Pearce recounted.

"And so I fired the present under the Christmas tree. After my family opened their gifts at Christmas, there was still one Christmas gift left and it's the gift this girl Vicki had given me. I told my family I'm never going to open that present."

He never did.

Pearce says Vicki's younger sister approached him a few years after the breakup and gave him some contact numbers, saying Vicki wanted to see him again. He said he saw his old flame a couple of times but they realized they weren't interested in dating again, and soon after they lost touch.

For years, Pearce continued placing the present under the tree, even after he got married and had children. His kids kept asking him if they could open it, but Pearce refused. Eventually, his wife put her foot down and said it wasn't welcome under the tree anymore.

Now, he just pulls out the old gift, which is wrapped in shiny blue paper that's fading, and just looks at it before putting it away again.

Is it a photograph of her? A book? Chocolates? He doesn't know. Some of the tape doesn't stick so well because one year, in a moment of weakness, Pearce started to open it and then stopped himself.

"I kept it initially because I guess I had hopes that we would get back together and open it together. Now it's just become a habit after 47 years of looking at it and having the pleasure of not opening it," Pearce said.

"Maybe I don't want to know what's inside it. It's more exciting right now not opening the thing."

Pearce said his wife is OK with it, and kind of likes the mystery of the unopened present, too, He said he's considering opening it on the 50th anniversary of receiving it and having a contest to guess what's under the wrapping, with a fee to enter and the proceeds going to a Christmas charity.

"Perhaps she can be found and share in the celebration," Pearce said.

Adventure Features

Adventure features describe unusual and exciting experiences—perhaps the story of someone who fought in a war, survived an airplane crash, climbed a mountain, sailed around the world, or experienced another country. Many writers begin with the action—their stories' most interesting and dramatic moments, and use quotations and descriptions. Sometimes the adventure can be a personal reconnection, such as in this story by *Globe and Mail* writer Justin Giovannetti about how he rediscovered and made new bonds with his father during a food tour of his home province of Quebec (Figure 10.2).[3] Giovannetti opens his story with childhood memories of his father. He starts his feature with

Fred Lum/Globe and Mail

Figure 10.2
Photographer Fred Lum's photo of *Globe and Mail* writer Justin Giovannetti, and his father Laurent Lamothe, eating poutine at the Cantine W in Warwick, Que.

the background information to give his readers the context for the father–son adventure. Giovannetti is directly involved in the story, which is told in a first-person narrative structure. But he does not fall into writing opinion. Giovannetti uses his father's words and describes his father's movement and feelings with factual descriptions rather than emotional ones to tell the story.

> I grew up in an ocean of French on the outskirts of Trois-Rivières. However, from an early age, I felt more at ease operating in English, and, though it was never my explicit intention, began focusing on, and absorbing, the culture of my Anglophone mother. It helped that her extended family was emotionally closer to us; I spent most summers in Nova Scotia with my maternal grandparents.
>
> My father, Laurent Lamothe, is a 73-year-old French-Canadian I would describe as *de souche*, old stock. Like many in La Belle Province, he can trace his lineage back to before the arrival of soldiers carrying the British flag. He has broad shoulders from a lifetime of hard labour; and he has little formal education. He left the family farm for work Down East during the Quiet Revolution and came back a few years later with an English girl from the Maritimes on his arm. A federalist, he had no time for Quebec's last independence referendum— but he is a staunch Quebec nationalist nonetheless, proud of his province's culture and language.
>
> As I got older, my dad could only watch in horror as I seemed to inch away from the French side of my family tree. Even my name shifted: The less French I felt, the more the Lamothe half fell out of usage. By my last year in elementary school I was firmly a Giovannetti, plain and simple. The choice would, understandably, remain a sore spot with my father for decades. After I moved to Montreal to study at Concordia, our communications pretty much consisted of a quick monthly phone call that ended with our joint lament for the Montreal Canadiens' weak defence.
>
> Then, in 2013, as I was readying for a move to Toronto to work for The *Globe*, my dad paid me a rare in-person visit, and we chatted awkwardly over dinner in my small Montreal apartment. Staring at my plate of pasta, and searching for something to talk about other than what he called my "move to Canada," I began babbling about poutine. I told him that the dish had always been one of my favourite things about Quebec, and how I would be interested in knowing more about its backstory, beyond the basic fact—on which I'd already stumbled—that a number of Quebeckers in the farmland south and east of Trois-Rivières claimed to have invented the dish in the late 1950s and early 1960s.
>
> "Oh, tell me their names," said my father, suddenly perking up. He might know who they were, he explained: In that same era, in that same region, he had worked at a *fromagerie*, helping to make cheese curds—which, along with french fries and gravy, constitute any *poutine authentique*. He also confessed to having a weak spot for greasy diners back then. His arms began waving as he spoke.

It would take us four years to turn our plan into action. But this past summer, we finally set out on a day-long road trip on the trail of poutine, across the countryside my dad had called home long before I came into his life.

Seasonal Features

Editors and news directors often assign feature stories about seasons and holidays. Stories about international holidays, such as the one below written by Claire Loewen for the *Montreal Gazette* in June 2017,[4] also are informative and entertaining.

Muslims in Montreal and around the world are celebrating the end of the holy month of Ramadan with Eid al-Fitr, a celebration that started Saturday evening.

While the tradition is centuries old, the month of reflection offers those who practise the faith the chance to reflect on the world around them.

Samah Jebbari, a Montreal high school teacher and member of the Canadian Muslim Forum, did things a little differently this year. On top of the traditional Ramadan fast, which lasts from dusk until dawn, she decided not to cook for her children until the food she had already prepared was finished—it was a month of leftovers.

"(My children) really liked the idea because it reminded them every night that, for example, children in Syria don't have this," Jebbari said.

The idea came as a result of the violence and attacks that have happened in the past year, she said. Ramadan gave her an opportunity to discuss the idea of sharing and thinking of others with her students and children.

Fasting can be taxing, but Jebbari wanted to dispel stereotypes that every Muslim is tired during the holy month—which coincided with exam preparation. She made sure to hydrate at night and eat very healthy food.

Along with prayer, charity and faith, a big part of Ramadan is spending time with one's family—Jebbari said she made time with her children—who are 17, 14 and 8—a priority.

"It's a time to reconnect," she said.

Explanatory Features

Explanatory features provide more detailed descriptions or explanations of organizations, activities, trends, or ideas in the news. These stories might localize national events or personalize an issue or event. After news stories describe an act of terrorism, an explanatory feature might highlight individual victims, discussing their lives, hopes, and dreams, or survival through interviews with family and friends. An editor might couple a story about a new science fiction movie with an explanatory feature on the makeup and costumes actors needed to become alien beings.

In 2014, *Globe and Mail* reporters Grant Roberson and Karen Howlett won the NNA for their explanatory work on how a drug patent led to Canada's opioid crisis.[5] Their extensive feature was a multimedia package of content that included graphics, photographs, and sidebar stories. The following is an excerpt from the main story that introduces the audience to the extensive project.

> In the fall of 1992, a relatively unknown pharmaceutical company based in Pickering, Ont., filed a 47-page document with the Canadian Intellectual Property Office, seeking to patent a new invention it said could transform the way doctors treat pain.
>
> Like the millions of patent applications before it, the one filed in Gatineau, Que., by the Canadian subsidiary of U.S. drug giant Purdue Pharma promised remarkable things.
>
> The company's researchers had "surprisingly" discovered a new way to treat pain. Purdue's innovative pill would substantially improve the "efficiency and quality of pain management," because it didn't need to be taken as often as other medications.
>
> Most importantly, it was safer. In a section of the application called "Summary of the Invention," where the benefits of the innovation are recorded, Purdue said its new pill could treat pain "without unacceptable side effects."
>
> The drug was awarded Canadian Patent No. 2,098,738. Its official title in the paperwork was listed as: controlled release oxycodone compositions. But Purdue called it OxyContin.
>
> It would go on to become a blockbuster drug—the most popular long-acting prescription painkiller in Canada for more than a decade, and one of the most lucrative pharmaceutical inventions to hit the market. . . .
>
> This is the story of how Patent '738 sparked the opioid crisis in Canada, with OxyContin serving as the gateway to an epidemic of addiction that has since spread to other, more hazardous substances such as fentanyl. It has left many dead, and many more ravaged by the drug and its implications.

No matter the type of feature story, the fundamental pursuit for a successful journalist is finding the human-interest angle in all kinds of beats and topics—politics, medicine, business, technology, education, and science. In the *Globe and Mail* multimedia piece on opioids, many of the sidebar features focused on paramedics, first responders, families, and victims affected by opioid addiction. Reporters look for individuals affected by the status quo or by change. They look for emotion. The narratives may portray typical conditions or unique aberrations to common systems, but they all include a human element. Reporters gather facts from documents, experts, and individuals affected by a situation to give a story context and to present it on a personal level. They might talk to family and friends of individuals who are subjects for the story. They use quotations, allowing subjects to tell about their experiences and feelings. Journalists go to the scene of the story—a person's home or a place of business, for example. They observe the details found in the physical surroundings and in people's mannerisms and body language. Other elements such as smell, sounds, taste, or texture make the story more interesting and realistic, drawing the reader into the narrative.

Parts of Feature Stories

Journalists can be creative in writing human-interest stories. Skilled writers use different techniques for the lead, body, and ending, depending on the type of feature.

The Lead of a Feature Story

Some features begin with summary leads. However, features also may start with quotations, anecdotes, questions, action, descriptions, shocking facts, delayed leads, or a combination of these alternative leads, which are described in Chapter 7. The only requirements are that the lead interests people, luring them into the story, and that the lead chosen is the best way to start showing the details of the story to be told.

In this Canadian Press story, Morgan Lowrie opens with a description that sets the somber tone for the remembrance service marking the 28 years since the shooting of 14 women at École Polytechnique, also referred to as the Montreal massacre (Figure 10.3).[6]

THE CANADIAN PRESS/Paul Chiasson

Figure 10.3

A woman reflects by the commemorative plaque during a ceremony marking the 28th anniversary of the Montreal Massacre on Dec. 6, 2017, in Montreal.

Bouquets of red, pink and white roses were laid outside École Polytechnique on Wednesday at the foot of a plaque bearing the names of the 14 women who were killed there 28 years ago.

The two dozen or so people who attended the brief outdoor ceremony stood in silence, some wiping away tears as they remembered the Montreal Massacre, when a gunman shot the 14 women to death and injured 14 other people on Dec. 6, 1989.

Industrial engineering student Blanche Mageau-Beland said she believes the anniversary is especially meaningful to the school's female engineering students.

"It's with the presence of those women and all the women who were in engineering before us that we're able to study," she said after the ceremony.

"They're the women who cleared the path."

The Body of a Feature Story

Like the lead, the body of a feature story can take many forms. The inverted-pyramid structure may be appropriate for some features, while chronological order works best for others. The point is to gather all of the details for the story first. Then, based on the details gathered, decide on the best structure to use. The structural support in a feature story must help the story details flow so the journalist is showing not telling the audience the story. The show–don't tell guideline is just as important in feature writing as it is in straight news reporting. The guideline means the journalist shows the audience all of the parts of a story, rather than just tells the facts without background, context, and—particularly in the case of feature writing—nuance. Each of the feature examples used in this chapter use the following structural points to let a story flow by showing, not just telling the details.

Structural Points

Every feature must be coherent. All the facts must fit together smoothly and logically. Transitions must guide the audience from one segment of the story to the next and clearly reveal the relationship between those segments. Transitions should be brief. They might ask a question, announce shifts in time or place, or link ideas by repeating key words or phrases.

Reporters should be concise and never waste their audience's time. Features should emphasize lively details—the action—and they should provide an occasional change of pace. A good reporter never writes a story consisting only of quotations or summaries. Instead, the reporter might use several paragraphs of summary, followed by some quotations to explain an idea, then some description, and finally more quotations or summary.

Good reporters illustrate character and personality. Instead of telling, they show; instead of saying that a person is generous or humorous, reporters should give specific examples of the subject's generosity and humour.

Successful feature writers also use elements such as characterization, setting, plot and subplot, conflict, time, dialogue, and narrative.

Reporters reveal the character of the people they write about with quotations and descriptions of mannerisms, body language, appearance, dress, age, preferences, prejudices, use of personal space, and a host of other traits. The setting reveals the subject's character and provides context for the audience to understand the subject. Geography shapes physical and mental traits, determines lifespan, and influences ways of earning a living. Reporters should tell where a subject grew up, what the person's surroundings are now, and how these factors contribute to who he or she is. Such touches of description sprinkled throughout a story show what the subject is like.

The plot of feature stories is often a description of the obstacles that lie between the subjects of the stories and their goals. The resolution of conflict (frustration induced by the obstacles) presents the theme of every human-interest story. The main variations of the plots are the conflicts between humans and nature, humans and humans, and humans and the inner self. As reporters interview people and ask them about events in their lives, plots naturally emerge. Often a subplot emerges, a secondary line of action that runs in counterpoint to the main action, sometimes helping and sometimes hindering the progress. If a reporter listens and identifies plot and subplot elements as the subject tells the story, a natural order emerges.

Time can be handled in a variety of ways. To organize some types of features, reporters can use a dramatic episode in the present as an opener, then flash back to the beginning of the story and bring it forward in chronological order. Reporters can foreshadow the future or build in a series of flashbacks, arranged in the order in which they happened.

Feature stories need dialogue. Reporters use dialogue to show temperament, plot, events, time, customs, colour, or continuity. They must be careful to choose only the best, most revealing quotations.

Reporters use narrative to weave a story together. Narrative is what summarizes, arranges, creates flow and transitions, and links one idea to the next. Narrative should be unobtrusive and subtle.

The Ending of a Feature Story

A feature should have a satisfying conclusion, perhaps an anecdote, quotation, key word, or phrase repeated in some surprising or meaningful way. Often called the kicker, the ending of a feature story should be given as much consideration as its beginning. Some of the best endings bring the story full circle back to the lead.

One type of profile feature often written by journalists is the obituary. An obituary is not the same as a death notice, which is placed as a type of paid notice in the pages of a newspaper or through a funeral home's website. An obituary is a written feature detailing a prominent person's life—beginning, middle, and end.

This obituary written by the CBC Sports' Bob Elliott about former Toronto Maple Leaf goalie Johnny Bower (Figure 10.4) shows all the elements of feature writing discussed in this chapter, and also how the ending of a well-written piece can bring the audience back to the story's beginning.[7]

Figure 10.4

The late Leafs goaltender Johnny Bower was always generous with an autographed photo for fans.

A man has to trust his barber.

And Johnny Bower trusted Tony Baggetta.

The Maple Leafs legend, who died Dec. 26 at the age of 93, first met Baggetta in the fall of 1961, when he was cutting hair at the Royal York Plaza in Etobicoke.

Ten years later, Baggetta opened Anthony's Family Hairstyling inside the Woodchester Mall on Dundas Street in west Mississauga. There are not a lot of pictures on the wall, but one stands out. A young Baggetta standing beside his barber's chair with the Leafs goalie smiling for the cameras.

Bower eventually moved west to Oakville, but remained a regular until Tony retired in the fall of 2015.

"Johnny Bower was one of the nicest men to ever come into the store," said Rosemarie, Tony's wife. "He had zero anger, he was always smiling and he was such a great guy. He was such a generous man. He always gave of his time. People he didn't know would ask to have their picture taken with him and he would say, 'Of course.'"

Const. Todd Clark, 44, is in his eighth year on the job with the Peel Regional Police.

One Sunday this summer he was assigned to work a charity event, and remembers how he "assumed that it was going to be a bad chore."

Instead, he was assigned to drive Bower to a charity torch ride for Special Olympics and then bring him home.

Bower deserved the special treatment since he was a) the force's first and only honourary chief in the 40-year history of Peel Regional Police, and b) he was Johnny Bower. As honourary chief, Bower was given the same dress uniform as the official chief. A Peel honour guard was there for Bower's funeral.

"I assumed he was living with his daughter, but Mr. Bower answered the door and was pretty spry for a 93-year old," Clark said.

En route, Bower asked Clark questions and Bower told stories.

Like the one about when Bower stole his old cotton Maple Leafs jersey after the final game of a season.

Clark remembers Bower telling him that former Leafs owner Harold Ballard came by to collect the players' jerseys, and in Bower's mind, "I never took anything from them and they never gave anything to me."

As Bower told it, "Just as he gets near me, a writer walks by, Ballard started swearing at him. [I] hid the jersey, went to the showers and then left."

The next day Ballard phoned Bower asking, "Where's your jersey?" Bower told him, "I gave it to you when you were yelling at the writer." Ballard, unsure of what really happened, then let it go.

Bower told the constable that Eddie Shack would ask players to sign his cowboy hat, then sell it for $200 and how Bower's wife, Nancy, banned Shack from the house.

"Mr. Bower said Nancy wouldn't let him in the house because he would use four-letter words and drink our wine, so any time Shack came over, Mr. Bower would stand and talk to him in the driveway," Clark recalled Bower telling him.

Bower told Clark of attending a charity event with Mississauga mayor Hazel McCallion. The mayor would take five shots and if she scored the charity was the winner. However, Bower had a stick and zero equipment, while McCallion was shooting one of those hard, orange balls. And Bower was not wearing a jock and, of course, that is where he was plunked. He allowed the last shot to get past him.

And Bower told Clark how, if he would "let in a stinker of a goal," defenceman Tim Horton would chew him out.

"Mr. Bower said it was only years later that he found out that [Horton] had a bonus for the total number of goals against."

At the Special Olympics event, Bower sat in a chair, posed for pictures and gave out autographed coloured pictures.

"Any time a woman would come along, he would demand to stand up," Clark said. "He was such a gentleman the whole day."

Then deputy chief Brian Adams brought the group together and recognized "one of the best goalies of all time." As Bower headed toward the podium, people clapped and it quickly turned into a standing ovation.

"You should have seen Mr. Bower light up," Clark said. "He had been shuffling all morning, but he walked to the podium with a purposeful stride and his face lit up. His first line was, 'I didn't get a hand like that at the Gardens.'"

On the drive home, Clark told Bower that he also was a goalie.

"Were you any good?" Bower asked.

"Well, Mr. Bower, I had a different strategy, I let the net stop most of my pucks," Clark said, eliciting a laugh from the Hall of Famer.

Clark also worked as a referee, and any time Bower was there for a ceremonial faceoff, he would drop by the referee's room.

"He'd come in with signed pucks and give each official a puck," said Clark, who admits he is a Philadelphia Flyers fan.

"Mr. Bower treated our service really well," Clark said. "He was not a celeb, just a good down-to-earth man. He was an old school gentleman. It's kind of a cliché, but they don't make them like that anymore."

Anthony's Family Hairstyling was sold to Marlene Carrasco 2016. And soon Carrasco had her picture taken with Bower, framed and posted on the wall.

So, outside of a few months, Bower's picture has been hanging from a wall every day inside the shop since 1971 as Cheryl, Big Tony, Luanne, Rose, New Tony, Ron, Johan, Tammy and others went about their work. And it will still hang there now that Bower has passed away.

Carrasco admits she knows more about soccer than hockey.

"I did not follow hockey too much," Carrasco said. "But Johnny Bower was so famous. He was with the Maple Leafs the last time that they won [the Stanley Cup.] He was our VIP. He was so nice, so famous. People would stop, ask him to have a picture taken with him."

Carrasco said Bower was a regular until a couple of months ago.

"The short time I was lucky to meet him it was an honour, he let me take his picture," she said. "Such a nice sweet man. He would give us a hug when he came in the shop. I was upset when I heard he passed. We had heard that he was not doing well."

Bower's picture hangs in such famed places as the Hockey Hall of Fame and the Air Canada Centre, fitting tributes to a legendary NHL career.

And just as fitting is its place in Anthony's Family Hairstyling, and in the many living rooms and offices and thousands of other places where Leafs fans live and remember.

Good journalists gather details and write stories that "inform and shape" life's beginning, middle, and end. These are also the marks of a well-written feature story.

✓ Checklist for Features

1. Select a topic likely to interest a large number of readers. Often a spin-off from a major event can be such a topic.
2. Profiles or personality features should reveal the character of the person about whom they are written.
3. Historical features may be pegged to anniversaries, describe famous leaders or landmarks, or illuminate trends.
4. Adventure features describe what happened to people who had unusual experiences, such as climbing a mountain or surviving a plane crash.
5. Seasonal features are tied to holidays, annual events, or changes in the weather.
6. Explanatory features might illuminate new scientific discoveries or describe how people are coping with the aftermath of a disaster.

7. Feature stories are more likely to use alternative leads—ones that describe a scene or tell an anecdote—than they are to use a summary lead.

8. Features can use an inverted-pyramid form, but often they develop chronologically or use flashbacks or foreshadowing.

9. The ending of a feature story should not summarize the story, but it should use some scene, quotation, or anecdote that brings it to a conclusion. Often the ending hearkens back to the lead.

 ## The Writing Coach

This piece by David Hayes aptly described the show–don't tell guideline that digital journalists use today.

Telling Pictures: Reporting and Reconstructing Scenes

By David Hayes

Early in my career, I was assigned by *Toronto Life* magazine to write a story about pimps and prostitutes in Toronto. In their efforts to charge pimps—who, in addition to being brutal employers, are notoriously elusive—morality squad cops often target their "girls." I tagged along for a couple of nights with two undercover cops and at one point stood inside the tiny rented room belonging to a bespectacled young prostitute, nicknamed "Goggles," who, they knew, was being victimized by a pimp. (As one of the officers pointed out later, she was making several hundred dollars a night, yet neither her surroundings nor her clothing reflected a fraction of that.) Of course, I'd been taught to "show, don't tell" in journalism school, and it was obvious, at this moment, that the details of the young woman's life were telling:

> Goggles is sitting on a narrow cot in a room the size of a walk-in closet. A cracked mirror is propped above an old porcelain sink. A makeshift table is covered in bottles and tins of makeup. There are posters on the walls that might have been taken from the covers of pulp fantasy novels and several photographs of a graceless Goggles modeling department store fashions. A tiny kitten named Minou squeaks querulously under the bed. The room is clean and very neat, as though someone is expecting guests.

When you're in the middle of a scene, the heat of the moment can be distracting. Strangers may stare at you. People may ask why you're there. Resentment, even hostility, may be in the air. It can be hard to stay cool and do your job, and even the most experienced feature writers can miss things that they can never go back and retrieve. Sometimes I repeat a mantra in my head at moments like this: take a deep breath, focus . . . think . . . focus . . . think . . .

continued

When I was standing in Goggles's room, there was another detail that I sensed might be important. Later in the story, this is what I wrote:

> A piece of yellow paper is taped to the wall beside her closet. On it is a handwritten poem that includes the line: Then love still taunts me with its thorny path.

The symbolism might have been too neat for fiction, but when you're writing non-fiction the things that really happen, and are really there, nearly always work. Afterward I always feel exhilarated, almost like a runner's high. It's what I call the thrill of the scene.

"Show, don't tell," the fundamental rule in non-fiction writing as well as fiction, refers in large part to letting action and dialogue reveal information to readers through the use of dramatic scenes. This kind of narrative storytelling has long been published in magazines and used by writers of non-fiction books (not to mention documentary filmmakers). But in recent years there has also been a narrative revolution in newspapers in Canada and the United States as publishers and editors have come to realize that old-fashioned storytelling is the unique strength that print journalism has over other media. At the heart of this kind of reporting and writing is an ability to capture the essence of people, environments, and situations as they unfold.

If "show, don't tell" were as simple as it sounds, aspiring writers could transform themselves into working professionals without much effort. Although words can paint pictures that are rich in vivid detail, learning how to gather those details, when you've gathered enough raw material to tell your story, which details are most important, and where in your manuscript everything should go is what distinguishes the skilled craftsperson from the amateur.

Source: Reproduced with permission from: Ivor Shapiro, ed., *The Bigger Picture: Elements of Feature Writing* (Toronto: Emond Montgomery, 2009), pp.91–94; First published as "Tales from the Track" by David Hayes in *Toronto Life* magazine, January 1985. Copyright © 2009 Emond Montgomery Publications.

 ## The Writing Coach

What Does It Take to Be a Top-Notch Features Writer?
By Bryan Denham, Associate Professor, Clemson University

- Descriptive writing skills. The features writer should be able to "paint a picture" and capture the essence of a subject.
- Good reporting skills. Without the ability to gather information in an efficient manner, the writer will have nothing to discuss.
- Good interviewing skills. It's one thing to conduct a basic interview; it's quite another to draw from a source sensitive or controversial information.

- Good research skills. What, if anything, has been written about the subject you are addressing?
- Respect for sources. Treat people with respect and dignity.
- Ethics. Always use good judgment and attribute quotes carefully.
- Persistence. Good writers don't give up on a story if it gets off to a slow start.
- Confidence. Sources have faith in people who appear confident and professional.
- Experience. The more experiences you have in life, the more perspective you will bring to your writing.
- Curiosity. Great writers are curious about the social world and can distinguish good story ideas from bad ones.
- Eagerness to explore. The best writers crave "small adventures."
- Broad-mindedness. Keep your mind open to new perspectives.
- Appreciation for cultural diversity. Embrace individuals who can offer you insight into different cultural values and traditions.
- Familiarity with trends in popular culture. Always keep "an ear to the ground" and stay attuned to what's going on around you.
- Vision. Great writers can picture how their articles will look in print, and they create the articles to fit in the space allotted for newspaper features.
- Reliability. As with hard news reporting, failure to show up for an interview or return a phone call will undermine your ability to produce good work.
- Appreciation for subtlety. Sometimes the most interesting aspects of an individual do not "leap out" at the writer. Students of the social world and human behaviour can observe things that go straight by others.
- Ability to seek out sources apart from the primary source. If you're profiling someone, for instance, you should talk to a few people who know the person.

Notes

1. Klinkenberg, Marty. 2016. "Survivor, Trailblazer, Leader, Hero." *The Globe and Mail*, December 23. Updated November 12, 2017. Accessed June 15, 2018, https://www.theglobeandmail.com/sports/hockey/fred-sasakamoose/article33409416/. Reprinted with permission of Globe and Mail, Inc.
2. "Edmonton Man Keeps Unopened Christmas Gift from Girl Who Dumped Him 47 Years Ago." 2017. Canadian Press, December 24. Accessed June 15, 2018, http://www.cbc.ca/news/canada/edmonton/edmonton-man-keeps-unopened-christmas-gift-from-girl-who-dumped-him-47-years-ago-1.4464205. CBC Licensing.
3. Giovannetti, Justin. 2017. "Poutine on the Side: A Father and Son Rediscover Each Other on a Québécois Culinary Journey." *Globe and Mail,* December 29. Accessed June 15, 2018, https://www.theglobeandmail.com/news/national/poutine-on-the-side-a-father-and-son-rediscover-each-other-on-a-quebecois-culinaryjourney/article37455104/?click=sf_globefb. Reprinted with permission of Globe and Mail, Inc.
4. Loewen, Claire. 2017. "For Montreal's Muslim Communities Eid al-Fitr Is a Chance to Reflect." *Montreal Gazette*, June 26. Accessed June 15, 2018, http://montrealgazette.com/news/local-news/for-montreals-muslim-communities-eid-al-fitr-is-a-chance-to-reflect. Reprinted with the express permission of: Montreal Gazette, a division of Postmedia Network Inc.
5. Robertson, Grant, and Karen Howlett. 2016. "How a Little Known Patent Sparked an Opioid Crisis. *Globe and Mail*, December 30. Updated November 17, 2017. Accessed June 15, 2018, https://www.theglobeandmail.com/news/investigations/oxycontin/article33448409/. Reprinted with permission of Globe and Mail, Inc.

6.   Lowrie, Morgan. 2017. "Montreal Marks Anniversary of 1989 École Polytechnique Shootings." Canadian Press, December 6. Accessed June 15, 2018, https://www.theglobeandmail.com/news/national/montreal-marks-anniversary-of-1989-ecole-polytechnique-shootings/article37221014/

7.   Elliott, Bob. 2017. "Memories of Johnny Bower Still Warm Hearts of Those Touched by Late Leafs Goalie." CBC Sports. February 2. Accessed June 15, 2018, https://www.cbc.ca/sports/hockey/nhl/johnny-bower-memories-warm-hearts-bob-elliott-1.4517474. CBC Licensing.

Suggested Readings and Useful Websites

Bulguth, Mark. 2015. *That's Why I'm a Journalist: Top Canadian Reporters Tell Their Most Unforgettable Stories.* Madeira Park, B.C.: Douglas and McIntyre.

Clark, Roy Peter. 2006. *Writing Tools: 50 Essential Strategies for Every Writer.* New York: Little, Brown.

Off, Carol. 2017. *All We Leave Behind: A Reporter's Journey into the Lives of Others.* Toronto: Random House.

Popova, Maria. 2012. "E.B. White on the Responsibility and the Role of the Writer." *The Atlantic*, April 17. Accessed June 15, 2018, https://www.theatlantic.com/entertainment/archive/2012/04/eb-white-on-the-responsibility-and-role-of-the-writer/256005/

Rowe, Dan. 2016. *Feature Writing for Journalism and Media Student.* Toronto: Oxford University Press.

Shapiro, Ivor, ed. 2009. *The Bigger Picture: Elements of Feature Writing.* Toronto: Emond Montgomery Publications.

Talaga, Tanya. 2017. *Seven Fallen Feathers: Racism, Death and Hard Truths in a Northern City.* Toronto: Anansi Press.

Poynter Institute: http://www.poynter.org

Exercise 1   Feature Stories

Generating Ideas and Selecting a Topic

1. Canada's national statistical agency, Statistics Canada, has a helpful website to ignite the imagination on story ideas. The department provides economic, social, and census data. Its special-topics areas, studies, and media releases offer history and statistics on many subjects. Get to the home page here: www.statcan.gc.ca. Develop as many stories ideas as you can from latest data releases.

2. The concept of "universal needs" can help reporters choose a topic. Everyone is interested in the needs all human beings have in common and the ways of satisfying these needs. Universal needs are food, clothing, shelter, love, health, approval, belonging, self-esteem, job satisfaction, and entertainment. The following exercise demonstrates how students can use universal needs to find a story idea: Write the universal needs (food, clothing, shelter, love, health, etc.) across

the top of a piece of paper. Down the left side, list some current topics in the news or pressing social issues (concerns of the elderly or students or parents, health care, unemployment, and teen suicide). Draw lines to form a grid. Fill in the spaces in the grid with "hybrid" story ideas created by combining the two topics, such as free medical clinics for students (combining the topics of students and health) or suicide rate among the homeless (combining the topics of self-esteem and unemployment).

3. Listen and observe to find a feature topic. Ride a city bus to the end of the line, or sit in the student union or in a cafeteria. Watch what people do, and listen to what people are talking about. Make a list of potential feature topics.

4. Survey students to get a story idea. Stand in the lobby of the student union or administration building or other popular places on campus, and ask students about their major concerns. If several students have a similar response, you might find that you have a good feature topic and angle. Qualify or narrow your questions to get informative responses. Do you want students to let you know what they think about Canada's policies on climate change, student accommodation on campus, dating practices among teenagers, national politics, or alternative medicine?

5. Read blogs and discussion groups on a news website, citizen journalism website, or other interactive places online. What are the issues people are discussing? What seems to be uppermost on their minds?

6. Google the top 10 searches for the day or week. These topics list subjects that are interesting to people and can provide the seeds of ideas for feature stories.

7. Pair up with another student. Set a timer and write for 10 minutes, completely free and uncensored, about one or more of the following personal topics: pet peeves, things I avoid writing about, things I am curious about, favourite places in my hometown, a specific holiday, my biggest problem as a child (or teenager). Take turns reading your papers aloud to your partner. Discuss how you could conduct research and interviews to make a story from one of the ideas you generated.

8. This time when you pair up with a student, list school experiences, such as advice to first-year students, what you wish you'd known when you first came to your school, good experiences, bad experiences, medical facilities, making friends, and living arrangements. Which ones would generate the most interest for a school newspaper? How would you conduct research, and whom would you interview? What type of research is needed for context?

9. Observe your surroundings as you walk to class. Make a list of 10 potential story ideas, such as dangerous traffic circles, bicycle safety, students who talk on cell phones while walking to class, or places to eat on campus.

10. The Poynter Institute offers this top 10 quick tips to develop story ideas. Develop a list of story ideas using these tips. https://www.poynter.org/news/10-ways-generate-story-ideas

Exercise 2   Feature Stories

Ideas for Campus Features

Here are 20 ideas for feature stories that you can write on your campus. Interview some students affected by the issues as well as authoritative sources.

1. Tuition is increasing nationally. What is the situation on your campus? How are students paying for their education?

2. Do more students today than 10 years ago work to support themselves? What are the numbers of students who work full- or part-time? Do they work on campus or elsewhere? How hard is it to find a job on campus?

3. Is the number of international students increasing on your campus? Compare your local statistics to national levels. Why do international students attend undergraduate or graduate programs in Canada instead of elsewhere?

4. What does your campus to do assimilate international students into the student body? Are international students comfortable pursuing a degree on your campus and in your city?

5. Campuses have counselling centres. Who frequents them the most often—undergraduate, master's, or doctoral students? What are the most common reasons that students visit counselling centres?

6. Students often experience stress while completing a college or university education. Is there a different type of stress associated with undergraduate, master's, or doctoral students?

7. Does your campus have an ombudsman? What are the most frequent problems he or she hears?

8. Many colleges and universities have study-abroad programs in which faculty members take students to another country to study a topic for credit in a particular class. What are the most popular programs? Why are they so popular? Are there programs in warring countries, and if so, what safety provisions are made? You should get some quotations from students who have participated in these programs.

9. Plagiarism and fabrication seem to be increasing on campuses nationally. What is the situation on your campus? Compare it to national figures. What are the punishments for cheating?

10. Think about a national issue or trend, and make a local comparison, using the people on your campus.

11. What are the best part-time jobs for students on your campus? Who earns the most money and enjoys the best hours and benefits? (Students who earn tips—bartenders, baggage handlers, servers in restaurants—often earn hundreds of dollars during weekend shifts.)

12. Write about your institution's use of part-time faculty members. Are part-timers well paid? What are the advantages and disadvantages of employing them? Why do they teach, and compared to your full-time faculty members, how qualified are they?

13. To obtain more practical experience, many students complete internships, and some students must do so. Typically, many interns are not paid. Discuss the advantages and disadvantages of internships.

14. Write about the problems and perceptions of physically challenged students. You might look specifically at the problems of students who are blind or use wheelchairs.

15. If some buildings on your campus are named after individuals, write about several of these individuals, explaining who they were and why they were honoured.

16. What, if any, are the advantages to being an athlete (or an honours student) at your institution? Do athletes have to meet the same entrance requirements as other students? Do they enjoy special housing, food, or financial aid? Do they have special tutors or registration times?

17. How easy is it for the students on your campus to obtain credit cards, how many overspend, and where do they find help?

18. Interview people who come to your campus to interview and hire graduating seniors. What do they look for? What common mistakes should job seekers avoid? What advice would they give students interviewing for jobs?

19. Write about student loans and the ability of students to repay the loans after graduation.

20. Interview the oldest student or faculty member on your campus. What was schooling, fashion, work, or etiquette like when that person was growing up? Choose one topic for an in-depth story.

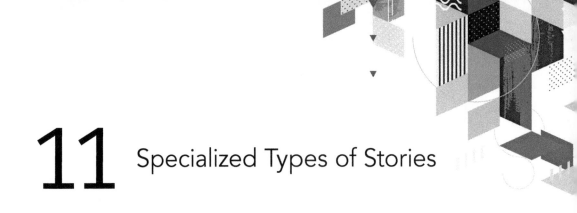

11 Specialized Types of Stories

"Two people, one of whom was a four-year-old boy, spent nearly three hours locked in a UPS store in Moncton, N.B., before the store owner, a UPS manager, RCMP officers and a locksmith were able to get them out."

—Written by online producer/reporter Alexander Quon for Global News, posted September 17, 2017

Rookie reporters assigned to write about a speech or meeting know how to cover an event with a set time and place. But a novice in a newsroom might not know how to write a specialized story. There are two kinds of specialized stories: brights and enhancers. Brights are stories that are novel because the facts are unique, like this Global News report about how long and how many people it took to free two people locked in a UPS store. Enhancers add to the coverage of a news event using different story forms.

Digitization means story forms are constantly changing. This chapter explains the following basic specialized story forms: follows/developing stories, roundups/newsletters, sidebars/graphics, backgrounders, and timelines. In addition, the chapter details content curation and multimedia projects as innovations in digital journalism.

Brights

Brights are short, sometimes humorous stories that surprise. Brights are also often called novelty, oddity, or offbeat stories. Some brights are written in inverted-pyramid style: After a summary lead, the story reports the remaining details in descending order of importance. Other brights have unexpected or bizarre twists, and reporters withhold those twists until the stories' final paragraphs. To keep their endings a surprise, these stories often begin with intriguing or suspenseful facts likely to interest readers but withhold until the end facts that are the most newsworthy or put the rest of the story in a new and surprising light. A bright with a surprise ending cannot begin with a summary lead because it would give away the ending.

Editors and news directors search for brights and display the best ones in their newspapers, news broadcasts, and websites. Brights entertain viewers and readers, arouse their emotions, and provide relief from the seriousness of the world's problems. Here is an example of a bright with a summary lead:

GREENCASTLE, Ind. (AP)—A consonant-loving thief has police and business owners baffled after dozens of Rs were stolen from signs around the community.

"We've lost our Rs. And we want them back," said Randall Jones, president of Headley Hardware.

The weekend caper targeted gas stations, restaurants, repair shops, and medical offices in the city of 10,000 people about 40 miles west of Indianapolis.

The thief also nabbed half a dozen letters from a lighted marquee in front of a National Guard post.

"I don't know if they think it's a joke, but to me it's just theft," said National Guard Sgt. Robert Lamb. "I just think it's disturbing."

Putnam Inn manager Jane Hansen isn't sure how the thief climbed more than six feet off the ground to take Rs from a sign in front of her motel.

"Whoever's doing it needs to put their talents to something more constructive," she said.

Greencastle Police said they've been notified about the stolen letters, but many business owners are choosing not to file reports.

The suspended-interest story that follows begins so routinely that at first it might mislead the audience; its bizarre twist is not revealed until the final paragraphs:

Police killed an intruder after he set off a burglar alarm in a clothing store on Main Street shortly after 1 a.m. today.

Police entered the store after customers in a nearby tavern heard the alarm and surrounded the building until the officers arrived.

Police found the intruder perched on a counter and killed it with a fly swatter.

"It was my third bat this year," declared a police officer triumphantly.

Animals are a favourite topic for brights. One big-city newspaper tracked down rumours that a cat had made its home in a busy subway station. The rumours were true, and the cat had been surviving on mice and tins of cat food left by subway passengers. Other brights draw their humour from the stupid things people do, as in the newspaper story that told of a rookie police officer who left his patrol car running with a suspect handcuffed in the back seat while he investigated a domestic disturbance. The suspect managed to free himself of his cuffs, climbed into the front seat of the car, and drove away.

Writers of brights need to be careful. A story that seems to make fun of a tragedy is tasteless, not funny.

Animal story brighteners are particularly prominent online, as the content can work well on Twitter, Facebook, and Instagram to draw the audience to the media's online news site. But be wary of writing brights for "click bait." Click bait is content that lacks news value, is not factual, and exaggerates, speculates, and sensationalizes to lure people to click on the item. Brights should have news value and be factual.

Enhancers

An enhancer is content that adds to a story in a separate article, either by updating that story after it has been published through follow-up coverage, or by having additional angles to the initial story detailed in smaller content pieces, known as sidebars. Enhancers can also be pieces that are summaries, such as newsletters and roundups that wrap up the news for the day, or highlight a media outlet's coverage of an issue. Another type of enhancer are hyperlinks that link related content to the story. The hyperlinks can also be to content that has been previously been published about the topic. Hyperlinks enhance by giving context and background to previous content, summaries enhance by giving snapshots of news coverage, and the other enhancers accentuate different angles to a story.

Most news stories are enhanced by these types of content. Reporters starting out in newsrooms are expected to know how to produce these content pieces.

Followups/Developing Stories

Followups, which are also called developing stories, report new developments in stories that were reported earlier. Followups were traditionally for newspaper stories when the next-day story would follow up on the first story reported in the paper the day before. Now breaking news is followed as soon as new information becomes available—and that can be every few minutes, even seconds online. The terms "followups" and "developing" are used interchangeably by online and broadcast media.

The Las Vegas massacre in October 2017 where 58 people were killed and hundreds injured by a lone gunman who shot multiple rounds from the 32nd floor of a Las Vegas hotel on crowds attending an outdoor country music festival is an example of breaking news story that was covered minute by minute online and extensively in the weeks after the event by traditional and online media.

Followup stories to the Las Vegas shooting detailed eyewitness accounts, rescue efforts, identification of the person who carried out the attacks, and interviews with friends and family of the victims. Although the followup story is tied to a past event, its lead always emphasizes the latest developments. Followups might summarize previous developments, but that information is presented as concisely as possible and placed later in the story.

Followup stories about disasters are especially common. In the spring of 2017, floods in southern Quebec from melting snow and heavy rainfalls forced the evacuation of many neighbourhoods with more than 2,500 people having to leave their homes. The following examples show the first day coverage of the height of the flood and followup stories in the *Montreal Gazette* (Figure 11.1)*. The paragraphs highlighted in bold show the angles for the followup stories.

FIRST STORY

May 7, 2017—Quebec's once-in-a-century flood appeared to reach its worst on Sunday, but it will be many days before the cresting river levels subside, Quebec's civil protection agency says.

The prognosis for the Montreal region is for river levels to stabilize on Monday and Tuesday, Gilles Desgagnés, regional director for Montreal, Laval, Lanaudière and the Laurentians said on Sunday evening after watching the des Prairies River along the northern edge of Montreal Island rise by 13 to 15 centimetres over the course of the day and inundate new areas that had thus far been spared, including Ahuntsic-Cartierville borough.

"We can say we have reached the peak," Desgagnés said, adding that the rise in water levels had already begun to slow by late Sunday. His agency is part of Quebec's public-safety department.

"It should stabilize on Monday and Tuesday and then it will begin to drop. But it will be very slow. It could take several days, a week or more, for the levels to drop."

The forecast for the next several days, which calls for rain and windy conditions in the Montreal and Laval area, will factor into whether flooding revisits some areas or even advances into new areas if there's strong wind, he said.

Desgagnés called the situation in Quebec "historic" and said the flooding that has punished several parts of the province, including areas of Montreal, is a once-in-a-century event.

"We call it a 100-year flood," he said, adding that it penetrated buildings that had not in living memory ever been flooded. "It happens once every 100 years."

Montreal Mayor Denis Coderre declared a 48-hour state of emergency at 1 p.m. on Sunday when an earlier forecast called for the des Prairies River to rise by 20 centimetres by Monday night.

The state of emergency gives Montreal fire department director Bruno Lachance, whose department serves the city and the island suburbs, the power to force evacuations anywhere on the island if lives are at risk.

Coderre said the agglomeration council, which includes Montreal and the island suburbs, will be convened for a special meeting on Tuesday to decide whether to extend the state of emergency by an additional five days.

The mayor said that municipal authorities are in "observation mode" and not projecting ahead to cleanup plans. But that time will come, he added.

* Excerpts reprinted with the express permission of: Montreal Gazette, a division of Postmedia Network Inc.

THE CANADIAN PRESS/Ryan Remiorz

Figure 11.1
Montreal Mayor Denis Coderre walks through flooded street of Île-Bizard, Quebec.

FOLLOWUP STORY

May 9, 2017—Along with a glimmer of sun and glimpses of blue sky, another rarity emerged from the gloom of this rain-drenched, disastrous Quebec spring Tuesday: signs of hope.

Water levels stabilized and even went down in some regions. The Galipeault Bridge, a major conduit on the western tip of the island that was forced to close Sunday due to high water levels, reopened in the afternoon.

After nearly six weeks of fending off the elements and trying to protect their homes, with and without success, exhausted men and women were caught on camera breaking into tears.

FOLLOWUP STORY

May 9, 2017—Montreal's city and agglomeration councils voted Tuesday morning to extend its local state of emergency, declared Sunday, for another five days.

The vote gives Montreal fire chief Bruno Lachance, who is also responsible for co-ordinating civil security on Montreal Island, the power to shut down roads, requisition personnel or equipment or compel residents to evacuate their homes if their security is deemed at risk.

"First, I'd like to address our citizens," Mayor Denis Coderre told the council. "I understand your frustration, I know when we lose our property . . . when we can't do anything against the force of the flooding, it hits us hard and it's traumatic.

"We're trying as much as we can to save neighbourhoods. But our No. 1 priority is that your lives aren't in danger. We have to ask for your patience, because even if the water level has dropped slightly, there's still a lot to do. And it won't necessarily be easy."

FOLLOWUP STORY

July 5, 2017—Saying that municipal officials continued to work on the issue well after news cameras left the scene, Mayor Denis Coderre pledged to raise concerns and complaints expressed by some Montreal flood victims over the pace of Quebec's assistance plan.

"I've noticed that some of the victims of the flooding are not necessarily happy with the speed with which the compensation is being made and where it seems there's something of a bureaucratic maze," Coderre said Wednesday at a public meeting of the city's executive committee. "I'll ask the Quebec government to make certain verifications. Everybody's working hard, there's supposed to be a certain flexibility in (compensation) programs . . . (but) it seems there are cases (where some victims) find themselves in a particular situation."

Coderre's comments follow several reports detailing complaints from residents in boroughs hit by last May's flood waters. Many residents said that, despite original pledges from the province that their compensation would be a priority for the government, some requests for assistance and information had gone unheeded for weeks.

Coderre said he wants "to send the message to our flooding victims that they're not alone. Whether at the city or borough level, we're there for them. We're working in concert with the Quebec government, but I think we'll ensure that things are proceeding well and not leave people with the impression they've been left on their own because that's not the case."

The mayor said he intends to speak with Quebec public security minister Martin Coiteux about government compensation "to make sure things are working properly . . . We're in solution mode and we'll work accordingly."

Roundups and Newsletters

To save space or time, news organizations summarize several different but related events in roundup stories. Traffic roundups are most common; instead of publishing separate stories about each traffic death that occurs in a single weekend, reporters might summarize several fatal accidents in a single story. News organizations might report all the weekend crimes, fires, drownings, graduation ceremonies, or sports games in roundup stories.

Here is an example of a weekend roundup sports story from the *Saskatoon Star Phoenix*'s website.*

The UBC Thunderbirds were crowned champions of the University of Saskatchewan Huskies men's basketball team's Ron & Jane Graham pre-season tournament at the PAC on the weekend.

The Thunderbirds defeated the Mount Royal Cougars 100–82 on Saturday to run their tournament record to 3–0. The Huskies finished their home tournament 1–2 with their lone win an 85–77 triumph over Mount Royal on Thursday. Lawrence Moore averaged 26.3 points per game for the Huskies.

The Huskies men's hockey team continued their perfect 4–0–0 start to the season with a weekend sweep over the visiting Lethbridge Pronghorns. The Huskies won 4–3 in double overtime on Friday and a 5–2 on Saturday. Logan McVeigh was the second overtime hero. Josh Roach had two goals and two assists for Saskatchewan on Saturday.

Meanwhile the women's hockey team split a weekend set in Lethbridge, falling 2–1 in overtime on Friday while winning 3–1 on Saturday. Pronghorn rookie Ali Borrow scored the overtime winner. Emily Upgang's game winner on Saturday helped the Huskies to improve to 2–1–0.

In soccer action the women came back from a 2–0 deficit to claim a 2–2 draw with the host Fraser Valley Cascades on Friday before being blown out 5–0 by the Trinity Western Spartans. The win was the Spartans ninth straight shutout, a streak which has reached 826 minutes. The Huskies have a 5–3–4 record, good enough for second place in the Prairie Conference.

The Huskie men were shutout 3–0 by host Calgary on Saturday before claiming a 1–1 draw with Mount Royal on Sunday. Tobias Hyrich-Krueger's goal helped the Huskies to improve to 7–5–2, second in Prairie Conference.

Another type of roundup story deals with a single event but incorporates facts from several sources. Reporters might interview half a dozen people to obtain more information about a single topic, to verify the accuracy of facts they have obtained elsewhere, or to obtain new perspectives. Such roundups are often included in another specialized digital story form called the newsletter. The newsletter uses digital media to give the audience a daily roundup of several news events. People can subscribe to a newsletter to be sent to their email or social media feed.

Here's an example of the *Globe and Mail*'s roundup newsletter from Tuesday, Oct. 24, 2017, which led off with that day's release of the federal budget (Figure 11.2).[1] Note the words in bold are links to complete news stories on the *Globe and Mail* website.

Evening Update newsletter: Federal deficit shrinks on strong economic growth, Liberals say in fall update; Quebec softens some provisions of face-covering law Bill 62

---

* Reprinted with the express permission of: Saskatoon StarPhoenix, a division of Postmedia Network Inc.

Good evening,

This is the daily Evening Update newsletter, a roundup of the important stories of the day and what everyone is talking about that will be delivered to your inbox every weekday around 5 p.m. ET. If you're reading this online, or if someone forwarded this e-mail to you, you can sign up for Evening Update and all Globe newsletters **here**. As we continue to grow the newsletter over the coming months we'd love to hear your feedback. Let us know what you **think**.

WHAT YOU NEED TO KNOW

Federal deficit shrinks on strong economic growth, Liberals say in fall update

Finance Minister Bill Morneau gave an **update** on the state of Canada's finances today. In Budget 2017, the deficit was forecast to be $28.5 billion but will now come in at $19.9 billion because of the country's roaring economic growth in 2017. The Liberals also announced increased funding for programs for the middle class and lower-income Canadians. The Canada Child Benefit will be indexed to inflation starting in July 2018, instead of 2020 as was originally planned. The Working

THE CANADIAN PRESS/Adrian Wyld

Figure 11.2
Finance Minister Bill Morneau receives applause after delivering his fall economic statement in the House of Commons in Ottawa, Tuesday, Oct. 24, 2017.

Income Tax Benefit will have a $500-million injection starting in 2019, but the government says that more details would be released in next year's budget.

Here's Campbell Clark's **take** on the update: "Mr. Morneau has had to learn some hard lessons in politics this year, and one of them is that subtlety is not a virtue. The point of making those announcements about the CCB and the WITB now is to claim credit for a good economy, and in doing so, draw attention to the strong economy. If Conservatives in opposition claim it's the wrong prescription, and he should instead have been more cautious, and cut the deficit, Mr. Morneau should be happy to fight that out. That might just put him past those small-business tax troubles." (for subscribers)

And this is what Barrie McKenna **thinks**: "The one thing Canadians can be assured of is that the latest fiscal update will prove to be just as unreliable as the last budget—and the next one—in predicting how big the deficit will be two and three years out, or whether it's likely to shrink or grow. The update projects the budget deficit will shrink to $12.5 billion in 2022–23 from $19.9 billion in 2017–18. A whole lot could happen in the next few months to blow a big hole in these projections." (for subscribers)

The *Globe and Mail*'s newsletter starts up with a roundup of the budget, giving the viewpoint of main source of the story, the federal finance minister, followed by comments from two *Globe and Mail* journalists, which serve as access for subscribers to their columns. The links in the newsletter lead directly to the full stories on the website. The newsletter lists 10 other items that were newsworthy that day and links to each of the stories on those items that are in the newspaper—both the print and online versions.

Some newsletters are structured to not only show the highlights of what is newsworthy but also what is trending on any specific day. "Trending" is a category that has evolved with the growth of digital media. Trending is a measurement tool the media relies on to understand what people are interested in and how to develop content that meets those interests.

In a roundup story, the lead emphasizes the most important or unique developments and ties all the facts together by stressing their common denominator, as in the following example from the Reuters reporting on the tensions of 2016 New Year's Eve celebrations around the world:

European capitals tightened security on Friday ahead of New Year's celebrations, putting up concrete barriers in city centres and boosting police numbers after the Christmas market attack in Berlin that killed 12 people Dec. 19.

In the German capital, police closed the Pariser Platz square in front of the Brandenburg Gate and prepared to deploy 1,700 extra officers, many along a party strip where armoured cars will flank concrete barriers blocking off the area.

The story's lead enhances the urgency of the news value with the security measures being taken in European capitals on the eve of the world's annual celebration. After this lead, the story is structured by detailing what measures each capital city is taking on Dec. 31, 2016.

This security roundup was part of a larger collection of stories covering New Year's Eve 2016. Digital media has increased the number of stories produced on a topic, and easily connects stories on the same topic together, giving the audience instant access to all of the coverage. Traditional newspaper layout is one-dimensional and finite in design. Readers see the photos and stories on a pre-determined number of papers allotted for coverage on a particular news event. With online media, the number of stories connected to one topic are not limited by space considerations. Hyperlinking can be endless. For example, at the end of the Reuters piece on security for European capitals, there was a link to a localized story about the Canadian government's steps to increase security ahead of the New Year's kick-off to the country's 150th birthday. And that story linked back to worldwide fireworks celebrations, which linked back to the European story. And all of these stories linked back to older stories about security, the Berlin attack, and Canada's 150th.

It literally is a web of current and connected content tied together by a click on a keyboard.

Sidebars and Graphics

Sidebars are separate stories that describe developments related to a major event. They are used to break long, complicated stories into shorter, more easily understood ones or to report information of secondary importance. Sidebars can give readers additional information about the main topic, usually from a different source or perspective. They can provide background information, explain a topic's importance, or describe the scene, emphasizing its colour and mood. The following example includes one main story (Conference Board study finds Canada lags when it comes to programs for preschoolers) and one sidebar story (child-care costs in Canada among highest in the world, OECD says)*.

MAIN STORY
Canada is lagging the world in spending on early childhood education—and it's going to cost the economy in the long run, a new report from the Conference Board of Canada suggests.

In a paper published Thursday, the think-tank argues that for every dollar spent on early childhood education programs, the economy gets about $6 worth of economic benefits down the line.

Not only do such programs give kids a head start, but they free up parents to work and increase the family's income, too.

"The science is unquestioning," said Craig Alexander, the group's chief economist and one of the authors of the report.

"There's clear evidence that kids develop better and stronger essential skills," he said, "and we can basically show that this does act to reduce income inequality."

Currently, public education starts at around six years old but "an awful lot of brain development happens in the early years before five," he said.

---

* Main story and sidebar courtesy of CBC Licensing.

Recent changes to parental leave policies now allow some parents to stay off work for up to the first 18 months, but between that and the school years, "we have a gap where parents are left to their own."

The Kenny family of Calgary knows all too well the benefits that come from filling in that gap. The Kennys pay out of pocket for one child in junior kindergarten and one in senior, and they see the benefits of that decision first hand, in terms of helping their kids—as dad Patrick puts it—"to hit the ground running."

"Education is paramount to any child development and what we've experienced is, 'the earlier the better,'" Patrick says.

The numbers back that up.

While Canada does a pretty decent job once kids reach about five, only about 58 per cent of Canadian kids between two and four have access to some sort of educational program. Among developed OECD nations, the average is 69 per cent. In some places—like Belgium, Germany, Croatia, Ireland, and France—it's 90 per cent.

"We should be aiming for more than that," Alexander said.

Publicly funded programs to help get Canada up to the average for kids between two and four would help 134,000 Canadian families. Jumping to among the leaders would boost almost 400,000.

But a key consideration, Alexander says, is that such programs need to be educational focused—not just child-minding.

"Many people see investments in early childhood education as glorified babysitting," Alexander said. "But we're not talking about kids sitting in school rooms. We're talking about play-based learning."

"There's an awful lot that kids can learn through play if you have a good curriculum and a good qualified teacher helping them develop."

Vicki Chamberlain-Polson, a junior kindergarten teacher at Calgary's Webber Academy for the past 15 years, is one such educator who knows the value of play.

"We like to think of play that's like building blocks," she said in an interview. "[They're] learning and building upon what they've already learned."

And the kids aren't the only ones building better foundations for their lives. Early childhood education programs help families by giving them the option of two income providers.

The Conference Board's report shows that after Quebec implemented its subsidized program in 1997, over the next two decades work force participation rate for women in the 20 to 44 age cohort increased from 76 to 85 per cent—much more than it increased by in the rest of the country [Figure 11.3].

That helps buoy the entire economy. In 2015, Canadian families with young children where the mother didn't work made up 43 per cent of low income households, compared with just 12 per cent of those with working mothers, the board noted in its report.

Figure 11.3

Quebec's subsidized child-care program helped boost the female participation rate in the labour force by almost 10 percentage points.

Costs can seem prohibitive to families, but as with many government programs, when they are scaled up to a national level the price comes down.

The Conference Board calculates that creating enough early childhood educational spots to get Canada up to the OECD average would cost $8,162 for every child between two and three, and $6,219 for older four- and five-year-olds.

Add it all up and the report calculates that full day kindergarten for every four-year-old in Canada would cost about $1.8 billion to set up, and about $2 billion a year to run—but it would benefit at least 316,500 kids that are currently disadvantaged.

Alexander says early childhood education is one of the best tools policy makers have at their disposal if they want to make a more equitable yet growing economy.

"We want the economy to expand," he said, "But we want all Canadians to benefit."

SIDEBAR

Canadian families spend almost one-quarter of their income on child care, a ratio that is much higher than in other parts of the world, the Organization for Economic Co-operation and Development says.

In a wide-ranging report on the status of young people around the world, the group of wealthy nations found Canada to be among the most expensive for daycare among its 35 members.

Across the OECD, the average two-income family spends about 15 per cent of its net income on child care. In Canada, that ratio is as high as 22.2 per cent of net income. That's higher than all but five countries that the OECD monitors. The U.K. led the way, where the average two-income family spends 33.8 per cent of its money on child care.

The figure would be even higher were it not for government subsidies and rebates.

And single parents, not surprisingly, fare much worse. Single parents in Canada spend, on average, almost a third or 32 per cent of their income on child care.

Only two countries—the United States and Ireland—fare worse than Canada, with ratios of 52 and 41 per cent of single parents' income on child care.

"Such high costs are a strong deterrent to employment," the paper says. "It may not be financially worthwhile for both partners to work, especially in families with several children."

The OECD says child-care costs are a major issue for young people, since many are forced to take time away from the workforce while their children are young. "It is usually the mother who stays at home," the report says. "Resuming employment after some years out of the workforce is difficult, and women often face wage penalties upon their return to work."

That's bad news for those families, but it's also bad news for the economy and society, as they pay less tax and have less money to spend.

The group says it's a particular issue for what they call NEETs—a term for young people of working age but who are "Not in education, employment, or training." It's a demographic group whose members are at risk of becoming permanently unemployed as they go through life, and likely to pass on that status to their offspring.

The OECD singles out affordable child care as of the easiest and most affordable way of targeting and limiting the number of NEETs.

"NEETs are not only more likely to have lower educational attainment and skills, but are also more likely themselves to have parents with low educational attainment and parents who are out of work," the OECD said. "Ensuring access to high-quality child care can, therefore, help to break the cycle of disadvantage from one generation to the next."

The paper singles out a number of programs for having shown quick and easy benefits:

- In Denmark, municipalities are obliged to offer all children older than six months a place in publicly subsidized child care.
- In Sweden, municipalities must provide at least 15 hours of child care per week to children over one. This obligation rises to full-time hours in cases where both parents are employed or in education.

Figure 11.4 Median monthly child-care fees for infants

Source: CBC News, data from Canadian Centre for Policy Alternatives: http://www.cbc.ca/news/business/child-care-costs-1.3888199

- In Iceland, the government provides greater subsidies for single parents needing child-care spaces.

Sidebars can also be information graphics instead of text pieces. Figure 11.4 was created to illustrate a sidebar issue for the CBC's coverage of the conference board report on preschool programs.

In addition to using information graphics, sidebars are also used to list highlights of a news story or for a question-and-answer (also called Q&As) interview with a person connected or affected by the story.

Here is an example from The Canadian Press of a highlight sidebar from news coverage of the federal Liberal budget tabled in February 2018.

Highlights from Federal Budget 2018

OTTAWA (CP)—Highlights from the federal Liberal budget tabled Tuesday by Finance Minister Bill Morneau:

- "Proactive" pay equity legislation, as well as $3 million over five years for a "pay transparency" measure, to close the wage gap among federal workers and in federally regulated sectors, impacting some 1.2 million people.

- The "Advisory Council on the Implementation of National Pharmacare," to be headed by former Ontario health minister Eric Hoskins, which will explore ways to establish a national drug program.
- $3.2 billion over five years for Canadian science and research, including money for granting councils and Canada Research Chairs, upgrading outdated laboratory facilities, and harnessing the power of "Big Data."
- $2.6 billion over five years for a wide array of measures to encourage and foster scientific innovation and gender equality in the field, including encouraging female entrepreneurs and business leaders, revamping procurement, and expanding access to broadband internet.
- A federal deficit of $18.1 billion, including a $3-billion "risk adjustment," down from $19.3 billion last year, that's projected to decline slowly over the next several years, reaching $12.3 billion ($9.3 billion without the $3-billion cushion) by 2022–23.
- About $1.4 billion over six years to support Indigenous children in foster care and promote family reunification, plus $400 million over 10 years to upgrade and expand Inuit housing and $500 million for Métis housing.
- Higher excise taxes on tobacco products, including a $1 increase on a carton of 200 cigarettes and an adjustment that would see taxes increase with inflation every year, rather than every five years.
- $1.2 billion over five years and $344.7 million a year afterward for a new employment insurance parental sharing benefit that would provide additional "use-it-or-lose-it" benefits for non-birthing parents to encourage women to re-enter the workforce.
- $2 billion over five years for international aid through a new International Assistance Innovation program, designed to come up with flexible new financing arrangements, and the Sovereign Loans program.
- $155.2 million over five years for a new Canadian Centre for Cyber Security and $116 million over five years for the RCMP to create a National Cybercrime Co-ordination Unit.
- $448.5 million over five years to double the number of placements under the Canada Summer Jobs program by 2019–20.
- $172 million over five years and $42.5 million a year afterward for the Canada Media Fund to foster the growth of Canadian-produced content.
- $50 million over five years to support "local journalism in underserved communities," and plans to explore new models that would allow private and philanthropic support for "non-profit" journalism, including allowing Canadian newspapers to receive charitable status.
- $75 million over five years, with $11.8 million a year afterward, to bolster Canada's trade ties with China and Asia.
- $191 million over five years to support jobs in the softwood lumber industry, including litigation under the World Trade Organization and NAFTA's dispute resolution mechanism.

- $90.6 million over five years to track down tax evaders and avoiders, plus $41.9 million over five years and $9.3 million a year thereafter to help Canada's courts deal with the additional caseload.
- Changes to income sprinkling, passive investment income, and the small business tax rate that are expected to save the government $925 million a year by 2022–23.
- $173.2 million in 2018–19 to support claim processing and to improve border security to better manage the increased number of people seeking asylum in Canada.

This sidebar is a text piece that would also be turned into an information graphic. Displaying data and figures with graphic illustrations can also help the audience understand the material.

Backgrounders and Timelines

Terms in journalism are literal at best. Backgrounders are just that—articles that give the background information of a particular news story. Backgrounders are usually longer form pieces that take an aspect of a main news story and go into greater detail about that aspect. In coverage of the Las Vegas shooting, there were backgrounders done on U.S. gun laws, mass shootings in that country, and on the killer himself.

Here is a backgrounder written for the *Washington Post* by Dan Zak a week after the shooting at the Mandalay Bay hotel in Las Vegas.[2]

> "Ship me somewheres east of Suez, where the best is like the worst, Where there aren't no Ten Commandments an' a man can raise a thirst . . ."
> —Rudyard Kipling, "Mandalay"

LAS VEGAS—The original name was Project Paradise. It was to be a 42-storey, billion-dollar resort featuring "an exotic South Seas theme," a swim-up shark exhibit and a trefoil footprint with a facade of gold leaf. By the time it was built on the burial ground of the 11-story Hacienda—an antique family-centric hotel and casino that was imploded on live TV on New Year's Eve 1996—Project Paradise had been renamed after a British poet's nostalgic (and imperial) ode to the exoticism of south Asia.

Mandalay Bay is "a world of escape where entertainment has the edge over reality," said the president of its parent company when it opened on March 2, 1999, in the new era of the Vegas mega-resort—a place where you can eat, shop, sleep, dance, go to the beach, get a tattoo, get a facial, get married, win a fortune, lose your shirt, drink your heartache away, see a prizefight, see a Broadway show.

"It's the embodiment of today's Las Vegas" says Thomas LaBue.

"You don't have to leave if you don't want to," says Joni Seto.

The 26th floor. Seto, 29, and her fiancé, LaBue, 32, are both entrepreneurs from Los Angeles. They love Mandalay Bay. Their room's floor-to-ceiling windows overlook everything. Straight ahead, the Luxor's Sphinx and the deep-focus length of the glittering strip. To the left, one of the windows blown out by the mass shooter, a jagged black blemish in the gold. To the right, the concert venue, empty except for the hoodies and beer cans and camping chairs left behind by the fleeing and the dying. When hysterical concertgoers stormed in, Seto and LaBue raced to a basement kitchen.

"I thought maybe we'd hide in the fridge," says LaBue.

"And I thought, 'There's no way I'm dying in a fridge,'" says Seto.

Here, they are not tourists. They are resortists, which is what Mandalay calls its guests. It was their first time back in two years, but a bellhop remembered their names and a cocktail waitress remembered their drinks. Mandalay remembers all their bets, too; it tracks them via electronic rewards cards. They prefer high-stakes baccarat. Their stay is fully comped. They have a host to manage their needs.

Yes, Mandalay Bay is open for business. It never closed. There are no memorials inside Mandalay—but then, no innocent deaths happened inside Mandalay. Instead there are discreet black placards offering counseling. Seto and LaBue took advantage of it Tuesday. There was a vast empty ballroom and counselors at far-flung tables and handouts titled "COPING AFTER A CRISIS."

They love Mandalay Bay.

"If there's any issue," LaBue says, "they will correct it."

"It's like two separate worlds," Seto says, after flinching at the sound of a police siren 26 stories below. "Inside, and out."

Vegas is full of mini-civilizations. Circus Circus is for middle-class families. Aria is definitely on the bougie side. The Linq is for college revelers. The Wynn, the Venetian, the Bellagio—the clientele's a bit old, kind of posh. Caesar's is garish, the Tropicana's homely. The three MGM-owned resorts on this end of the strip ascend in order of ritziness as you move south: Excalibur, then Luxor, then Mandalay Bay—the grandest of the trio, and the first resort Californians hit on their way into town.

Nevada had a monopoly on gambling until New Jersey legalized it for Atlantic City in the 1970s, forcing Las Vegas to strategize. What else could they offer, besides poker and blackjack and roulette?

The answer: Everything.

"And that's what you see with Mandalay Bay and other properties of the 1990s—whether it's entertainment, or high-end shopping, or the nightclubs or the pools," says Michael Green, associate professor of history at the University of Nevada at Las Vegas. "Mandalay Bay is part of a movement in that direction: the notion that you can go somewhere and you can bathe in an Egyptian pyramid, or whatever else you might want."

Mandalay Bay has 3,039 hotel rooms. The casino is 130,000 square feet; the adjoining convention space is 2 million. Five of Mandalay Bay's upper floors are actually a Four Seasons, a caste within a caste. Just below those floors was the temporary and final home of Stephen Craig Paddock, a lover of casinos and mass murder, now linked forever to the strip's southernmost resort, the safe haven from which death rained down.

"Las Vegas is one of the best, the safest, in terms of surveillance and security," says Norm Clarke, a veteran Associated Press reporter and former *Las Vegas Review-Journal* gossip columnist. "But they always thought the threat would come through the door, not from above. And that's changed the dynamic."

There are security officers at each of the lobby's three elevator bays. There is crime-scene tape across a couple of exits.

There have been no cancellations at Mandalay's wedding chapel as of Wednesday. But on Monday, several companies recalled their people from a data convention being held among huge multipurpose rooms with names like Lagoon, Islander and Shellseeker. Mandalay Bay is a conventioneer's resort, despite its quarter-mile walks between activities.

"The layout is jacked," complains one conventioneer from the East Coast, on his way from the craps table Wednesday evening to get a Sazerac. "I mean, I don't mind, but the women wear heels. The layout in the Aria is better because the conference space is vertical."

He was asleep a couple floors below the shooter and didn't wake up until SWAT barreled into his room at 3:30 a.m. Monday.

"Vegas is surreal no matter where you are," he says, ashing a Marlboro right on the stone bar. "Mandalay at least has some class."

Mandalay may have some class, but that's only because it has everything. It has "Walking Dead" slots and Elvira slots and a high-stakes slot room that no one ever seems to occupy. It has sushi, Wolfgang Puck, a headless statue of Lenin near a Russia-themed restaurant, a 10-foot statue of Michael Jackson on a 10-foot pedestal in the lobby, a shop named Essentials that sells $60 "Earth-friendly" headphones, and a beach-like pool whose artificial wave system was said to have been operated at one point by a man named Moses. Walking around the casino floor must be what the early stages of Alzheimer's feels like; everything looks vaguely familiar and strangely alien, and you're in a constant state of being vaguely lost and strangely soothed.

It is stimulant and tranquilizer.

There is no Mandalay Bay aesthetic, because it has every aesthetic—art deco, mid-century modern, 1980s brass works, 1990s proportions—until you meander into the Four Seasons wing, and the busy blues and golds and reds, and the Jurassic-scale foliage, quickly give way to grays and creams and orchids and succulents. This is how they tell you that you don't belong: They make you feel it.

Back to Mandalay.

"The smell here," says Lori Bubenicek, who works for Hilton in Illinois and is in town for a convention of the wedding-industrial complex. "You smell it?"

No . . .

Exactly, she says. "You walk into other hotels and smell smoke."

In Mandalay, you smell nothing. Or is it everything? Here you smell the sweetness of industrial cleaner, the savoriness of the buffet, the perfume of a passing waitress in her teal miniskirt uniform—but not in offensive quantities, and never for too long. Here, strands of crystal in the chandeliers get wiped in the middle of the night. The footrests at the slot machines get scrubbed with a small brush.

It's always just a little too cold.

"All eyes are on guest operations right now," emails Yvette Monet, corporate communications manager for MGM Resorts International, Mandalay's parent company, while declining to comment further. "I am sorry about that. One thing I can tell you is that Mandalay Bay pays close attention to its Wikipedia page to ensure accuracy."

The Wikipedia page says Mandalay Bay was the setting of a "Modern Family" episode in 2014, and used for various shots in "Ocean's Eleven," "Ocean's Thirteen" and "The Hangover." It has "the largest unobstructed ballroom" in the country, at 100,000 square feet—nearly twice the floor space of the entire White House. The page has a section titled "2017 shooting," though there's no mention of the only other comparable Vegas tragedy, in terms of casualties: the 1980 fire at the former MGM Grand, where the blaze travelled the 100-yard casino floor in less than 20 seconds, eventually killing 85 people and injuring 650.

"It led to a revolution in Nevada in fire safety," says Green, the UNLV professor.

"The question was, 'Is this fire going to kill Las Vegas? Will this scare people away?'" says Clarke, who was reporting for the AP that day. "So I went to a pit boss in the casino—and it was deserted just like on 9/11—and I asked . . . and he just kind of gave me a little laugh and said, 'The only thing stronger than garlic is gambling. Vegas will survive.'"

And so it does. Mandalay Bay is getting back to normal, after a Monday that one resortist called "morose" and a Tuesday that another called "surreal."

About 8:15 p.m. Wednesday, Billy Idol took the stage in the House of Blues, a venue that's kind of plopped in the middle of Mandalay Bay, about 200 feet from where the Sinatra impressionist is appearing, near the escalators to the Luxor (if you want to bathe in a pyramid). This is the first night of Idol's residency in Mandalay. Idol thought briefly about cancelling the show but then realized that the shooting victims had gathered to hear music, and so he should play his own, in tribute.

"They came to Vegas to have that experience," he says from the stage, about the victims. "They love this place." And then, about reality intruding on entertainment: "They can't break me! And they can't break Las Vegas!"

Backgrounders are often enhanced with timelines which are used as graphic representations of important moments in the narrative. Timelines are illustrated using still photos, videos, and audio clips. Examples of timelines are provided as links in the Suggested Readings and Useful Websites section at the end of this chapter.

An innovation in timelines was developed by the *New York Times* in its followup coverage of the Las Vegas massacre. The *Times* developed a way of showing the timeline of the shooter's rampage by gathering all of the visual and audio clips on social media, and researching other source material from officials involved in the investigation to compile a video piece that digitally mapped what happened second by second in the 10-minute rampage.

Content Curation

As the *Times*' Las Vegas timeline project shows, digital media delivers information every second from multiple platforms. This endless supply of information means reporters have more potential sources of information and more ways to access those sources. As a reporter's means of gathering and verifying information has increased, so have the ways of presenting those stories. Content curation means gathering content from social media platforms and using that content to build another story. The term "content curation" comes from the original role of a newspaper rewrite editor. A rewrite editor had many jobs, one of them being to compile stories using information gathered by other news organizations. Before the internet became a tool in newsrooms in 1995, rewrite editors would be responsible for putting together stories if their own newsroom could not assign a reporter to cover it. A rewrite editor would take a breaking news story from the Canadian Press wire service, and monitor television and radio news casts to gather more information. Using these three sources, the rewrite editor would put together a story, making sure to give proper attribution to CP and the broadcast media sources used in the rewrite story.

Today this happens on a wider media landscape and takes less time to do because of digital media. Rewriting has become curation because there is so much more information to sort through to determine what is fact and what is speculation before writing a credible story.

Twitter is a valuable content curation tool. Using free applications such as TweetDeck, journalists can search for tweets about specific news topics from credible sources by using key words and following trusted news sites and sources on Twitter.

Reporters also use Twitter to take their notes to help them later when they write their full text stories. Reporters covering speeches, meetings, court cases, and other set events also use Twitter to send immediate updates on the event as new facts emerge. Live-tweeting helps in two ways—as the reporter's notes, and informing the public and other media outlets of what is happening at the news events.

Other reporters and people can retweet the reporter's original tweet and help spread the information.

Another method of curation is using an application service that helps create stories from social media postings. These applications work by gathering the best photos, videos,

GIFs, and tweets about a specific topic that the reporter uses to weave a selection of the best of these social media bits into a story form to explain the news event to the audience.

Multimedia

Text, audio, and visuals were aligned with their media—text and photographs were print, and video and audio were broadcast. But digitalization was the great harmonization of these two media streams which meant they all came together into one form, providing more storytelling options.

A multimedia story is one that uses words, pictures moving and still, and audio to give the audience many layers to take in information. The multimedia approach gives nuances and levels of meaning to a story that lets journalists go deeper in their reporting and have a stronger relationship with the audience. The audience is given more entry points into the narrative—and has a deeper understanding of that story.

A groundbreaking multimedia project was done by the *New York Times* in 2012. "Snow Fall: The Avalanche at Tunnel Creek" tells the story of the skiers caught in an avalanche in a pass in the Cascade Mountains in Washington state. The multi-chapter series written by features reporter John Branch weaves text with video, photos, and graphics seamlessly and gives the audience the feeling of being immersed in the story.

Reaction to this innovation in journalism was wide-ranging. Margaret Sullivan wrote in the *New York Times* public editor's journal about the piece:

> The effort . . . received around 2.9 million visits, and the visitors shared some qualities that are much desired by the *Times*. First, many of them—maybe as many as one-third—were new visitors to the *Times*. Second, they spent a lot of time with the project, about 12 minutes, which amounts to eons for a single digital story.
>
> In an e-mail to the newsroom, Jill Abramson, the executive editor, called it a "wildly new reading experience." She summed it up by noting that "rarely have we been able to create a compelling destination outside the home page that was so engaging in such a short period of time on the web."

The series had such an impact that the "snowfall effect" became a term journalists started to use for this type of long-form immersive journalism.

✔ Checklists for Writing Specialized Stories

Brights

1. Choose either an inverted-pyramid style or a suspended-interest style for the story.
2. If you use a suspended-interest approach, write a lead that will intrigue readers without revealing the bizarre or amusing twist the story takes at the end.

Followups

1. Write a followup each time something newsworthy develops in a continuing story.
2. Stress the new developments in the lead and body of the story.
3. Summarize the important background and earlier developments.

Roundups

1. Emphasize the most important or unique incident or development in the lead.
2. Explain in the lead what is common to all the incidents reported in the roundup.
3. Organize facts and quotations by topic, not by source.

Sidebars

1. Focus the lead on background, colour, mood, or some other aspect of the story different from the one emphasized in the lead to the main story.
2. Summarize the news event described in the main story.

 The Writing Coach

Interview with John Branch

Capilano University student Taylor Campbell had a Q&A interview over email in 2014 with *New York Times* feature writer John Branch. The interview was conducted as part of Campbell's graduation project on digital journalism.

The following interview took place on Monday, November 10, 2014, and was conducted over email. The questions asked were specific to writing as a journalist for a digitally produced story, namely, "Snow Fall: The Avalanche at Tunnel Creek."

Taylor Campbell: Was "Snow Fall" always meant to be a digital piece from its conception? If so, what was the reasoning behind that decision?

John Branch: Not at all. The story started as most stories do: Something happens, and we go check it out. It wasn't until I had done about two months of reporting that there was any consideration for something different. I had done many, many interviews, and I was trying to make sense of everyone's version of events and how they matched up with one another and with all the records of the day—911 calls, text messages, time stamps on GoPro videos, police/sheriff reports, etc. Mostly for my own sanity, I created a minute-by-minute timeline, and cut and pasted all the info I had into it. In the end, I had a huge file, a minute-by-minute (roughly)

continued

account, told through the words of the survivors. I had moved from New York to California in the middle of all this, and to show my editors that I had been plugging away, I sent them that file—something I've never done before. They read through it and found it compelling, and then passed on the file to the heads of several NYT departments—graphics, interactive, photo, video. The message was essentially this: "Branch is working on something that we think could be quite compelling, and we'd love your help on this. Take a look and let us know what you think." And then is when the size and scope of the project changed. A few guys on our multimedia team saw potential in doing something out of the ordinary.

Taylor Campbell: To what extent did you as the writer have control over the story? (Such as anything including font size, page layout, video and audio format?) Likewise, how much thought goes into the level of control the reader has while viewing the article?

John Branch: I'd like to think I had total control of the story. All the words were mine, and they were not changed to accommodate the various multimedia elements. But how those words are presented were (and always are) mostly out of my control. We don't write headlines or captions, for example. In this case, I was basically a consultant as the digital piece was being designed (and, it's important to note, "Snow Fall" was also a 14-page special section in print, which was extraordinary in its own way). I had many conversations with the graphic artists and designers along the way, mostly on the graphic elements. As for the "look" of the piece, mine was just one opinion.

Taylor Campbell: Does a project of this magnitude require a team? If so, how large and what was the composition? What kinds of costs are required for a project like this?

John Branch: Yes, of course, there was a team. In the end, I think 16 people had a hand in it. I was involved from start to finish. A photographer and video journalist were assigned to it fairly early. And then, once we decided on which graphics to construct, about 6–8 graphic artists got involved. There were page designers and 2–3 coders, applying the digital magic to all forms of devices (various browsers, from IBM desktops to iPhones, etc.). We've never added up the number of hours or the costs involved. We don't divide our work that way. (I can't, for example, even guess how many hours I've been working on a current project. We don't sign in and sign out when we move from one story to another, which might happen many times in a day.)

Taylor Campbell: As a story that includes multiple forms of media, why choose to keep the videos, audio clips, and imagery as supplementary information as opposed to integral elements to the story? Was this an author's decision?

John Branch: Ha. I would say that they were/are "integral" parts of the story. But I know what you mean. Those are decisions made by our interactive web editors and graphics editors. As it is, most of the elements start playing without prompting from the reader; it is the flashing cursor that triggers photos or parts of graphics. There was talk of making this something that could be viewed/read without a mouse click. But that proved a bit elusive. Should videos just start playing while someone is reading? Should the voice of the interview subject replace the text words? But people engage in different ways, in different places. What if someone is at work and doesn't have the sound up? What if they are looking at an iPhone, not a laptop? Certain limitations were put in place. The reader can't just sit back and experience it, entirely, as if it's a movie.

Taylor Campbell: What does a lengthier, investigative narrative format achieve with regards to "Snow Fall," as opposed to a shorter piece?

John Branch: Detail. Context. Richness. Could "Snow Fall" have been 1,000 words, like a typical NYT story, instead of 17,000? Of course. But you'd probably have a news story, with quotes from a few people about what happened. And readers would have digested it and, more than likely, forgotten it shortly after clicking on the next 1,000-word story. We felt this story deserved a full airing, from all the perspectives, to make it both more compelling and more educational.

Taylor Campbell: Did writing for a digital medium alter your writing process? If it did, in what ways?

John Branch: No. For a short time, there was talk that we might change chapter breaks, or alter transitions as the text blended into graphics or photos or whatever. In the end, we didn't do it, because it didn't seem necessary. But I imagine those are the types of conversations we'll have, more and more, in the coming months and years.

Taylor Campbell: With the flexibility that the digital medium offers, can aspects of journalism such as the lead or the hook on a new form in an image or video for example?

John Branch: Sure. I think we're limited only by our imagination, and we're learning that the "old" way of presenting or structuring a story does not always need to apply. I've joked that "Snow Fall," if not the longest story the NYT has ever run (it's close), is certainly the longest without a nut graph. You have to read, what, 15,000 words before you know who lives and who dies. That's not very newspaper-like.

Taylor Campbell: Are there any pieces that you have read that you feel have fully taken advantage of the tools offered by the digital medium?

John Branch: I'm a writer, so I'm not out searching for digital pieces. But many of them get passed on to me, because of "Snow Fall." And I'm proud that "Snow Fall" holds up so well after two years. I've seen lots of imitators, but they all seem to be forgetting the core magic of "Snow Fall"—each element added to the story, provided extra

continued

information. The graphics were visual storytelling elements, built in science and data and research. Most "Snow Fall" imitators seem to try to emulate the look, but do it with nothing more than large photos and slowly moving, evocative photos. Those are bells and whistles. Nothing about "Snow Fall" was done simply to dazzle the reader. Each element was specifically designed to inform the reader. That's a huge difference.

Notes

1. *Globe and Mail* newsletter, October 24, 2017: https://beta.theglobeandmail.com/news/national/evening-update-newsletter-federal-deficit-shrinks-on-strong-economic-growth-liberals-say-in-fall-update-quebec-softens-some-provisions-of-face-covering-law-bill-62/article36705284/?ref=http://www.theglobeandmail.com&

2. Zak, Dan. "Mandalay Bay embodied everything modern Las Vegas wanted to be. Until this week." The Washington Post. 5 October 2017. https://www.washingtonpost.com/lifestyle/style/mandalay-bay-embodied-everything-modern-las-vegas-wanted-to-be-until-this-week/2017/10/05/b55170ba-a990-11e7-b3aa-c0e2e1d41e38_story.html?utm_term=.0cb7123b57e7. Reprinted with permission of Washington Post News Media Services; permission conveyed via Copyright Clearance Center, Inc.

Suggested Readings and Useful Websites

Boynton, Robert, ed. 2005. *The New New Journalism: Conversations with America's Best Nonfiction Writers on Their Craft.* New York: Vintage Books.

Branch, John. 2012. "Snow Fall: The Avalanche at Tunnel Creek." *New York Times.* Accessed June 20, 2017, http://www.nytimes.com/projects/2012/snow-fall/#/?part=tunnel-creek

Browne, Malachy, 2017. "Reporting on Las Vegas, Pixel by Pixel." *New York Times*, October 23. Accessed June 20, 2018, https://www.nytimes.com/2017/10/23/insider/reporting-on-las-vegas-pixel-by-pixel.html?_r=0

Campbell, Taylor Adam. 2014. "A Study on Digital Journalism." Updated December 14, 2014. Accessed June 20, 2018, http://scalar.usc.edu/works/digital-journalism/index

Ellis, Sherry. 2009. *Now Write! Nonfiction: Memoir, Journalism, and Creative Nonfiction Exercises from Today's Best Writers and Teachers.* New York: Tarcher.

Grabowicz, Paul, Richard Hernandez, and Jeremy Rue. 2014. "Tutorial: Taxonomy of Digital Story Packages." UC Berkeley, Graduate School of Journalism, Advance Media Institute. Accessed June 20, 2018, https://multimedia.journalism.berkeley.edu/tutorials/taxonomy-digital-story-packages/

McCarten, James, ed. 2015. *The Canadian Press Caps and Spelling,* 21st edn. Toronto: The Canadian Press.

———. 2017. *The Canadian Press Stylebook: A Guide for Writers and Editors,* 18th edn. Toronto: The Canadian Press.

Shapiro, Ivor, ed. 2009. *The Bigger Picture: Elements of Feature Writing.* Toronto: Emond Montgomery Publications.

Lin, Mu. MulinBlog: A Digital Journalism Blog: http://www.mulinblog.com/

Exercise 1　Specialized Types of Stories

Brights

Use the following information to write brights, taking care not to reproduce any errors (e.g., spelling, style) that might appear in the information. Write some brights with a summary lead and others with a surprise ending.

Squirrels

University officials are blaming squirrels for a rash of problems students, teachers, and staff members have been experiencing with their cars. One person whose car has been damaged by squirrels is Oliver Brooks, an associate professor of English. One of the headlights in his van went out a few weeks ago. He replaced it, but it still didn't work. When he opened the hood, however, he was surprised to find a squirrel's nest. "There was a big squirrels nest in the corner where the light wires were," he said. Brookes spent $184 to get the wiring replaced. Linda Kasparov, university dietitian, had a similar experience. She was driving home one night when the headlights, speedometer, and oil-pressure gauge on her new sedan all quit working. She pulled into a service station and asked the attendant what was wrong. She said, "The attendant put up the hood and then jumped back exclaiming, 'My God, what have you got in there!'" She said there was a nest made of sticks, string, and plastic bags. One of the bags started moving, and when the attendant pulled it out, he discovered three baby squirrels. The squirrels had chewed through every wire in the engine compartment except two. The repair bill for Kasparov was $425. Laura Ruffenboch, a wildlife professor at the university, said the insulation on many electrical wires is made from a soybean derivative, and the squirrels may find that attractive. She also said it was unusual for squirrels to make nests in cars that are used regularly.

Underage Driver

Charles Todd Snyder was charged with drunk driving following a traffic accident in your city one week ago. He was also charged with driving without a driver's licence in his possession. He was scheduled to appear in court at 9 a.m. this morning. He failed to appear in court. As a consequence, Judge Edward Kocembra ordered police to go to Snyders home and to haul Snyder into court. Police went to the address Snyder had given officers at the time of the accident. The police returned to the court at approximately 10:15 a.m. and appeared before Judge Kosembra with Snyder. Snyder was in his mothers arms. He is a 13-month-old child, and his mother insisted that he drinks only milk and that the only vehicle he ever drives is a stroller. So the judge apologized for the inconvenience and told the officers to give Snyder and his mother a ride back to their home. Snyder, apparently frightened by the unfamiliar surroundings and people, cried. Police said that whoever was stopped had falsely given the arresting officers Snyders name and address when he signed the drunken driving ticket and the ticket for driving without a drivers licence in his possession. They told the judge that they have no idea who that person might be.

Exercise 2   Specialized Types of Stories

Followup Stories

Write a story summarizing the initial set of facts and then just the lead for a followup story about the later developments. Or your instructor might ask you to write a complete news story about each day's developments. Be sure to correct any errors of grammar, spelling, and style in the notes.

Yesterday

Two boys were playing in Nichols Lake in Lakeside Park in your town. They were wading along the shore of the lake at about 12 noon at a point where the bottom drops off steeply. The two boys were Randy Stockdale, age 9, son of George and Lillian Stockdale, and Edward McGorwan, age 10, son of Karen McGorwan. Edward waded too far from shore, lost his footing, and was unable to get back to shore. He and Randy started to yell for help. A man whose name has not been released by police heard their screams and ran to the lake to help. James Kirkman, a cab driver who was taking his lunch break in the park, heard the screams, too. He radioed his dispatcher who called 911. Kirkman said later that the unidentified man waded out as far as he could and tried to reach out to Edward, but the boy had drifted too far from shore. "When the boy went under and didn't come back up for air, this guy dove under to find him. But he didn't come back up, either," Kirkman said. Police Officers Kevin Barlow and Eddie Linn arrived on the scene at 12:18. Barlow immediately stripped to his shorts and started diving into the lake to find the victims. After several dives, he came back up with Edward McGorwan, who was unconscious. Linn tried to resuscitate the boy, but he was still unconscious when he was taken by ambulance to the Regional Medical Centre. Barlow continued to search for the unidentified man for another 20 minutes until Dorothy Heslin, a scuba diver who assists the police on a volunteer basis, arrived. She pulled him from the water about 1:15 p.m. Wayne Svendson, a paramedic, tried to resuscitate the man. Svendson said the water was unusually cold and hypothermia had set in, which was indicated by the fact the mans skin had started to turn blue. The man was taken to the Regional Medical Centre. Dr. Catrina Lowrie, a physician at the Medical Centre, said the man was pronounced dead when he arrived. She also said that Edward McGorwan was in critical condition. Officer Barlow also was treated at Regional Medical Centre for minor shock caused by the long period of time he spent in the water looking for the victims. He was released that afternoon.

Today

This morning, the police department released the name of the man who died trying to save Edward McGorwan from Nichols Lake. His name is William McDowell and he is an unemployed housepainter. He was 30 years old. Police Chief Barry Kopperud said, "McDowell risked his life without hesitation to try to save someone in trouble. He was a real hero." Also this morning, Dr. Lowrie at the Regional Medical Centre announced that Edward McGorwan had died. "He spent the night on a respirator, but his condition did not improve. This morning, at his mothers request, we took Edward off the respirator.

He died less than half an hour later." McDowells sister lives in your town. Her name is Janice Carson. She said her brother had dropped out of Colonial High School one year before graduating and joined the navy. He spent six years in the navy and after he left he held a succession of jobs, including electronics technician, cook, construction worker, and painter. She said he always enjoyed his jobs but was too restless to stay at one for more than a couple of years. "I guess some people would call him a drifter, but to me he was a free spirit. He loved people but he didn't want to be tied down with a house and a mortgage and all of that. There were only two things he never learned how to do. He couldn't hold a job for more than two years and he could never say no to anyone who needed help," she said with tears in her eyes.

Exercise 3   Specialized Types of Stories

Roundups—Multiple Sources

Write a single news story that summarizes the following information. Organize the information in a clear, logical, cohesive manner. As you write the story, correct the spelling, style, grammatical, and vocabulary errors. Also be thorough; report every issue in depth. Notice that the sources' comments appear in quotation marks, so you can quote them directly.

Background

The Sunnyview Retirement Home is an 8-storey brick building located on Hillcrest Street in your community. The building is a former hotel. Ten years ago it was renovated and turned into apartments for retirees. It is privately operated, for profit, with 110 apartments, including 30 for a single resident and 80 for two residents, often couples, sharing an apartment. About 175 people were living there when a fire broke out at approximately 7:10 a.m. this morning. As many as 150 firefighters from throughout your region, including nearby communities, were called in for assistance in battling the blaze and assisting in rescuing all the victims from their peril.

Fire Chief Tony Sullivan

"Its the worst damn fire I've ever seen. We've got seven dead we know of and maybe 20 more that've been taken to hospitals with various injuries, some pretty serious. We just can't tell for sure. There could be lots more in the building, people who couldn't get out. I can't send my men in yet to look for them, not at this point, because its not safe. We've got the fire out, but it was a fierce one, and some floors and walls were weakened and are liable to collapse at any time. We may have to pull them down or they could fall on my men. It may be another day before we're able to make a thorough search and recover all the bodies."

Rescue Worker John Charlton

"People I've talked to say the fire started on the first or second floor. The fire itself wasn't so bad, except on the first couple of floors. Everything on those floors is gone. The fire didn't spread to the upper floors, but most of the deaths occurred up there. It was the smoke that did it. People said they couldn't breathe, and then a lot of them were old and in bad shape to begin with. We've taken the survivors that weren't hurt none to a church just across the street, and they're mostly resting there now. I don't know where they'll go tonight, where they'll sleep. The Red Cross is setting up an information centre for relatives at the church. We've, uh, got all sorts of relatives that've been in and out all morning, looking for their people and apparently bringing them home with them, so we don't know who's missing or dead or home safe with their families."

Retirement Home Director Mildred Anchall

"We don't know how the fire started, just that it started somewhere on the second floor, and our alarms sounded at 7. It happened so fast, it spread so fast, that all we could do was try and get everyone out. No one had time to stop and get a list of all our residents, and now they've been taken a half-dozen different places. We don't have any way of knowing who's safe and who's missing. Besides our residents, I've got my staff to worry about, and some visitors who were in the building. It's a tragedy, a real tragedy, something like this. You hear about things like this happening but never think it could happen at your home."

Building Inspector Ralph Schweitzer

"We inspected the building just a couple weeks ago, and it satisfies all our codes. When it was remodelled 10 years ago we didn't require sprinklers, and they would have saved everyone, would have put the fire out in a minute or two, so they would have really prevented a tragedy like this. Anyone building a nursing home today is required to put in sprinklers, and this is what we have in mind to prevent, a real serious tragedy like this one."

Survivor Steven Minh

"I'm 82, and I've been living here since it opened 10 years ago. Nothing like this ever happened here before. Its like I was back in World War II or something. I lived on the eighth floor, and people up there were screaming for help. The smoke was real bad, and some of us don't move so quick anymore. The firemen got up there real fast and led us down the stairs. There were some real heroes up there. I saw firemen carrying a half-dozen people down 6 or 8 flights of stairs when they could hardly breath themselves, and a lot of us would be dead without them. We couldn't have lasted much longer with the smoke and all. I'd just like to know what started the fire because it spread so fast. One minute everything was OK, then we were all choking on the smoke."

Survivor Betsy Aaron

"It was terrible in there. We began hearing fire alarms, but they weren't loud enough. By the time we realized what it was and went out into the hall it was full of smoke. I had a third-floor apartment, so I was able to get right out. I just took an elevator downstairs. Other people said they weren't working, but that must have been later, after I was out, that the elevators stopped working. When I got out on the street and looked up I saw people I knew leaning out their windows and shouting, 'Help me! Help me!' I couldn't do anything for them, not anything at all."

Fire Chief Marshal R.J. Hilton

"We haven't pinpointed the cause of the fire yet. It's too early, but my personal feelings are, strictly on a preliminary basis, it seems to have been an accidental fire that started in one of the apartments. It'll be at least a day or two before we have anything official on that."

Exercise 4   Specialized Types of Stories

Sidebars

Use the following information to write two separate stories: first a news story reporting the fire, then a sidebar based on the interviews with Mrs. Noffsinger.

Main Story

The Grande Hotel is located downtown at the corner of Manitoba and Barber Avenues. It is a seven-storey structure with a total of 114 rooms. It was constructed and opened for business in the year 1924. In recent years the hotel has been in an obvious state of decline, unable to compete with new facilities in the city and with the convenience of motels located along highways which now bypass the city. Many of the hotel rooms have been rented on long-term leases, often to elderly persons who like its downtown location, which is more convenient for them, since many facilities they use are in walking distance and buses are easily available for other trips they want to make. Three persons died in a fire at the hotel last night. The cause of the fire is undetermined. It started in a third-floor room. It spread and also destroyed the fourth, fifth, sixth, and seventh floors before it was brought under control at 4:30 a.m. today. At about 11 p.m. a guest called the lobby to report the odour of smoke. A hotel employee used a passkey to enter the third-floor room where the fire originated and found it totally engulfed in flames. The room is believed to have been vacant at the time. The employee sounded a fire alarm in the hotel and called firefighters. It was the first five-alarm blaze in the city in more than 10 years. Every piece of fire equipment in the city was rushed to the scene, and off-duty firefighters were called in to assist. Fortunately, said Fire Chief Tony Sullivan, no other fires were reported in the city at the same time or he would have had to send a truck and men from the scene of the hotel blaze. Hotel records indicate that 62 persons were registered in the hotel at the time the blaze initiated; 49 had long-term leases and 13 were transients. All the transients were located on the second floor and escaped safely. The dead, all of whom had long-term leases, have been identified as Mildred Haserot, age 58; Willie Hattaway, age 67; and Pearl Petchsky, age 47. The bodies of all three victims were found on the fourth floor, where they lived. Fire Chief Tony Sullivan said this morning the hotel is a total loss and that some walls are in danger of collapse. He said: "The fire was already out of hand when our first units reached the scene. I was called from home, and by then the flames were breaking out through the third- and fourth-floor windows. We were really lucky there weren't more people killed, but the hotel people knocked on the door of every room that was occupied to get everybody out. Most guests used a back stairway, and we were lucky the elevators kept working for awhile even after my men got into the building, otherwise the loss would have been worse. I'm also told that the top two floors were empty, and that helped keep down the loss of lives."

The Red Cross is caring for survivors, finding them new rooms and providing clothes and emergency allocations of cash, a total of $250 per person. Five people were injured, including one fireman who suffered from smoke inhalation. The others suffered from burns, some serious, and also from smoke inhalation. Three are being treated at Mercy Hospital. Two have been released, including the fireman. Their names and conditions are unknown at this time.

Sidebar

Nora Noffsinger, 74, has been a resident of the Grande Hotel for the past nine years. She paid $880 a month rent for one room on the fifth floor. A retired bookkeeper, she said afterward: "It was dreadfully expensive, but it was a charming old building and I had lots of good friends living there. I was asleep last night when I heard someone pounding on my door. I don't know who it was, but he told me to get out fast, and I did. All I had on were my pyjamas and a robe, but I could see the smoke, even up there on the fifth floor, and I was scared; I knew right away that it was bad. Everyone else was scared too, but we all knew what to do. We'd talked lots about what we'd do if there was ever a fire because you hear so often about fires in old hotels, and we wanted to be prepared. We all kept flashlights in our rooms and planned to go down the back stairway unless the fire was there, and it wasn't. The lights were still on, so we didn't even need our flashlights. Now the Red Cross put me in a motel room a few blocks away, and I guess I should be happy I'm safe, but I lost everything—my clothes, a little money I'd kept hidden in a secret place, all my photographs. My husband's dead, you know, and I lost all my pictures of him. I don't know what I'll do now; I don't have any children. I'm all by myself, except for my friends, and they all lived at the hotel with me."

12　Grammar and Spelling

"The English language is tough to master—apparently even for those paid to write and edit it. Yes, that means newspaper pros. And readers notice when they get it wrong. They contact me about misplaced homophones, apostrophes and spelling errors. Bad grammar, however, tops readers' lists of pet peeves."

—Sylvia Stead, public editor for the *Globe and Mail*. Reprinted with permission of Globe and Mail, Inc.

Journalists earn their living by writing. To become effective writers, they must understand more than the basics of grammar and word usage. They must become experts.

Good reporters have good news judgment and the ability to write well. Some students taking their first journalism class have wonderful news sense but do not know the basics of good grammar. They perform poorly in class because they cannot communicate news and ideas in ways others can easily understand.

Understanding the following areas of good grammar will help.

Sentence Diagram

Words are classified as different parts of speech depending on what work they do in a sentence.

This chapter is about grammar, and it summarizes the basics adequately.

Here is the part-of-speech category for each word in the sentence above:

- The word "this" is a demonstrative pronoun modifying the noun "chapter."
- The word "is" is the present tense, third-person form of the verb "to be."
- The word "about" is a preposition introducing the noun "grammar."
- The word "and" is a co-ordinating conjunction that joins the two independent clauses.

- The word "it" is a third-person pronoun whose antecedent is "chapter."
- The word "summarizes" is a verb in the third person, present tense.
- The word "the" is the definite article before the noun "basics."
- The word "adequately" is an adverb modifying the verb "summarizes."

The Parts of Speech

All words are classified as one or another of the eight parts of speech—noun, verb, pronoun, adjective, adverb, preposition, conjunction, and interjection. Understanding grammar begins with an understanding of the parts of speech and how they are used.

Nouns

A noun is a name for any animate or inanimate thing: people, animals, places, qualities, acts, or ideas.

Common nouns name any member of a class of things: "cow," "town," "soldier," "refrigerator," "computer," "honesty." Proper nouns are names for specific individuals, animals, places or things: "Robert," "Melissa," "House of Commons," "Vancouver." The first letter of a proper noun is always capitalized; the first letter of a common noun is capitalized only when it is the first word in a sentence.

Nouns are also classified as concrete or abstract. Concrete nouns name tangible objects such as "table," "book," or "tree." Abstract nouns name intangible things or ideas: "laziness," "creativity," "beauty." Nouns may indicate various levels of abstraction, becoming more abstract as they become more general. "Animal" can refer to any of millions of kinds of organisms from bacteria to humans. "Mammal" is more specific, referring to thousands of species that share certain physiological characteristics. "Dog" is still more specific, identifying a particular species of mammal. "Fido," a name for a specific dog, represents the most concrete level.

News writers try to use the most concrete and most specific nouns possible. Stories filled with such words are easily understood and more interesting than stories filled with abstract nouns.

Verbs

Verbs are the most important part of speech. Whereas nouns are static, verbs describe action; they tell what things and people do. Examples are "run," "steal," "hesitate," and "reflect." Verbs not only show action but also change form to tell the reader who is doing the acting and when. For example, past tense tells the reader that the action being described has been completed.

All verb tenses use one of four main forms of the verb: the infinitive (to walk), or present-tense form (I walk); the present participle, which is the "-ing" form of the verb (I am walking); the simple past-tense form (I walked); and the past-perfect tense (I have walked). These are called the principal parts of a verb. Regular verbs add "-ed" to form the past and past-perfect tenses, and they add "-ing" to form the present participle. For an

Table 12.1 Principal Parts of Verbs

Infinitive	Present	Present Participle	Past Tense	Past Participle
to sail	sail	sailing	sailed	sailed
to talk	talk	talking	talked	talked
to write	write	writing	wrote	written
to run	run	running	ran	run

irregular verb, consult a dictionary for the verb's principal parts. Table 12.1 presents the principal parts of a few common verbs ("sail" and "talk" are regular verbs; "write" and "run" are irregular verbs).

English has a dozen possible tense variations to show the time of the action but only three main tenses: present, past, and future. The most often-used tenses are the three simple tenses (present: talk; past: talked; future: will talk) and the three "perfect" or compound tenses (present perfect: have talked; past perfect: had talked; future perfect: will have talked). A verb can also be used in a progressive tense, to show that an action is continuing (present progressive: am talking; past progressive: was talking; future progressive: will be talking). Finally, a verb can be in a perfect-progressive tense (present perfect-progressive: have been talking; past perfect-progressive: had been talking; future perfect-progressive: will have been talking). Here's an example of what a verb ("to vote") looks like in all twelve possible tenses:

Simple present: I vote.
Simple past: I voted.
Simple future: I will vote.

Present perfect: I have voted.
Past perfect: I had voted.
Future perfect: I will have voted.

Present progressive: I am voting.
Past progressive: I was voting.
Future progressive: I will be voting.

Present perfect-progressive: I have been voting.
Past perfect-progressive: I had been voting.
Future perfect-progressive: I will have been voting.

Verbs give readers hints about who is doing the action. For most verbs, the third-person singular in the present tense has a distinct form, usually created by adding "-s" to the end of the verb (I vote, you vote, but he *votes*). "Argues," for example, tells the reader that the arguing is going on in the present, and a person other than the speaker of the sentence is doing the arguing.

Because verbs pack so much information, good writers pay close attention to the selection of verbs. The best verbs convey strong actions that readers can easily visualize. Sentences with strong verbs and concrete nouns need little help from adjectives and adverbs.

Adjectives

Adjectives describe nouns and pronouns. In many instances, the adjectives precede the nouns they modify: the *thick* book, the *yellow* flower, the *sleepy* town. Other times, the adjective follows some form of the verb "to be"—the town is *sleepy.*

Adjectives may have "more," "most," "less," or "least" before them or have "-er" or "-est" attached at the end to indicate degrees of comparison. English has three degrees of comparison: positive, comparative, and superlative. The positive degree is the basic form of the adjective and merely states that a particular thing possesses a quality. The comparative degree is used when comparing two things in the degree to which they possess a quality. The superlative degree is used when three or more things are being compared. Table 12.2 shows some examples of regular forms.

Some adjectives take irregular forms for the comparative or superlative degree. Table 12.3 has a few examples.

Almost any word can be used as an adjective to modify nouns. Two or more words can be combined to create adjectival phrases, as in these examples:

Nouns modifying nouns: *car* insurance, *school* assignments, *government* official
Present participles modifying nouns: *soaring* airplane, *ironing* board, *winding* road
Past participles modifying nouns: *hardened* criminal, *trusted* friend, *softened* butter
Adjectival phrases: *sky-blue* shirt, *full-time* employee, *man-eating* shark

Note that the words combined to form adjectival phrases are often hyphenated.

Table 12.2 Degrees of Comparison

Positive Degree	Comparative Degree	Superlative Degree
the thick book	the thicker book	the thickest book
the beautiful flower	the more beautiful flower	the most beautiful flower
the popular candidate	the less popular candidate	the least popular candidate

Table 12.3 Irregular Forms of Degrees

Positive Degree	Comparative Degree	Superlative Degree
good	better	best
bad	worse	worst
little	less	least

Articles

The indefinite articles are "a" and "an." The definite article is "the." Most grammarians consider the three articles special kinds of adjectives. The use of an indefinite article implies that the writer is referring to any member of a class of people or things. The definite article implies that the writer is referring to a specific member of a class.

Jane checked out a book from the library. (The book could be any in the library.)

Jane checked out the book from the library. (A given book has already been specified.)

"A" is used before nouns that begin with consonant sounds; "an" is used before nouns that begin with vowel sounds. In most cases, the choice is obvious, but some words that start with consonants sound as if they start with vowels. In "honour," for example, the "h" is silent, so it requires "an" instead of "a."

He received an honorary degree.

In other cases, words that start with vowels sound as if they start with consonants. "Europe" sounds as if it starts with a "y"; therefore, it uses the indefinite article "a."

They plan a European vacation.

Reporters who misuse the definite article confuse readers by implying that an object being referred to is the only such object in existence. If a reporter writes that three people were taken to "the hospital," yet the story's earlier paragraphs never mentioned any hospital, then the use of "the" implies the area has only one hospital. Similarly, a story reporting someone had coffee at "the Second Cup in Vancouver, British Columbia," implies, wrongly, that there is only one Second Cup in the city.

Adverbs

Adverbs modify verbs, adjectives, and other adverbs. Like adjectives, adverbs describe the words they modify. They may show manner, degree, direction, cause, affirmation, negation, frequency, time, or place. Many (but not all) adverbs end in "-ly." The following sentences illustrate some of the uses of adverbs. The adverbs are italicized:

Rose *quickly* paid her bills.

Canadian Forces are *fully* committed to the mission.

He recited the alphabet *backward*.

Gordon travels *weekly* to Toronto.

The couple walked *arm in arm* down the aisle.

Like adjectives, adverbs can show degrees of comparison. Most adverbs form the comparative and superlative degrees by combining with "more," "most," "less," or "least." Here are some examples:

Positive degree: The Queen Mary bus runs *frequently*.

Comparative degree: The Peel bus runs *more frequently* than the Queen Mary bus.

Superlative degree: The 27th Street bus runs *most frequently* of all city buses.

Pronouns

Pronouns can replace proper or common nouns, allowing the writer to avoid needless and confusing repetition of a noun. The noun the pronoun replaces is called its antecedent. "Antecedent" means "that which goes before," and the pronoun usually (but not always) follows its antecedent.

Bill overcame his fear and took the test.
In spite of his fear, Bill took the test.

In both of these sentences, "Bill" is the antecedent for the pronoun "his," but in the second sentence, the pronoun precedes the antecedent. Whether the pronoun follows or precedes its antecedent, the writer must be sure the meaning is clear. Sometimes the pronoun "it" is used as the subject of sentences that state the time, describe the temperature or weather, or suggest some other environmental fact: for example, in "It often rains in Vancouver."

Grammarians generally recognize six kinds of pronouns: demonstrative, indefinite, interrogative, reflexive, relative, and personal.

Demonstrative

Demonstrative pronouns designate or point out the things referred to. English has two demonstrative pronouns: "this" and "that," and their plural forms, "these" and "those." "This" and "these" refer to things that are close in time and space; "that" and "those" refer to things that are more remote. Demonstrative pronouns are used alone (Give me *that*); when they are used to describe a noun or pronoun, they are called demonstrative adjectives (Give me *that* book).

You neglected to mention *that*. (demonstrative pronoun)

This piece of fruit is sweeter than *that* one. (demonstrative adjective)

Demonstrative pronouns may have specific nouns as their antecedents, or they may have entire phrases or clauses as antecedents. In the following sentence, the antecedent for "that" is the entire opening clause:

The bill may be amended before it is enacted, but *that* will be up to the committee.

Indefinite

Indefinite pronouns refer to objects or people generally or indeterminately. The pronoun may refer to any of a class of people. In the next sentence "each" is an indefinite pronoun:

Each of the workers received a pay raise.

Some of the common indefinite pronouns include these: "all," "another," "any," "anybody," "anyone," "both," "each," "either," "every," "everybody," "everyone," "few," "little," "many," "much," "neither," "nobody," "none," "one," "other," "several," "some," "somebody," "someone," and "such."

Interrogative

Pronouns used to ask questions—such as "who," "which," and "what"—are called interrogative pronouns; they have no antecedents. Here are some examples:

Who has the key?
Which are yours?
What are her reasons?

Reflexive

Reflexive forms of personal pronouns add "-self " or "-selves" at the end; they are used when the subject and object of the verb are the same (as in the first sentence below) and for emphasis (as in the second sentence). When they are used for emphasis, they are called intensive pronouns rather that reflexive pronouns.

Hiroshi cut *himself* while slicing the carrots. (reflexive pronoun)

The plumber fixed the drain, but I *myself* replaced the faucet. (intensive pronoun)

Relative

The main relative pronouns are "that," "which," and "who" (also "whom" and "whose"). Relative pronouns are used to join relative (or adjective) clauses to the main clause in a sentence, as in these examples:

The mayor promised a plan *that* will hold down costs.

The plan, *which* was announced yesterday, won approval at council.

The members, *who* were eager to call it a day, fidgeted noisily in their seats.

"Who" should be used to refer to people. "Which" and "that" can be used for animals, inanimate things, and abstractions.

Personal

Personal pronouns are the most easily recognized pronouns. They take the place of names of people, although the third-person neutral "it" can replace a noun for any living or inanimate object or abstraction.

The personal pronouns are the most fully "inflected" words in English. That means the pronouns change their form to show whether they are the subject of the sentence, a direct or an indirect object, or a possessive (Table 12.4). The form used for subjects is called the subjective (or nominative) case. The correct form for objects is the objective case, and that for possessives is the possessive case. Note that when possessive pronouns are used to modify nouns (*my* coat, *his* hat, *their* jackets, etc.), they are, strictly speaking, functioning as adjectives rather than as pronouns.

Personal pronouns must agree with their antecedents in number and can agree according to gender. However, efforts should be made to use gender-neutral pronouns, and reporters should ask sources what their preferred pronouns are. When gender-neutral pronoun use is not required, a singular masculine antecedent requires a singular masculine pronoun; a plural antecedent requires a plural pronoun. The correct case of a pronoun depends on its function within a sentence or clause. In the following examples, the personal pronouns are italicized:

The president says the company will send the order directly to *him*.

Coach Raphael Morales told the players *they* would make the playoffs this year.

I told Sooyoung this side of the fence is *mine* and that side is *hers*.

Table 12.4   Personal Pronouns

Person	Subjective Case	Objective Case	Possessive Case
1st-person singular	I	me	my or mine
2nd-person singular	you	you	your or yours
3rd-person masculine	he	him	his
3rd-person feminine	she	her	her or hers
3rd-person neutral	it	it	its
1st-person plural	we	us	our or ours
2nd-person plural	you	you	your or yours
3rd-person plural	they	them	their or theirs

In the first example, "president" is the antecedent of "him," which is in the objective case because it functions as an indirect object of the verb "will send." In the second example, "players" is the antecedent for "they," which is in the subjective case because it functions as the subject of the verb "would make." In the final example, "I" is the subject of the sentence (its antecedent is understood to be the speaker), and the words "mine" and "hers" are pronouns in the possessive case because they indicate ownership, in this case of a fence (the antecedent "mine" is "I," and the antecedent of "hers" is "Sooyoung").

Prepositions

A preposition shows a relationship to the word that it introduces, called the object of the preposition. The object of a preposition is a noun or pronoun (or noun/pronoun phrase). The following sentence contains two prepositional phrases. In the first, the preposition "from" introduces its object, "headquarters," and in the second, the preposition "to" introduces the indefinite pronoun "everyone":

The new order from headquarters will apply to everyone.

Here are some of the more common prepositions:

at	from	through
about	in	throughout
above	inside	till
after	into	under
along	of	until
below	on	up
beside	onto	upon
between	opposite	with
beyond	outside	within
by	over	without
down	since	
for		

English also has some prepositions that consist of more than one word. Some of the common ones are "because of," "in spite of," "on account of," "out of," "owing to," "with respect to," "in addition to," and "together with." The word or words that a preposition introduces have the effect of describing something, as in these examples: a book *about genetics*, a brownie *with ice cream*, the beach *beside the lake*, the rocks *on the mountainside*.

The uses of prepositions are highly idiomatic in English. Writers cannot simply rely on dictionary definitions to know which preposition best fits a sentence. Instead, they must become familiar with the language through reading and listening. Use of the wrong preposition can convey a false or misleading meaning. The following sentences are the same except for the preposition, but their meanings differ:

> I bought a book by Professor Smith.
> I bought a book from Professor Smith.

The first sentence tells the reader who wrote the book but nothing about from whom the speaker bought it. The second tells the reader from whom the speaker bought the book but not who wrote it.

Sometimes prepositions combine with verbs to create idiomatic phrases. The addition of the preposition can dramatically change the meaning of the verb. "To break" means something different from "to break into" or "to break down." The last of these three illustrates the idiomatic nature of prepositions. A person whose car has stopped running might say, "My car broke down." Logic does not compel this use of "down"; it's just the way people speak.

Conjunctions

Conjunctions are words, phrases, or clauses that connect other words, phrases, and clauses in sentences. Conjunctions are generally classified as co-ordinating or subordinating. Co-ordinating conjunctions connect elements of equal grammatical standing—words to words, phrases to phrases, clauses to clauses. Subordinating conjunctions connect dependent clauses to the main or independent clauses in sentences.

The seven most common co-ordinating conjunctions are "and," "or," "but," "nor," for," "yet," and "so." Conjunctions show different relations—for example, addition, contrast, separation, and consequence. Writers can make transitions smooth and clear by selecting the conjunction that most accurately reflects their meaning.

Subordinating conjunctions are more numerous than co-ordinating conjunctions, but they too can show a variety of relationships: cause, comparison, concession, condition, manner, place, purpose, or time. Here are some of the more common subordinating conjunctions:

after	in order that	until
although	rather than	when
because	since	whenever
before	so that	where
hence	though	whether
if	unless	while

Independent clauses joined by a co-ordinating conjunction should use a comma before the conjunction.

The message arrived, but he ignored it.

The afternoon was hot, so I went for a swim.

If the independent clauses have no co-ordinating conjunction linking them, use a semicolon.

The company issued its report Wednesday; the price of its stock fell 40 per cent the next day.

Use a semicolon, too, if the independent clauses are linked by a conjunctive adverb. Some of the conjunctive adverbs are "however," "moreover," "nevertheless," and "therefore."

The premier agreed to the tax increase; however, he opposed the plan for a new prison.

We were out of town last week; therefore, we missed the show.

Some conjunctions come in pairs. They are called correlative conjunctions and include the following:

both-and: Both the president and the vice-president will attend the dinner.

either-or: Either the president or the vice-president will attend the dinner.

neither-nor: Neither the president nor the vice-president will attend the dinner.

whether-or: Whether the president or the vice-president will attend the dinner is unclear.

as-as: Workers hope their pay increase will be as large this year as it was last year.

if-then: If the company refuses to increase pay, then the workers will strike.

Interjections

Interjections are words or short phrases that express strong emotions. Interjections bear no grammatical relation to the rest of the sentence and are considered independent or absolute constructions. Some common interjections are "aw," "bravo," "goodbye," "hey," "hush," "nonsense," "oh," "oh, dear," "ouch," "well," "whew," and "wow."

Interjections usually are punctuated with exclamation points, which can come either after the interjection itself or at the end of the sentence containing the interjection.

Nonsense! I never said such a thing.

Nonsense, I never said such a thing!

The placement of the exclamation point depends on whether the strong emotion attaches to the interjection alone or to the entire sentence.

Basic Sentence Structure

Simple sentences usually include a subject, a verb, and an object. The subject is the person or thing doing the action. The verb describes the action. The object is the person or thing acted on. Consider this sentence:

The batter hit the ball.

"Batter" is the actor (the subject of the sentence). "Hit" is the action (the verb), and "ball" is the thing acted on (the object).

Sometimes sentences include indirect objects, which tell to whom or for whom an action was done. The test for an indirect object is to place "to" or "for" before the word. The following sentences have both direct and indirect objects (Table 12.5).

Juan sent Maria a Valentine card.

Samantha bought her mother a new television.

When a noun alone is used as an indirect object, it usually comes between the verb and the direct object, as in the preceding examples. But when the indirect object takes the form of a prepositional phrase, it usually follows the direct object.

Juan sent a Valentine card *to Maria*.

Samantha bought a new television *for her mother*.

Verbs that have direct objects are called transitive verbs; verbs without direct objects are called intransitive verbs. Many verbs can be used in both transitive and intransitive ways. Take the normally intransitive verb "to walk," for instance. In the sentence "I walk every evening," the subject ("I") is doing something, but not to or for anyone or anything. Here is the same verb as a transitive verb: "I walk the dog every evening."

In the sentence "She flew the flag," "flew" is used as a transitive verb: the verb has a direct object ("flag"). But in this next sentence: "The flag flew from the pole," "flew"

Table 12.5 Direct and Indirect Objects

Subject	Verb	Indirect Object	Direct Object
Juan	sent	Maria	a Valentine card
Samantha	bought	her mother	a new television

is used as an intransitive verb (the flag did something, but not to or for anyone or anything).

A complete grammatical sentence needs only a subject and a verb, but sentences usually contain other words, including direct and indirect objects. Writers can embellish the simple sentence (which has one main clause) in various ways. For example, they can combine two main clauses to make a compound sentence.

Ice skating is her favourite sport, but she enjoys roller blading too.

She is an engineer, and he is a teacher.

Another way is to combine an independent clause with a dependent one to make a complex sentence. Dependent clauses are introduced by subordinating conjunctions and are unable to make sense standing alone (they need to be attached to an independent clause to make sense).

As noted, subordinating conjunctions are words and phrases like "because," "as a result of," "after," "before," "whenever," and "as long as."

I eat dinner *after my last class is over.*

I visit my aunt *whenever I go home for the holidays.*

Writers may use one or more dependent clauses together with two or more independent clauses to create compound-complex sentences.

I visit my aunt whenever I go home for the holidays, but I call her almost every week.

Sentences can also contain phrases, which are related groups of words that lack a subject-verb combination. Prepositional phrases and verbal phrases are common types. They may be incorporated in the body of the sentence, or they may introduce the main (or independent) clause. The first of the following sentences ends with a prepositional phrase, and the second begins with a verbal phrase:

People spend more time outdoors *in the springtime.*

Tired from her bicycle ride, Suzanna took a nap.

Sentence parts can be combined and arranged in many ways. Writers vary sentence structure to keep their prose from becoming too predictable and simplistic, but as a general rule, simple sentences that stick to subject-verb-object order are the clearest and most easily understood in news writing.

Active and Passive Voice

Sentences that use the subject-verb-object order are sentences in active voice. A sentence in passive voice turns that order around. The direct object of the active-voice sentence becomes the subject of the passive-voice sentence; the subject becomes part of a prepositional phrase; and the verb is replaced with its past participle and some form of the verb "to be."

Notice that in the following examples, the passive-voice sentence takes two words more than the active-voice sentence to say the same thing. Those extra words are unnecessary stumbling blocks for readers.

> **ACTIVE VOICE:** The batter hit the ball.
> **PASSIVE VOICE:** The ball was hit by the batter.

Notice, too, that the actor or subject can disappear from a passive-voice sentence:

> **ACTIVE VOICE:** The mayor gave Alex an award.
> **PASSIVE VOICE:** An award was given to Alex.

Some writers make the mistake of using the indirect object as the subject of the passive-voice sentence. This mistake is most common with verbs like "give" or "present." In the preceding example, for instance, some writers might try to make "Alex" the subject of the passive-voice sentence. Some grammarians call this a false passive and consider it an error.

> **FALSE PASSIVE:** Alex was given an award.
> **TRUE PASSIVE:** An award was given to Alex.

The false passive is an error because it suggests that "Alex" is what was given. But the award is what was given, and Alex was the recipient of the award.

Writers should avoid the passive voice not only because it is wordier than the active voice but also because it often camouflages responsibility. If a disaster strikes or a defective product harms someone, then government or business officials may admit "mistakes were made," but that passive construction reveals nothing about who made the mistakes or why. The passive voice is the ally of all who seek to evade responsibility; it is the enemy of all who seek clarity.

Agreement

Nouns, pronouns, and verbs are either singular or plural. Nouns and pronouns also indicate gender: masculine, feminine, or gender neutral. A basic principle of grammar is that nouns and verbs should agree with each other and so should nouns and pronouns. Singular subjects should have singular verbs, and plural subjects should have plural verbs; plural nouns should have plural pronouns; and so forth. The principle is simple, but the opportunities for error are numerous.

Subjects and Verbs

If the subject of a sentence is singular, use a singular verb, and if the subject is plural, use a plural verb. Getting subjects and verbs to agree is easy when sentences are simple. But when prepositional phrases separate subjects and verbs or when the subject is a collective noun, agreement becomes trickier. In the first example shown next, the singular noun "team" is the subject, and the prepositional phrase "of researchers" describes the subject. The verb must agree with the singular "team," not the plural "researchers." In the following examples, the subjects are in italics, and the verbs are underlined:

WRONG: A *team* of researchers <u>have gathered</u> the information.
CORRECT: A *team* of researchers <u>has gathered</u> the information.

WRONG: Three *teams* from the university <u>is gathering</u> the information.
CORRECT: Three *teams* from the university <u>are gathering</u> the information.

Some nouns may appear to be plural because they end in "s," but they are considered singular in some senses. Some examples are "economics," "politics," and "physics."

WRONG: *Economics* <u>are</u> a required course.
CORRECT: *Economics* <u>is</u> a required course.

Nouns that refer to a group or a collection of individuals as one whole are called collective nouns. Words like "committee," "club," "jury," "regiment," and "team" are examples. Proper nouns that identify organizations also are collective nouns: "Parliament" and "Microsoft," for instance. Usually, collective nouns are considered singular and require singular verbs and pronouns:

WRONG: The *jury* <u>announce</u> their verdict.
CORRECT: The *jury* <u>announces</u> its verdict.

WRONG: The *Canadian Association of Journalists* <u>have begun</u> a program to help reporters with their writing.
CORRECT: The *Canadian Association of Journalists* <u>has begun</u> a program to help reporters with their writing.

Nouns and Pronouns

Nouns and pronouns must agree with verbs; they must also agree with their antecedents in number. Pronouns can agree in gender, but gender-neutral language should be acknowledged when a source requests it. A singular feminine noun requires a singular feminine pronoun, and a plural neutral noun requires a plural neutral pronoun.

The following examples use gender-specific pronouns, which are underlined, and their antecedents are in italics.

> *Rachael* took <u>her</u> work with <u>her</u> when <u>she</u> visited New York.

> The carpenter replaced the *nails* in <u>their</u> container.

Collective nouns like "team," "jury," "group," "committee," "family," and "faculty" cause the most problems with noun-pronoun agreement. Unsure whether a collective noun is singular or plural, beginning writers try to have it both ways. They use singular verbs with collective nouns but then use plural pronouns to take their place:

> **WRONG:** *General Motors* is expanding <u>their</u> product line.
> **CORRECT:** *General Motors* is expanding <u>its</u> product line.

> **WRONG:** The *team* wins <u>their</u> third victory in a row.
> **CORRECT:** The *team* wins <u>its</u> third victory in a row.

If a collective noun is used in a plural form, then a plural pronoun is needed:

> **WRONG:** The *committees* reviewed <u>its</u> goal of curbing children's access to internet pornography.
> **CORRECT:** The *committees* reviewed <u>their</u> goal of curbing children's access to internet pornography.

Ambiguous Pronouns

Pronouns can lead to ambiguity. In the following example, readers do not know whose mother is being asked for permission:

> Walter and Taylor went to his mother for permission to stay out late.

Too many pronouns within one sentence or paragraph can perplex readers:

> The committee took its recommendation to the board. It discussed it before returning it to it for further consideration.

Limit the use of pronouns, and make sure each one has a clear antecedent. Revised, the sentence in the preceding example might read, "The committee took the recommendation to the board, which revised and returned it to the committee for further consideration."

Reporters use words such as "this" and "those" with caution because their meanings often are unclear. Reporters are particularly careful to avoid starting a sentence or paragraph with "it," "this," "these," "those," or "that." When one of these words starts a sentence, readers may have trouble determining its antecedent. Reporters can avoid confusion by repeating a key word or rewriting a foggy sentence:

ORIGINAL: Commissioner Terry Benham, who represents Scott County on the Transit Authority, said it has stopped losing money. He attributed this to the elimination of routes that had proven consistently unprofitable.

REVISED: Commissioner Terry Benham, who represents Scott County on the Transit Authority, said the bus system is no longer losing money because consistently unprofitable routes have been eliminated.

Plurals and Possessives

Nouns can be singular ("cat") or plural ("cats"). Generally, one makes a noun plural by adding an "s" at the end. For example, the plural of "student" is "students."

The plural of nouns ending in "s," "z," "x," "sh," and "ch" is often formed by adding an "es." For instance, "church" becomes "churches," "dish" becomes "dishes," "business" becomes "businesses," and "cake mix" becomes "cake mixes."

Other plural endings are irregular. A method left over from old English is to add "en," as in "child" to "children" and "woman" to "women." Some nouns ending in "f," such as "wolf," change to "ves" to become "wolves."

Possessives sometimes show ownership of one noun by another (Susan's glove), but they may indicate other kinds of relationships. Possessives may classify or describe nouns (province's rights) or describe purpose (a children's book). Possessives and plurals are easily confused because an "s" is used to form both.

Singular and plural nouns not ending in "s" require adding an apostrophe and "s" ('s) to become possessive (Table 12.6).

Plural nouns ending in "s" need just an apostrophe (') to form a possessive (Table 12.7).

Singular common nouns that end in "s" need an apostrophe and an "s" ('s) to form the possessive (Table 12.8).

Table 12.6 Possessives with Nouns Not Ending in "s"

Noun not ending in "s"	Possessive	Sentence
singular: dog	dog's	The dog's water dish was empty.
singular: Jean	Jean's	Jean's bracelet was missing.
plural: children	children's	The children's party was successful.
plural: geese	geese's	The geese's formation was in a "V."

Table 12.7   Possessives with Plural Nouns Ending in "s"

Plural noun ending in "s"	Possessive	Sentence
monkeys	monkeys'	The monkeys' antics were hilarious.
churches	churches'	The churches' pastors meet weekly.

Table 12.8   Possessives with Singular Common Nouns Ending in "s"

Singular common noun ending in "s"	Possessive	Sentence
witness	witness's	The witness's testimony failed to sway the jury.

Table 12.9   Possessives with Singular Proper Names Ending in "s"

Singular proper name ending in "s"	Possessive	Sentence
Chris	Chris's	Chris's proposal was approved.
Strauss	Strauss's	Strauss's operas are still performed.

Grammarians differ on this point, but according to *The Canadian Press Stylebook*, singular proper names that end in "s" (or an "s" sound) normally take an "'s" to form the possessive (Table 12.9).

Pronouns have distinct possessive forms and do not need an apostrophe or an "s" to show possession: mine, yours, his, hers, its, ours, theirs.

Many students confuse "its" with "it's." The first is the possessive pronoun, which does not need an apostrophe. The second is the contraction for "it is," and the apostrophe substitutes for the "i" in "is." Similarly, the possessive pronouns "his" and "hers" do not need apostrophes. Students also confuse the plural possessive pronoun "their" with "there," which refers to a place, or "they're," which is the contraction for "they are."

"That" and "Which"

"That" and "which" are little words, but they can make a big difference in the meaning of a sentence. The following sentences illustrate how changing "that" to "which" changes the meaning of the sentence:

She told Shannon to take the lawn mower that is in the barn to Jason.

She told Shannon to take the lawn mower, which is in the barn, to Jason.

In the first sentence, the use of "that" suggests there is more than one lawn mower on the property—in the yard, the garage, and the barn, for instance—but Shannon should take the one from the barn. In the second sentence, the clause introduced by "which" suggests there is only one lawn mower on the property, so it is the only one Shannon can take to Jason.

In the first sentence, the clause is restrictive and uses "that" and no commas; in the second, the clause is non-restrictive and uses "which" and commas. Note that the second sentence adds information but not information that is essential to the meaning of the sentence.

Here's a rule that can help decide between "that" and "which": If the subordinate clause can be removed and the sentence meaning does not change, use "which" and commas. Otherwise, use "that" and no commas.

"Who" and "Whom"

"That," "which," and "who" (also "whom" and "whose") are relative pronouns. "That" and "which" introduce clauses referring to ideas, inanimate objects, or animals without names; "who" is for clauses that refer to people and animals with names.

> **WRONG:** It was Morgan that came by the house yesterday.
> **CORRECT:** It was Morgan who came by the house yesterday.

> **WRONG:** It was a stray cat who ate the bird.
> **CORRECT:** It was a stray cat that ate the bird.

The distinction between "who" and "whom" torments some writers. "Who" is the subject of a clause; "whom" is the object of a verb or a preposition. Whether the word is a subject (in subjective case) or an object (in objective case) might not always be clear in sentences that depart from normal word order, such as questions. Whether "who" or "whom" is correct depends not on word order but on the word's grammatical relationship to the rest of the sentence. These two sentences illustrate the difference:

> Who gave you the scarf?

> Whom do you prefer as student council president?

In the first example, "who" is the subject of the clause, the initiator of the action "gave." In the second sentence, "whom" is the direct object of the verb "prefer." Here are two more examples:

> **WRONG:** Who did you speak to?
> **CORRECT:** Whom did you speak to? (To whom did you speak?)

> **WRONG:** The report names the man who the police suspect of the crime.
> **CORRECT:** The report names the man whom the police suspect of the crime.

In the first sentence, the relative pronoun is the object of the preposition "to." In the second, it is the direct object of the verb "suspect"; it refers to the person the police suspect. Both should be "whom."

One way to avoid or reduce confusion over "who" and "whom" is to replace them with a more familiar personal pronoun. Isolate the "who" or "whom" phrase. If "he" or "she" is required, then use "who." If "him" or "her" is needed, use "whom." Do that in the following sentence, and it is easy to see that "whom" is wrong:

The candidates discussed whom was responsible for the tax increase.

At first, the pronoun "whom" might sound correct, but when the pronoun is replaced with the more familiar "him" or "her," the error becomes apparent. The pronoun is the subject of the clause "was responsible for the tax increase" and so must be in subjective case. No one would say "her" was responsible or "him" was responsible; it's obvious that "she was responsible" or "he was responsible" are correct. The relative pronoun to use here is "who."

Misplaced Modifiers

Modifiers are words or phrases that limit, restrict, or qualify some other word or phrase. Modifiers should appear as close as possible to the word or phrase they modify. Misplaced modifiers can make sentences ambiguous, confusing, or nonsensical:

CONFUSING: She retold the ordeal of being held hostage with tears running down her cheeks.
REVISED: With tears running down her cheeks, she retold the ordeal of being held hostage.

CONFUSING: The gunmen tied the victim and left him with his hands and feet taped and lying on the back seat.
REVISED: The gunmen tied the victim, taped his hands and feet, and left him lying on the back seat.

In the first example, the phrase "with tears running down her cheeks" follows "hostage," and readers might think the phrase modifies "hostage"—that she was crying while she was a hostage. But the phrase really tells how the woman behaved as she talked about her ordeal. The second revision shows that the victim, not just his hands and feet, is left lying on the back seat.

Sometimes the meaning of a sentence can change dramatically simply by the positioning of a modifying word or phrase. Look at how the following sentences change in meaning by moving the word "only":

Only Smith's farm produces the best apples in the county.

Smith's only farm produces the best apples in the county.

Smith's farm only produces the best apples in the county.

Smith's farm produces only the best apples in the county.

Smith's farm produces the best apples only in the county.

Careful writers choose the word order that accurately conveys their meaning.

Dangling Modifiers

Modifiers dangle when the word or phrase they are supposed to modify does not appear in the sentence. That may happen when a thoughtless or hurried writer starts a sentence intending to state an idea one way and then switches in mid-sentence to express it in another way:

CONFUSING: Pleased with everyone's papers, the class received congratulations.
REVISED: Pleased with everyone's papers, the teacher congratulated the class.

Modifiers should be placed as close as possible to the word or phrase they modify; when they aren't correctly placed, they cause confusion.

CONFUSING: Angered by the unannounced closure of the plant, security guards hurriedly cleared the area.
REVISED: Security guards hurriedly cleared the area of employees angered by the unannounced closure of the plant.

Readers understand introductory words to modify the subject of the sentence, "security guards." The first sentence suggests it was the security guards who were angered by the closure; the revision makes it clear that the employees were the ones angered.

Personification

Avoid treating inanimate objects or abstractions as if they were human. Objects such as buildings, cars, stores, and trees cannot hear, think, feel, or talk. Yet some writers treat them as people. The writers see—and repeat—the error so often they fail to recognize it and continue to personify such things as corporations, countries, and machines.

Memorial Hospital treated her for shock and a broken arm.

She was driving west on Columbia Street when two cars in front of her slammed on their brakes.

Can a hospital treat patients, or is that the job of a hospital's staff? Can a car slam on its own brakes? Of course not. Such personifications are easy to correct:

ORIGINAL: The store said it will not reopen.
REVISED: The owner of the store said she will not reopen it.

ORIGINAL: The intention of the road was to help farmers transport their crops to market.
REVISED: Highway planners intended the road to help farmers transport their crops to market.

Personification also contributes to two other problems. First, audiences cannot determine a story's credibility if reporters fail to identify their sources. Readers can assess the credibility of a statement attributed to a mayor or premier but not the credibility of a statement attributed to a city or province.

Second, personification allows people to escape responsibility for their actions. Individual officials cannot be held responsible for their actions if reporters attribute those actions to a business or government.

Parallel Form

When writers link similar ideas, they do so with parallel structures. Grammatically parallel structures create harmony and balance in writing, and they help readers compare and contrast the ideas that are linked within the sentence.

The principle of parallelism requires that every item in a series take the same grammatical form: all nouns, all verbs, or all prepositional phrases. If the first verb in a series uses the past tense, every verb in the series must use the past tense, or if the first verb ends in "-ing," all must end in "-ing." If reporters fail to express like ideas in the same grammatical form, their sentences become convoluted and confusing:

NOT PARALLEL: She enjoys writing, researching, and reading her published work is great fun, too.
PARALLEL: She enjoys writing, researching, and reading her published work.

NOT PARALLEL: Police said the plastic handcuffs are less bulky, not as expensive, and no key is needed to remove them from a suspect's wrists than metal handcuffs.
PARALLEL: Police said plastic handcuffs are less bulky, less expensive, and less difficult to remove from a suspect's wrists than metal handcuffs.

NOT PARALLEL: The Greenes have three children: 4-year-old Gordon, Andrea, who is 3, and little Fielding is not quite 25 months.
PARALLEL: The Greenes have three children: Gordon, 4; Andrea, 3; and Fielding, 2.

"Because" and "Due To"

Students often misuse "because" and "due to." "Because" is a subordinating conjunction, used to introduce a subordinate clause, as in the following sentence: "The train arrived late because it encountered bad weather between Saskatoon and Edmonton. "Due to" is a preposition meaning "ascribed to" or "attributed to"; it is used after a noun (the train's late arrival, due to bad weather, forced a change in their itinerary) or after a linking verb (the delay was due to bad weather). "Due to" is always followed by a noun or noun phrase. Using "due to" to mean "because of" (the train was late due to bad weather) is common but considered incorrect in formal usage.

Spelling

People complain about inaccuracies in news stories, and they are often referring to spelling errors. Misspellings reflect laziness on the part of the writer, and they sometimes cause readers to doubt the facts in the story.

Commonly misspelled words make up some of the exercises at the end of this chapter. A common phrase such as "a lot" is frequently misspelled. Three other words that students often misspell are "medium," "criterion," and "phenomenon." All three are singular forms. Students often use the plural form instead: "media," "criteria," and "phenomena." Thus it would be correct to say, "The four criteria are adequate" but not "The media is inaccurate" or "The phenomenon are unusual."

Reporters usually follow formal rules for spelling. For example, they normally use "until" rather than "till" and "although" rather than "though." They also avoid slang.

A final point about spelling: Spell-check programs help many writers, but a program can look only at the spelling of a word, not at how it is used. If a student were to write, "There cats name is Savannah," the spell-checker would note that every word in the sentence is spelled correctly. It would miss two errors: "There" should be "Their" and "cats" should be "cat's." No one should depend solely on a spell-check program.

Words that look or sound alike but have different meanings, such as "accept/except" and "capital/capitol," can also be confusing.

✔ Checklist for Grammar

1. Use subject-verb-object order for sentences.
2. Use verbs in active voice, not passive voice.
3. Use singular verbs with singular subjects and plural verbs with plural subjects.
4. Make sure that pronouns agree with their antecedents.
5. Spell plurals and possessives correctly.
6. Use "that," "which," "who," and "whom" correctly.
7. Place modifiers immediately before or after the word they describe.
8. Avoid personification; do not suggest inanimate objects can talk, think, or feel.

9. List items in a series in parallel form.
10. Use the articles "a," "an," and "the" correctly.
11. Reread copy several times for spelling and other writing errors.
12. Do not depend solely on spell-check programs to find misspelled words.

 The Writing Coach

The section on sensitive subjects in *The Canadian Press Stylebook* details how to decide on when to use gender-neutral pronouns.

Whenever possible, confirm with the person how they wish to be described in print, including their preferred pronouns—male, female, or gender-neutral pronouns like "they" and "them." Such pronouns can be used sparingly to refer to a single individual who expresses such preferences but be careful—it can get confusing for a reader. Always explain the person's preference in copy, and make generous use of the person's chosen name as an alternative in order to foster as much clarity as possible.

Suggested Readings and Useful Websites

Barber, Katherine, and Robert Pontisso, eds. 2006. *Oxford Canadian A–Z of Grammar, Spelling, & Punctuation.* Don Mills, ON: Oxford University Press.

Barber, Katherine, Heather Fitzgerald, Tom Howell, and Robert Pontisso, eds. 2006. *Paperback Oxford Canadian Dictionary,* 2nd edn. Don Mills, ON: Oxford University Press.

Bell, James B., and Edward P.J. Corbett. 1977. *The Little English Handbook for Canadians.* Toronto: Wiley Canada.

Cragg, Catherine, et al., eds. 2003. *Editing Canadian English,* 2nd edn. Prepared for the Editors' Association of Canada. Toronto: McClelland and Stewart.

Fee, Margery, and Janice McAlpine. 2007. *Oxford Guide to Canadian English Usage,* 2nd edn. Don Mills, ON: Oxford University Press.

Hacker, Diana. 2007. *A Canadian Writer's Reference,* 4th edn. Boston: Bedford/St. Martin's.

McCarten, James, ed. 2017. *The Canadian Press Stylebook,* 18th edn. Toronto, ON: The Canadian Press.

Ruvinsky, Maxine. 2009. *Practical Grammar: A Canadian Writer's Resource,* 2nd edn. Don Mills, ON: Oxford University Press.

Red River College, Interactive Grammar Lessons: http://blogs.rrc.ca/asc/faculty/online-study/

University of Victoria Language Centre: http://web2.uvcs.uvic.ca/elc/studyzone

Exercise 1   Recognizing and Correcting Newswriting Errors

Answer key provided: see Appendix B.

Section I: Agreement
Edit the following sentences, correcting agreement and other errors.

1. The committee submits their data this weekend which they expect will help their church.
2. She said the company failed to earn enough to repay their loans, and she does not expect them to reopen.
3. The jury reached their verdict at 1 a.m., concluding that the media was guilty of libelling the restaurant and their twenty-two employees.
4. The decision allowed the city council to postpone their vote for a week, and they suggested that the sites developer design a plan to save more of it's trees.
5. A representative for the organization said they help anyone that is on welfare obtain some job training and raise their self esteem.

Section II: Plurals and Possessives
Edit the following sentences, correcting for plurals, possessives, and other errors.

1. The womens car was parked nearby, and sheriffs deputies asked to see the owners drivers licence.
2. The juror said she opposes assisted suicide "because a doctors job is to save peoples lives, not end them."
3. Last years outstanding teacher insisted that peoples complaints about the schools problems are mistaken.
4. Manvel Jones parents said there younger childrens teacher earned her bachelors degree in philosophy and her masters degree in eductaion.
5. Everyones money were stolen, and the neighbourhood associations president warned that the police are no longer able to guarantee peoples safety in the citys poorest neighbourhoods.

Section III: Placement
Rewrite these sentences, keeping related words and ideas together. Correct all errors.

1. The board of trustees voted 8–1 to fire the college president for his sexual misconduct during an emergency meeting Thursday morning.
2. On their arrival, the hotel manager took the guests' bags to their rooms.

3. The union representative urged Canadians to support better working conditions for the country's immigrant workers at the Unitarian church Sunday.
4. Jogging around campus, a thorn bush ripped a hole in Zena's shirt.
5. A suspect in the burglary case was arrested after a high-speed chase involving two lawn mowers stolen from a hardware store.

Section IV: Personification
Rewrite the following sentences, eliminating personification and other errors.

1. Slamming on its brakes, the car turned to the left, narrowly missing the dog.
2. The city said it cannot help the three businesses who asked for better lighting.
3. After detecting the outbreak, the hospital admitted that 7 babies born this month were infected, including one that died.
4. The Fire Department treated the child for smoke inhalation, then transported her to Mercy Hospital, which treated her broken legs.
5. The corporation, which denied any responsibility for the deaths, will appear in court next month.

Section V: Parallel Form
Rewrite these sentences in parallel form, and correct all errors.

1. He was charged with drunken driving and an expired drivers licence.
2. Karen Kim was a full-time student, Air Force reservist, and she worked part-time for a veterinarian.
3. To join the club, one must be a sophomore, junior, or senior; studying journalism; be in good academic standing; and have demonstrated professional journalistic ability.
4. The mayor warned that the neighbourhoods high crime rate causes residents to flee, contributes to more unemployment for workers, and the city loses tax revenue, along with lowering everyones property values.
5. She said the other advantages of owning her own business include being independent, flexible hours, and less stress.

Section VI: Multiple Errors
Rewrite the following sentences, correcting all errors. Most sentences contain more than one kind of error.

1. A sheriffs deputy saw the teenagers Chevrolet pull out of the alley, driving recklessly without its headlines on, and arrested it's driver.
2. The city also said that they cannot silence Sooyoung Li, the woman that fears pollution is likely to effect the neighbourhoods 300 residents.

3. Seeking more money, publicity, and to help the poor, the churchs members said it wants the city to help it by providing food and offer housing for the homeless.

4. The Public Works Department said they could pave the developments road themselves for less than $1.2 million, the Roess Company submitted a bid of $2.74 million.

5. A jury awarded almost $10.5 million to the operators of an abortion clinic that charged that picketers tormented them and there clients. The clinics operators praised the jury's verdict, saying their courage and understanding set a needed precedent.

Exercise 2   Recognizing and Correcting Newswriting Errors

Section I: Agreement
Edit the following sentences, correcting agreement, ambiguity, and other errors.

1. Every one of the news stories were accurate in their description of the accused.
2. Are seven dollars enough to buy the book?
3. Spagetti and meatballs are my favourite dish.
4. The board voted to raise they're salaries 10 per cent.
5. The cat and dog, whom ate off her plate, was punished severely.

Section II: Plurals and Possessives
Edit the following sentences, correcting errors in plurals and possessives as well as any other errors.

1. The women's liberation movement continue to help champion their cause for equality.
2. Experts fear the grey wolfs are a endangered species.
3. The fishes scales glowed in the dark from being exposed to pollution.
4. She acknowledged that the mistake was her's.
5. Their going to take they're trip to Jamaica this year.

Section III: Placement
Rewrite these sentences, keeping related words and ideas together. Correct all errors.

1. While baring it's teeth, the dogcatcher caught the racoon.
2. The teacher said that grading was tiring and exhausting for her students papers.
3. Too cold to move, her coat was inadequate for her outing.

4.   The mother knew that going to war would be hard for her baby, who was a sergeant in the military.
5.   The firefighter saved the child as she ran into the burning house.

Section IV: Personification
Rewrite the following sentences, eliminating personification and other errors.

1.   The jets unloaded their bombs in the no-fly zone.
2.   The funeral home said the former mayors burial was at 4 p.m.
3.   What the newspaper says is all ways right.
4.   The governors meeting voted to raise taxes.
5.   Her watch said it was noon time.

Section V: Parallel Form
Rewrite these sentences in parallel form, and correct all errors.

1.   She goes to university majoring in journalism to write news.
2.   The mayor promised improvements in employment, education and to fix up roads in the city.
3.   Tracy went to the store for eggs and butter and also to buy milk.
4.   Sept. 11, 2001, was sad, had offensiveness and many students believe it is upsetting to their classmates.
5.   She asked the victim to describe the muggers's height, weight and if he knew what she wore.

Section VI: Multiple Errors
Rewrite the following sentences, correcting all errors. Most sentences contain more than one error.

1.   As it rolled along the floor, her foot was run over by the chair.
2.   The electricians's union told their members to go on strike and to also demonstrate their disagreement.
3.   Detailed and tricky, the class finished their exams.
4.   The hockey team was given their five goals by their principal player, Annie Bearclaw.
5.   None of the witnesses were available to the reporter that had a deadline.
6.   The beautiful flower, black and blue, was stepped on by the gardeners dog.
7.   The teacher that was interviewed by the reporter asked for her email.
8.   All the people in the neighbourhood was given a good citizenship award by the mayor.
9.   The woman could not be a juror due to she said the judge was an hypocrite with her rulings.
10.   He likes to watch movies which make him cry and also gets him to feeling sentimental.

Exercise 3   Recognizing and Correcting Newswriting Errors

Section I: Modifiers
Edit the following sentences, correcting for misplaced or dangling modifiers.

1. Riddled with errors, the teacher graded the assignment.
2. The president met with the committee wearing a blue suit today.
3. Although it had a slightly green peel, the monkey at the zoo ate the banana.
4. The rancher wore a leather belt into the church with a bronze bull-riding buckle.
5. The mayor gave an emotional speech to the spectators outside the new library that had stood there for hours.

Section II: "Who" and "Whom"
Choose the correct relative pronoun in the following sentences.

1. To (who/whom) did you hand your article?
2. You chose (who/whom) to write a series of stories on Hurricane Katrina?
3. (Who/Whom) is going to receive the award this year?
4. On (who/whom) did she blame the robbery?
5. (Who/Whom) asked for the story on the fighting in Afghanistan?

Section III: Plurals and Possessives
Edit the following sentences, correcting errors in plurals and possessives as well as any other errors.

1. The hostess's stool was missplaced during the rearrangement of the restraunt.
2. The poker player's finally agreed to end thier game at 3 a.m.
3. "Its Kris' turn to drive the race car," said the manager of the team.
4. The monkeys's cages was cleaned out Saturday by the small team of zookeepers.
5. Looking really nice in her new dress, the gloves were new ones for Loreli.

Section IV: Active and Passive Voice
Edit the following sentences, changing passive to active voice.

1. The pitchfork was thrown into the corner by the farmer.
2. An antique train engine will be sold by the Smith Auctioneers next month.
3. The child was handed a football by his uncle on Thanksgiving.
4. A new movie was watched by several students during the festival.
5. The stolen car was given a new paint job.

Section V: Agreement

Read the following sentences, correcting for subject-verb agreement and subject-pronoun agreement.

1. The congregation of the church were playing bingo on Wednesday evenings.
2. The family walking into the store are going to buy their groceries for the week.
3. The bar association says they will enforce stricter rules in the conducting of their examinations.
4. The emails from the office of the dean deals with the new policy on student loans.
5. The group of journalism designers want training in Flash.

Exercise 4   Spelling

Cross out the word that is misspelled in each of the following pairs. Always use the spelling recommended by the Canadian Press.

1. a lot/alot
2. acceptable/acceptible
3. accidently/accidentally
4. accommodate/accomodate
5. advertising/advertizing
6. adviser/advisor
7. afterward/afterwards
8. alright/all right
9. baptize/baptise
10. boy friend/boyfriend
11. broccoli/brocolli
12. canceled/cancelled
13. catagorized/categorized
14. cemetery/cemetary
15. comming/coming
16. commited/committed
17. congradulations/congratulations
18. conscious/concious
19. contraversial/controversial
20. credability/credibility
21. critized/criticized
22. cryed/cried
23. defendant/defendent

24. desert/dessert (food)
25. despite/dispite
26. deterrant/deterrent
27. dilema/dilemma
28. disastrous/disasterous
29. dispise/despise
30. elite/elete
31. embarass/embarrass
32. emphasize/emphacize
33. employe/employee
34. endorsed/indorsed
35. exhorbitant/exorbitant
36. existance/existence
37. explaination/explanation
38. fascination/facination
39. favoritism/favouritism
40. Febuary/February
41. fourty/forty
42. fulfil/fulfill
43. glamour/glamor
44. goverment/government
45. guerrilla/guerilla
46. harassment/harrassment

47. humorous/humerous
48. independant/independent
49. indispensable/indispensible
50. infered/inferred
51. innuendo/inuendo
52. irrate/irate
53. irregardless/regardless

54. it's/its (possessive pronoun)
55. janiter/janitor
56. judgement/judgment
57. kindergarten/kindergarden
58. license/licence (noun)
59. lightning/lightening
60. likelyhood/likelihood

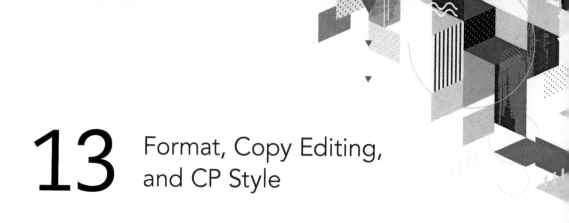

13 Format, Copy Editing, and CP Style

*"I write every day. I walk around in silent conversation with
my latest unfinished songs."*

—Gord Downie, songwriter and lead singer of The Tragically Hip, 2009

Gord Downie was known as Canada's poet because the songs he wrote as a solo artist and as lead singer with The Tragically Hip told stories that had powerful connections with people.

In 2016, the year before he died from a brain tumour, Downie wrote and recorded the album *A Secret Path*, which tells the story of a 12-year-old Ojibwa boy Chanie Wenjack, who died after he ran away from a residential school in 1966. Downie found out about Chanie's story in 2013 when his brother Mike told him about a CBC report based on an investigative piece in *Maclean's* magazine written by Ian Adams in 1967. Downie wanted to tell Chanie's story to show the public the hardships and racism faced by the country's Indigenous people. He wrote Chanie's story through poems and songs and started the Gord Downie & Chanie Wenjack Fund to increase the public's awareness of the need for reconciliation with Canada's Indigenous people.

A Secret Path and Downie's other works show how dedication to research and a thorough writing process can produce powerful messages to communicate to an audience. Downie's description of his daily writing process is similar to the process journalists need to use after they have gathered source material for their stories. Downie's "silent conversation" describes the review and revision process reporters do once they gather all the information they need to write a story. Reporters have these silent conversations as they review their content and revise their words to produce stories that their editors and producers will review and revise again before publishing them. The editing process *is* a "silent conversation" reporters have with their content to produce informative stories that speak clearly to the audience.

Journalism is a rewarding but challenging profession, and it requires honest hard work and dedication to the principles of the craft. News judgment, critical thinking, and good writing are the foundations of solid and responsible journalism. Learning how to report and write in journalistic style through practice in identifying leads, researching events and issues, organizing thoughts, and writing clearly for an audience will help you to develop as a journalist. Clarity of writing is the key to effective reporting. Reporters achieve clarity by reviewing the source materials they have gathered, then writing the source material into a story form, and then revising until the story is clear. Revision takes time, patience, and persistence; reporters will revise a story many times before it is good enough to be revised by an editor or a producer, and then to be published. Being a journalist is a privilege and a responsibility. Journalists have the unique opportunity to record people's private thoughts and enjoy the advantages of sometimes being one of the first to learn about new issues, ideas, and events. Yet journalists must be accountable for the decisions they make, because journalists express the news and information that people need to make productive decisions about their lives.

Although the purpose of reporting the news has remained the same for decades, the tools for gathering, producing, presenting, and disseminating news and information have changed. Twenty-five years ago, few editors knew what an online database was, and most thought it unimportant. Today, reporters must know how to gather and present information using databases, Twitter, Snapchat, Instagram, and Facebook in addition to traditional reporting skills.

The essential skills of journalism are astute news judgment, reporting aptitude, and writing ability. All journalists, whether traditional, visual, or digital, use basic news judgment skills. Once journalists understand the fundamentals of writing clearly and concisely, they can transfer these skills to different media. This chapter focuses on revision using basic print copy-editing skills and Canadian Press style as a starting point.

Producing Copy

More changes than ever are happening in newsrooms. Until about 45 years ago, reporters rolled two sheets of paper divided by a carbon into their manual typewriters. Reporters kept one copy of the story in case the editor lost the other. These copies were called hard copies— and one hard copy was called the carbon copy. Reporters used pencils to correct their errors with copy-editing marks in the story before handing it to an editor. The editor would often make further changes on the paper using pencils to make copy-editing symbols before giving the reporter's story to a typesetter to compose stories on the news page. Starting in the 1970s, media organizations experienced a period of rapid technological change from manual typewriters to electric typewriters to video display terminals to computers to tablets and cell phones, which are now used in all stages of the news process, ranging from writing stories to producing high-resolution digital images of news pages. Journalists now write their stories on cell phones, tablets, laptops, and computers and correct their errors instantly. When journalists finish their work, their stories are reviewed by an editor or a producer on another device. The final edited stories are posted online, in print or broadcast over the web, radio, and TV. Everything is done digitally, and stories are placed on multiple platforms.

Newsrooms use software that tracks the editing changes made for each revision. As an editor edits the copy that a reporter has submitted digitally, the changes are noted in the text in a different colour, and notations of those changes are made in the margins of the text. As with most technology, this has streamlined and sped up the editing process. But before the development of tracking software and computer technology, stories were edited on paper using traditional copy-editing symbols.

The ability to edit hard copies may seem outdated, but it is still an essential tool for reporters to have for three reasons. First, technology does fail and when working out in the field, sometimes paper edits are the only resources available. Second, many people prefer hard-copy edits to software-tracked editing because traditional editing is less invasive in the body of the text. Pencil edits are drawn out to the margins for notes and changes, and symbols are used to suggest changes. Tracking software makes the changes within the text, although editors do have the option to suggest rather than make in-text edits. Third, the traditional format and copy-editing symbols are also helpful for students whose stories are printed for instructors' comments and editing. Students are expected to make corrections using the same format, editing, and style guidelines professional journalists use for hard-copy revisions. Knowledge of both the old and new forms of editing is valuable for student journalists. The guidelines presented here are standard, but some news organizations may have slightly different practices.

News Story Format

Reporters have developed a unique format for their stories, and each story they write follows the guidelines presented here. Although minor variations exist from one news organization to another, most publications are remarkably consistent in their adherence to these rules. Also, most computer word-processing programs in the newsroom are programmed for standard margins and provide a special space for the reporter's name, the date, and the slug (a short description of the story).

- Print each news story on one side only of separate 8 1/2-by-11-inch sheets of paper.
- Leave a one-inch margin on each side and at the bottom of every page. Standard margins help editors and production workers gauge the length of each story. Instructors use this space to write comments.
- Type your name as the journalist, the date the story is written, and a slug on the upper left-hand corner of the first page:

Maxine Ruvinsky

July 14, 2019

GIRLHERO

Slugs help editors identify and keep track of stories that are being prepared for publication. They also provide a quick summary of each story's topic. Slugs, or slug-lines as they used to be called, are usually one word, written all in capitals, that accurately describe the story. A story that reports an increase in college tuition might be slugged "TUITIONHIKE"; a story about a fundraiser dance for charity might be slugged "DANCEFUND." Slugs need to be as specific as possible. Vague slug-lines, such as "dance" or "fundraiser" or "charity," might be used on more than one story, and the stories, their headlines, and their placement in the paper might then become confused.

When deciding on a slug, journalists should avoid jokes, sarcasm, insensitivity, and statements of opinion that would cause embarrassment if the slug were accidentally published or posted outside the newsroom.

- Begin each story about one-third of the way down the first page. The space provides room for editors to comment and for instructors to evaluate students' work.
- Set the tab key to indent a half-inch at the beginning of each paragraph.
- Double-space and type each story so that it is neat, uniform, and easy to read.
- Editing should be placed clearly above the typed lines in the skipped spaces. The spacing should make editing easier to do and see. Do not leave any extra space between paragraphs.
- Use left justification, and avoid hyphenating words at the end of a line.
- Traditionally, journalists never divide a paragraph across pages. Keeping a paragraph together keeps its information together should following pages be misplaced. Word-processing programs can be set up to automatically keep paragraphs together.
- If a story is continued on a second page, type the word "more" centred at the bottom of the first page to indicate to the editor and production staff that the story does not end on the first page; more information is on an additional page.
- Begin the second page and all later pages about one inch from the top of the page. Type your last name, the slug-line, and the page number of the story in the upper left-hand corner:

Ruvinsky

GIRLHERO

Page 2

- At the end of the story, type an end mark to show that the story is complete. The most common symbols are "30," "###" or the journalist's initials. Telegraphers used the Roman numerals "XXX" to indicate the end of a message. Eventually, editors put it at the end of a story indicating its completion, and the Roman numerals were ultimately changed into the Arabic "30." Traditional end marks to Linotype operators were "-30-" or three pound signs ("###"). Printers preferred "#" because it avoided confusion between "30" and "—3—" or "3-em," a sign that called for the insertion of a dash to separate parts of a story.

The news business has its jargon, and some of the terms have unusual spellings. Instead of using the word "paragraph," some journalists call it a "graph" or "graf." Other journalists refer to a page of a story as an "add" or a "take." Sometimes reporters use the word "copy" instead of "story" to refer to the written version of a news report. The first sentence of a story is often referred to as a "lead" or "lede."

News organizations also vary on the use of datelines (also called placelines), which indicate the place where the event occurred. Datelines are placed at the beginning of the story and normally include the name of the city, printed in capital letters and followed by a comma, the abbreviation for the province in upper and lowercase letters, and a dash (for example: BRANTFORD, Ont.—). Names of major cities that have large populations and are synonymous with a province or nation (Montreal, New York, or Tokyo) are used without the name of the province or country. Most news organizations do not use datelines for stories that originate within their own communities. When they use the names of other cities within their own province, they omit the name of the province.

Datelines routinely used to include the date the story was written. Because communication was slower in the nineteenth century, the dates in datelines helped readers know how fresh the news was. Now, many stories are published the day they are written or the day after. In the rapidly expanding world of online news, publication is nearly instantaneous and updating is continual.

News organizations also have different policies about when to use datelines. Some organizations tell their reporters to use datelines to indicate where the basic information in the story came from even if the writer of the story was in another city. A more rigorous standard, and the one followed by the Canadian Press, says datelines should be used only when the principal reporter of the story is in the city named in the dateline.

Copy-Editing Symbols

Reporters should review and revise their stories before submitting them to their editors. This review and revision is called editing. Reporters edit their stories and correct all errors before giving the final version to an editor. If the editor finds a problem, the story is often returned to the reporter for more revisions.

Stories written for reporting classes should be neat and easy to read. To edit a story on paper, use a pencil to insert the copy-editing symbols shown in the following paragraphs.

Ink cannot be erased, and the original markings might be confused with revised editing. Editing online obviously does not allow for this sort of traditional editing, but learning the copy-editing symbols and how to apply them is still the best way to become proficient (and good editors are still in high demand, regardless of medium).

If several errors appear within one word, draw one line through the word, and place the correct spelling above it. Make these copy-editing symbols and corrections plain and obvious. If several major errors appear in a paragraph or section of a story, retype that section. If corrections become too numerous and messy, retype the entire story so that it is easy to read. The following is an example of copy-editing for print publications. Copy-editing symbols are on the inside front and back covers of the textbook.

Double-space your story. Indent every paragraph in a news story, and mark the beginning of each paragraph with the proper copy-editing symbol: |_____ If you want to mark a paragraph to be divided into two shorter paragraphs, you can use either the same copy-editing symbol or this one: ¶ .

If you indent a line and then decide that you do not want to start a new paragraph, link the lines together with a pencil, as shown here.

The same symbol is used to link the remaining parts of a sentence or paragraph after a major deletion, ~~involving the elimination of a great many words and more than one line of type, or even a complete sentence or two,~~ as shown here.

Always use a pencil, not a pen, to correct any errors that appear in your stories. If you make a mistake in correcting your story with a pen, the correction will be difficult to change.

Write "OK" above facts or spellings that are so unusual that your editors are likely to question their accuracy, and circle the letters. (For example, you might need to check again the spelling of Suzanne Schlovitkowitz, when writing that she became a millionaire at the age of 13.) The notation "OK" indicates that the information is correct, regardless of how odd, unlikely or bizarre it may appear to be.

If you accidentally type an extra word or letter, cross out with one line the word or ~~or~~ letter, then draw an arc above it to link the remaining portions of the sentence. An arc drawn above a deletion indicates that the remaining segments of the sentence or paragraph should be moved closer together, but a space should be left between them. To eliminate a space within a word, draw an arc both above and below it. To eliminate an unnecessary letter, draw an arc both above and below it, plus a *vertical* line through it. To delete a letter or punctuation at the end of a word, you can draw a symbol through it like this.

When two words or letters are inverted, use symbol this to indicate that they should be transposed. If you want to move an entire paragraph, retype that portion of the story. Particularly if the transposed paragraphs are on different pages, several errors are likely to occur if you fail to retype them.

draw three lines under a letter to indicate that it should be capitalized. If a letter is capitalized, but should not be, draw a *slanted* line through it. If two words are incorrectly run to-gether, draw a *straight*, vertical line between them to indicate that a space should be added.

If you make a correction and then decide that the correction is unnecessary or mistaken, write the word "stet" (from the Latin word "stare," meaning "let it stand") alongside the correction to indicate that you want to retain the original version.

If you want to add or change a letter, word or phrase, write or type the change above the line, then use a caret to indicate where it fits into the sentence. Many punctuation marks, includ-ing colons, semicolons, exclamation points and question marks, are added in the same manner (for example: When will he have din-ner ready). Make certain that your caret is legible by insert-ing it in the space above or below the text line.

To add a comma, draw a comma in the proper place and put a caret *over* it (for example: The dog is big black and furry.). If you add an apostrophe or quotation mark, place a caret *under* it (for example: He said, "Im going to the store.). To add a pe-riod, draw either a dot or a small "x" and circle it. A hyphen is indicated by the symbol⸗, and a dash by the symbol)—(.

Never type or write over a letter or word. Also, place all corrections above (never below) the typed line and error. Other-wise, an editor won't know if your correction goes with the line above or below it.

As you examine various newspapers, you will see that they never underline, ~~because typesetters do not have a key to under-line.~~ However, you can use the symbol shown here to indicate that a word needs to be set in _italics_, and you can use the symbol shown here to indicate that a word needs to be set in **boldface**. You can use this symbol to center a line on the page:

]By Gordon Elliott[

☐ This symbol means flush left. This symbol means flush right.☐

Spell out most numbers below 10 and use numerals for the number 10 and most larger numbers. Consult The Associated Press Stylebook and Libel Manual for more exact guidelines. If you type a numeral, but want it spelled out, circle it (for example: She has ④ dogs.). If you spell out a number, but want to use the numeral, circle it (for example: She has (twelve) horses.). Similarly, circle words that are spelled out, but should be abbreviated (for example: He is from Madison, (Wisconsin)), and words that are abbreviated but should be spelled out (for example: Her dad is from (Tex.). Do not use a circle to indicate that a letter should or should not be capitalized.

Below the last line of each news story, in the center of the page, place one of these "end marks":

-30-
-0-
###

The Canadian Press Stylebook

Most Canadian news organizations have adopted *The Canadian Press Stylebook*. The stylebook contains a briefing on Canadian media law and lists hundreds of rules for abbreviations, capitalization, punctuation, grammar, spelling, and word usage. Students should have their own copies of *The Canadian Press Stylebook* as well as *The Canadian Press Caps and Spelling*, as the books are valuable reference tools for all of their journalism courses and their work in the field. Both books are available at most campus and community bookstores and online.

The stylebook helps journalists avoid misspellings and errors in grammar and word usage. In addition, the stylebook saves journalists time, because in a single volume it answers most of the questions they are likely to ask about the proper use of the language.

News organizations large and small rely on consistent standards. By specifying a single set of rules for everyone to follow, *The Canadian Press Stylebook* encourages consistency. Without a single set of rules, news organizations would publish more errors, which could be both costly and embarrassing. For example, four reporters within the same news organization might write the same phrase in four different ways. One reporter might spell "per cent" as two words (17 per cent); another might use one word (17 percent); a third might use the percentage sign (17%); and a fourth might spell out the number 17 (seventeen per cent). The first version (17 per cent) is correct. Reading newspapers is also easier if the style is consistent. Consistency in style and spelling also adds to a medium's credibility.

Over the years, the stylebook has grown to include information necessary for journalists, such as guidelines for the internet, sports and business, media law, and photo captions. In addition to its other uses, the stylebook helps students prepare for their first jobs. If beginning journalists learn the book's basic rules while enrolled in college or university, they can easily begin writing for the media—and move from one employer to another. Because most news organizations have adopted *The Canadian Press Stylebook*, reporters do not have to learn a new set of rules each time they move to another newsroom.

Many large newsrooms have style manuals of their own—such as the *Globe and Mail* and the CBC—which also deal with specifics of how online content should be presented. Some other large news organizations publish books that specify the rules for handling stylistic problems particular to their fields or disciplines. Similarly, some college and university newspapers specify a standardized set of rules for common usage.

Accuracy of Names and Facts

Editors, instructors, and the public do not tolerate sloppiness, and they are particularly critical of errors in spelling, names, and facts because there is rarely any excuse for them.

Be especially careful to check the spelling of people's names. Most misspellings are the result of carelessness, and they anger two sets of people—those whom the reporter intended to name as well as those who were inadvertently named. Most editors require their reporters to consult a second source, usually a telephone or city directory (hard-copy or online) to verify the way names are spelled. Always confirm the spelling of a source's name and title before ending an interview.

In the real newsroom, of course, reporters would check the spelling with the source and in the appropriate directory. For the exercises in this chapter, assume that a name is spelled correctly the first time it is used in the story, and make subsequent references conform to that spelling. To avoid inconsistent spelling of names, check a name every time it appears in a news story, not just the first time it is used.

Journalists understand the importance of double-checking the accuracy of every fact in every news story. Any factual error will damage a news organization's reputation and could seriously harm people mentioned in the stories. Because of the serious consequences of inaccuracies, an instructor is likely to lower grades significantly for a factual error. Students are also penalized for errors in diction, grammar, and style. If an instructor accepts late assignments (most do not), grades may be lowered because of a missed deadline. All media organizations must meet rigid deadlines, and editors expect work to be turned in on time.

How to Revise and Rewrite Content

Every reporter and editor has a different way of editing content. One editor needs to take a quick walk around the newsroom before sitting back down to edit a story. One reporter needs to listen to her favourite song before editing her story. Whatever the personal preferences, there are some fundamental routines that need to be followed. There are two types of editing—the line edits and the structural edit. Before either a line or structural edit is done, the story must be read through from beginning to end. A proper edit of any content cannot be done until the entire story is read. Revision cannot be effective if a reporter/editor does not have a full grasp of the story's angle and its content.

First, read the whole story. Do not make any edits or changes during this first read-through of the story. Reporters and editors must remember that if they if don't understand the story, the readers won't understand it. There are no stupid questions in journalism, so do not hesitate to ask questions when a story does not make sense.

After the first read-through, read the story again, this time editing each line to check for the following:

1. Check word meanings and cut wordiness.
2. Check facts, spellings, capitalization, numbers, grammar, and punctuation.
3. Use S-V-O sentence structure.
4. Use concise and clear sentences and paragraphs.
5. Keep opinions, assumption, and "you," "me," and "I" out of copy.
6. Be specific.

7. Cut repetition.
8. Cut needless adjectives, adverbs, and descriptive clauses.
9. Use CP style.
10. Check attribution.

After the line edit is completed, read the story a third time for structural edits, checking for the following.

1. Is the lead the right one for this story?
2. Are the 5Ws plus H questions answered?
3. Is the lead supported by factual information in the story?
4. Is there proper context for the story?
5. Is there a nut graph in the story? Is it in the right place?
6. Do the paragraphs flow into one another?
7. Is there a chronology to the narrative that is easy to follow?

One traditional method editors used for structural edits was to number each paragraph in sequence and use the numbers to propose a new structural sequence to the reporter for revision.

An essential consideration for all editors is to review all changes made to content with the reporter who gathered and wrote the content.

✔ Checklist for Copy Preparation

1. Devise a slug that specifically describes the story's content. Type your name, the date, and the slug in the upper left-hand corner of the document.
2. Begin typing the story one-third of the way down the first page and one inch from the top of all following pages.
3. Double-space each story.
4. Indent each paragraph.
5. Use a pencil and the proper copy-editing symbols to correct errors on hard copy.
6. Make certain no words are divided and hyphenated at the end of a line and no paragraphs are divided across pages.
7. Print separate stories on separate pages, and do not use the back of pages.
8. If the story continues on a second page, type "more" at the bottom of the first page; type your name, the page number and the slug-line at the top of the second and subsequent pages; and type an end mark at the end of the story.
9. If the story originated outside your community, add the proper dateline.
10. Consult the appropriate directory to verify the spelling of all names used in the story; check these names every time they are used.

The Writing Coach

Russell's Rules for Good Writing

By Nick Russell, journalist and author, Victoria, B.C.

1. Editing. Good copy editors polish, without imposing on a piece. They make good copy even better. But brilliant copy editors draw out the possibilities of the story, the possibilities of the writer; they identify the fine writer's style, discreetly refining it, so the writer sees the published piece and says to herself: "Yeah, that's what I meant to say," or "Good, they never touched it."

2. Sentence length. There is no iron rule, and no ideal length. But we need to wonder why the average sentence in daily papers is generally 50 per cent longer than in popular American bestsellers. A sentence in a news story can be immensely long—if it's for some deliberate effect. Short, staccato sentences can add speed and excitement to a story, but they don't work all the time. Best is a mix. And if your lead sentence is more than 20 words long, it had better be damn good!

3. Verbs. The most important word in most sentences is the verb. Verbs need to be strong, vivid, clear, and ACTIVE. It follows that the verb in the lead is likely the most important word in the entire story. The second-weakest verb in the journalist's vocabulary is "is." The weakest verb is "'s," as in, "There's a new yadda yadda."

4. Vocabulary. Words are our tools. The fine cabinet-maker never uses all her tools, but they are there when she needs them, shining and sharp. They need TLC: cleaning, polishing, careful storage for quick retrieval. Journalists should not be the first to use a new word, nor the last to use an old word. Every word needs to communicate clearly and instantly exactly what the writer wants it to communicate.

5. Loaded language. Some words carry a burden of emotion—words such as "censor," "reform," "admit," "disabled." They are effective, powerful weapons in our arsenal, but they must be used very carefully; a loaded word is an editorial opinion.

6. Bafflegab. We're not just in the reporting business—we are in the translation business. As the world gets more complex, each specialist develops special vocabulary, and it's up to us to make these fields accessible, without getting sucked into the techno-babble of the experts we cover—the computer geeks, the sewage engineers, the rocket scientists.

7. Syntax. The rules of English grammar are often arcane and illogical. But if you break them unknowingly, you'll probably confuse the reader to the point of irritation and turn-off. If you know the rules, you can break them—occasionally—with great effect.

8. Style. Good writing will be tight, clear, crisp, and accurate, drawing vivid word-pictures for the reader. But VERY good writing will also have flair: a sensitive, crafted use of pace and rhythm and mood. And the best copy editor looks at that with enthusiasm and respect, thinking, "I wish I'd written that," and leaves it alone.

Source: Reprinted with permission of Nick Russell.

Suggested Readings and Useful Websites

Adams, Ian. 1967. "The Lonely Death of Chanie Wenjack." *Maclean's*. February 1. Accessed June 20, 2018, http://www.macleans.ca/society/the-lonely-death-of-chanie-wenjack/

Barber, Katherine. 2004. *The Canadian Oxford Dictionary*. Don Mills, ON: Oxford University Press.

———. 2007. *Only in Canada, You Say: A Treasury of Canadian Language*. Don Mills, ON: Oxford University Press.

Barber, Katherine, Heather Fitzgerald, Tom Howell, and Robert Pontisso, eds. 2006. *Paperback Oxford Canadian Dictionary*, 2nd edn. Don Mills, ON: Oxford University Press.

Editing Canadian English: The Essential Canadian Guide Revised and Updated. 2000. 2nd edn. Toronto: Editors' Association of Canada. (First published by Macfarlane Walter and Ross in 2000; second printing published by McClelland and Stewart in 2003).

McCarten, James, ed. 2015. *The Canadian Press Caps and Spelling*, 21st edn. Toronto: The Canadian Press.

———. 2017. *The Canadian Press Stylebook: A Guide for Writers and Editors*, 18th edn. Toronto: The Canadian Press.

Messenger, William E., et al., eds. 2008. *Canadian Writer's Handbook*, 5th edn. Don Mills, ON: Oxford University Press.

Porter, Jody. 2016. "Meet the Journalist Who Inspired Gord Downie and Joseph Boyden to Write about Chanie Wenjack." CBC News. October 21. Accessed June 20, 2018, http://www.cbc.ca/news/canada/thunder-bay/ian-adams-gord-downie-1.3813737

Strunk, W., Jr., & White, E.B. (2009). *The Elements of Style*, 4th edn. New York: Macmillan.

Truss, Lynne. 2003. *Eats, Shoots & Leaves: The Zero Tolerance Approach to Punctuation*. New York: Penguin.

Zinsser, William. 2006. *On Writing Well*, 6th edn. New York: HarperCollins.

The Canadian Press: http://www.thecanadianpress.com

Editors' Association of Canada: http://www.editors.ca/index.htm

Journalist's Resource: https://journalistsresource.org/tip-sheets/style/copyediting-for-reporters

Purdue Online Writing Lab: https://owl.english.purdue.edu/owl/

Sources for Students: http://www.sources.com/students.htm

Exercise 1   Format and Copy-Editing Symbols

Using the proper copy-editing symbols, correct the errors in the following stories. Use the reference chart for copy-editing symbols on the inside of the front cover to help you. Use the *Canadian Press Stylebook* for help with possessives.

1. Background Investigations

    for $150, threee retirde detective s will Help you investigate a potential date roommmate, emploeye or anyone else you are curous about.

    one year ago, the detectivrs openedBackgroundds Unlimited and, for $150, will conduct a basic background investigation. The investigation includes on an examinatino of an Indi-viduals criminal record, driving record, employment history credit historyy and educational background

"People have started coming to us, askingus to on check there spouses, tenants nannies—anyone you nac can imagin," said Roger datolla, retired who after wworking 26 years for the city s police department,. HIS partners, Betsy Aaron and Myron Hansen, retired after 20years "We re friendds, and this seemed like a natural for us," Datolla said. "Were all familiar with the routnie, and its catching on faster than we expected. Of coarse, some people want us condcutt more detailed investigations, and we chagre more for that."

Lar ge corporations ask bBackgrounds Unlimited to investigate potential employes. "They want to find out about soneone before they hire the person, before its two late,"" Datolli continued "A charming personality isn't enough these days for someone loking for a good job. People in personnel offices realizze they can't rely on instinct, refences, or even diplomas or written employment histories. Its too easy to fake all that.plus, small businessses, especially, don"t have the contacts or know-how to conduct good background checks."

Aaronadded: "WE started fo off thinking almost all our worlk would be from businesses, mainly checking on ojb applicamnts, possibly employee thefts and that type of thing. Sudenly, we re getting other people, and that part of our business is mushrooming, almost half ofwhatdo we now. We ve had mothers comein,checking on guys their daughterss are dating, and couples checking onneighbors. We even had a colllege teacher ask u s to cheCk on a student he thought was dangereous.

2.   Jury Award

A judge Monday ordered the cityy to pay $2.8 million too Caleb Draia, a thieve from Calgary shot in the back

A polic officer fired threee shotsat Dr aia, and one hit him, paralyzing him for live.

Draia admitted that he grabed a purse from 74 year old Celia Favata as she as was returning to hwrher car in parking lot at cColonial Mall. He pleaded guilty to a charge of robbary and was sentenced to five yearns in prison, a ternm he;s now serving.

Draias lawyer argued that the police were not justified in shooting, his client in the bcak as he fled. A judge agree, ruling that Draia was the victim of excessive, deadly policcpolice force.

Favata testified tht she was nearly chokked todeath. "I tried to holler for help, and he threatened to choke me to death if I didn't shut up," she said Her glassses were broken her dress torn, her nose bloodied and her left arm broken when Draia through her to tHE ground.

"Thiis wasn't just a mugigng," city atorney Allen Farci argud."This was really a case of attempted murder."

After Judge Marilyn PIcot annnounced her verdict, FAvata said: "Its not right. I never got 10 centts, and now this thug gets nearly $3 million. He deserved to be hurt,."

Police officer George Oldaker was shoppiing at the hall heard Favatas cries, and asw her lying injued on the ground. "Officer Oldaker was justified in shooting Draia because he was preventing the flight of a violent felon," the citey attorney argued. "Theirwas no other way to stop Draia, to keep from him escaping. N o one know who he was, so if he got away, chances were he'd never be CAUGHT."

Farci said hewill apppeal the judges decison. "Its ludicrous," he siad said. "This verdict sends a message to people that you can be rewarded if anything happens to you, even iff you're hurt while connitting a very serious crime. HE could've killed thtat poorold woman.

Exercise 2   Format and Copy-Editing Symbols

Using the proper copy-editing symbols, correct the errors in the following stories. Use the reference chart for copy-editing symbols on the inside of the front cover to help you.

1.   Truancy
     REGINA — premier Brad wall is looking to change labour legislatiion on under-age workers.

     Earlier th is week, 20 15-yeearr-old Dairy Queen employees wer laid off in northwes Regina, becccause they were undreage according to Saskatchewan labour standard's legislation.

     The legislation, which has been in effect since 1971, states: "you have to be at least 16 years old tO work in hotels, restaurants, educational institutions, hospitls and nursing homes."

     The controversy around the ississue has Pemier Brad Wall and Advanced Eddducattion, Employment and Labour Minister Rob Norris talking abouttry-ing to change the legislation.

     "It doesn't make a lot of sense that you CAN maybe pump gas and sell a person a muffin across a counter at a certain age, but you couldn't go acccross the street and hand a person a wrapped cheeseburge at a fAst food Place," said Wall, who was in White City discussing saskatchewan's role in thaNational Job Fair in Toronto.

     Wall anndd Norris both ssaidd that safetyand ecudation for childrem is im-portant, but that "commoonsense" is needed in labor legislation.

     "As we look at the job market as it evolves in Ssaskchewan in the twenty-first century, its time that WE take a sensible appraoch," said Norris. "What that in-cludes is having an iinfoormed approach, taking a look acrossjurisdictions . . . and common sense is goingg to prevail on this."

     According to Wall, the Government was already looking at The legislaton before the layoffs happened, but the labour standards officer haad no choice But to followthe law.

     "When a complaint is recieved and its the law of the province, I think there's a duty there to enforce that. But it doesn't Channge the fact that we need to find somme answers," Wallsaid.

     However, Larry Hubich, president of the Saskatchewan Federation ofLabour, said that the soluution is more complex than justchanging Legislation.

"Why not change it in the Ohter direction and say, in odrder for you to work in any occupation in Saskatchewan, you need to be at least 16," hubich said.

"I would be very intersted in having a respectfuull and comprehensssive consultation on what is an apropriate age (to work) and to take into consideration What our inetrnational obligations are wiht respect to the minimum age for Child lbour."

He also said that truancy laws in the Province exist that reqiure childrem to be in shool until Thye turn 16.

2. Police Sting

The policehavearrested 114 people who thought they inherited $14,000.

"Most evrey criminal i s greedy," PoliceChief Barry Kopp errud said, "and we appealed to their greed."

The police created a fictitious law firm, then spent $1,100 for a fake sign and for pprinting and postage send to letters to 441 peeple wanted on warrants issued in the past three year. Each leterletter was mailed to the persons last known a ddress and said the recipient had inherited $14,200 from a distaant relative. The letter set An appointment time for each person to come to the firm and pick up acheck.

Fourteen officers posing as lawyers and their asistants were assigned to donated space and workeed from there 8 a.m.to 9 p.m monday through Friday last week. Recipients who appeared to collect their money were led to a back room and quietly arrested.

Koperrud siad offficers are often unable to find people wanted on w arrants. "When we go to tyhere homes and try to pick these peopl up, we often mis s them, and that warnz them we're after them.They disappear, staying with friends or relatives or moving toother cities."

DetectiveManuel Cortez added: "Ths was a good tactic. I dont have any qualms about tell-ing a little white lie to criminls trying to ezcape the law. Be sides, it saved a tonn of money. Normally, too make these arrests would take hundreds of hoUrs of our time, and some of these people would commit new crimes before we caught hemthem, if we caught them at all."

Most of the people policc arrested weer wanted for probation violations drunken driving writing bad checks failure to pay child support and other nonviolent crimes. However, seven were wanted for burglary, thee for car theft, thre for robbery and one for aiding an escape

Exercise 3   CP Style

Circle the correct CP style within the parentheses. Use *The Canadian Press Stylebook* for help.

1. Sooyoung ran a red light at the intersection of Brown and Grant (Streets/streets).
2. The (prime minister/Prime Minister) will return to the (Parliament Buildings/parliament buildings) at 3 p.m.

3. The ophthalmologist's office is at (nine/9) Westwind (Avenue/avenue/Ave./ave.).

4. Emily is taking a course in the (Sociology/sociology) and (English/english) (Departments/ departments).

5. Copy-editing symbols have not changed much since the (1920s/1920's).

6. Only (three/3) (%/per cent/percent) of the U.S. population in 2003 bought duct tape and plastic for their windows when (President/president) Bush put the country on high alert for terrorist attacks.

7. (Mrs. Fred Greene/Josephine Greene) won the (womans/womens/woman's/women's) (golf/Golf) (Tournament/tournament).

8. The (winter's/Winter's) lowest temperature was (minus/-) (fourty/forty/40) (degree's/ degrees/0).

9. One of the (potato/potatoe) sacks weighted (4/four) (lbs./pounds), and the other weighed (11/eleven) (oz./ounces).

10. The Italian flag is (red, white, and green/red; white; and green/red, white and green/red, white & green).

11. Many people in Canada and the (US/U.S./United States/united states) are worried about the sars (Virus/virus).

12. The textbook cost (forty dollars/40 dollars/$40).

Exercise 4   Format, Copy-Editing, and CP Style

Circle the correct CP style within the parentheses. Use *The Canadian Press Stylebook.* Answer Key provided; see Appendix B.

1. The (priest/Priest) (said/celebrated) (Mass/mass) during their marriage ceremony.

2. Morgan's new book is (entitled/titled) ("Rachael's New Glasses"/*Rachael's New Glasses*).

3. Her (dad/Dad) celebrates his birthday in (August/Aug.).

4. The jury found him (not guilty/innocent).

5. The miniature ponies were (reared/raised) in Elliott (county/County).

6. The mayor lives on Morning Glory (Street/St.).

7. Seven of the (people/persons) in the room were reading newspapers.

8. (Jean and Diane's/Jean's and Diane's) room was in a mess.

9. Neither Jason nor his friends (was/were) going to the party.

10. The wine was bottled in (October 2002/Oct. 2002/October, 2002).

11. Most news organizations want a reporter with a (Bachelor's degree/Bachelor degree/bachelor degree/bachelor's degree) in journalism.

12. The (Police/police) clocked the (mayor/Mayor) going (thirty/30) (km/h/k.m.h/ kilometres per hour) over the speed limit.

13. She will remember (September 11, 2001/Sept. 11, 2001,) always.

14. Manuel (Middlebrooks, Jr./Middlebrooks Jr.) works for the (Canadian Security Intelligence Service/C.S.I.S./CSIS).

Exercise 5   CP Style and Copy Editing

Use the proper copy-editing symbols to correct the mechanical, spelling, and stylistic errors in the following sentences. Refer to *The Canadian Press Stylebook* and the copy-editing symbols on the inside of the front cover to help you.

Remember that none of the possessives has been formed for you. If you need help in forming the possessives, use *The Canadian Press Stylebook*.

1. Next Summer, Maurice Reimer, an accountant with an office on Bender Ave., wants to buy a 4-door toyota avalon that costs about 29000 dollars.
2. Atty. Miguel Acevedo, who lives on Bell Ave. said his seven-yr.-old son received serious injuries when hit by the drunk driver in a ford van.
3. Canadian Senator Connie Mack, a conservative from Alberta, said the social security system is bankrupt and, in ten years, the Federal Government will slash its benefits.
4. Prof. Denise Bealle, a member of the History Dept., estimated that one third of her students will seek a Masters Degree within 5 years.
5. Fire totally destroyed the Dries Manufacturing Company at 3130 River Rd., and the damage is estimated at 4,000,000 to 5,000,000 dollars.
6. The boy, an 18 year old College Freshman, arrived in Flin Flon Man.at 12 noon and will stay until February 14th.
7. 50 youths met in the ymca at 3010 1st Avenue yesterday and agreed to return at 7:00PM October 4 to view the film titled Sports.
8. Irregardless of the investigations outcome, the thirty two White youths at Colonial high school want Mr. Tony Guarinno to continue as their Coach.
9. During the 1920s, the Federal Government allocated 820000 dollars for the project, and Mrs. Mildred Berg, who has a Ph.D. in Sociology, said 8% of the money was wasted.
10. On February 14 1996 the temperature fell to 0 in Moosejaw Saskatchewan and on February 15th it fell to -14.
11. Yesterday the United States President promised that the United States Congress would help the flood victims in Miss., Ala., Ga., and La.
12. He wants to duplicate copies of the e mail he received last Spring and to mail copies to 8 members of the Eastwind Homeowners Assn.
13. The jury reached their verdict at 12 midnight November 4th, finding Kevin Blohm, age 41, not guilty of the 3 charges.
14. Doctor Rachael Rosolowski, of Toronto, said the X rays taken yesterday reveal that the Popes cancer is spreading.
15. Police said the ford mustang driven by Anne Capiello of University Boulevard was traveling sixty mph when it collided with a tree at the corner of Wilson and Hampshire Avenues.

16. The building on Grand Av. was totally demolished during the 1990s, and the state legislature yesterday voted 120-14 to spend 14,300,000 million dollars to rebuild it.

17. Four fifths of the hispanic medical students said they watched the television program entitled "ER" at 10:00PM last Thur. night.

18. 24 women, led by Prof. Maxine Cessarini, met at 9:00p.m. last night and concluded that their childrens 3rd grade teacher lacks a Bachelors Degree and lied at the P.T.A. meeting held last Aug. 29th.

Exercise 6 CP Style and Copy Editing

Use the proper copy-editing symbols to correct mechanical, spelling, and stylistic errors in the following sentences. Remember that none of the possessives has been formed for you. For help, refer to *The Canadian Press Stylebook*.

1. After earning her Masters Degree the Mayor of Lethbridge Alberta resigned and, on January 1st, established the Alberto Corporation at South Hawkins Dr.

2. On September 27 2005 Haitian born Michaelle Jean made history by becoming the 1st black Governor General of Canada and the 2nd immigrant in a row named to be Canada's titular head of state.

3. Ms. Delta Comanche, the Companys Number 1 choice for the job of Head of Purchasing, estimated that 80% of the Department Heads favor the new Plan.

4. In January as the Priest celebrated a high mass at St. Margaret Mary Church on Park Ave., Ronal Sheppard, Junior, age 3, fell asleep.

5. The Canadian Civil Liberties Association (C.C.L.A.) was founded in Toronto Ontario in 1964 to defend civil rights country-wide and uphold the constitution.

6. The ford mustang driven by a white male in his 20s sped South on Pennsylvania Av., then turned left onto Franklin Dr. at speeds up to 80 m.p.h.

7. Chapter 20 in the book entitled Wasteful Solutions charges that in May, 2004 the parliamentary committee wasted 2 to 2.3 million dollars sightseeing in the gaspesie and the Queen Charlotte islands.

8. James Eastland, III, a Lieutenant Colonel in the Canadian forces, received an M.A. in Business Administration and will speak at 2:00pm Sunday afternoon to the Small Business Owners Assn. at 626 North 3rd Street.

9. Reverend Audrey Van Pelt, of North Wilkes Rd., arrived October 20th at 6:00 p.m. in a white Cadillac he bought last Summer.

10. The twelve youths from Montreal Quebec said yesterday that their number one fear is the rising cost of College tuition.

11. The President of People's Gas Company said the new building at 1840 North Hampton Rd. will cost $12,400,000 dollars and be completed in 2 years.

12. Two teenagers saw the 8 year old boy in a car and said the driver was about 30, 6 ft. tall, and weighed 180 lbs.

13. The conference started at 12 noon yesterday and, ten minutes later, the groups President introduced the 3 mps from Ont.

14. Prof. Mayerline Valderama of Kelowna British Columbia arrived for work on February 23 2004 when two college Freshmen, both majoring in Political science, stepped towards her and demanded her resignation.

15. The clubs Vice-President said his seven year old son found a wallet containing $1434, and that 7 persons have claimed it.

16. Afterwards, the Sask. Premier estimated that 1/4 the teenagers and 80% of their parents favor tougher standards, but implementing them would cost $1,000,000,000 a year.

17. The woman was born in the town of Cache Creek in January 1986 and is minoring in german. At 8:00pm Tuesday night, she attended a meeting of the German Friendship Assn. with 3 friends.

18. After leaving the official residence on Sussex Drive, Prime Min. Stephen Harper retired from the Federal Government and moved to southern British Columbia but continued to meet with conservative leaders.

Appendix A

Copy-Editing Practice

Using copy-editing symbols and a pencil, and referring to your *Canadian Press Stylebook, Caps and Spelling* and *Canadian Oxford Dictionary*, make all the necessary corrections to the news stories that follow. Look for errors in grammar, spelling, punctuation and CP style. There are two review tests (with two stories in Test A and two stories in Test B). When you've completed each test, check your work against the original versions of these stories (you will find stories A1 in Chapter 8, A2 in Chapter 9, and stories B1 and B2 in Chapter 10). There is a total of 100 errors in all the tests, with a tally listed at the end of each story. You can count the errors you have found and corrected and then gauge your progress in terms of a total percentage grade at the end. Some important notes to remember as you do your editing: If capital letters are needed for proper nouns such as "House of Commons," capitalizing the "h" in "house" and the "c" in "commons" counts as one error/ correction (not two); please use Canadian spellings; and the first references of names are spelled correctly, so check all names against the first reference to them.

From Chapter 8

A1

TORONTO—The last thing Benjamin ever thought he'd have to do is too help his father die.

But after a cancer diagnosis in the prime of life, his father gathered his wife, 20-year-old Benjamin and his older brother around the kitchen table in there Toronto home to discuss exactly that.

"We faced his death together, as a challenge," recalls Benjamin, who asked that his surname not be used to protect the privacy of his greiving mother. "When he knew the end was near, he asked that something good come out of it and that his body be used to help others".

Benjamin struggled to accept the fact that his father, a successful businessman and enthusiastic skier, golfer and runner in his late 50's, had only months to live. Just over a year, as it turned out, from diagnosis to his death last January. When aggressive treatment failed to stop the spread of pancreatic cancer to his internal organs, his father opted for pallaitive care.

"There was no sugarcoating. We knew he was going to die," says Benjamin, a posed and thoughtful business student. "We were involved in every decision. We normalized it by talking about everything, including all the therapies and procedures my father went through."

With every passing year, as live expectancies increase, there is an allusion we will all last forever. Medical stories often focus on the sexier aspect of medicine—the cure.

But palliative-care experts say the bulk of medicine is about something less cherry: how to manage the care of terminally ill people. Research shows that many doctors, as well as patients, are reluctant to initiate this conversation. A recent study by Queen's University in Kingston found that only 18% of 440 patients with endstage disease talked to doctors about their prognosis, even though most were likely to die within a few months.

The time has come to put death back on the table for discussion, says Gary Rodin, the head of psychosocial oncology and palliative care at Princess Margaret Hospital in Toronto.

"For years there was a feeling in the medical community that you shouldn't talk about death. This created a conspiracy of silence." Says Dr. Rodin, who is also a University of Toronto prof. "But someone who is seriously ill knows it, so if you dont talk about it they feel very alone."

Today, medicine students are being taught empathy and communication along with anatomy and physiology.

Doctors understand that terminally ill patience don't want sympathy, or to be deprived of hope. "But hope isn't just about how long you live," says Dr. Rodin, "but about knowing you are loved, and that your life is meaningful."

Researchers have found that the final daze of a person's live are often the most expensive, and medical complicated. In many cases, active treatment are maintained, or another round of chemotherapy administered, even if there is no chance it will improve the patient's quality of life.

"There are cases where futill treatment, such as chemotherapy, is given because people are reluctant to have these conversations," Dr. Rodin says, "and patients fear they will be abandoned. Far too often, people are refered to palliative care too late."

If patients plan ahead, there is a greater likelyhood that there passing will be more pieceful, and that their death won't in any way deminish the life they have lived. Planning includes a discussion about how and where to dye and the writing of a living will and a do not resuscitate order (dnr).

Though Dr. Rodin helped Benjamin and his family cope, a recent U.S. study found that forty percent of people with family members in hospice care were provided no information about the loved one's life expectancy, and 20% were never told the illness could not be cured. The study, published last year in the journal of palliative Medicine, concluded that the most common question was: "How long does my loved one have?" and "What is happening with my loved one." Many were afraid to ask doctors for a physical description of a dying person's last moments, which can be quite frightening.

In his recent book The Welcome Visitor, legendary bbc broadcaster John Humphrys writes about people who are afraid of living too long and having no control over how there lives end.

"Society's approach to death must change as we all live longer," Mr. Humphrys says. He was inspired to write the book by his father's "final sad, lingering and undignified" years. "My father's last year's cast a shadow over what had been a good life," he says.

Benjamin knows he is blessed to have well-adjusted parents who helped him face death: "We saw it as our family responsibility."

Dr. Rodin also helped the family decide how to manage their father's care, including weather he should participate in a clinical trail and when to stop aggressive cancer therapies in favor of enjoying the few months he had left. Ultimately, his father decided to work a half-day at the office, and ski and travel as long as he could. The summer after his diagosis, he even completed a two-day, 200-kilometre bike race to raise money for cancer research.

By the fall of 2008, when his illness became debiltating, he chose to be cared for at home. A palliative-care team installed a hospital bed in his bedroom, and a physcian was on call 24 hours a day. His sons and wife helped him with his medication and going to the bathroom.

Two days before he died, his father checked into Princess Margaret's palliative-care unit. A colorful mural decorated the wall of his room, and soothing music from a cd player on his bedside table filled the room. A physician told the family what to expect when his time came, and explained that he wouldn't be in pain.

"He told us it could be a few days or hours. We held my father's hand and told him we loved him, because he could still feel our presence, even though he wasn't responding," Benjamin says. His breathing became laboured toward the end, which was a little scarie, but the palliative-care team insured he had the right balance of drugs.

In his greif, Benjamin felt supported by his close-knitt pear group, but also found he had no script for his journey. "I didnt want my friends to pity me or for them to feel hurt. I wanted them to know that I was still the same person," he recalls.

In this, too, his father and Dr. Rodin helped him, advising him how to share news of the illness with friends.

Dr. Rodin notes that things rarely go as smoothly as they did for Benjamin's family. Sometimes, the dying person changes his wishes as he becomes sicker. There is no prescription for a "good death," as it is strongly influenced by a person's religion, culture, age, background and psychology.

But every family can benefit from open communication, early planning and attention to pain relieve, Dr. Rodin says. "Birth and death are two major life events. We go to prenatal classes to prepare for birth, and we also need to prepare for death."

TALLY   /50

From Chapter 9

A2

The most important thing woman's basketball coach Vance Coleman carries in his briefcase is not a sketch of a new defencive scheme, a game plan for the upcoming oponent, or even the phone number of a basketball colleague.

It's a crumpled, yellowed piece of paper with a list full of scratches and re-do's. It's his list of 5 life goals. Coleman lists living a long and healthy life, playing the roll of a good father and husband, and earning a million dollars as his top 3 goals. The other 2, he said, constantly change as he ages.

But the point, Coleman said, is to always have them.

"There is an equation I use that works on the basketball court, on the playing field, in business, and in life," Colman said, "and that is performance equals ability times motivation. You may have all the ability in the world, but with no motivation, you won't acomplish anything. 0 times anything is nothing.

"No matter what you do in live, you have to have goals. And you have to stick to those goals."

Colemann, now in his second year at the university and his 17th year of coaching, spoke about goals and motivation to nearly three hundred students at the Student alumni association Conference Friday.

"The first thing you need is a good attitude." Coilman said, "When you get up at 7 a.m., do you say, 'Good morning, God,' or 'Good God, morning'? Same words, big difference in attitude."

Next, the coach shifted gears to the importance of beliefs.

"When someone asks you what you belief in, tell them with conviction," Coleman said. "Say, 'I belief in myself and what I think with my whole heart and nothing less.'"

TALLY   /20

From Chapter 10

B1

Muslims in Montreal and around the world are celebrating the end of the wholy month of Ramadan with eid-al-fitr, a celebration that started Sat. evening.

While the traditions is centuries old, the month of reflection offers those who practice the faith the chance to reflect on the World around them.

Samah Jebbari, a Montreal high school teacher and member of the canadian muslim forum, did things a little differently this year. On top of the traditional ramadan fast, which lasts from dusk until dawn, she decided not to cook for her children untill the food she had already prepare was finish—it was a month of left overs.

"(My children) really liked the idea because it reminded him every night that, for example, children in syria don't have this," Jebbari said.

The idea came as a result of the violent and attacks that have happened in the past year, she said. ramadan gave her an opportunity to discus the idea of sharing and thinking of others with her students and children.

Fasting can be taxing, but Jebbari wanted to dispell stereotypes that every Muslim is tired during the holy month—which coincided with exam preparation. She made sure to hydrate at night and eat very healthy food.

Along with prayer, charity and faith, a big part of Ramadan is spending time with one's family—Jebaddi said she made time with her children—who are seventeen, fourteen and eight—a priority.

"It's a time to reconnect," she said.

TALLY   /20

From Chapter 10

B2

A man has to trust his barber.

And Johnny Bower trusted Tony Baggetta.

The Maple Leafs legend, who died Dec. 26 at the age of 93, first met Baggetta in the fall of 1961, when he was cutting hair at the royal york plaza in Etobicoke.

Ten years later, Bageta opened Anthony's Family Hairstyling inside the Woodchester Mall on Dundas Street in west Mississauga. There are not alot of pictures on the wall, but one stands out. A young Baggetta standing beside his barbers chair with the Leafs goalie smiling for the cameras.

Bower eventually moved west to Oakville, but remained a regular till Tony retired in the Fall of 2015.

"Johnnie Bower was one of the nicest man to ever come into the store," said Rosemarie, Tony's wife. "He had zero anger, he was always smiling and he was such a grate guy. He was such a generous man. He always gave of her time. People he didn't know would ask to have their picture taken with him and he would say, 'Of course.'"

TALLY   /10

TOTAL   /100

Appendix B

Answer Key

Chapter 3

Exercise 1   Editing

Section I: Being Concise
1. The contractor ~~did a totally complete job on the~~ <u>completed</u> the renovation.
2. The candidates for mayor will ~~conduct a~~ poll ~~of~~ the residents.
3. She said the ~~new~~ innovation would save the company money.
4. He said the birthday party was ~~an unexpected~~ surprise.
5. The police officer tried to calm ~~down~~ the accident victim.

Section II: Rewriting Wordy Sentences
1. The mayor said everyone had to co-operate ~~together~~ or someone would <u>sue</u> ~~file a lawsuit against~~ the city.
2. ~~It would appear that~~ <u>The</u> new school mascot, which ~~got a stamp of approval from~~ <u>alumni approved</u>, will <u>be</u> at Saturday's game.
3. ~~As a matter of fact,~~ <u>Some</u> ~~of the~~ tickets were free ~~of charge~~ to the contest winners while other tickets cost ~~the sum of~~ $50 for handling fees.
4. Police ~~claimed~~ <u>said</u> the ~~armed~~ gunman <u>entered the bank to rob it.</u> ~~was carrying a dangerous weapon when he entered the bank with the underlying purpose of robbing it.~~
5. Local residents said they <u>would leave if</u> ~~planned to evacuate in the event that~~ the floodwaters reached the <u>riverbanks.</u> ~~and completely destroyed the town.~~

Section III: Using Powerful Verbs
1. The car needs new paint job.
2. He plans to open a restaurant in Moncton.
3. Many students are interested in the professor's classes.
4. The province pays for the preschool nutrition program.
5. A short circuit in the church's electrical wiring caused the fire.
6. Admission to the amusement park is $25.
7. Karen and David are planning a trip to the beach this summer.
8. John has picked up a second job to help pay for university.
9. The moderator suggested panel participants take a break.
10. She reserved three hotel rooms.

Exercise 2   Vocabulary

1. The mayor (accepted) the offer from the university board of directors to (aid) the city in its (cleanup) efforts after the storm.
2. The professor (alluded) to the chapter in the book that mentions that people will (alter) their behaviour if they are (assured) their efforts will be rewarded.
3. The (site) of the new World War II memorial (piqued) the interest of many (people) in the neighbourhood.
4. (Personnel) were asked to evaluate their (peers) in regard to (their) job performance.
5. She was afraid the club members would (waver) in defence of their actions when it was determined the (principal) planned to (censure) them for demonstrating in front of the school.
6. The restaurant (complemented) the meal with a delicious (dessert).
7. The team's (morale) was higher (than) ever after (its) undefeated season became a reality.
8. Police said the car was (stationary) when the truck (collided with) it, causing a quite a (sight) for passersby.
9. The beautiful (weather) was one of the reasons that thousands of Canadians turned out to demonstrate at the (Parliament Buildings).
10. The snowstorm during the (ascent) of the mountain peak hampered the rescue workers from reaching the climber who (suffered) a broken leg (because of) a fall from a ledge.

Chapter 9

Exercise 2   Quotations and Attribution

Wording, Placement, and Punctuation
1. "Our goal is peace," the prime minister said. (Use a comma, not a period, before the attribution, and place the punctuation mark inside the quotation mark. Transpose the attribution's wording so the subject appears before the verb. Avoid using "claimed" as a word of attribution.)
2. Benjamin Franklin said, "Death takes no bribes." (Use a comma, not a colon, before the one-sentence quotation. Because it is a complete sentence, capitalize the first word of the quotation. Place the final period inside the quotation mark.)
3. She said her son calls her literary endeavours "mom's writing thing." (Condense the attribution, and place the period inside the quotation mark. Normally, you do not need a comma before a partial quotation. Also an apostrophe is needed in mom's.)
4. He is a scuba diver and pilot. He also enjoys skydiving and explains, "I like challenge, something exciting." (Clearly attribute the direct quotation.)
5. The Mideast crisis is likely to last indefinitely, the prime minister said. (The quotation can be paraphrased more clearly and simply. Place the paraphrase before the attribution.)

6. Albert Camus wrote: "A free press can of course be good or bad, but, most certainly, without freedom it will never be anything but bad. . . . Freedom is nothing else but a chance to be better, whereas enslavement is a certainty of the worse." (Place the attribution at the beginning, not the end, of a long quotation, and use a colon to introduce the quotation. Quotation marks do not have to be placed around every sentence in a continuing quotation. Use normal word order in the attribution.)

7. "I think that America has become too athletic," Jesse Owens said. "From Little League to the pro leagues, sports are no longer recreation. They are big business, and they're drudgery." (The attribution "expressed the opinion that" is wordy. Do not place quotation marks around every sentence in a continuing quotation. If it remains at the beginning of the quotation, the attribution should be followed by a colon. Attribute a continuing direct quotation only once.)

8. The man smiled and said: "It's a great deal for me. I expect to double my money." (Because the quotation contains more than one sentence, "said" should be followed by a colon, not a comma. Do not use "smiled" as a word of attribution. Place quotation marks at the beginning and end of the direct quotation, not at the beginning and end of every sentence. Attribute a continuing direct quotation only once.)

9. The woman said she likes her job as a newspaper reporter and explained: "I'm not paid much, but the work is important. And it's varied and exciting. Also, I like seeing my byline in the paper." (Reporters should stress their source's answer to a question, not the question. Attribute a continuing quotation only once. Avoid "grinned" as a word of attribution. The attribution "responded by saying" is wordy.)

10. The librarian said the new building will cost about $4.6 million. (The attribution can be condensed, and by paraphrasing, you can simplify the quotation. Also, virtually all the news published in newspapers is given to reporters. You do not have to mention that routine detail in every story.)

Chapter 12

Exercise 1   Recognizing and Correcting Newswriting Errors

Section I: Agreement

1. The committee submits its data this weekend and expects the data to help the church.

2. She said the company failed to earn enough to repay its loans, and she does not expect it to reopen.

3. The jury reached its verdict at 1 a.m., concluding that the media were guilty of libelling the restaurant and its 22 employees.

4. The decision allowed the city council to postpone its vote for a week, and council members suggested that the site's developer design a plan to save more trees.

5. A representative for the organization said it helps people who are on welfare obtain some job training and raise their self-esteem.

Section II: Plurals and Possessives

1. The women's car was parked nearby, and the sheriff's deputy asked to see the owner's driver's licence.
2. The woman said she opposes assisted suicide "because a doctor's job is to save people's lives, not end them."
3. Last year's outstanding teacher insisted that people's complaints about the school's problems are mistaken.
4. Manvel Jones's parents said their younger children's teacher earned her bachelor's degree in philosophy and her master's degree in education.
5. Everyone's money was stolen, and the neighbourhood association's president warned that the police are no longer able to guarantee people's safety in the city's poorest neighbourhoods.

Section III: Placement

1. The Board of Trustees voted 8–1 during an emergency meeting Thursday morning to fire the college president for his sexual misconduct.
2. When the guests arrived, the hotel manager took their bags to their rooms.
3. At the Unitarian church on Sunday, the union representative urged Canadians to support better working conditions for the country's immigrant workers.
4. As Zena jogged around campus, a thorn bush ripped a hole in her shirt.
5. A suspect in the burglary case involving two lawn mowers stolen from a hardware store was arrested after a high-speed chase.

Section IV: Personification

1. Slamming on the brakes, the driver turned the car to the left, narrowly missing the dog.
2. The city officials said they cannot help the three businesses whose owners asked for better lighting.
3. After detecting the outbreak, the hospital administrators admitted that seven babies born this month were infected, including one who died.
4. Firefighters treated the child for smoke inhalation, then transported her to Mercy Hospital, where her broken legs were treated.
5. The corporation officers, who denied any responsibility for the deaths, will appear in court next month.

Section V: Parallel Form

1. He was charged with driving drunk and having an expired driver's licence.
2. Karen Kim was a full-time student, Air Force reservist, and part-time worker for a veterinarian.
3. To join the club, one must be a sophomore, junior, or senior; study journalism; be in good academic standing; and have demonstrated professional journalistic ability.

4. The mayor warned that the neighbourhood's high crime rate causes residents to flee, contributes to more unemployment for workers, deprives the city of tax revenue, and lowers everyone's property values.
5. She said the other advantages of owning her own business include being independent, having flexible hours, and enduring less stress.

Section VI: Multiple Errors

1. A sheriff's deputy arrested the driver after he saw the teenager pull the Chevrolet out of the alley and drive recklessly without headlights.
2. City officials also said that they cannot silence Sooyoung Li, the woman who fears pollution is likely to affect the neighbourhood's 300 residents.
3. Seeking more money, publicity, and help for the poor, the church's members said they want the city to help them by providing food and housing for the homeless.
4. A spokesperson said the Public Works Department could pave the development's road itself for less than $1.2 million. The Roess Company submitted a bid of $2.74 million.
5. A jury awarded almost $10.5 million to the operators of an abortion clinic who charged that picketers tormented them and their clients. The clinic's operators praised the jury's verdict, saying the jurors' courage and understanding set a needed precedent.

Chapter 13

Exercise 4   Format, Copy Editing, and CP style

1. The priest celebrated mass during their marriage ceremony.
2. Morgan's new book is titled *Rachael's New Glasses*.
3. Her dad celebrates his birthday in August.
4. The jury found him not guilty.
5. The miniature ponies were raised in Elliott County.
6. The mayor lives on Morning Glory St.
7. Seven of the people in the room were reading newspapers.
8. Jean and Diane's room was in a mess.
9. Neither Jason nor his friends were going to the party.
10. The wine was bottled in October 2002.
11. Most news organizations want a reporter with a bachelor's degree in journalism.
12. The police clocked the mayor going 30 km/h over the speed limit.
13. She will remember Sept. 11, 2001, always.
14. Manuel Middlebrooks Jr. works for CSIS.

Index

Note: Page numbers in italics refer to photographs.

Aboriginal Peoples in Canada

Eighth Edition

James S. Frideres
University of Calgary

René R. Gadacz
Grande Prairie Regional College

PEARSON

Prentice
Hall

Toronto

Library and Archives Canada Cataloguing in Publication

Frideres, James S., 1943-
    Aboriginal peoples in Canada / James S. Frideres, René R. Gadacz. — 8th ed.

Fourth ed. published under title: Native peoples in Canada. 2nd ed. published under
    title: Native people in Canada. 1st ed. published under title: Canada's Indians.
Includes bibliographical references and index.

ISBN 978-0-13-205187-3

    1. Native peoples—Canada. 2. Native peoples—Canada—Social conditions.
3. Native peoples—Canada—Politics and government. I. Gadacz, René R. II. Title.
E78.C2F7 2007   971.004'97   C2007-902558-7

ISBN-13: 978-0-13-205187-3
ISBN-10: 0-13-205187-7

Vice-President, Editorial Director: Gary Bennett
Senior Acquisitions Editor: Laura Paterson Forbes
Marketing Manager: Sally Aspinall
Developmental Editor: Alexandra Dyer
Production Editor: Katie Hearn
Copy Editor: John Firth
Proofreader: Molly Wolf
Production Coordinator: Avinash Chandra
Composition: Laserwords
Art Director: Julia Hall
Cover Design: Julia Hall
Cover Image: Getty Images

Statistics Canada information is used with the permission of Statistics Canada. Users are
forbidden to copy the data and redisseminate them, in an original or modified form, for
commercial purposes, without permission from Statistics Canada. Information on the
availability of the wide range of data from Statistics Canada can be obtained from Statistics
Canada's Regional Offices, its World Wide Web site at http://www.statcan.ca, and its toll-free
access number 1-800-263-1136.

1 2 3 4 5   11 10 09 08 07

Printed and bound in the United States of America.